Frommer's®

Fiji

2nd Edition

by Bill Goodwin

WILEY

Wiley Publishing, Inc.

Published by:

WILEY PUBLISHING, INC.

111 River St.

Hoboken, NJ 07030-5774

ISBN 978-0-470-61827-1 (paper); ISBN 978-0-470-90498-5 (ebk); ISBN 978-0-470-40707-3 (ebk); ISBN 978-0-470-92914-8 (ebk)

Editor: Chris Summers
Production Editor: Jana M. Stefanciosa
Cartographer: Nick Trotter
Photo Editor: Richard Fox
Production by Wiley Indianapolis Composition Services
Front Cover Photo: A deserted beach on Kadavu Island, Fiji ©Douglas Peebles / AGE Fotostock, Inc. / PhotoLibrary
Back Cover Photo: An orange-fin anemonefish (*Amphiprion chrysopterus*) off the coast of Fiji © Dave Fleetham / Pacific Stock / SuperStock, Inc.

For information on our other products and services or to obtain technical support, please contact our Customer Care Department within the U.S. at 877/762-2974, outside the U.S. at 317/572-3993 or fax 317/572-4002.

Wiley also publishes its books in a variety of electronic formats. Some content that appears in print may not be available in electronic formats.

Manufactured in the United States of America

5   4   3   2   1

CONTENTS

LIST OF MAPS

To my father,
with love and with grateful thanks for supporting my being a writer
rather than a lawyer.

ACKNOWLEDGMENTS

I owe a debt of gratitude to many individuals and organizations without whose help this book would have been impossible to research and write. You will become acquainted with many of them in these pages, and it will be your good fortune if you meet them in the islands.

My good fortune was to be assisted by Valerie Haeder, who had the enviable task of reporting on Fiji's beautiful Yasawa Islands. You will read her well-chosen words in chapter 6.

I am particularly grateful to Cherill Watson, Ili Matatolu, Thomas Valentine, Susan Bejeckian, and especially to Keti Wagavonovono of the Fiji Visitors Bureau, who went out of their way to help me research this book.

My deep personal thanks go to Connie Haeder, Curtis and Judy Moore, Anne Simon, Suzanne McIntosh, Nancy Monseaux, and Max Parrish, who have tended the home fires while I have been away in paradise over the years; to my sister, Jean Goodwin Santa-Maria, who has consistently given much-needed moral support; and to Dick Beaulieu, always a font of information, advice, and ice-cold Fiji Bitters.

I am truly blessed to have all of them in my life.

—Bill Goodwin

HOW TO CONTACT US

In researching this book, we discovered many wonderful places—hotels, restaurants, shops, and more. We're sure you'll find others. Please tell us about them, so we can share the information with your fellow travelers in upcoming editions. If you were disappointed with a recommendation, we'd love to know that, too. Please write to:

Frommer's Fiji, 2nd Edition
Wiley Publishing, Inc. • 111 River St. • Hoboken, NJ 07030-5774
frommersfeedback@wiley.com

AN ADDITIONAL NOTE

Please be advised that travel information is subject to change at any time—and this is especially true of prices. We therefore suggest that you write or call ahead for confirmation when making your travel plans. The authors, editors, and publisher cannot be held responsible for the experiences of readers while traveling. Your safety is important to us, however, so we encourage you to stay alert and be aware of your surroundings. Keep a close eye on cameras, purses, and wallets, all favorite targets of thieves and pickpockets.

ABOUT THE AUTHOR

Bill Goodwin is one of the world's experts on travel to Fiji and the South Pacific. Before falling in love with the islands, he traveled widely as a decorated officer in the U.S. Navy and was an award-winning newspaper reporter for the *Atlanta Journal,* which sent him to Washington, D.C., as a political correspondent. He then served as legal counsel and speechwriter for two influential U.S. senators—Sam Nunn of Georgia and the late Sam Ervin of North Carolina. In 1977, he and a friend sailed a 41-foot yacht from Annapolis, Maryland, to Tahiti. He left the boat in Papeete and, with girlfriend and backpack, spent more than a year exploring French Polynesia, American Samoa, Samoa, Tonga, Fiji, New Zealand, and Australia. After another stint with Senator Nunn and a year in Hawaii, he researched and wrote the first edition of *Frommer's South Pacific* in 1986–87. He also is the author of *Frommer's Tahiti & French Polynesia* and, at home, *Frommer's Virginia.* Visit him at www.billgoodwin. com.

FROMMER'S STAR RATINGS, ICONS & ABBREVIATIONS

Every hotel, restaurant, and attraction listing in this guide has been ranked for quality, value, service, amenities, and special features using a **star-rating system.** In country, state, and regional guides, we also rate towns and regions to help you narrow down your choices and budget your time accordingly. Hotels and restaurants are rated on a scale of zero (recommended) to three stars (exceptional). Attractions, shopping, nightlife, towns, and regions are rated according to the following scale: zero stars (recommended), one star (highly recommended), two stars (very highly recommended), and three stars (must-see).

In addition to the star-rating system, we also use seven feature icons that point you to the great deals, in-the-know advice, and unique experiences that separate travelers from tourists. Throughout the book, look for:

special finds—those places only insiders know about

fun facts—details that make travelers more informed and their trips more fun

kids—best bets for kids and advice for the whole family

special moments—those experiences that memories are made of

overrated—places or experiences not worth your time or money

insider tips—great ways to save time and money

great values—where to get the best deals

The following abbreviations are used for credit cards:

AE	American Express	DISC	Discover	V	Visa
DC	Diners Club	MC	MasterCard		

TRAVEL RESOURCES AT FROMMERS.COM

Frommer's travel resources don't end with this guide. Frommer's website, **www.frommers. com**, has travel information on more than 4,000 destinations. We update features regularly, giving you access to the most current trip-planning information and the best airfare, lodging, and car-rental bargains. You can also listen to podcasts, connect with other Frommers. com members through our active-reader forums, share your travel photos, read blogs from guidebook editors and fellow travelers, and much more.

THE BEST OF FIJI

The best thing about Fiji isn't its palm-draped beaches, blue lagoons, or rugged mountains. You can find those elsewhere on many tropical islands, including Fiji's neighbors in the South Pacific Ocean. I think it's the enormous friendliness of the Fijian people. They make it a special place.

Picking the best of everything else in Fiji is no easy task, for this is a diverse tropical country with many choices. In this chapter, I point out the best of the best—not necessarily to pass qualitative judgment, but to help you choose among many options. I list them here in the order in which they appear in the book.

Your choice of where you go and what you do will depend on why you are coming to Fiji and how much money you have to spend while you're here. You can scuba dive to exhaustion over some of the world's most beautiful reefs or just laze on the beach with a trashy novel. You can share a 300-room hotel with package tourists, or get away from it all on a tiny islet. Even out there, you can be left alone with your lover or join your fellow guests at lively dinner parties. You can totally ignore the islanders around you or enrich your own life by learning about theirs. You can listen to the day's events on CNN International or get out and see what Fiji was like a century ago. Those decisions are all yours.

Regardless of where you stay and what you do, you are in for a memorable time. The friendly Fijians will see to that.

THE most BEAUTIFUL ISLANDS

"In the South Seas," Rupert Brooke wrote in 1914, "the Creator seems to have laid himself out to show what He can do." How right the poet was, for in Fiji lie some of the world's most beautiful islands. I think the following stand out.

o **Monuriki:** Tom Hanks spent a lot of time filming *Castaway* on lovely Monuriki, one of the westernmost of the Mamanuca Islands. A rocky central mountain drops down to the beach where Hanks figured out how to pry open a coconut. See chapter 6.

o **Yasawa:** This long, narrow island off the northwest coast of Viti Levu has several of Fiji's best beaches scattered among its rolling hills. It's also home to Yasawa Island Resort and Spa, one of Fiji's top offshore hotels. See chapter 6.

o **Waya:** Near the southern end of the Yasawa chain, Waya Island is one of the few in Fiji with the combination of cliffs and sheer basaltic peaks I find so appealing in the Pacific islands. See chapter 6.

o **Beqa:** Off Viti Levu's southern coast, Beqa has no roads cutting through its hills. Lovely Malumu Bay, one of Fiji's more scenic spots, nearly bisects Beqa, and it's all surrounded by the magnificent Beqa Lagoon. See chapter 8.

o **Kadavu:** About 60km (37 miles) long and just 14km (8½ miles) across at its widest point, Kadavu is Fiji's unspoiled nature preserve. Native birds and other wildlife live in abundance on Kadavu, given the absence of mongooses, iguanas, myna birds, and other introduced predators. The Great Astrolabe Reef provides great diving off the eastern and southern shores. See chapter 9.

o **Ovalau:** The sheer cliffs of Ovalau kept the town of Levuka from becoming Fiji's modern capital, but they create a dramatic backdrop to an old South Seas town little changed in the past century. Ovalau has no good beaches, which means no resorts alter its landscape. See chapter 12.

o **Savusavu:** Savusavu isn't an island but almost seems like it is, as it sits on a peninsula separated from the main part of Vanua Levu by spectacular, mountain-surrounded Savusavu Bay, which is so large that the U.S. Navy considered hiding the Pacific fleet there during World War II. See chapter 13.

o **Qamea and Matagi:** These little jewels off the northeastern coast of Taveuni are lushly beautiful, with their shorelines either dropping precipitously into the calm surrounding waters or forming little bays with idyllic beaches. See chapter 14.

THE best BEACHES

Because all but a few islands in Fiji are surrounded by coral reefs, it has no real surf beaches like those so common in, say, Hawaii and Florida. Most islands have bathtublike lagoons lapping on coral sands draped by coconut palms. Needless to say, resort developers have placed their establishments on most of the best.

Unfortunately, most lagoons in Fiji are very shallow at low tide, thus limiting water sports for half the day. In other words, they are deep enough at low tide for walking, not swimming. The very best beaches do have lagoons deep enough for swimming and snorkeling at all tides, and I point them out in this section.

It seems to me that every nook and cranny in the Yasawa Islands is blessed with a white-sand beach. Certainly those gorgeous little islands have more than their fair share of Fiji's best beaches.

o **Qalito (Castaway) Island** (the Mamanucas): Better known as the home of **Castaway Island Resort** (p. 129), hilly Qalito Island ends at a point flanked on both sides by beaches of deep white sand, which helps make Castaway one of Fiji's most popular resorts.

o **Malolo Island** (the Mamanucas): The beach fronting **Malolo Island Fiji** resort (p. 127) has deep sand, and the lagoon here is deep enough for swimming and snorkeling at most tides. The resort has one of Fiji's best beach bars.

Fiji's Best Beaches

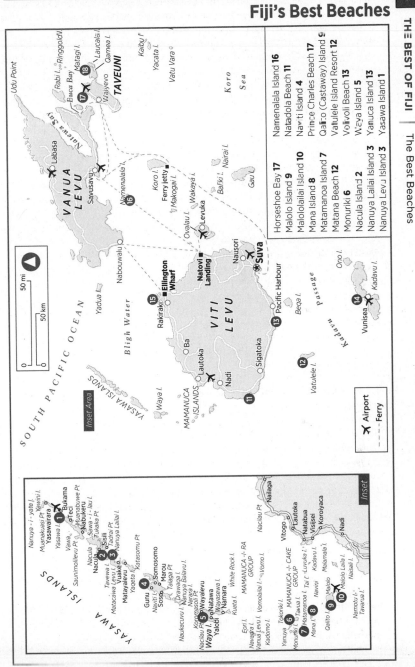

Namenalala Island **16**
Natadola Beach **11**
Naviti Island **4**
Prince Charles Beach **17**
Qamea (Castaway) Island **5**
Vatulele Island Resort **12**
Volivoli Beach **13**
Weya Island **5**
Yanuca Island **13**
Yasawa Island **1**

Horseshoe Bay **17**
Malolo Island **9**
Malololailai Island **10**
Mana Island **8**
Matamanoa Island **7**
Matana Beach **12**
Monuriki **6**
Nacula Island **2**
Nanuya Lailai Island **3**
Nanuya Levu Island **3**

○ **Mana Island** (the Mamanucas): Mana Island has beaches on both its sides, but the one on the south coast is worth writing home about. It's so long that it's shared by **Mana Island Resort** (p. 129) and bottom-end backpacker hostels.

○ **Matamanoa Island** (the Mamanucas): Just enough room exists between Matamanoa's rocky central hill and its beach to shoe-horn in **Matamanoa Island Resort** (p. 129). Both the sands and the lagoon here are deep enough to enjoy all the time.

○ **Malololailai Island** (the Mamanucas): Connected to the larger Malolo Island by a marshy isthmus, Malololailai is home to three resorts: **Musket Cove Island Resort** (p. 125), **Lomani Island Resort** (p. 125), and **Plantation Island Resort** (p. 126). Although the lagoon is shallow, the beach in front of Lomani and Plantation Island resorts is one of Fiji's most picturesque, with coconut palms hanging over it in places.

○ **Waya Island** (the Yasawas). A small bay on the northwest corner of dramatically beautiful Waya is bordered by a long stretch of deep white sand. Near the center of it stands the eclectic **Octopus Resort** (p. 134).

○ **Naviti Island** (the Yasawas). The western side of Naviti Island, about midway up the Yasawas, is indented with several bays with beaches. Best is at **Botaira Beach Resort** (p. 135), with excellent snorkeling just offshore.

○ **Nanuya Levu Island** (the Yasawas). One of the most picturesque of any resort in Fiji, the venerable **Turtle Island** (p. 139) sits beside one of a dozen beaches on Nanuya Levu Island, some of which starred in the Brooke Shields version of *The Blue Lagoon.*

○ **Nanuyalailai Island** (the Yasawas): Next door to its larger sister, Nanuyalailai is skirted on its south side by a long beach that wraps around a coconut palm–studded peninsula. **Nanuya Island Resort** (p. 139) sits on its western end, while **Blue Lagoon Cruises** (p. 122) uses the other to take its guests ashore.

○ **Nacula Island** (the Yasawas): It is my opinion that the world-class beach fronting **Blue Lagoon Beach Resort** (p. 140) and the adjacent **Oarsmans Bay Lodge** on Nacula Island is the best in Fiji. This curving strip of white sand reaches far out into the lagoon, so you can swim and snorkel at any time.

○ **Yasawa Island** (the Yasawas): Several of Fiji's best beaches are on Yasawa, the northernmost island in the Yasawa chain. One long stretch of sand near the north end is divided by big black rocks flanked by two Fijian villages. Another in front of **Yasawa Island Resort and Spa** (p. 141) also has rocks plus waves, a rarity among Fijian beaches.

○ **Natadola Beach** (the Coral Coast): One of only two beaches on Fiji's main island worth writing home about, Natadola is home to the **InterContinental Fiji Golf Resort & Spa** (p. 149) and the country's top golf course. The reef is far offshore here, allowing a bit of surf to hit the beach.

○ **Vatulele Island Resort** (Vatulele): The 1km (½ mile) of sand in front of luxurious **Vatulele Island Resort** (p. 157) is one of the most brilliant white beaches in Fiji, and the lagoon is deep enough for all-tide water sports.

○ **Yanuca Island** (Beqa Lagoon): I think the beach in front of **Batiluva Beach Resort,** a funky little surf camp (p. 163), is second best in Fiji, behind only the sands on Nacula Island in the Yasawas. Resorts at Pacific Harbour on Viti Levu bring their guests out here for excellent snorkeling around coral heads just off the beach.

- **Matana Beach** (Kadavu): On Kadavu's north shore, Matana Beach combines deep white sand with a deep lagoon. Bordered by a Fijian village and **Dive Kadavu/ Matana Beach Resort** (p. 170), Matana has a fine view westward along Kadavu's shore.
- **Volivoli Beach** (Rakiraki): At the very northern tip of Viti Levu, a few kilometers from Rakiraki, lovely Volivoli has a deep lagoon and a spectacular view southwestward toward Viti Levu's mountains. You don't have to pay a fortune either, with inexpensive **Volivoli Beach Resort** (p. 195) just around the corner.
- **Prince Charles Beach** (Taveuni): The northern coast of Taveuni has three great beaches within walking distance of each other, the best being Prince Charles Beach, so named because said prince once took a dip in its warm lagoon. See p. 226.
- **Horseshoe Bay** (Matagi Island): Matagi is an extinct volcano whose crater fell away on one side and formed picturesque, half-moon-shaped Horseshoe Bay. Guests at **Matangi Private Island Resort** (p. 233) can have one of its two fine little beaches all to themselves.

THE most ROMANTIC RESORTS

Fiji is a marvelous place for honeymoons and other romantic escapes. I've never stayed anywhere as love-enhancing as a thatched-roof bungalow beside the beach. You'll find lots of these in Fiji. A few are built on stilts out over the lagoon, while others have their own swimming pools and hot tubs.

Fiji's numerous small, relatively remote offshore resorts offer as much privacy as you are likely to desire. Many are even on islands all by themselves. Most of these establishments have less than 20 bungalows each, instead of the 40 or more found in French Polynesia and elsewhere, which means their units are usually widely spaced.

They are so romantic that a friend of mine says her ideal wedding would be to rent an entire small resort, take her wedding party with her, get married in Fijian costume beside the beach, and make the rest of her honeymoon a diving vacation.

Every offshore resort in Fiji qualifies as a very good romantic retreat, but I'm headed to one of the following when Cupid strikes. Most have full-service spas for your pampering pleasure.

- **The Westin Denarau Island Resort & Spa** (Denarau Island, Nadi; *C* **800/325-3535** or 675 0000; www.westin.com): Of the large hotels on Denarau Island, The Westin is the most romantic, with dark wood beams and tapa cloth giving its spacious rooms more Fijian charm than any of the others. The spa is very good, too. See p. 105.
- **Likuliku Lagoon Resort** (Malolo Island, the Mamanucas; *C* **672 4275** or 666 3344; www.likulikulagoon.com): This exquisitely designed resort is tops in the Mamanuca Islands, primarily because it's the first in Fiji with overwater bungalows. See p. 127.
- **Tokoriki Island Resort** (Tokoriki Island, the Mamanucas; *C* **666 1999;** www. tokoriki.com): The beach at Tokoriki has erosion problems, but it has bungalows with their own plunge pools (p. 131).

- **Matamanoa Island Resort** (Matamanoa Island, the Mamanucas; ℂ **666 0511**; www.matamanoa.com): It's less luxurious than Tokoriki, but Matamanoa is a good choice for cost-conscious honeymooners, and it has one of Fiji's best beaches. See p. 129.

- **Turtle Island** (Nanuya Levu Island, the Yasawas; ℂ **800/225-4347** or 672 2921; www.turtlefiji.com): Fiji's first top-end resort continues to offer romance beside its seemingly landlocked "Blue Lagoon." Its bungalows are among the most charming in Fiji. See p. 139.

- **Yasawa Island Resort and Spa** (Yasawa Island, the Yasawas; ℂ **672 2266**; www.yasawa.com): Sitting on one of the prettiest beaches in Fiji, Yasawa Island Resort and Spa has a very low-key, friendly ambience to go with its very large bungalows, the choicest being the secluded honeymoon unit with its own beach (it has a private pool). See p. 141.

- **Navutu Stars Resort** (Yaqeta Island, the Yasawas; ℂ **664 0553**; www.navutustarsfiji.com): Also in the Yasawa Islands, Navutu Stars Resort has a spa and yoga sessions in addition to fine food brought to you by its Italian owners. A salt-water pool compensates for a poor beach. See p. 138.

- **InterContinental Fiji Golf Resort & Spa** (ℂ Natadola Beach, the Coral Coast; **800/424-6835**; www.ichotelsgroup.com): Although the InterContinental attracts families, couples can entertain themselves in the Cleopatra bathtubs on each room's large private balcony. See p. 149.

- **Vatulele Island Resort** (off the Coral Coast; ℂ **672 0300**; www.vatulele.com): One of Fiji's top beaches fronts Vatulele Island Resort, which, after 2 decades of providing luxury, has attained venerable status among the country's top hotels. Romantic couples can have dinner out on the beach, or get a bird's-eye view from a private gazebo overlooking the sands. See p. 157.

- **The Wakaya Club** (Wakaya Island; ℂ **344 0128**; www.wakaya.com): In central Fiji near Ovalau Island, the Wakaya Club has long been at or near the top of Fiji's best resorts. It has some of the country's largest bungalows, plus a palatial mansion with its own pool, perched high atop a ridge. The staff leaves the guests to their own devices, and you might see a movie star or two relaxing here. See p. 207.

- **Jean-Michel Cousteau Fiji Islands Resort** (Savusavu; ℂ **800/246-3454** or 885 0188; www.fijiresort.com): "Cousteau" is Fiji's best family hotel but it expertly herds the kids away in the award-winning Bula Club so the young ones do not interfere with couples (including their own parents) in search of romance. The beautiful honeymoon villa has its own swimming pool. See p. 214.

- **Coconut Grove Beachfront Cottages** (Taveuni; ℂ/fax **888 0328**; www.coconutgrovefiji.com): Ronna Goldstein's charming three-unit, bed-and-breakfast-like hotel is one of Fiji's best bargains for anyone, including honeymooners on a budget. See p. 228.

- **Maravu Plantation Beach Resort & Spa** (Taveuni; ℂ **866/528-3864** or 888 0555; www.maravu.net): Maravu is not directly on the beach (a picturesque one is just across the road), but bungalows come equipped with hot tubs, and two of the honeymoon units have spectacular views of the Somosomo Strait. See p. 228.

- **Matangi Private Island Resort** (Matagi Island, off Taveuni; ℂ **888/628-2644** or 888 0260; www.matangiisland.com): One of the widely spaced bungalows at Matangi Private Island Resort is built up in a Pacific almond tree, while two others are carved in the side of a cliff. They all have outdoor bathrooms. See p. 233.

GETTING HITCHED IN FIJI

These romantic islands are marvelous places to get married, and becoming officially hitched is relatively easy in Fiji. You do not have to be a resident, and obtaining the necessary licenses and permits requires only a few days. Most resorts will take care of the formalities and organize traditional ceremonies (which can take place on the beach, if you like). Their wedding coordinators will tell you what documents you will need to bring (or send in advance) and what local formalities you will need to execute. *Note:* Do not even think of making the arrangements yourself.

○ **Qamea Resort and Spa** (Qamea Island, off Taveuni; ℂ **866/867-2632** or 888 0220; www.qamea.com): Among my favorite places to stay are the charming, old South Seas–style bungalows at Qamea Island Resort and Spa. More luxurious still are the two bungalows specifically designed for honeymooners and two villas with their own plunge pools. Kerosene lanterns romantically light the 16m-high (52-ft.) thatched roof of Qamea's main building at night. See p. 234.

THE best PLACES TO GET AWAY FROM IT ALL

Some of Fiji's offshore resorts are better at getting away from it all than others. The ones I list below are small enough that you won't have a lot of company, and, because they are on islands all by themselves, you won't have people from another property walking along your stretch of private beach.

○ **Wadigi Island Resort** (Wadigi Island, the Mamanucas; ℂ **672 0901**; www.wadigi. com): On a tiny islet, Wadigi Island Resort has just three units, all on top of a peak with a glorious view of nearby Malolo Island and the surrounding Mamanucas. Celebrities love it because it's very private. See p. 132.

○ **Matamanoa Island Resort** (Matamanoa Island, the Mamanucas; ℂ **666 0511**; www.matamanoa.com): In the westernmost portion of the Mamanucas, this remote little resort is one of Fiji's most reasonably priced romantic resorts, and its beach is superb. See p. 129.

○ **Botaira Beach Resort** (Naviti Island, the Yasawas; ℂ **603 0200**; www.botaira. com): The country's best Fijian-owned resort sits by itself beside a great beach and colorful lagoon. Your mobile phone won't work here, nor will you be able to log onto the Internet. See p. 135.

○ **Turtle Island** (Nanuya Levu Island, the Yasawas; ℂ **800/225-4347** or 672 2921; www.turtlefiji.com): Fiji's first top-end resort has all of Nanuya Levu Island to itself. Sitting on a ridge by itself, the most private bungalow has a 180-degree view of the lagoon and surrounding islands. See p. 139.

○ **Yasawa Island Resort and Spa** (Yasawa Island, the Yasawas; ℂ **672 2266**; www. yasawa.com): Another fine honeymoon choice, Yasawa Island Resort and Spa has no neighbors and, therefore, is very private. Its secluded honeymoon *bure* (bungalow) has its own private beach and pool. See p. 141.

o **Lalati Resort & Spa** (Beqa Island; © **347 2033;** www.lalati-fiji.com): Beside picturesque Malumu Bay and enjoying a fine view of the Beqa Lagoon and Viti Levu's southern shore, Lalati appeals to couples looking to dive, or to just get away. The full-service spa is augmented by an air-conditioned lounge with TV and DVD player, and the outdoor pool helps compensate for a poor beach. See p. 164.

o **Lawaki Beach House** (Beqa Island; © **992 1621** or 368 4088; www.lawakibeach housefiji.com): Beside a beach, this homestay is the best place in Fiji for anyone on a tight budget to escape from it all. See p. 165.

o **Royal Davui Island Fiji** (in Beqa Lagoon; © **330 7090;** www.royaldavui.com): On a tiny, rocky islet in Beqa Lagoon, this luxury resort is set above a small beach. Bungalows are built in an old-growth hillside, but guests are compensated by marvelous views from each unit's plunge pool–equipped veranda. See p. 165.

o **Dive Kadavu/Matana Beach Resort** (Kadavu Island; © **368 3502;** www.dive kadavu.com): Only a 10-minute boat ride from Kadavu's airstrip, this little resort has been a top dive base since 1983, but it uses the name Matana Beach Resort to take advantage of its location on one of Fiji's most beautiful beaches. See p. 170.

o **Matava—The Astrolabe Hideaway** (Kadavu Island; © **333 6222;** www.matava. com): Much farther than Dive Kadavu/Matana Beach Resort from the airstrip—at least 45 minutes by small boat—Matava is so eco-friendly that it has no air-conditioners and turns on the solar-powered lights only at night. Made primarily of thatch and other natural materials, its spacious bungalows are nevertheless charming. It's close to many Great Astrolabe Reef dive sights, but it also specializes in kayaking trips, bird-watching, and deep sea fishing. See p. 171.

o **Koromakawa Resort** (Ono Island; © **603 0782;** www.koromakawa.com.fj): You are guaranteed to be by yourselves at this remote resort, which has a single two-bedroom cottage beside a beach on Ono Island off Kadavu's northwest coast. See p. 171.

o **The Wakaya Club** (Wakaya Island; © **344 0128;** www.wakaya.com): Except for a few private villas owned by Hollywooders and other well-heeled types, one of Fiji's top resorts has all of Wakaya Island to itself. Nicole Kidman, Russell Crowe, and other Aussies like to take breaks at Wakaya on their way home. See p. 207.

o **Matangi Private Island Resort** (Matangi Island, off Taveuni; © **888/628-2644** or 888 0260; www.matangiisland.com): This couples-only resort's honeymoon bungalow up in a Pacific almond tree is both charming and private, and you can walk over the hill and have the gorgeous beach in Horseshoe Bay all to yourselves. See p. 233.

o **Qamea Resort and Spa** (Qamea Island, off Taveuni; © **866/867-2632** or 888 0220; www.qamea.com): Qamea's two luxurious honeymoon bungalows are situated on one end of the resort, although I prefer the two other villas with their own plunge pools. See p. 234.

THE best FAMILY RESORTS

There are no Disney Worlds or other such attractions in Fiji. That's not to say that children won't have a fine time here, for Fiji draws many Australians and New Zealanders on family holidays. It has one of the South Pacific's finest family resorts, and others make provisions for families as well as honeymooners. Kids who are at home in the water will enjoy themselves most.

With their innate love of children, Fijians are very good at babysitting and staffing the kids' programs at the major resorts.

On the other hand, many of Fiji's small resorts do not accept young children. I point these out in my hotel reviews.

o **Radisson Resort Fiji Denarau Island** (Denarau Island, Nadi; ✆ 800/395-7046 or 675 1264; www.radisson.com/fiji): All of the large resorts on Denarau are well equipped for families with children, but I am especially fond of the Radisson because of its large, charming, and safe swimming pool complex. Some of its condo units even have washers and dryers. See p. 102.

o **Treasure Island Resort** (Luvuka Island, the Mamanucas; ✆ 666 6999; www. fiji-treasure.com): Modest but comfortable Treasure Island occupies a tiny, beach-fringed islet, the middle of which has a children's program, a miniature golf course, and baby sea turtles swimming in a breeding pool. See p. 123.

o **Castaway Island Resort** (Qalito Island, the Mamanucas; ✆ 800/888-0120 or 666 1233; www.castawayfiji.com): One of Fiji's oldest resorts but thoroughly refurbished over the years, Castaway has plenty to keep both adults and children occupied, from a wide array of water sports to a kids' playroom and a nursery. See p. 129.

o **Malolo Island Fiji** (Malolo Island, the Mamanucas; ✆ 666 9192; www.malolo island.com): This sister of the adults-only Likuliku Lagoon Resort has a fine beach, as well as a shaded swimming pool designed with children in mind. See p. 127.

o **Mana Island Resort** (Mana Island, the Mamanucas; ✆ 665 0423; www.manafiji. com): Relatively large Mana Island Resort caters to everyone and gets many day-trippers from Nadi; but the beach is safe, and it has one of the better children's programs in the Mamanuca Islands. See p. 129.

o **Plantation Island Resort** (Malololailai Island, the Mamanucas; ✆ 666 9333; www.plantationisland.com): The largest resort in the Mamanucas has long appealed to Australian families, offering a wide range of accommodations and activities, including a children's program with a full-time babysitter. See p. 126.

o **InterContinental Fiji Golf Resort & Spa** (✆ Natadola Beach, the Coral Coast; 800/424-6835; www.ichotelsgroup.com): Fiji's swanky golf resort also caters to families with a state-of-the-art children's center and a large, shallow swimming pool. See p. 149.

o **Outrigger on the Lagoon Fiji** (Korotogo, the Coral Coast; ✆ 800/688-7444 or 650 0044; www.outrigger.com): The beach and shallow lagoon at the Outrigger leave much to be desired, but it has an exceptional swimming pool. See p. 150.

o **Shangri-La's Fijian Resort & Spa** (Yanuca Island, the Coral Coast; ✆ 866/565-5050 or 652 0155; www.shangri-la.com): The country's largest resort with 442 units, "The Fijian" has a better beach and lagoon than its big rivals on Denarau Island and the Coral Coast. You may exhaust yourself chasing the youngsters around its sprawling grounds, but the hotel has plenty of activities for all ages. See p. 149.

o **Jean-Michel Cousteau Fiji Islands Resort** (Savusavu; ✆ 800/246-3454 or 885 0188; www.fijiresort.com): Although it appeals equally to couples, Fiji's finest family resort encourages parents to enroll their kids in its exceptional Bula Club, thus keeping the youngsters educated, entertained, and out of sight from break-fast to bedtime. See p. 214

THE best CULTURAL & ENVIRONMENTAL EXPERIENCES

The Fijians are justly proud of their ancient culture, and they eagerly inform anyone who asks about both their ancient and modern ways. Here are some of the best ways to learn about their lifestyle and explore the environment of their islands.

o **Fijian Village Visits** (nationwide): Many tours from Nadi, the Coral Coast, and most offshore resorts include visits to traditional Fijian villages, whose residents stage welcoming ceremonies (featuring the slightly narcotic drink kava, or *yaqona* as it's known in Fiji). The hosts then show visitors around and explain how the old and the new combine in today's villages. See "Exploring the Nadi Area," p. 90.

o **Sigatoka Sand Dunes National Park** (near Sigatoka, the Coral Coast; ✆ 652 0243; www.nationaltrust.org.fj): Ancient Fijian burial grounds and pieces of pottery dating from 5 B.C. to A.D. 240 have been found among these dunes, which stretch for several miles along Viti Levu's southern coast. See p. 146.

o **Tavuni Hill Fort** (near Sigatoka, the Coral Coast; ✆ 650 0818): This best example of a traditional Fijian fort stands atop a hill east of Sigatoka. It renders both a glimpse of what war was like in the old days and a splendid view over the Sigatoka River Valley. See p. 147.

o **Kula Eco Park** (Korotogo, the Coral Coast; ✆ 650 0505; www.fijiwild.com): Opposite the Outrigger on the Lagoon Fiji, this nature park exhibits most of Fiji's endemic species of birds, reptiles, and mammals. Children are given a chance to handle some of the creatures in a petting zoo. See p. 148.

o **Waterfall and Cave Tours** (the Coral Coast): On walking tours offered by **Adventures in Paradise Fiji** (✆ 652 0833; www.adventuresinparadisefiji.com), you will be welcomed into a Fijian village plus see a cave and one of the country's many waterfalls. See p. 148.

o **Arts Village Cultural Centre** (Pacific Harbour; ✆ 345 0065; www.artsvillage. com): A reconstructed traditional Fijian village built of thatch and other local materials is the centerpiece of this cultural center, which has fire-walking shows in addition to demonstrations of old-time Fijian skills. See p. 159.

o **Rafting on the Navua River** (Pacific Harbour): The Navua River begins in the highlands and ends on the southern coast of Viti Levu, on the way cutting two gorges, one of them dubbed the "Grand Canyon of Fiji." Rafting on the river— either by inflatable raft through the white-water gorge with **Rivers Fiji** (✆ 800/446-2411 in the U.S., or 345 0147; www.riversfiji.com) or while riding lashed-together bamboo poles (a bilibili raft) through the lazy lowlands with **Discover Fiji Tours** (✆ 345 0180; www.discoverfijitours.com)—is one of Fiji's top outdoor experiences. See p. 161.

o **Fiji Museum** (Thurston Park, Suva; ✆ 331 5944; www.fijimuseum.org.fj): The small but very good Fiji Museum has a terrific collection of war clubs, cannibal forks, and other ancient artifacts, plus the rudder of HMS *Bounty*. See p. 177.

o **Suva Municipal Market** (Usher St. at Rodwell Rd., Suva; no phone): You'll see an enormous amount of tropical produce for sale at Suva's main supplier of food. The market is especially active on Saturday morning. See p. 177.

- **Rainforest Walks** (Savusavu): No wires are in place to allow exploration of the canopy, but earthly gravel pathways lead to a waterfall in **Waisali Rainforest Reserve** (℗ 330 1807; www.nationaltrust.org.fj), a 116-hectare (290-acre) national forest up in the central mountains of Vanua Levu. See p. 211.

- **Adventure Cruises on the Tui Tai** (Savusavu; ℗ 885 3032; www.tuitai.com): Passengers on the small but luxurious sailing ship *Tui Tai* spend much of their time snorkeling, diving, and mountain biking, but they also get to visit Fijian villages on remote islands such as Kioa. See p. 211.

- **Bouma Falls and Lavena Coastal Walk** (Taveuni): Although Taveuni is best known for world-class scuba diving, it's also one of the best places in Fiji to explore the mountainous interior. **Bouma National Heritage Park** (℗ 888 0390; www.bnhp.org) has three waterfalls, and the **Lavena Coastal Walk** (℗ 820 3639) leads along the island's nearly deserted east coast to yet another falls—though you'll need to swim to reach it. See p. 222.

THE best OF THE OLD SOUTH SEAS

Fiji is developing rapidly, with modern, fast-paced towns replacing what were once small villages and sleepy backwater ports. However, a few places still hearken back to the old South Sea days of coconut planters, beach bums, and missionaries.

- **Lautoka:** Fiji's second-largest city is still small enough to walk around, and its genteel citizens normally won't hassle you to "come in, take a look" at their shops. The town was laid out by the British, with broad streets, shady sidewalks, and pleasant parks. See "Lautoka," in chapter 5.

- **Sigatoka:** The riverfront town of Sigatoka, on the Coral Coast, isn't as pleasing to the eye as Lautoka, but it still makes its living not from tourists but from trading with the farmers in the picturesque Sigatoka River Valley. Across the river from today's downtown is LasiLasi, an early 20th-century European settlement and a candidate for heritage site status. See chapter 7.

- **Kadavu:** The long, skinny island of Kadavu, some 100km (60 miles) south of Viti Levu, has a road on one end, but you must take a boat to reach all its best spots. That's one bit of evidence of how little Kadavu has changed. Unlike Fiji's other large islands, it has no sugar-cane farms, no mongooses, no iguanas, no myna birds, and few if any Fiji Indians. The result: It's like the rest of Fiji used to be. See chapter 9.

- **Suva:** The British are long gone, and Suva today is the largest, most vibrant city in the South Pacific islands. But among its new high-rise office towers are grand colonial buildings, orderly parks, and a mixed population that dates back to the days of the Raj. See chapter 10.

- **Rakiraki:** On the northern tip of Viti Levu, the Fijian village of Rakiraki and its surrounding countryside seem caught in a time warp, provided you don't notice the few small real-estate developments creeping into the hills (will we Westerners ever stop wanting to buy our own piece of paradise?). See chapter 11.

- **Levuka** (Ovalau Island): No other town has remained the same after a century as much as has Levuka, Fiji's first European-style town and its original colonial capital in the 1870s. The dramatic cliffs of Ovalau Island hemmed in the town and prevented growth, so the government moved to Suva in 1882. Levuka looks very much as it did then, with a row of clapboard general stores along picturesque Beach Street. See chapter 12.

o **Savusavu:** You're apt to see more Americans strolling the streets of picturesque Savusavu than anywhere else in Fiji, as so many of them have purchased land near there, but the town still has the feel of the days when schooners would pick up cargo at such places as the Copra Shed. See chapter 13.

o **Taveuni:** Fiji's lush "Garden Island" has changed little since Europeans bought land holdings and started coconut plantations in the 19th century. With a large population of indigenous plants and animals, Taveuni is a nature lover's delight and the best place to go hiking in Fiji. See chapter 14.

THE best DINING EXPERIENCES

You won't be stuck eating only island-style food cooked in an earth oven (see "Eating & Drinking in Fiji," in chapter 2), nor will you be limited by New Zealanders' and Australians' traditionally bland tastes, which until recently predominated at many restaurants in Fiji. The Indians brought curries to Fiji, and exciting new restaurants are offering cuisine from around the world.

Here are some of my favorites.

o **Indigo** (Denarau Island; ✆ 675 0026): In the Port Denarau shopping and dining complex, Indigo is the second-best Indian restaurant in Fiji, behind Saffron (see below), but it also pulls from Southeast Asian culinary tradition with Thai-style crab and Rendang curry. Most dining is alfresco. See p. 112.

o **Bulaccino** (Nadi Town; ✆ 672 8638): I've had terrific breakfasts and lunches at this sophisticated coffee shop beside the Nadi River. Unfortunately, it is not open for dinner. See p. 112.

o **Saffron** (Nadi Town; ✆ 670 1233; www.chefsfiji.com): Part of the Jack's of Fiji shopping complex in downtown Nadi, Saffron consistently serves some of Fiji's best northern Indian cuisine, and it's tops for vegetarians, too. See p. 113.

o **Nadina Authentic Fijian Restaurant** (Queen's Rd., Martintar, Nadi; ✆ 672 7313): While most resorts serve native food only on the buffets at their nighttime island feasts, this little restaurant serves great Fijian fare—such as the luscious *ota miti,* the tender young shoots of the wood fern served with coconut milk—my favorite Fijian vegetable. See p. 114.

o **Sitar Indian and Thai Restaurant** (Queen's Rd., Martintar, Nadi; ✆ 672 7722; www.sitar.com.au): Predominately alfresco, the casual Sitar serves very good Indian and Thai cuisine in a setting more reminiscent of an Australian pub complete with chest-high drinking tables and a big sports TV. See p. 115.

o **Vilisite's Seafood Restaurant** (the Coral Coast; ✆ 653 0054): This seaside restaurant, owned and operated by a friendly Fijian woman named Vilisite, doesn't look like much from the outside, but it offers a handful of excellent seafood meals to augment a terrific view along the Coral Coast. See p. 156.

o **Hare Krishna Restaurant** (16 Pratt St., Suva; ✆ 331 4154): I always have at least one lunch at this clean, casual vegetarian restaurant. Choosing is easy, as everything is presented cafeteria-style. See p. 187.

- **Maya Dhaba** (281 Victoria Parade, Suva; ✆ **331 0045**): Although inexpensive, Maya Dhaba is Suva's most sophisticated restaurant, offering authentic Indian cuisine at extraordinarily reasonable prices in a hip, urbane environment. Both meat and vegetarian dishes appear here. See p. 188.

- **Old Mill Cottage** (47–49 Carnavon St., Suva; ✆ **331 2134**): Diplomats and government workers pack this old colonial cottage at breakfast and lunch for some of the region's best and least-expensive local fare. Offerings range from English-style roast chicken with mashed potatoes and peas to Fijian-style *palusami* (fresh fish wrapped in taro leaves and steamed in coconut milk). See p. 188.

- **Surf 'n' Turf** (Copra Shed, Savusavu; ✆ **881 0966**): A veteran of Jean-Michel Cousteau Fiji Islands Resort, Chef Vijendra Kumar is very good with tropical lobsters, and he often accompanies them with *ota*, my favorite Fijian vegetable. See p. 219.

- **Coconut Grove Restaurant** (Matei, Taveuni; ✆ **888 0328;** www.coconutgrove fiji.com): I love the fresh banana bread and the fish curry at Ronna Goldstein's little hotel on Taveuni. Adding to the enjoyment is the view from her veranda of the rocky islets off Taveuni. See p. 231.

- **Tramontu Bar & Grill** (Matei, Taveuni; ✆ **888 2224**): The pizzas and other fare at this local restaurant aren't that great, but it has a million-dollar view of the Somosomo Strait from its clifftop perch. See p. 232.

- **Vunibokoi Restaurant** (Matei, Taveuni; ✆ **888 0560;** www.tovutovu.com): This plain restaurant on the front porch of the inexpensive Tovu Tovu Resort has one of the best Friday-night buffets of Fijian *lovo* food (cooked in an underground oven). See p. 232.

THE best DIVING & SNORKELING

With nutrient-rich waters welling up from the Tonga Trench offshore and being carried by strong currents funneling through narrow passages, Fiji is famous for some of the world's most colorful soft corals.

All the islands have excellent scuba diving and snorkeling, and all but a few of the resorts either have their own dive operations or can easily make arrangements with a local company. Many dive operators will take snorkelers along; that's my favorite way to go snorkeling in Fiji.

The best areas to dive are listed here. See "Diving & Snorkeling," under "The Active Traveler," in chapter 3, for additional advice and information, especially about live-aboard dive boats, which will take you to reefs beyond those reachable from the resorts.

Most lagoons in Fiji become extremely shallow at low tide, which means you may do little more than wade in the water for half the day. I tell where you can swim and snorkel at all tides under "Fiji's Best Beaches," earlier in this chapter.

- **Shark Diving** (Pacific Harbour): The dive masters lure tiger, bull, and other sharks by feeding them in these exciting dives off southern Viti Levu. It's not for novices. See chapter 8.

- **Beqa Lagoon** (off Beqa Island): Beqa Lagoon has soft corals, especially at Frigate Passage, where they seem to fall over one another. See chapter 8.

o **Great Astrolabe Reef** (off Kadavu): Skirting the eastern and southern sides of Kadavu, the Great Astrolabe Reef has lost much of its reef-top soft corals but still has plenty over the sides. It also attracts Fiji's largest concentration of manta rays. See chapter 9.

o **Bligh Water** (off Rakiraki, northern Viti Levu): Although not as dramatically beautiful as elsewhere, the reefs off northern Viti Levu have colorful soft corals, and with less current, you can see them in most tidal conditions. It is Fiji's best for wreck diving. See chapter 11.

o **Lomaiviti Passage** (btw. Ovalau and Wakaya islands): With both soft and hard corals, the dive sites in the waters between Ovalau and Wakaya islands are among the most diverse in Fiji. And since there are few resorts in the area, you could have them all to yourself. See chapter 12.

o **Namena Marine Protected Reserve** (off Savusavu): This magnificent barrier reef that nearly surrounds Moody's Namena resort is now a protected marine reserve populated by both soft and hard corals. See chapter 13.

o **Somosomo Strait** (off Taveuni): The narrow passage between Vanua Levu and Taveuni is Fiji's most famous site for soft corals, especially its Great White Wall and Rainbow Reef. The snorkeling is very good here, too, but watch out for strong currents and sharks. See chapter 14.

FIJI IN DEPTH

I will say this often: The thing I like best about Fiji is its enormously friendly people. You'll see what I mean as soon as you get off the plane, clear Customs and Immigration, and are greeted by a procession of smiling faces, all of them exclaiming an enthusiastic *"Bula!"* That one word—"health" in Fijian—expresses the warmest and most heartfelt welcome I have ever received anywhere.

Fiji's great diversity will also be immediately evident, for the taxi drivers who whisk you to your hotel will not be Fijians of Melanesian heritage, but Indians whose ancestors migrated to Fiji from places such as Calcutta and Madras. Now about 40% of the population, these Fiji Indians have played major roles in making their country the most prosperous of the independent South Pacific island nations.

Fiji has a lot to offer in terms of raw material for building the region's largest tourism industry. In the most-visited areas—and especially on Fiji's marvelous offshore islets—you'll find gorgeous white-sand beaches bordered by curving coconut palms, azure lagoons, and colorful reefs offering world-class scuba diving and snorkeling, green mountains sweeping to the sea, and a tropical climate in which to enjoy it all.

Fiji has something for every budget. Its wide variety of accommodations ranges from deluxe resorts nestled in tropical gardens beside the beach to down-to-basics hostels that cater to the young and young-at-heart. Out on its 300-plus islands is one of the largest and finest collections of small, Robinson Crusoe–like offshore resorts I have ever seen.

Although it has been in the news because of its military coups (four of them, most recently in Dec 2006), visitors have not directly been affected by the political tensions. From a traveler's point of view, everything was working normally. Travel advisories by the New Zealand government notwithstanding, politics in Fiji, to my mind, should not determine whether you visit these marvelous islands and their extraordinarily friendly inhabitants.

Before you start making your plans, let's see what Fiji is like today, review the fascinating story of how it got to this point, take a look at its mix of cultures and languages, and get a glimpse of its natural environment.

FIJI TODAY

About half the people in Fiji reside in urban areas and deal with typical matters such as traffic jams, while the others live out in the countryside trying to squeeze a living from sugar-cane farms, or to provide provisions for their traditional Fijian villages.

Thanks to its industrious Indian residents, Fiji is a relatively developed Third World country. With a multitude of buses and taxis, the transportation system is efficient and relatively inexpensive, though service from the one domestic airline tends to be a bit pricy. The electrical system is reliable, as are communications. Two over-the-air TV stations serve the country's viewers, and they can pay for satellite service. Despite periodic disruptions in some areas, the water pipes provide clean water to the taps.

All of which means that travel in Fiji, overall, is both efficient and comfortable.

Government

Fiji had a Westminster-style government prior to the 2006 coup. A 71-member parliament consisted of 23 seats reserved for Fijians, 19 for Indians, 1 for Rotuma (a Polynesian island north of Viti Levu), 3 for general electors (anyone who's a Fijian, Indian, or Rotuman), and 25 for any citizen regardless of race. The Great Council of Chiefs picked the country's largely figurehead president, who presided over an appointed senate with relatively little power.

> **Impressions**
>
> *There is no part of Fiji which is not civilized, although bush natives prefer a more naked kind of life.*
> —James A. Michener, *Return to Paradise*, 1951

Since the coup, the country has had an interim government headed by the military commander, navy Commodore Frank Bainimarama, who overthrew elected Prime Minister Laisenia Qarase's Fiji nationalist government, which Bainimarama accused of being both corrupt and racist. His interim government consists of a broad range of local leaders, and despite its suppressing political dissent and the local media, is seen by many locals as more progressive than its elected predecessor.

Bainimarama has abolished the constitution and has promised to hold elections in 2014 after the country writes a new constitution without the race-based electoral system by which nationalist Fijians maintained a majority in parliament.

While the Fijian-Indian racial divide gets most of the blame for the coups, the situation is more complicated. Many indigenous Fijians are educated, live in urban areas, hold responsible positions in tourism and other industries, and deal with Indians on a daily basis. They are at opposites with other Fijians, especially some fundamentalist Christians of the Methodist persuasion, who see Indians as heathens who should be deported.

In addition, the country has a hereditary system of Fijian chiefs, some of whom have always been rivals. Some descendants of Cakobau, the chief of tiny Bau Island who rose to national power with the help of European settlers in the 1840s (see "Looking Back at Fiji," below), were prime backers of the Fiji nationalist government ousted in 2006. Others are serving in today's interim government, including Ratu Epeli Nailatikau, the President of Fiji.

Economy

Tourism is far and away Fiji's largest industry. Although the number of visitors dropped off following the December 2006 coup, earlier record demand spurred a hotel construction boom. Sugar and garment manufacturing—Fiji's other economic mainstays—have also fallen off. Grown primarily by Indian farmers on land leased from Fijians, the sugar cane is harvested between June and November and crushed in five aging sugar mills—all of which need repair and upgrading—operated by the government-owned Fiji Sugar Corporation. The number of farmers has decreased because Fijian landowners did not renew many of their land leases (some displaced farmers have moved into shanties around Suva). In addition, the country lost European Union sugar price supports and favorable trade preferences for garments sold to the United States and Australia.

Behind sugar, the country's leading exports are the famous "Fiji" mineral water, fresh and frozen fish, tuna canned at Levuka, timber and wood products, taro and cassava, and gold mined in northern Viti Levu. For domestic consumption, Fiji produces furniture, coffee (you'll get a rich, strong brew throughout the country), and other consumer goods (the Colgate toothpaste you buy in Fiji most likely will have been made here). Suva is also a major transshipment point for goods destined for other South Pacific islands. Remittances from locals overseas also contribute significantly to the economy.

Nevertheless, unemployment is a persistent problem in Fiji. More than half the population is under 25, and there just aren't enough jobs being created for young people joining the workforce. About 50% of all households live below the official poverty line or just above it. As a consequence, the country has seen a marked increase in burglaries, robberies, home invasions, and other crimes.

LOOKING BACK AT FIJI

Fiji's oral history goes back some 2,500 years, when the current indigenous residents' ancestors landed on Viti Levu, but the first European eyes in these parts belonged to Dutch navigator Abel Tasman, who sighted Vanua Levu Island and some others in 1643. British Capt. James Cook, the famous South Pacific explorer, visited one of the southernmost islands in 1774. Capt. William Bligh was the first European to sail through and plot the group, after the mutiny on HMS *Bounty* in April 1789. Bligh and his loyal crew sailed their longboat through Fiji on their way to safety in Indonesia. They passed Ovalau and sailed between Viti Levu and Vanua Levu. Large Fijian *druas* (war canoes) gave chase near the Yasawas, but with some furious paddling and the help of a fortuitous squall, Bligh and his men escaped to the open ocean. For a while, Fiji was known as the Bligh Islands, and the passage between Viti Levu and Vanua Levu still is named Bligh Water.

The Tongans warned the Europeans, who made their way west across

---

Recovering the *Bounty*'s Rudder

Sunk at Pitcairn Island by the mutineers in 1789, HMS *Bounty* remained in its watery grave until it was discovered by a *National Geographic* expedition in the 1950s. The *Bounty*'s rudder is now on display at the Fiji Museum in Suva (p. 177).

History of Fiji

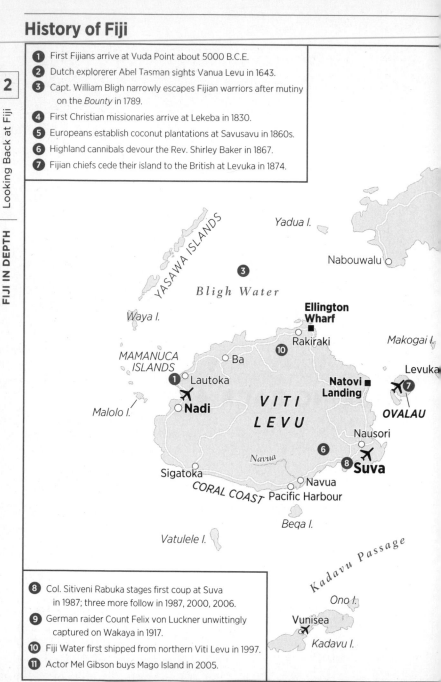

1. First Fijians arrive at Vuda Point about 5000 B.C.E.
2. Dutch explorerer Abel Tasman sights Vanua Levu in 1643.
3. Capt. William Bligh narrowly escapes Fijian warriors after mutiny on the *Bounty* in 1789.
4. First Christian missionaries arrive at Lekeba in 1830.
5. Europeans establish coconut plantations at Savusavu in 1860s.
6. Highland cannibals devour the Rev. Shirley Baker in 1867.
7. Fijian chiefs cede their island to the British at Levuka in 1874.

Yadua I.

Nabouwalu

YASAWA ISLANDS

Bligh Water

3

Waya I.

Ellington Wharf

Rakiraki

Makogai I.

MAMANUCA ISLANDS

Ba

10

Levuka

1 Lautoka

Natovi Landing

Malolo I.

Nadi

VITI LEVU

OVALAU

7

Nausori

Navua

6

8 Suva

Sigatoka

CORAL COAST Pacific Harbour

Navua

Beqa I.

Vatulele I.

Kadavu Passage

Ono I.

Vunisea

Kadavu I.

8. Col. Sitiveni Rabuka stages first coup at Suva in 1987; three more follow in 1987, 2000, 2006.
9. German raider Count Felix von Luckner unwittingly captured on Wakaya in 1917.
10. Fiji Water first shipped from northern Viti Levu in 1997.
11. Actor Mel Gibson buys Mago Island in 2005.

Udu
Point

Airport

SOUTH
PACIFIC
OCEAN

Labasa

VANUA
LEVU

Natewa

Rabi I. Ringgold I.

Buca Bay

Savusavu

Matagi

Waiyevo

Namenalala I.

Qamea

TAVEUNI

Naitaba I.

Koro I.

Kaibu I.

Vanua Balavu I.

Yacata I.

Ferry jetty

Koro
Sea

Mago

Vatu
Vara

Tuvuca I.

Wakaya I.

Cicia

LAU
GROUP

Nairai I.

Nayau I.

Gau I.

Lekeba I.

Vanua Vatu I.

Oneata I.

Moala I.

Komo

Moce I.

MOALA
GROUP

Vuaqava I.

Namuka-i-lau I.

Kabara I.

Totoya I.

Matuku I.

Fulaga I.

0   50 mi
0   50 km

the South Pacific, that Fiji was inhabited by ferocious cannibals, and the reports by Bligh and others of reef-strewn waters added to the dangerous reputation of the islands. Consequently, European penetration into Fiji was limited for many years to beach bums and convicts who escaped from the British penal colonies in Australia. There was a sandalwood rush between 1804 and 1813. Other traders arrived in the 1820s in search of *bêche-de-mer* (sea cucumber). This trade continued until the 1850s and had a lasting impact on Fiji because along with the traders came guns and whiskey.

Cakobau Rises & Falls

The traders and settlers established Fiji's first European-style town at Levuka on Ovalau in the early 1820s; but, for many years, the real power lay on Bau, a tiny island just off the east coast of Viti Levu. With the help of a Swedish mercenary named Charlie Savage, who supplied the guns, High Chief Tanoa of Bau defeated several much larger confederations and extended his control over most of western Fiji. Bau's influence grew even more under his son and successor, Cakobau, who rose to the height of power in the 1840s. Cakobau never ruled over all the islands, however, for Enele Ma'afu, a member of Tonga's royal family, moved to the Lau Group in 1848 and exerted control over eastern Fiji. Ma'afu brought along Wesleyan missionaries from Tonga and gave the Methodist church a foothold in Fiji (it still is the predominate denomination here).

Although Cakobau governed much of western Fiji, local chiefs continued to be powerful enough to make his control tenuous. The lesser chiefs, especially those in the mountains, also saw the Wesleyan missionaries as a threat to their power, and most of them refused to convert or even to allow the missionaries to establish outposts in their villages. Some mountaineers made a meal of the Rev. Thomas Baker when he tried to convert them in 1867 (see the "A Holy Meal" box, later in this chapter).

Cakobau's slide from power began in earnest July 4, 1849, when John Brown Williams, the American consul, celebrated the birth of his own nation. A cannon went

DATELINE

1500 B.C. Polynesians arrive from the west.

500 B.C. Melanesians settle in Fiji, push Polynesians eastward.

A.D. 1300–1600 Polynesians, especially Tongans, invade from the east.

1643 Abel Tasman sights Vanua Levu, other islands in Fiji.

1774 Capt. James Cook visits Vatoa.

1789 After the mutiny on the HMS Bounty, Capt. William Bligh navigates his longboat through Fiji and is nearly captured by a war canoe.

1808 Swedish mercenary Charlie Savage arrives at Bau and supplies guns to Chief Tanoa in successful wars to conquer western Fiji.

1822 European settlement begins at Levuka.

1830 First Christian missionaries arrive at Lakeba in the Lau Group.

1840 A U.S. exploring expedition under Capt. John Wilkes visits the islands.

1848 Prince Enele Ma'afu exerts Tongan control over eastern Fiji from outpost in Lau Group.

off and started a fire that burned Williams's house. The Fijians promptly looted the burning building. Williams blamed Cakobau and demanded US$5,000 in damages. Within a few years the U.S. claims against the chief totaled more than US$40,000, an enormous sum in those days. In the late 1850s, with Ma'afu and his confederation of chiefs gaining power—and disorder growing in western Fiji—Cakobau offered to cede the islands to Great Britain if Queen Victoria would pay the Americans. The British pondered his offer for 4 years and turned him down.

> **Impressions**
>
> *Many of the missionaries were eaten, leading an irreverent planter to suggest that they triumphed by infiltration.*
> —James A. Michener, *Return to Paradise*, 1951

Cakobau worked a better deal when the Polynesia Company, an Australian planting and commercial enterprise, came to Fiji looking for suitable land after the price of cotton skyrocketed during the U.S. Civil War. Instead of offering his entire kingdom, Cakobau this time tendered only 80,000 hectares (200,000 acres). The Polynesia Company accepted, paid off the U.S. claims, and, in 1870, landed Australian settlers near a Fijian village known as Suva. The land was unsuitable for cotton, and the climate was too wet for sugar; so the speculators sold their property to the government, which moved the capital there from Levuka in 1882.

Fiji Becomes a Colony

The Polynesia Company's settlers were just a few of the several thousand European planters who came to Fiji in the 1860s and early 1870s. They bought land for plantations from the Fijians, sometimes fraudulently and often for whiskey and guns. Claims and counterclaims to land ownership followed; and, with no legal mechanism to settle the disputes, Fiji was swept to the brink of a race war. Things came to a head in 1870, when the bottom fell out of cotton prices, hurricanes destroyed

---

1849 U.S. Consul John Brown Williams's home is burned and looted during July 4 celebrations; he blames Cakobau, high chief of eastern Viti Levu.

1851 U.S. warship arrives, demands that Cakobau pay $5,000 for Williams's losses.

1853 Cakobau is installed as high chief of Bau, highest post in Fiji.

1855 United States claims against Cakobau grow to $40,000; U.S. warship arrives, claims some islands as mortgage.

1858 Cakobau offers to cede Fiji to Britain for $40,000.

1862 Britain rejects Cakobau's offer.

1867 Unrest grows; Europeans crown Cakobau King of Bau; Rev. Thomas Baker is eaten.

1868 Polynesia Company buys Suva in exchange for paying Cakobau's debts.

1871 Europeans form central government at Levuka, make Cakobau king of Fiji.

1874 Cakobau's government collapses; he and other chiefs cede Fiji to Britain without price tag.

continues

the crops, and anarchy threatened. Within a year, the Europeans established a national government at Levuka and named Cakobau king of Fiji. The situation continued to deteriorate, however, and 3 years later Cakobau was forced to cede the islands to Great Britain. This time there was no price tag attached, and Queen Victoria accepted. The Deed of Cession was signed on October 10, 1874, at Nasovi village near Levuka.

Britain sent Sir Arthur Gordon to serve as the new colony's first governor. He allowed the Fijian chiefs to govern their villages and districts as they had done before (they were not, however, allowed to engage in tribal warfare) and to advise him through a Great Council of Chiefs. He declared that native Fijian lands could not be sold, only leased. That decision has to this day helped to protect the Fijians, their land, and their customs, but it has fueled the bitter animosity on the part of the land-deprived Indians.

Gordon also prohibited the planters from using Fijians as laborers (not that many of them had the slightest inclination to work for someone else). When the planters switched from profitless cotton to sugar cane in the early 1870s, Sir Arthur convinced them to import indentured servants from India. The first 463 East Indians arrived on May 14, 1879 (see "The Islanders," later in this chapter).

Following Gordon's example, the British governed "Fiji for the Fijians"—and the European planters, of course—leaving the Indians to struggle for their civil rights. The government exercised jurisdiction over all Europeans in the colony and assigned district officers (the "D.O.s" of British colonial lore) to administer various geographic areas. There was a large gulf between the appointed civil servants sent from Britain and the locals.

Fiji Becomes Independent

One of the highest-ranking Fijian chiefs, Ratu Sir Lala Sukuna, rose to prominence after World War I. Born of high chiefly lineage (*ratu* means "chief" in Fijian), Sukuna was educated at Oxford, served in World War I, and worked his way up through the

1875	Sir Arthur Gordon becomes first governor.	1956	First Legislative Council established, with Ratu Sir Lala Sukuna as speaker.
1879	First Indians arrive as indentured laborers.	1966	Fijian-dominated Alliance Party wins first elections.
1882	Capital moved from Levuka to Suva.	1969	Key compromises pave way for constitution and independence. Provision guarantees Fijian land ownership.
1916	Recruitment of indentured Indians ends.		
1917	German raider Count Felix von Luckner captured at Wakaya.	1970	Fiji becomes independent; Alliance party leader Ratu Sir Kamisese Mara chosen as first prime minister.
1917–18	Fijian soldiers fight with the Allies in World War I.		
1942–45	Fijians serve as scouts with Allied units in World War II; failure of Indians to volunteer angers Fijians.	1987	Fijian-Indian coalition wins majority, names Dr. Timoci

The Count Confounded

In 1917, Count Felix von Luckner arrived at Wakaya Island off eastern Viti Levu in search of a replacement for his infamous World War I German raider, the *Seeadler,* which had gone aground in the Cook Islands after shelling Papeete on Tahiti. A local constable became suspicious of the armed foreigners and notified the district police inspector. Only Europeans—not Fijians or Indians—could use firearms, so the inspector took a band of unarmed Fijians to Wakaya in a small cattle trading boat. Thinking he was up against a much larger armed force, von Luckner unwittingly surrendered.

colonial bureaucracy to the post of chairman of the Native Land Trust Board. Although dealing primarily with disputes over land and chiefly titles, he used that position as a platform to educate his people and to lay the foundation for the independent state of Fiji. As much as anyone, Sukuna was the father of modern, independent Fiji.

After the attack on Pearl Harbor began the Pacific War in 1941, the Allies turned Fiji into a vast training base. They built the airstrip at Nadi, and several coastal gun emplacements still stand along the coast. Thousands of Fijians fought with great distinction as scouts and infantrymen in the Solomon Islands campaigns. Their knowledge of tropical jungles and their skill at the ambush made them much feared by the Japanese. The Fijians, said one war correspondent, were "death with velvet gloves."

Although many Indo-Fijians at first volunteered to join, they also demanded pay equal to that of the European members of the Fiji Military Forces. When the colonial administrators refused, they disbanded their platoon. Their military contribution was one officer and 70 enlisted men of a reserve transport section, and they were

continues

promised that they would not have to go overseas. Many Fijians to this day begrudge the Indo-Fijians for not doing more to aid the war effort.

Ratu Sukuna continued to push the colony toward independence until his death in 1958, and although Fiji made halting steps in that direction during the 1960s, the road was rocky. The Indo-Fijians by then were highly organized, in both political parties and trade unions, and they objected to a constitution that would institutionalize Fijian control of the government and Fijian ownership of most of the new nation's land. Key compromises were made in 1969, however, and on October 10, 1970—exactly 96 years after Cakobau signed the Deed of Cession—the Dominion of Fiji became an independent member of the British Commonwealth of Nations.

Under the 1970 constitution, Fiji had a Westminster-style Parliament consisting of an elected House of Representatives and a Senate composed of Fijian chiefs. For the first 17 years of independence, the Fijians maintained a majority—albeit a tenuous one—in the House of Representatives and control of the government under the leadership of Ratu Sir Kamisese Mara, the country's first prime minister.

Then, in a general election held in April 1987, a coalition of Indians and liberal Fijians voted Ratu Mara and his Alliance party out of power. Dr. Timoci Bavadra, a Fijian, took over as prime minister, but his cabinet was composed of more Indians than Fijians. Animosity immediately flared between some Fijians and Indians.

Rambo's Coups

Within little more than a month of the election, members of the predominantly Fijian army stormed into Parliament and arrested Dr. Bavadra and his cabinet. It was the South Pacific's first military coup, and although peaceful, it took nearly everyone by complete surprise.

The coup leader was Col. Sitiveni Rabuka (pronounced "Ram-*bu*-ka"), whom local wags quickly nicknamed "Rambo." A career soldier trained at Britain's Royal Military Academy Sandhurst, the then 38-year-old Rabuka was third in command of the army. A Fijian of non-chiefly lineage, he immediately became a hero to his

2001 Fiji's supreme court upholds 1998 constitution; Qarase's Fijian nationalist party wins parliamentary majority in new elections.	**2007** Bainimarama promises new elections by 2009.
	2009 President Ratu Josefa Iloilo abolishes constitution, appoints Bainimarama to head appointed government. Bainimarama pushes elections back to 2014.
2002-04 Qarase releases some coup participants from prison, proposes "reconciliation" bill seen by others as amnesty.	
2006 Citing corruption and racism, Commodore Frank Bainimarama overthrows Qarase, installs interim government with Chaudhry as finance minister.	

"commoner" fellow Fijians. Rabuka at first installed a caretaker government, but in September 1987 he staged another bloodless coup. A few weeks later he abrogated the 1970 constitution, declared Fiji to be an independent republic, and set up a new interim government with himself as minister of home affairs and army commander.

In 1990, the interim government promulgated a new constitution guaranteeing Fijians a parliamentary majority—and rankling the Indians. Rabuka's pro-Fijian party won the initial election, but he barely hung onto power in fresh elections in 1994 by forming a coalition with the European, Chinese, and mixed-race general-elector parliamentarians.

Rabuka also appointed a three-person Constitutional Review Commission, which proposed the constitution that parliament adopted in 1998. It created a parliamentary house of 65 seats, with 19 held by Fijians, 17 by Indians, 3 by general-electors, 1 by a Rotuman, and 25 open to all races.

The 2000 Insurrection & Coup

A year later, with support from many Fijians who were unsettled over the country's poor economy, rising crime, and deteriorating roads, labor union leader Mahendra Chaudhry's party won an outright majority of parliament, and he became Fiji's first Indian prime minister. Chaudhry had been minister of finance in the Bavadra government toppled by Rabuka's coup in 1987.

Chaudhry appointed several well-known Fijians to his cabinet, and the revered Ratu Mara encouraged his fellow Fijians to support the new administration. It didn't work, and in May 2000 a disgruntled Fijian businessman named George Speight led a gang of armed henchmen into parliament. Demanding the appointment of an all-Fijian government, they held Chaudhry and several members of parliament hostage for the next 56 days. While negotiating with Speight, the military under Commodore Frank Bainimarama suspended the constitution and appointed an interim government headed by Laisenia Qarase, a Fijian banker. Speight released his hostages after being promised amnesty, but the army arrested him 2 weeks later and charged him with treason. His death sentence was later commuted to life in prison.

Fiji's supreme court then ruled that the 1998 constitution was still in effect and ordered fresh parliamentary elections to be held in 2001. Under the watchful eye of international observers, the Fijians won an outright majority, and caretaker leader Qarase became the legal prime minister. Chaudhry also was returned to parliament.

A Fiji nationalist, Qarase proposed a "Reconciliation, Tolerance, and Unity" bill, which opponents—including Bainimarama—claimed would grant amnesty to Speight and other participants in the 2000 insurrection. The proposed legislation was the most contentious issue in the general elections of May 2006, which returned Qarase's party to power.

The 2006 Coup

Qarase further incensed the military by releasing some 200 coup participants from prison, and he continued to push his controversial reconciliation bill. He also proposed transferring ownership of Fiji's foreshore and lagoons from the government to indigenous seaside tribes, who would then be free to charge resorts, dive operators, fishers, and others to use their lagoons and coastal waters. This proposal created a firestorm of protest from the tourism industry as well as from Fijians who do not live by the sea—and thus presumably would have to pay to go fishing.

> ### 💬 Bainimarama Explains His Coup
>
> *It must therefore be understood that the events of 05 December 2006 were clearly not a 'grab of power.' It was rather about rescuing a young and fragile nation which was being plunged into abyss and darkness by political leaders who were manipulative, frequently flaunted the law, and openly encouraged corruption and divisive policies to promote racism to suit their own agenda and needs.*
>
> —Commodore Frank Bainimarama, 2006

Bainimarama warned Qarase for most of 2006 that the military would take power if he did not abandon the proposals. On December 5—a date Fijians refer to as "5/12"—the military drove from Queen Elizabeth Barracks into downtown Suva and staged an entirely peaceful coup. Despite some protestors being taken to the barracks for a bit of persuasion, life outside tourism returned to normal relatively quickly. The initial military roadblocks and checkpoints markedly reduced Fiji's crime rate (it went back up when the soldiers were withdrawn, prompting some merchants to call for permanent checkpoints).

The interim regime has been surprisingly progressive. In addition to abandoning overtly racist government policies, Bainimarama has cracked down on corruption and uncontrolled government spending, which had become rampant under Qarase. Among actions with long-lasting consequences, he has opened Fiji's formerly monopolized communications industry to competition, which resulted in a second over-the-air television channel and lower prices for phone and Internet services. He also has encouraged the thousands of Indian professionals who had fled the country to return home by letting them hold dual citizenship in Fiji and another country.

Opposition to Bainimarama continued into 2009, when he instituted controls over the news media. When the country's Supreme Court ruled his coup to be unconstitutional, he had the president abrogate the 1998 constitution. He then fired all of the judges. While he had earlier promised elections for 2009, he instead ordered national consultations for a new constitution before elections, now planned for 2014.

LAY OF THE LAND & THE SEA

A somewhat less-than-pious wag once remarked that God made the South Pacific islands on the 6th day of creation so He would have an extraordinarily beautiful place to rest on the 7th day. Modern geologists have a different view, but the fact remains that the islands of Fiji and the surrounding sea are possessed of heavenly beauty and a plethora of life forms.

The Fiji archipelago forms a horseshoe around the shallow, reef-strewn **Koro Sea,** much of which was dry land some 18,000 years ago during the last Ice Age. More than 300 islands and islets range in size from Viti Levu (10 times the size of Tahiti) to tiny atolls that barely break the surface of the sea. The total land area is 18,187 sq. km (7,022 sq. miles).

The islands were created by volcanic eruptions along the collision of the Indo-Australian and Pacific tectonic plates. Although the main islands are quiet today, they are part of the volcanically active and earthquake-prone "Ring of Fire" around the Pacific Ocean.

From its strategic position in the southwestern Pacific some 5,152km (3,200 miles) southwest of Honolulu and 3,175km (1,972 miles) northeast of Sydney, Fiji is the modern transportation and economic hub of the South Pacific islands. **Nadi International Airport** is the main connection point for flights going to the other island countries, and Fiji's capital city, **Suva,** is one of the region's prime shipping ports and headquarters of many regional organizations.

Flora & Fauna

Most species of plants and animals now native to Fiji originated in Southeast Asia and worked their way eastward across the Pacific, by natural distribution or in the company of humans. The number of indigenous species diminishes the farther east one goes. Very few local plants or animals came from the Americas, the one notable exception being the sweet potato, which may have been brought back from South America by voyaging Polynesians.

PLANTS

The flora changes according to each island's topography. The mountainous islands make rain from the moist trade winds and thus possess a greater variety of plants. Their interior highlands are covered with ferns, native bush, or grass. The low atolls, by contrast, get sparse rainfall and support little other than scrub bush and coconut palms.

Ancient settlers brought coconut palms, breadfruit, taro, paper mulberry, pepper (*kava*, or *yaqona* in Fijian), and bananas because of their usefulness as food or fiber. Accordingly, they are generally found in the inhabited areas of the islands and not so often in the interior bush.

With a few exceptions, such as the *tagimaucia* found on Taveuni, tropical flowers also worked their way east in the company of humans. Bougainvillea, hibiscus, allamanda, poinsettia, *poinciana* (flame tree), croton, *frangipani* (plumeria), ixora, canna, and water lilies all give colorful testament to the islanders' love for flowers of every hue in the rainbow. The aroma of the white, yellow, or pink frangipani is so sweet it's used as perfume on many islands.

ANIMALS & BIRDS

The fruit bat, or "flying fox," and some species of insect-eating bats are the only mammals native to the South Pacific islands. The early settlers introduced dogs, chickens, pigs, rats, and mice. Fiji has one type of poisonous snake, but it lives in the mountains and is seldom seen. You will see lots of geckos and skinks, those little lizards that seem to be everywhere in Fiji. With their ability to walk upside-down across the ceiling at night, geckos are adept at scaring the devil out of unsuspecting tourists. They are harmless, however, and actually perform a valuable service by eating mosquitoes and other insects.

Most land birds live in the bush away from settlements and the accompanying cats, dogs, rats, and ubiquitous Indian myna birds. Mynas were brought to Fiji early in the 20th century to control insects and are now nuisances themselves (these fearless, aggressive creatures will steal the toast right off your breakfast table!). For this reason, the birds most likely to be seen are terns, boobies, herons, petrels, noddies,

Be Careful What You Touch

Fiji has laws protecting the environment, so *do not deface the reef.* You could land in the slammer for breaking off a gorgeous chunk of live coral to take home as a souvenir. The locals know what they can and cannot legally take from under the water, so buy your souvenir coral in a handicraft shop.

and others that earn their livelihoods from the sea. But if you keep your eyes and ears at the ready, you may see and hear some of the 26 species of birds that are endemic to Fiji, such as the barking pigeon, red-headed parrotfinch, and giant forest honeyeater. Taveuni is famous among birders for its orange dove, while Kadavu has its shining musk parrot, fantail, honeyeater, and whistling dove.

The Sea

The tropical South Pacific Ocean teems with sea life, from colorful reef fish to the horrific Great White sharks featured in *Jaws,* from the *paua* clams that make tasty chowders to the deep-sea tuna that keep the cannery going at Levuka.

More than 600 species of coral—10 times the number found in the Caribbean—form the great reefs that make this a divers' Mecca. Billions of tiny coral polyps build their own skeletons on top of those left by their ancestors, until they reach the level of low tide. Then they grow outward, extending the edge of the reef. The old skeletons are white, while the living polyps present a rainbow of colors. Corals grow best and are most colorful in the clear, salty water on the outer edge or in channels, where the tides and waves wash fresh seawater along and across the reef. A reef can grow as much as 5 centimeters (2 in.) a year in ideal conditions.

A plethora of tropical fish and other marine life fills most of the lagoons, which are like gigantic aquariums. Bookstores in the main towns sell pamphlets with photographs and descriptions of the creatures that will peer into your face mask.

Humpback whales migrate to the islands from June to October, and sea turtles lay their eggs on some beaches from November through February.

The Environment Today

Although pollution, rising seawater temperature, and a proliferation of crown-of-thorns starfish have greatly hampered reef growth—and beauty—in parts of Fiji, many areas are unmatched in their color and variety of corals.

Fiji has allowed some resort owners to blast away parts of the reef to create marinas and swimming areas, but it has laws protecting its lagoons, which are a major source of food for the locals. Fiji allows but restricts the use of spear guns, so ask before you go in search of the catch of your life.

Sea turtle meat is considered a delicacy in the islands, and Fijians are not above making a meal of turtles despite laws that make it illegal. Do not even think of bringing home one of their shells: Both sea turtles and whales are on the list of endangered species. Many countries, including the United States, prohibit the importation of their shells, bones, and teeth.

You can collect empty seashells on the beach, but not if they still have live animals inside. Likewise, you can make a souvenir of a dead piece of coral lying on the shore, but you cannot take coral directly from a reef.

THE ISLANDERS

Early European explorers were astounded to find the far-flung South Pacific islands inhabited by peoples who apparently had been there for thousands of years. How had these people— who lived a late Stone Age existence and had no written languages—crossed the Pacific long before Christopher Columbus had the courage to sail out of sight of land? Where had they come from? The questions that baffled European explorers continue to intrigue scientists and scholars today.

The First Fijians

The late Thor Heyerdahl drifted in his raft *Kon Tiki* from South America to French Polynesia in 1947, to prove his theory that the Pacific Islanders came from the Americas. Bolstered by linguistic and DNA studies linking the Polynesians to Taiwan, however, experts now believe the Pacific Islanders have their roots in eastern Asia.

The accepted view is that during the Ice Age, a race of humans known as Australoids migrated from Southeast Asia to Papua New Guinea and Australia, when those two countries were joined by dry land. Another group, the Papuans, arrived from Southeast Asia between 5,000 and 10,000 years ago. Later, a lighter-skinned race known as Austronesians pushed the Papuans out into the more eastern South Pacific islands. They became the Polynesians, whom archaeologists now believe

---

💬 "FIJI TIME"

There's an old story about a 19th-century planter who promised a South Pacific islander a weekly wage and a pension if he would come to work on his copra plantation. *Copra* is dried coconut meat, from which oil is pressed for use in soaps, cosmetics, and other products. Hours of backbreaking labor are required to chop open the coconuts and extract the meat by hand.

The islander was sitting by the lagoon, eating fruit he had picked from nearby trees while hauling in one fish after another. "Let me make sure I understand you," said the islander. "You want me to break my back working for you for 30 years. Then you'll pay me a pension so I can come back here and spend the rest of my life sitting by the

lagoon, eating fruit from my trees and the fish I catch? I may not be sophisticated, but I am not stupid."

The islander's response reflects an attitude still prevalent in Fiji, where many people don't have to work in the Western sense. Here life moves at a slow pace, which the locals call "Fiji Time."

Consequently, do not expect the same level of service rendered in most hotels and restaurants back home. The slowness is not slothful inattention; it's just the way things are done here. Your drink will come in due course. If you must have it immediately, order it at the bar. Otherwise, relax with your friendly hosts and enjoy their charming company.

A HOLY MEAL

When meeting and talking to the smiling Fijians, it's difficult to imagine that hardly more than a century ago their ancestors were among the world's most ferocious cannibals. Today the only vestiges of this past are the four-pronged wooden cannibal forks sold in handicraft shops (they make interesting conversation pieces when used at home to serve hors d'oeuvres).

Yet in the early 1800s, the Fijians were so fierce that Europeans were slow to settle in the islands for fear of literally being turned into a meal. Back then, Fijian society was organized by tribes, which constantly warred with each other, usually with brutal vengeance. The winners hung captured enemy children by their feet from the rigging of their canoes, and they sometimes consecrated new buildings by burying live adult prisoners in holes dug for the support posts.

The ultimate insult, however, was to eat the enemy's flesh. Victorious chiefs were even said to cook and nibble on the fingers or tongues of the vanquished, relishing each bite while the victims watched in agony. "One man actually stood by my side and ate the very eyes out of a roasted skull he had, saying, 'Venaca, venaca,' that is, very good," wrote William Speiden, the purser on the U.S. exploring expedition that charted Fiji in 1840.

More than 100 white-skinned individuals ended up with their skulls smashed and their bodies baked in an earth oven, including the Rev. Thomas Baker, who attempted to convert the Viti Levu highlanders in 1867. Instead of converting, they killed the reverend, tossed his body into an oven, and made a meal of him.

settled in Samoa more than 3,000 years ago and then slowly fanned out to colonize the vast Polynesian triangle stretching from Hawaii to Easter Island to New Zealand.

The most tangible remains of the early Austronesians are remnants of pottery, the first shards of which were found during the 1970s in Lapita, in New Caledonia. Probably originating in Papua New Guinea, Lapita pottery spread east as far as Tonga. Throughout the area it was decorated with geometric designs similar to those used today on tapa cloth, known in Fijian as *masi*. Apparently the Lapita culture died out in Polynesia some 2,500 years ago, for by the time European explorers arrived in the 1770s, only the Fijians still made pottery using Lapita methods. And they still do.

The islands settled by the Papuans and Austronesians are known collectively as *Melanesia*, which includes Papua New Guinea, the Solomon Islands, Vanuatu, New Caledonia, and Fiji. More specifically, Fiji is the melting pot of the Melanesians to the west and the Polynesians to the east.

The name Melanesia is derived from the Greek words *melas,* "black," and *nesos,* "island." The Melanesians in general have features more akin to sub-Saharan Africans, but interbreeding among the successive waves of migrants resulted in many subgroups with varying physical characteristics. Among them, the mountain tribes tend to have darker skin than the coastal dwellers, who interbred with the lighter-skinned Austronesians. The Fijian culture, on the other hand, has many Polynesian elements, brought by interbreeding and conquest.

Fiji's Mixed Population

Adding to the mix are Fiji Indians, most of whom are descendants of laborers brought to work the country's sugar-cane fields (see "The Fiji Indians," below). The official 2007 census found that of Fiji's total population of 827,900, indigenous Fijians made up 57%, Fiji Indians 38%, and other Pacific islanders, Chinese, Europeans, and persons of mixed race the other 5%. Thanks to a high Fijian birthrate, the overall population has been rising slightly despite the country's losing thousands of Fiji Indians since the first military coup in 1987.

It's difficult to imagine peoples of two more contrasting cultures living side by side than the indigenous Fijians and the Fiji Indians. "Fijians generally perceive Indians as mean and stingy, crafty and demanding to the extent of being considered greedy, inconsiderate, grasping, uncooperative, egotistic, and calculating," wrote Professor Asesela Ravuvu of the University of the South Pacific. On the other hand, he said, Indians see Fijians as *"jungalis"*—poor, backward, naive, foolish, and living on land they will not sell.

Given that these attitudes are not likely to change anytime soon, it is remarkable that Fijians and Fiji Indians actually manage to coexist. Politically correct Americans may take offense at things they overhear in Fiji, where racial distinctions are a fact of life—as you will notice on the country's immigration entry form.

From a visitor's standpoint, the famously friendly Fijians give the country its laid-back South Seas charm while providing relatively good if not altogether efficient service at the hotels. For their part, the Fiji Indians make this an easy country to visit by providing excellent maintenance of facilities and efficient and inexpensive services, such as transportation.

The 1998 constitution makes everyone, regardless of his or her race, a Fiji Islander.

The Indigenous Fijians

Today's indigenous Fijians are descended from a Melanesian people who came from the west and began settling here around 500 B.C. Legend says they arrived at Viseisei village, at Vuda Point on Viti Levu. Over time they replaced the Polynesians, whose ancestors had arrived some 1,000 years beforehand, but not before adopting much of Polynesian culture and intermarrying enough to give many Fijians lighter skin than that of most other Melanesians, especially in the islands of eastern Fiji near the Polynesian Kingdom of Tonga. (This is less the case in the west and among the hill dwellers, whose ancestors had less contact with Polynesians in ancient times.) Similar differences occur in terms of culture.

> ### Impressions
>
> *A hundred years of prodding by the British has failed to make the Fijians see why they should work for money.*
> —James A. Michener, *Return to Paradise*, 1951

For example, whereas Melanesians traditionally pick their chiefs by popular consensus, Fijian chiefs hold titles by heredity, in the Polynesian (or more precisely, Tongan) fashion.

Most Fijians still live in small villages along the coast and riverbanks or in the hills, and you will see some traditional thatch *bures*, or houses, scattered in the countryside away from the main roads. As in the old days, every Fijian belongs to a clan, or *matangali*, that was originally based on skills such as canoe making and

"grog" ETIQUETTE

Known as *kava* elsewhere in the South Pacific, slightly narcotic *yaqona* (yon-gon·na)—or "grog"—rivals Fiji Bitter beer as the national drink. In fact, Fiji has more "grog shops" than bars. You will likely have half a coconut shell of grog offered—if not shoved in your face—beginning at your hotel's reception desk.

And thanks to the promotion of *kava-lactone,* the active ingredient, as a health-food answer to stress and insomnia in the United States and elsewhere, growing the root is an important part of the South Pacific's economy. When fears surfaced a few years ago that kava could be linked to liver disease, locals commented that if that was true, there would be few healthy livers in Fiji.

Yaqona has always played an important ceremonial role in Fijian life. No significant occasion takes place without it, and a *sevusevu* (welcoming) ceremony is usually held for tour groups visiting Fijian villages. Mats are placed on the floor, the participants gather around in a circle, and the yaqona roots are mixed with water and strained through coconut husks into a large carved wooden bowl, called a *tanoa.*

The ranking chief sits next to the tanoa during the welcoming ceremony. He extends in the direction of the guest of honor a cowrie shell attached to one leg of the bowl by a cord of woven coconut fiber. It's extremely impolite to cross the plane of the cord once it has been extended.

The guest of honor (in this case your tour guide) then offers a gift to the village (a kilogram or two of dried grog roots will do these days) and makes a speech explaining the purpose of his visit. The chief then passes the first cup of yaqona to the guest of honor, who claps once, takes the cup in both hands, and gulps down the entire cup of sawdust-tasting liquid in one swallow. Everyone else then claps three times.

Next, each chief drinks a cup, clapping once before bolting it down. Again, everyone else claps three times after each cup is drained. Except for the clapping and formal speech, everyone remains silent throughout the ceremony, a tradition easily understood considering kava's numbing effect on the lips and tongue.

farming. Clan elders meet in each village to choose a *ratu,* or chief. Charged with caring for their land, villagers still grow food crops in small "bush gardens" on plots assigned to their families. More than 80% of the land in Fiji is communally owned by Fijians and managed for them by the Native Lands Trust Board.

A majority of Fijians are Methodists, their forebears having been converted by Wesleyan missionaries who came to the islands from Tonga in the 19th century. The Methodist Church is a powerful, pro-Fijian political force.

THE TABUA

The highest symbol of respect among Fijians is the tooth of the sperm whale, known as a *tabua* (pronounced "tam-*bu*-a"). In ancient times tabuas played a role similar to that of money in modern society and still have various ceremonial uses. They are presented to chiefs as a sign of respect, given as gifts to arrange marriages, offered to friends to show sympathy after the death of a family member, and used as a means to seal a contract or another agreement. It is illegal to export a tabua out of Fiji, and even if you did, the international conventions on endangered species prohibit your bringing it into the United States and most other Western countries.

FIRE WALKING

Legend says that a Fijian god once repaid a favor to a warrior on Beqa Island by giving him the ability to walk unharmed on fire. His descendants, all members of the

Sawau tribe on Beqa, still walk across stones heated to white-hot by a bonfire—but usually for the entertainment of tourists at the hotels rather than for a particular religious purpose.

Traditionally, the participants—all male—had to abstain from women and coconuts for 2 weeks before the ceremony. If they partook of either, they would suffer burns to their feet. Naturally a priest (some would call him a witch doctor) would recite certain incantations to make sure the coals were hot and the gods were at bay and not angry enough to scorch the soles.

Today's fire walking is a bit touristy but still worth seeing. If you don't believe the stones are hot, go ahead and touch one of them—but do it gingerly.

Some Fiji Indians engage in fire walking for religious purposes during an annual Hindu soul-cleansing festival (see "Fiji Calendar of Events," in chapter 3).

FIJIAN VILLAGE ETIQUETTE

Fijian villages are easy to visit, but keep in mind that to the people who live in them, the entire village—not just an individual's house—is home. In your native land, you wouldn't walk into a stranger's living room without being invited, so find someone and ask permission before traipsing into a Fijian village. The Fijians are accommodating people, and it's unlikely they will say no; in fact, they may ask you to stay for a meal or stage a small yaqona ceremony in your honor (see "'Grog' Etiquette" box, above).

> ### Impressions
>
> *It is doubtful if anyone but an Indian can dislike Fijians . . . They are one of the happiest peoples on earth and laugh constantly. Their joy in things is infectious; they love practical jokes, and in warfare they are without fear.*
> —James A. Michener, *Return to Paradise*, 1951

If you are invited to stay or eat in the village, a small gift to the chief is appropriate; F$10 per person or a handful of dried kava root from the local market will do. The gift should be given to the chief or highest-ranking person present to accept it. Sometimes it helps to explain that it is a gift to the village and not payment for services rendered, especially if it's money you're giving.

Only chiefs are allowed to wear hats and sunglasses in Fijian villages, so it's good manners for visitors to take theirs off. Shoulders must be covered at all times. Fijians go barefoot and walk slightly stooped in their bures. Men sit cross-legged on the floor; women sit with their legs to the side. They don't point at one another with hands, fingers, or feet, nor do they touch each others' heads or hair. They greet each other and strangers with a big smile and a sincere *"Bula."*

The Fiji Indians

The *Leonidas*, a labor transport ship, arrived at Levuka from Calcutta on May 14, 1879, and landed 463 indentured servants destined to work Fiji's sugar-cane fields.

The indigenous Fijians are justly renowned for their friendliness to strangers, and many Fiji Indians are as well educated and informed as anyone in the South Pacific. Together, these two peoples are fun to meet, whether it be over a hotel desk or while riding with them in one of their fume-belching buses.

As more than 60,000 Indians would do over the next 37 years, these first immigrants signed agreements (*girmits,* they called them) requiring that they work in Fiji for 5 years; they would be free to return to India after 5 more years. Most of them labored in the cane fields for the initial term of their girmits, living in "coolie lines" of squalid shacks hardly better than the poverty-stricken conditions most left behind in India.

After the initial 5 years, however, they were free to seek work on their own. Many leased plots of land from the Fijians and began planting sugar cane or raising cattle. To this day most of Fiji's sugar crop, the country's most important agricultural export, is produced on small leased plots. Other Fiji Indians went into business in the growing cities and towns; joined in the early 1900s by an influx of business-oriented Indians, they thereby founded Fiji's modern merchant and professional classes.

Of the immigrants who came from India between 1879 and 1916, when the indenturing system ended, some 85% were Hindus, 14% were Muslims, and the remaining 1% were Sikhs and Christians. Fiji offered these adventurers far more opportunities than caste-controlled India. In fact, the caste system was scrapped very quickly by the Hindus in Fiji, and, for the most part, the violent relations between Hindus and Muslims that racked India were put aside on the islands.

Only a small minority of the Fiji Indians went home after their girmits expired. They tended then—as now—to live in the towns and villages, and in the "Sugar Belt" along the drier north and west coasts of Viti Levu and Vanua Levu. Hindu and Sikh temples and Muslim mosques abound in these areas, and places such as Ba and Tavua resemble small towns on the Indian subcontinent. On the southern coasts and in the mountains, the population is overwhelmingly Fijian. Fiji Indians constituted more than half of Fiji's population prior to the 1987 coup, but emigration (not to India but to Australia, New Zealand, Canada, and the U.S.) reduced their share to 38% by 2007. It has grown lately as some expatriated Indians have returned home.

FIJI IN POPULAR CULTURE
Books

The National Geographic Society's book *The Isles of the South Pacific* (1971), by Maurice Shadbolt and Olaf Ruhen, and Ian Todd's *Island Realm* (1974), are out-of-date coffee-table books but have lovely color photographs. *Living Corals* (1979), by Douglas Faulkner and Richard Chesher, shows what you will see underwater.

HISTORY, POLITICS & CULTURE
Fiji-based writer Kim Gravelle has written several books about the country's history and culture. *Fiji's Times: a History of Fiji* (1980) is a compilation of his articles from

the pages of the *Fiji Times* newspaper. *The Fiji Explorer's Handbook* (1980) is a dated guide to the country, but the maps are still excellent. Gravelle travels from Fiji to other South Pacific countries in *Romancing the Islands* (1977).

Noted conservationist Joana McIntyre Varawa married Fijian Male Varawa, who was half her age, and moved from Hawaii to his home village. In *Changes in Latitude* (1989), she writes of her experiences, providing many insights into modern Fijian culture.

TRAVELOGUES

Sir David Attenborough, the British documentary film producer, traveled to Papua New Guinea, Vanuatu, Fiji, and Tonga in the late 1950s. Sir David entertainingly tells of his trips in *Journeys to the Past* (1983).

Travel writer and novelist Paul Theroux took his kayak along for a tour of Fiji and several other South Pacific islands and reported on what he found in *The Happy Isles of Oceania: Paddling the Pacific* (1992). The book is a fascinatingly frank yarn, full of island characters and out-of-the-way places.

Ronald Wright's enjoyable book *On Fiji Islands* (1986) is packed with insights about the Fijians and Indians.

John Dyson rode interisland trading boats throughout the South Pacific and wrote about his experiences in *The South Seas Dream* (1982). It's an entertaining account of the islands and their more colorful inhabitants. Julian Evans tells of a more recent trading-boat trip to Fiji, the Samoas, and Tonga in *Transit of Venus* (1992).

More recently, J. Maarten Troost tells some hilarious tales in *Getting Stoned with Savages: A Trip Through the Islands of Fiji and Vanuatu* (2006). He spins similar yarns about Micronesia in *The Sex Lives of Cannibals* (2004).

Film & TV

Fiji has provided the backdrop for several movies and television shows, the most recent being a season of CBS's *Survivor: Fiji*, which took place on the northern coast of Vanua Levu in 2007.

In the movies, Jean Simmons played a teenage girl shipwrecked with a boy on a deserted island in the 1949 version of *The Blue Lagoon*. The 1980 remake helped launch the career of Brooke Shields, then 14 years old. Both were shot on Nanuya Levu Island in the Yasawas, home of Turtle Island Resort. It inspired Richard Evanson, the resort's owner, to rename the surrounding waters "The Blue Lagoon." A 1991 sequel, *Return to the Blue Lagoon*, was made on Taveuni.

Tom Hanks starred in 2000 as a FedEx employee marooned on Modriki Island in the Mamanucas in *Castaway.* Hanks lost 55 pounds while making the movie, but not by roughing it on Modriki; he reportedly stayed in a suite at the Sheraton Fiji Resort and rode a helicopter out to the deserted island each morning.

Anacondas: The Hunt for the Blood Orchid was filmed in the winding, muddy waterways of Pacific Harbour in 2004. It was the sequel to 1997's *Anaconda*, which was shot in Brazil. Fiji, of course, has no real anacondas.

EATING & DRINKING IN FIJI

Fiji's dining scene was pretty bleak when I first visited in the 1970s. There was tasty food to be had at the country's numerous curry houses, which catered to the local Indian population; but other restaurants offered bland fare of the roast and grilled steak variety that predominated in Australia and New Zealand in those days. What a world of difference 3 decades make: Fiji today has some very good restaurants serving food from around the globe—although I never come here without also partaking of a native Fijian feast.

Lovos & Mekes

Like most South Pacific islanders, the Fijians in pre-European days steamed their food in an earth oven, known here as a *lovo*. They would use their fingers to eat the huge feasts (*mekes*) that emerged, and then would settle down to watch traditional dancing and perhaps polish off a few cups of yaqona.

The ingredients of a lovo meal are *buaka* (pig), *doa* (chicken), *ika* (fish), *mana* (tropical lobster), *moci* (river shrimp), *kai* (freshwater mussels), and various vegetables, such as dense *dalo* (taro root), spinachlike *rourou* (taro leaves), *lumi* (seaweed), and my favorite, *ota* (wood fern shoots). Most dishes are cooked in sweet *lolo* (fresh coconut milk) or *miti* (condensed coconut milk).

The most plentiful fish is the *walu*, or Spanish mackerel, from which Fijians make delicious *kokoda* (ko-*kon*-da), their version of fresh fish marinated in lime juice and mixed with fresh vegetables and coconut milk. Another Fijian specialty is *palusami,* a rich combination of meat or fish baked in banana leaves or foil with onions, taro leaves, and coconut milk.

Most resort hotels have mekes on their schedule of weekly events. Traditional Fijian dance shows follow the meals. Unlike the fast, hip-swinging, suggestive dancing of Tahiti and the Cook Islands, Fijians follow the custom of the Samoas and Tonga, with gentle movements taking second place to the harmony of their voices. The spear-waving war dances have more action.

Curry In Fiji

While not all menus include Fijian-style dishes, most offer at least one Indian curry, which bodes well for vegetarians, since most Hindus eat no meat or seafood.

Fijian curries traditionally are on the mild side, but you can ask for it spicy. Curries are easy to figure out from the menu: lamb, goat, beef, chicken, vegetarian. If in

---

The Best Fijian Chow

You'll be offered Fijian food during meke nights at the resorts, but I join the locals for the best Fijian chow at:
- o **Nadina Authentic Fijian Restaurant,** Nadi (© 672 7313; p. 114).
- o **Vilisite's Seafood Restaurant,** Korovou, Coral Coast (© 653 0054; p. 156).

- o **Hare Krishna Restaurant,** 16 Pratt St., Suva (© 331 4154; p. 187)
- o **Old Mill Cottage,** 47–49 Carnavon St., Suva (© 331 2134; p. 188)
- o **Surf 'n' Turf,** the Copra Shed, Savusavu (© 881 0966; p. 219)
- o **Vunibokoi Restaurant,** Matei, Taveuni (© 888 0560; p. 232)

Keep an Eye on Your Beer Mug

Bartenders in Fiji are taught to keep your beer mug full and your pockets empty. That is, they don't ask if you want another beer: They keep pouring until you tell them emphatically to stop.

doubt, ask the waiter or waitress. *Roti* is the round, lightly fried bread normally used to pick up your food (it is a hybrid of the round breads of India and Pakistan). *Puri* is a soft, puffy bread, and *papadam* is thin and crispy.

The entire meal may come on a round steel plate, with the curries, condiments, and rice in their own dishes arranged on the larger plate. The authentic method of dining is to dump the rice in the middle of the plate, add the smaller portions around it, and then mix them all together.

Wine, Beer & Spirits

Fiji does not produce wine, but connoisseurs will have ample opportunity to sample the vintages from nearby Australia, where abundant sunshine produces renowned full-bodied, fruit-driven varieties, such as chardonnay, semillon, Riesling, shiraz, Hermitage, cabernet sauvignon, and merlot. New Zealand wines are also widely available, including distinctive whites, such as chenin blanc, sauvignon blanc, and soft merlot.

The country does brew the robust Fiji Bitter beer—or "Stubbie" to locals because of its distinctive short-neck bottles. Fiji Gold is a somewhat lighter version, and Fiji Premium is more like a light, crisp American beer than the others. New to the scene is Vonu, a darker beer brewed north of Nadi Airport.

With all those sugar-cane fields, it's not surprising that Fiji produces a decent dark rum known as Bounty. A gin is produced here, too, but it's best used as paint thinner.

Freight and import duties drive up the cost of other spirits and all wines, so expect higher prices than at home. I always bring my two allowed duty-free bottles of spirits. You can buy from shops in the baggage claim area at Nadi Airport before clearing Customs, but I have found duty-free liquor to be less expensive in Los Angeles recently.

PLANNING YOUR TRIP TO FIJI

3

Fiji experienced a tourism boom prior to the December 2006 coup, with Australians and New Zealanders—for whom Fiji is as convenient as the Caribbean is to Americans and Canadians, or the Greek Isles are to Europeans—flocking to the islands in droves. That peak period saw numerous new resorts and other facilities being built. The country's tourism business dropped off significantly following the coup, however, and with fewer tourists, a glut of hotel rooms, and the worldwide economic recession, the local travel industry has been tempting visitors with reduced prices for hotel rooms, cruises, and airfares. As a result, this is an excellent time to visit Fiji—and save money.

Most resorts have been offering discount deals, such as stay 7 nights but pay only for 5. It's imperative, therefore, to check the website of your choice of airline, resort, or cruise for its current specials. No single clearinghouse markets the deals, but many show up on the Australian-oriented **www.etravelblackboard.com**. Also check with the Tourism Fiji website and contact travel agents who specialize in package tours and independent travel to Fiji (see "Packages for the Independent Traveler," later in this chapter).

Fiji's tourism industry is modern and advanced by Third World standards, and you should experience few unexpected bumps when planning your trip. Just remember that "Fiji Time" exists out here (see the box on p. 29), so don't expect instant answers to your queries.

For additional help in planning your trip and for more on-the-ground resources in Fiji, please turn to chapter 15, "Fast Facts."

WHEN TO GO
The Climate

Although local weather patterns have changed in the past 20 years, making conditions less predictable, local residents recognize a cooler and more comfortable **dry season** during the austral winter, from June to September. The winter trade winds blow fairly steadily during these months, bringing generally fine tropical weather. It's the best time of year to visit.

The austral summer, from November through April, usually is the warmer and more humid **wet season.** In a normal year, low-pressure troughs and tropical depressions can bring several days of rain followed by periods of intense sunshine at this time. Things have not been normal of late, however, for January of 2009 saw extremely heavy rains and the worst flooding in a generation, while January of 2010 had scant rain and record high temperatures. Whatever happens, an air-conditioned hotel room or bungalow can feel like heaven during this humid time of year. This is also the season for tropical cyclones (hurricanes), which should never be taken lightly. Fortunately, they usually move fast enough that their major effect on visitors is a day or two of heavy rain and wind. If you're caught in one, the hotel employees are experts on what to do to ensure your safety.

Another factor to consider is the part of an island that you'll visit. Because moist trade winds often blow from the east, the eastern sides of the high, mountainous islands tend to be wetter all year than the western sides. On the southeastern shore of Viti Levu, Suva gets considerably more rain than Nadi, which is on the island's dryer side. Consequently, most of Fiji's resorts are on the western side of Viti Levu.

Also bear in mind that the higher the altitude, the lower the temperature. If you're going up in the mountains, be prepared for much cooler weather than you'd have on the coast.

Fiji's average high temperatures range from 83°F (28°C) during the austral winter (June–Sept) to 88°F (31°C) during the summer months, which are December through March. Evenings average a warm and comfortable 70°F to 82°F (21°C–28°C) throughout the year.

The Fiji Meteorological Service (www.met.gov.fj) gives the current forecast.

Average Maximum Daytime Temperatures at Nadi

	JAN	FEB	MAR	APR	MAY	JUNE	JULY	AUG	SEPT	OCT	NOV	DEC
Temp °F	89	89	88	87	86	85	83	84	85	86	88	89
Temp °C	32	32	31	31	30	29	28	29	29	30	31	32

The Busy Season

July and August are the busiest tourist season in Fiji. That's when Australians and New Zealanders visit the islands to escape the cold back home.

There also are busy miniseasons, when it is school holiday time in Australia and New Zealand. These periods vary, but in general they are from the end of March through the middle of April, 2 weeks in late May, 2 weeks at the beginning of July, 2 weeks in the middle of September, and from mid-December until mid-January. You can get a list of Australian holidays at **www.oztourism.com.au** (click on the

The islands are extraordinarily beautiful anytime, especially so at solstice time in late September and late March, when the sun's rays hit the lagoons at just the right angle to highlight the gorgeous colors in the waters. The play of moonlight on the surface, and the black silhouettes the mountains cast against the sky, are even more magical when the moon is full. Keep that in mind when planning your trip—especially if it's your honeymoon.

"School Holiday" link); for New Zealand holiday schedules go to **www.tourism.org. nz** (the "Utilities and Holidays" link).

Some hoteliers raise their rates during the busy periods.

From Christmas through the middle of January is a good time to get a hotel reservation, but airline seats can be hard to come by, as thousands of islanders fly home from overseas.

Fiji Calendar of Events

Fiji has no grand nationwide festival around which to plan a visit, but there are local events that will enrich your time here. Many are Hindu festivals, whose timing changes from year to year. For an exhaustive list of events beyond those listed here, check **http://events. frommers.com**, where you'll find a searchable, up-to-the-minute roster of what's happening in cities all over the world.

FEBRUARY/MARCH

Hindu Holi, nationwide. Hindus throughout Fiji often squirt each other with colored water during Hindu Holi, their Festival of Colors. February or March.

JULY

Bula Festival, Nadi. The town goes all out in July for its annual big bash, with parades, music, and cultural demonstrations. Mid-July.

Hindu Fire Walking, nationwide. Some Hindus engage in fire walking during soul-cleansing rituals, but unlike Fijian fire walkers, they do not perform for tourists at hotels. July or August.

AUGUST

Hibiscus Festival, Suva. The capital city's Hibiscus Festival is as close to a national festival as Fiji has. A carnival atmosphere prevails as thousands gather in Albert Park.

See www.hibiscusfiji.com for details. Mid-August.

SEPTEMBER

Sugar Festival, Lautoka. Viti Levu's "Sugar City" gets into the act with its annual Sugar Festival.

Fiji Regatta Week, Mamanuca Islands. Cruising yachts from around the region gather at Musket Cove Island Resort in the Mamanucas for races, bikini contests, and the consumption of many thousands of Fiji Bitter beers. Some yachts then race to Port Vila in Vanuatu. Mid-September.

NOVEMBER

Diwali Festival, nationwide. Although it's the Hindu festival of lights, every Fiji resident seems to put candles in their yards and set off fireworks during this holiday. November 5, 2010, and October 26, 2011.

ENTRY REQUIREMENTS

Passports & Visas

All visitors must have a passport valid for 6 months beyond their visits and an onward or return airline ticket. See "Passports," in chapter 15, for information on how to get a passport.

Visitor permits good for stays of up to 4 months are issued upon arrival to citizens of the United States; all Commonwealth countries; most European, South American, and South Pacific island nations; and Mexico, Japan, Israel, Pakistan, South Korea, Thailand, Tunisia, and Turkey.

Citizens of all other countries must apply for visas in advance from the Fiji embassies or consulates. In the United States, contact the **Embassy of Fiji,** 2000 M St. NW, Ste. 710, Washington, DC 20007 (© **202/466-8320;** fax 202/466-8325; www. fijiembassy.org).

Other Fiji embassies or high commissions are in Canberra and Sydney, Australia; Wellington, New Zealand; London, England; Brussels, Belgium; Tokyo, Japan; Kuala Lumpur, Malaysia; Port Moresby, Papua New Guinea; New Delhi, India; and Beijing, China. Check your local phone book, or go to www.fiji.gov.fj and click on "Fiji Missions Overseas."

Persons wishing to remain longer than their initial permits allow must apply for extensions from the **Immigration Department,** whose primary offices are at the Nadi International Airport terminal (© **672 2454;** www.fiji.gov.fj) and in the Labour Department building on Victoria Parade in downtown Suva (© **321 1775**).

Note: Except for U.S. citizens, nationals, and resident aliens, everyone transiting through Los Angeles International Airport must either have a visa to visit the United States or be from a Visa Waiver country. See **http://travel.state.gov/visa** for more information.

Medical Requirements

Vaccinations are not required unless you have been in a yellow fever or cholera area shortly before arriving in Fiji.

Customs

WHAT YOU CAN BRING INTO FIJI

Fiji's **Customs allowances** are 200 cigarettes; 2 liters of liquor, beer, or wine; and F$400 worth of other goods in addition to personal belongings. Pornography is prohibited. Firearms and nonprescription narcotics are strictly prohibited and subject to heavy fines and jail terms. Any fresh fruits and vegetables must be declared and are subject to inspection and fumigation. You will need advance permission to bring any animal into Fiji; if you do not obtain it, your pet will be quarantined.

Note: Customs will x-ray *all* of your luggage upon arrival.

WHAT YOU CAN TAKE HOME FROM FIJI

U.S. citizens who have been in Fiji for at least 48 hours are allowed to bring back, once every 30 days, US$800 worth of merchandise duty-free. For specifics contact the **U.S. Customs & Border Protection (CBP),** 1300 Pennsylvania Ave. NW, Washington, DC 20229 (© **877/287-8667;** www.cbp.gov).

Canadian Citizens: Canada Border Services Agency, Ottawa, Ontario, K1A 0L8 (© **800/461-9999** in Canada, or 204/983-3500; www.cbsa-asfc.gc.ca).

U.K. Citizens: HM Customs & Excise, Crownhill Court, Tailyour Road, Plymouth, PL6 5BZ (© **0845/010-9000;** from outside the U.K., 020/8929-0152; www.hmce.gov.uk).

Australian Citizens: Australian Customs Service, Customs House, 5 Constitution Ave., Canberra City, ACT 2601 (© **1300/363-263;** from outside Australia, 612/6275-6666; www.customs.gov.au).

New Zealand Citizens: New Zealand Customs, The Customhouse, 17–21 Whitmore St., Box 2218, Wellington, 6140 (© **04/473-6099** or 0800/428-786; www.customs.govt.nz).

GETTING TO FIJI

The only practical way to Fiji is by air. Even though Australians and New Zealanders can be in Fiji in a few hours, the distances for the rest of us run into the many thousands of miles. So be prepared to fly 11 hours or more from Los Angeles to Fiji, much longer from the U.K. and Europe.

Because populations are small in this part of the world, flights are not nearly as frequent to and among the islands as we Westerners are used to with destinations closer to home. The local airlines have relatively few planes, so mechanical problems as well as the weather can cause delays.

The Airports

Most international flights arrive at **Nadi International Airport (NAN),** on the western side of Viti Levu about 11km (7 miles) north of Nadi Town. A few flights arrive from Samoa and Tonga at **Nausori Airport (SUV),** some 19km (12 miles) from Suva.

Nadi and Nausori are the only lighted airstrips in the country, which means you don't fly domestically after dark. Many international flights arrive during the night, so a 1-night stay-over in Nadi may be necessary before you leave for another island.

The Airlines

Following, in alphabetical order, are the airlines that actually fly their planes to and from Fiji. Most have code-share arrangements with other airlines, which sell tickets for their flights. Most also offer air-and-hotel packages on their websites.

o **Air New Zealand** (© **800/262-1234** or 310/615-1111 in the U.S.; www.airnewzealand.com) flies its own planes between Auckland and Nadi. Although it sells tickets for flights between Los Angeles and Fiji, the planes are flown by Air Pacific (see below), on a code-share basis. Air New Zealand links the U.K. and Europe to Los Angeles, where passengers connect to Fiji. It also flies from Japan, Hong Kong, Singapore, Seoul, Taipei, and Beijing to Auckland, with connections from there to Fiji. It is a member of the Star Alliance (www.staralliance.com), which includes United Airlines, Air Canada, and several European and Asian carriers.

o **Air Pacific** (© **800/227-4446** in the U.S.; www.airpacific.com), Fiji's international airline, has extensive service to Nadi from Sydney, Brisbane, and Melbourne in Australia, and Auckland, Wellington, and Christchurch in New Zealand. It is the only carrier flying its own planes between Nadi and Los Angeles, a service it code-shares with Air New Zealand and Qantas Airways. In other words, it doesn't matter which airline sells you a ticket between Los Angeles and Fiji, you will fly in an Air Pacific plane. Consequently, be sure to check Air Pacific's price before buying from another carrier. One of Air Pacific's flights between Nadi and Honolulu stops in Samoa going and coming. It also provides nonstop service between Fiji and Hong Kong, on which Europeans and Asians can connect to Fiji without having to go through the U.S. immigration hassles at Los Angeles International Airport. Within the region, Air Pacific links Nadi to Samoa and Tonga, and it goes west to Vanuatu and Solomon Islands.

o **Continental Airlines** (© 800/528-3273 in the U.S.; www.continental.com) sends a plane from Guam to Nadi and on to Honolulu, then back over the same route the next day. That means you can get to Fiji from Asia on Continental by connecting in Guam, and from North America through Hawaii. Alaska residents should investigate connecting with Continental (or Air Pacific) in Honolulu rather than flying all the way down to Los Angeles to change planes.

o **JetStar Airlines** (© 13-15-38 in Australia; © 0800/800-995 in New Zealand; www.jetstar.com), the cut-rate subsidiary of Qantas Airways, has service between Australia and Fiji.

o **Korean Air** (© 800/438-5000 in the U.S.; www.koreanair.com) has service between Seoul and Fiji. Although it's a longer distance, a connection through Seoul can be quicker from the U.K. and Europe than flying through Los Angeles, and you avoid the U.S. immigration headache. You'll have to overnight in Seoul on the return, at the airline's expense.

o **Pacific Blue** (© 13-16-45 in Australia; © 0800/670-000 in New Zealand; www.flypacificblue.com), the international subsidiary of the Australian cut-rate domestic airline Virgin Blue (itself an offshoot of Sir Richard Branson's Virgin Atlantic), has low-fare service from Australia and New Zealand to Fiji.

o **Qantas Airways** (© 800/227-4500 in the U.S.; www.qantas.com), the Australian carrier, has flights from several Australian cities and Fiji, and between Los Angeles and Fiji, although its Los Angeles–Fiji passengers fly on Air Pacific planes.

o **V Australia** (© 138-287 in Australia; © 0800/828-782 in New Zealand; www.vaustralia.com), another part of Sir Richard Branson's Virgin empire, has discount fares from Australia and New Zealand to Nadi. Americans can connect to V Australia's Los Angles-Sydney flights, and thence to Nadi, via **Virgin America** (© 800/444-0260; www.virginamerica.com).

Shopping for The Best Airfare

In addition to searching for the lowest airfare in the usual ways, I contact travel agents who specialize in Fiji. Which is to say, one who actually has been here—or better yet, who lives in Fiji—and is familiar with all it has to offer.

Following in alphabetical order are some reputable companies who specialize in Fiji and the South Pacific islands. Most make their money selling packages that include both airfare and accommodations. They don't turn as much profit from airline tickets as they do from hotel rooms, but some will discount air fare and hotel rooms separately; that is, not as part of a package. Be sure to shop for the best deal among them, and remember, it never hurts to ask.

- **Brendan Worldwide Vacations** (© 800/421-8446 or 818/785-9696; www. brendanvacations.com) provides packages to Fiji.
- **Costco Travel** (© 877/849-2730; www.costco.com) sells island packages to Costco members. The agency was a South Pacific specialist before Costco bought it.
- **Impulse Fiji** (© 253/617-1375 in the U.S.; www.impulsefiji.com) is a small Nadi-based firm owned by my American friend Dick Beaulieu, who has lived in Fiji since 1980. He and his staff arrange personalized travel to Fiji, including money-saving last-minute deals.
- **Islands in the Sun** (© 800/828-6877 or 310/536-0051; www.islandsinthesun. com), the largest and oldest South Pacific specialist, offers packages to Fiji.
- **Journey Pacific** (© 800/704-7094; www.journeypacific.com) is a Las Vegas–based agency offering Fiji packages.
- **Newmans South Pacific Vacations** (© 800/421-3326; www.newmansvacations. com), a long-established New Zealand–based company, offers packages to Fiji.
- **Pacific Destination Center** (© 800/227-5317; www.pacific-destinations.com) is owned and operated by Australian-born Janette Ryan, who offers some good deals to the islands.
- **Pleasant Holidays** (© 800/742-9244; www.pleasantholidays.com), a huge company best known for its Pleasant Hawaiian and Pleasant Mexico operations, offers packages to Fiji.
- **South Seas Adventures** (© 800/576-7327; www.south-seas-adventures.com) has adventure travel packages to Fiji.
- **Sun Vacations** (© 672 4293 in Fiji; www.sunvacationsfiji.com) is a small Nadi-based firm operated by Canadian-born Lynne Carlos, who has lived here since 1996. It has a walk-in office in the arrivals concourse of Nadi International Airport.
- **Sunspots International** (© 800/334-5623 or 503/666-3893; www.sunspotsintl. com), based in Portland, Oregon, has trips specifically tailored to Fiji.
- **Swain Tahiti Tours** (© 800/22-SWAIN (227-9246); www.swaintours.com) obviously knows a lot about Tahiti and French Polynesia, but it also sells packages to Fiji.
- **Travel2** (© 888/671-3986; www.travel2-us.com) puts together cost-effective packages to Fiji.
- **Travel Arrangements Ltd.** (© 800/392-8213; www.southpacificreservations. com) is operated by Fiji-born Ron Hunt, a veteran South Pacific travel agent who now lives in California. He sells packages and specializes in designing itineraries (and weddings) to suit your whims and pocketbook.
- **Travelwizard** (© 800/330-8820; www.travelwizard.com) specializes in designing luxury travel packages but also has less-expensive offerings. Among its offerings are adventure, diving, and surfing trips to Fiji.

Other companies have adventure travel packages combining outdoor activities with accommodations. See "The Active Traveler," below.

Arriving at Nadi

Arriving passengers can purchase duty-free items at two shops in the baggage-claim area before clearing Customs (they are in fierce competition, so it could pay to shop between them and ask for discounts). Imported liquor is expensive in Fiji, so if you drink, don't hesitate to buy two bottles here. Frankly, I've found duty-free liquor prices to be less at Los Angeles International Airport than here in Nadi.

After Customs runs your bags through an x-ray machine, you emerge onto an air-conditioned concourse lined on both sides by airline offices, travel and tour companies, car-rental firms, and a 24-hour branch of the **ANZ Bank** (see "Money & Costs," later in this chapter).

The Left Luggage counter at the far end of the departures concourse provides **baggage storage** for about F$3 to F$6 a day, depending on the size of the baggage. The counter is open 24 hours daily. The hotels all have baggage-storage rooms and will keep your extra stuff for free. The Left Luggage also has **showers** and rents towels.

A **post office,** in a separate building across the entry road from the main terminal, is open Monday to Friday from 8am to 4pm.

GETTING TO YOUR HOTEL FROM NADI AIRPORT

Representatives of the hotels and tour companies meet arriving visitors and provide free transportation to the hotels for those with reservations.

Taxis line up to the right outside the concourse. See the table under "Getting Around Fiji," below, for typical fares to the hotels. Only taxis painted yellow are allowed to take passengers from the airport. They have been inspected by the airport authority and are required to have air-conditioning, which most drivers will not voluntarily turn on.

Local buses to Nadi and Lautoka pass the airport on the Queen's Road every day. Walk straight out of the concourse, across the parking lot, and through the gate to the road. Driving in Fiji is on the left, so buses heading for Nadi and its hotels stop on the opposite side, next to Raffle's Gateway Hotel; those going to Lautoka stop on the airport side of the road. See "Getting Around Nadi," in chapter 5, for details.

Departing From Nadi

The Nadi domestic terminal and the international check-in counters are to the right of the arrival concourse as you exit Customs (or to the left, if you are arriving from the main road). The area is grossly under air-conditioned and often crowded, so don't change out of your shorts until you have cleared Immigration and are in the cooler international departure lounge.

There you will find a currency exchange counter, snack bar, showers, and large department stores. Duty-free prices, however, are higher here than you'll pay elsewhere in the country, and haggling won't change the set prices.

Passengers departing on flights bound for the United States must go through a body-pat security check in the departure lounge. (An Australian friend of mine wisecracked that we Americans "should change the name of your country to the United States of Paranoia.")

Fiji has no **departure tax** for either international or domestic flights.

Arriving & Departing at Suva

Nausori Airport is on the flat plains of the Rewa River delta about 19km (12 miles) from downtown Suva. The small terminal has a snack bar and an ATM but few other amenities. For more information, see "Getting to & Around Suva," in chapter 10.

Nausori Airport has a small duty-free shop in its departure lounge but no currency exchange facility. Some of Air Pacific's flights between Nadi and Samoa and Tonga stop first at Nausori, where you will deplane and clear Immigration and Customs.

GETTING AROUND FIJI

Fiji has an extensive and reliable transportation network of airplanes, helicopters, rental cars, taxis, ferries, and both long-distance and local buses. This section deals primarily with getting from one island or major area to another; see "Getting Around," in chapter 5, and "Getting to the Islands," in chapter 6, for details on transportation within the local areas.

By Plane & Helicopter

With a virtual monopoly since Air Fiji bit the dust in 2009, **Pacific Sun** (© **800/294-4864** in the U.S., 672 0888 in Nadi, or 331 5755 in Suva; www.pacific sun.com.fj) flies from Nadi to the major tourist destinations. (**Note:** It does not fly directly btw. Savusavu and Taveuni.) It operates a few 44-seat planes between Nadi, Suva, and Labasa, but don't be shocked when you climb off that gargantuan Boeing 747 and into an 18-seat Twin Otter for your 1-hour connecting flight to Savusavu or Taveuni, or a 9-seater to the smaller islands.

At this writing, **one-way fares from Nadi** start at F$58 to Malololailai Island (Lomani, Musket Cove, and Plantation Island resorts), F$68 to Mana Island, F$78 to Suva, F$176 to Savusavu, and F$230 to Taveuni.

You can save by booking round-trip fares; ask the airline for specifics. It also may pay to shop for the airline's Internet specials.

Pacific Sun is a wholly-owned subsidiary of Air Pacific, with which it shares offices in the international arrivals concourse at Nadi International Airport and on Victoria Parade in Suva.

Pacific Islands Seaplanes (© **672 5644;** www.fijiseaplanes.com) provides charter service throughout Fiji in its small, Canadian-built floatplanes, which use wheels to take off from Nadi airport and then use floats to land on water at the offshore resorts.

Island Hoppers (© **672 0140;** www.helicopters.com.fj) also will whisk you to the Mamanucas in one of its helicopters. If you have to ask how much these rides cost, you can't afford them. I would let my choice of resort arrange my transfers and tell me how much it will cost.

By Rental Car

Rental cars are widely available in Fiji. Each company has its own pricing policy, and you can frequently find discounts, special deals, and some give-and-take bargaining over long-term and long-distance use. All major companies, and a few not so major, have offices in the commercial concourse at Nadi International Airport, so it's easy to shop around. Most are open 7 days a week, some for 24 hours a day.

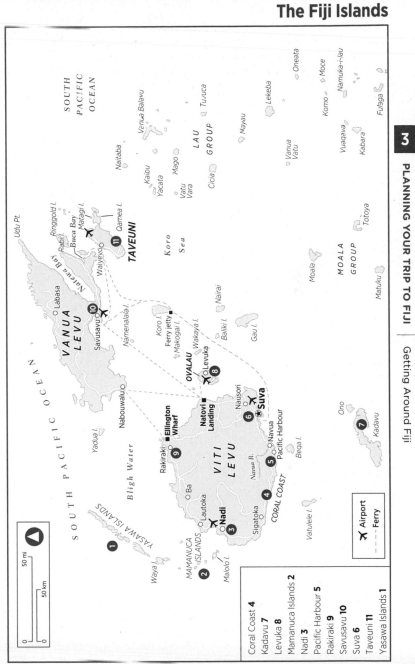

Coral Coast **4**
Kadavu **7**
Levuka **8**
Mamanuca Islands **2**
Nadi **3**
Pacific Harbour **5**
Rakiraki **9**
Savusavu **10**
Suva **6**
Taveuni **11**
Yasawa Islands **1**

How to Fly Smoothly in Fiji

Here are a few tips to help make flying in Fiji a smooth experience.

o Book your domestic interisland flights well in advance, preferably as part of your international ticket. You may not get on a plane at all if you wait until you arrive in Fiji to take care of this important chore.

o Pacific Sun does not fly directly between Savusavu and Taveuni. To get between them, you must backtrack to Nadi or Suva on the morning flight, and wait there for the afternoon flight to the other island. That's an expensive,

full-day proposition. The only alternative is a half-day journey on the bus-ferry *Amazing Grace* (see "By Ferry," below).

o Weigh your bag, because **baggage allowances** on domestic flights may be 10kg (22 lb.) instead of the 20kg (44 lb.) allowed on international flights. Usually you can check 20kg (44 lb.) if you're connecting from or to an international flight, but inquire with Pacific Sun to avoid showing up with too much luggage.

Give careful consideration to how far you will drive; it's 197km (122 miles) from Nadi Airport to Suva, so an unlimited kilometer rate could work to your advantage if you plan to drive that far.

Avis (© **800/331-1212,** or 672 2233 in Nadi; www.avis.com.fj) has more than 50% of the business here, and for good reason: The Toyota dealer is the local agent, so it has the newest and best-maintained fleet. In addition to the office at Nadi Airport, Avis can be found in Suva (© **331 3833**), in Korolevu on the Coral Coast (© **653 0176**), and at several hotels.

Thrifty Car Rental (© **800/367-2277,** or 672 2935 in Nadi; www.thrifty.com), which is handled by Rosie the Travel Service, is also a good choice. Its rates are comparable to Avis's but its cars tend to be older.

Other international agencies here are **Budget Rent A Car** (© **800/527-0700** or 672 2735; www.budget.com); **Hertz** (© **800/654-3131** or 672 3466; www.hertz. com), and **Europcar** (© **800/227-7368** or 672 5957; www.europcar.com).

The most reliable local companies are **Carpenters Rentals** (© **672 2772,** or 332 8628 in Suva; rentals@carpenters.com.fj), which also is operated by an automobile dealer, and **Khan's Rental Cars** (© **679 0617** or 338 5033 in Suva; www. khansrental.com.fj). I rent from other "kick-the-tires" local companies only when I need a car just to run around the Nadi area—not to take on a road trip.

Rates at all agencies range from about F$125 upward per day with unlimited kilometers. Add about F$25 a day to reduce your collision damage liability. Your home **insurance** policy might cover any damages that occur in Fiji, but I recommend getting local coverage when you rent a car. Even if you do, the local policies require you to pay the first F$500 or more of damages in any event. Underbody and overhead damage is not covered, so go slow when crossing Fiji's innumerable "road humps"—and do not park under coconut trees!

All renters must be at least 21 years old, and a few companies require them to be at least 25 or have at least 2 years driving experience.

Gasoline (petrol) is readily available at service stations in all the main towns. Expect to pay about twice what you would pay in the United States and Canada, about the same as elsewhere.

DRIVING RULES

Driving is on the left-hand side of the road throughout Fiji, as in the U.K., Australia, and New Zealand. Your valid home driver's license will be honored here. **Seat belts** are mandatory. **Speed limits** are 80kmph (48 mph) on the open road and 50kmph (30 mph) in the towns and other built-up areas. It's illegal to drive while talking on a **mobile phone.** You must **stop for pedestrians** in all marked crosswalks.

Driving under the influence of alcohol or other drugs is a criminal offense in Fiji, and the police frequently throw up roadblocks and administer Breathalyzer tests to all drivers. Even if I have a rental car, I take a taxi home after a session with friends at a local bar.

By Bus

Appealing to backpackers and other cost-conscious travelers, **Feejee Experience** (© **672 5959;** www.feejeeexperience.com) runs a bus counterclockwise around Viti Levu 4 days a week. The vehicles have local guides and stop for sightseeing and activities such as village visits, hiking, and river rafting.

You buy a pass, which allows you to get on and off the bus at will for up to 6 months. The "Hula Hoop" pass costs F$485 and includes the bus around Viti Levu. The "Lei Low" pass for F$725 adds a night in a dorm on Beachcomber Island Resort in the Mamanuca Islands off Nadi (see p. 130). The "Mangos & Mantarays" adds a trip to Mantaray Island Resort for F$865.

Driving in Fiji: Watch Out for Cows, Horses & Road Humps!

Most roads in Fiji are narrow, poorly maintained, and crooked. (Fixing pot-holes is not an art here!) The **Queen's Road** is paved between Nadi and Suva, but in most Western countries it would be described as a two-lane country road. Likewise the **King's Road,** around northern Viti Levu between Lautoka and Suva. About 30km (18 miles) of it through the mountains between Koro-vou and Rakiraki are still rough gravel and must be driven with the utmost caution. Only short sections of the two roads are within view of the ocean.

Not all local drivers are well trained, experienced, or skilled, and some of them (including bus drivers) go much too fast for the conditions.

Consequently, you should **drive defen-sively** at all times. Constantly be alert for potholes, landslides, hairpin curves, and various stray animals—cows and horses are a very real danger, especially at night.

Also keep an eye out for speed bumps, known in Fiji as **road humps.** Most Fijian villages have them. Although big signs made to resemble traditional Fijian war clubs announce when you're entering and leaving vil-lages on the Queen's Road, road humps are usually positioned between the clubs, so slow down! The humps are large enough to do serious damage to the bottom of a car, and no local rental agency's insurance covers that.

Feejee Experience will book and hold rooms or dorm beds at its preferred hostels, including Mango Bay Resort on the Coral Coast, Raintree Lodge in Suva, and Volivoli Beach Resort in Rakiraki.

You can get around by local bus for a lot less money, but you won't have the guides, the activities, or the companionship of youthful fellow travelers.

The most comfortable buses between Nadi airport and Suva are the air-conditioned **Fiji Express** (© 672 3105 in Nadi, or 331 2287 in Suva). One bus leaves Nadi airport daily at 7:30am and stops at the major hotels along the Queen's Road before arriving at Suva about 11:30am. It departs Suva at 3:30pm and returns to Nadi at 7:30pm. Another bus begins its daily run at 7:30am from the Holiday Inn Suva and arrives in Nadi about 11:30am. It begins its return to Suva at 1pm, arriving in the capital about 5pm. One-way fares run up to F$22, depending on how far you go. You can book at any hotel tour desk.

Sunbeam Transport Ltd. (© 666 2822 in Lautoka, or 338 2704 in Suva) and **Pacific Transport Ltd.** (© 670 0044 in Nadi, or 330 4366 in Suva) operate express and regular buses that go all the way around Viti Levu. They stop at the domestic terminal at Nadi Airport and the markets at Nadi Town, Sigatoka, and Navua. Express buses take about 4 hours between Nadi and Suva, compared to 5 hours on the local "stages." These buses cater to local residents, do not take reservations, and have no air-conditioning. The Nadi-Suva fare is about F$15, express or local.

In addition to Sunbeam Transport Ltd., **Reliance Transport Bus Service** (© 666 3059 in Lautoka, or 338 2296 in Suva) and **Akbar Buses Ltd.** (© 669 4760 in Rakiraki) have express and local service between Lautoka and Suva via the King's Road. The Lautoka-Suva fare is about F$13.

Public buses are plentiful and inexpensive in Fiji, and it's possible to go all the way around Viti Levu on them. I did it once by taking the Fiji Express (see below) from Nadi to Suva one morning, a local express to Rakiraki the next morning, and then another express to Lautoka and a local back to Nadi.

Fume-belching **local buses** use the produce markets as their terminals. The older buses have side windows made of canvas panels that are rolled down during inclement weather (they usually fly out the sides and flap in the wind like great skirts). They run every few minutes along the Queen's Road between Lautoka and Nadi Town, passing the airport and most of the hotels and restaurants along the way (see "Getting Around Nadi," in chapter 5).

Minivans scoot along the Queen's Road between the Nadi Town market and the Suva Municipal Market. Those with yellow license tags with the prefix "LM"

It Never Hurts to Bargain

In Nadi and on the Coral Coast, you will see the same taxi drivers stationed outside your hotel every day. Usually they are paid on a salaried rather than a fare basis, so they may be willing to spend more time than usual showing you around. Also, they might charge you less than the government-regulated fares for long-distance trips, such as from Nadi to the Coral Coast or Suva, because many would rather earn one big fare a day than several small ones. It never hurts to politely bargain.

(licensed minivan) are regulated by the government. I avoid the others, which can be unsafe, and I strongly suggest you do the same.

By Taxi

Taxis are abundant in Fiji. All taxis are required to have meters (and air-conditioners, if they serve Nadi airport), but most drivers will not turn them on unless you ask. Even with the meter running, settle on a fare to your destination before striking out (see the distance and fare chart below). Some drivers will complain about short fares and will badger you for more business later on during your stay; politely ignore these entreaties.

Not to be confused with minibuses, **"share taxis"** or "rolling taxis"—those not otherwise occupied—pick up passengers at bus stops and charge the bus fare. They are a particularly good value on long-distance trips. A taxi returning to Suva, for example, will stop by the Nadi Town market and pick up a load of passengers at the bus fare rather than drive back to the capital empty. Ask around the local market bus stops if share taxis are available. You'll meet some wonderful Fijians that way.

Although the government sets all taxi fares, it has not raised them for several years despite skyrocketing fuel prices. They may be higher by the time you arrive. In the meantime, many drivers will ask for a few dollars more than the official fare. Even if they don't, I usually give them a small tip anyway—provided they haven't pestered me, refused to turn on the air-conditioner, or blared Indian music from their radios. The following are distances from Nadi International Airport via the Queen's Road and the official government-regulated taxi fares at press time.

FROM NADI AIRPORT TO:	KM	MILES	APPROX. TAXI FARE
Tanoa/Novotel Hotels	1.3	0.8	F$3
Nomads Skylodge Hotel	3.3	2.0	F$4
Mercure/Sandalwood Inn/Nadi Bay Hotel	5.2	3.1	F$5
Wailoaloa Beach	8.3	5.0	F$8
Denarau Island	15	9.3	F$20
Nadi Town	9.0	5.4	F$10
Shangri-la's Fijian Resort and Spa	60	37	F$55
Sigatoka	70	43	F$60
Outrigger on the Lagoon Fiji	78	48	F$65
Hideaway Resort	92	57	F$68
The Warwick Fiji Resort & Spa	104	64	F$80
Pacific Harbour	148	92	F$145
Suva	197	122	F$165

By Ferry

Three reliable shuttle boats operated by Nadi-based **South Sea Cruises** (© 675 0500; www.ssc.com.fj) connect the Mamanuca and Yasawa islands to Denarau Island and Nadi. The *Tiger IV* and the *Cheetah* make three runs daily through the Mamanucas, while the *Yasawa Express* goes to the Yasawas and back once a day. See chapter 6, "The Mamanuca & Yasawa Islands," for details.

Vehicle- and passenger-carrying ferries also run between Suva and the main islands. Invariably they run overnight, and their schedules can change abruptly depending on the weather and the condition of the ships. Consequently I do not recommend them unless you have unlimited time and an adventurous spirit. Call the operators below for the latest information.

One boat you might consider riding is the passenger ferry **Amazing Grace** (© **888 0320** on Taveuni, 927 1372 in Savusavu), which takes about 90 minutes to cross the Somosomo Strait between Buca Bay on Vanua Levu, and Waiyevo on Taveuni. From Buca Bay, it's a 2½-hour bus ride over a gravel road to or from Savusavu. The boat-ferry trip begins at 9am on either island, and ends about 4½ hours later on the other. Used mostly by locals, the *Amazing Grace* is small and has wooden seats, and the bus is open-air with straight-back benches; therefore, you will not have a smooth ride, comfortable seats, or air-conditioning. But it is an alternative to spending all day getting between Taveuni and Savusavu by air. The one-way fare is F$25, including a bus ride. Reservations are strongly advised.

Bligh Water Shipping Ltd. (© **331 8247** in Suva, or 990 2032 in Lautoka; www.blighwatershipping.com.fj) operates the cleanest and most reliable ferries between Suva, Savusavu, and Taveuni. One departs Suva for Savusavu and Taveuni thrice weekly. Adult economy fare for the 11-hour, overnight run to Savusavu starts at F$55.

Patterson Shipping Services (© **331 5644** in Suva; patterson@connect.com. fj) has bus-ferry connections from Natovi Wharf (north of Suva on eastern Viti Levu) to Buresala Landing on Ovalau, and to Nabouwalu on Vanua Levu. You connect by bus from Suva to Natovi, from Buresala to Levuka, and from Nabouwalu to Labasa (local buses connect Labasa to Savusavu). The one-way Suva-Levuka fare is about F$25, while Suva-Labasa is about F$55. Patterson's office is in Ste. 1–2, Epworth House, Nina Street in Suva.

MONEY & COSTS

Fiji is a reasonably priced destination—much less expensive than big cities such as New York and London, more than some Southeast Asian countries. It became even more reasonably priced in 2009, when the national government devalued the Fiji dollar by 20%.

You will find a wide range of prices here. Domestic airfares are relatively high, but taxi and bus fares are cheap. Some luxury resorts charge more than F$3,000 a night, but you can get a clean, comfortable hotel room for F$75.

Much of the country's tourism infrastructure is oriented toward backpackers, but the resulting prices are attractive to travelers of any age who are on a tight budget.

Currency

The national currency is the Fiji dollar, which is divided into 100 cents. Dollar notes come in $2, $5, $10, $20, $50, and $100. Coins are 5¢, 10¢, 20¢, 50¢, and $1.

The Fiji dollar trades independently on the foreign exchange markets and is abbreviated "FID" by the banks and airlines. I use **F$** in this book.

Since the devaluation in 2009, some hotels and resorts quote their rates in U.S. dollars, indicated in this book by **US$**, or in Australian dollars **(A$).** Otherwise I give prices in Fiji dollars.

WHAT THINGS COST IN FIJI	US$/C$	UK£
Taxi from airport to Nadi Town	5	3.30
Bus from airport to Nadi Town	0.52	0.34
Moderate hotel room for two	250	165
Inexpensive hotel room for two	55	36
Moderate lunch for two, without alcohol	26	17
Moderate three-course meal for two, without alcohol	40	26.50
Bottle of Fiji Bitter beer in a bar	2.50	1.65
Cup of regular coffee	2.25	1.50

The currency conversions quoted in the table below were correct at press time. However, rates fluctuate, so before departing consult a currency exchange website such as **www.xe.com/ucc/full** and **www.oanda.com/convert/classic** to check up-to-the-minute rates.

THE VALUE OF THE FIJI DOLLAR VS. OTHER POPULAR CURRENCIES

F$	US$	Can$	UK£	Euro (€)	A$	NZ$
1	50¢	50¢	£.33	€37¢	A56¢	NZ74¢

How to Get Local Currency

ANZ Bank branches in the baggage claim area and in the international arrivals concourse at Nadi International Airport are open 24 hours a day, 7 days a week. Both have ATMs, where you can draw Fijian currency by using MasterCard or Visa credit or debit cards. **Fexco Pacific/Western Union** has exchange counters (but no ATMs) in the arrivals concourse and near the departures door.

ANZ Bank, Westpac Bank, and **Colonial National Bank** have offices throughout the country where currency and traveler's checks can be exchanged. They all have ATMs at their Nadi and Suva offices and at their branches in Savusavu. Colonial National Bank has an ATM on Taveuni. There's an ATM at the Nausori Airport terminal near Suva. Several large hotels on Viti Levu have ATMs in their lobbies. Elsewhere, bring credit cards, cash, and traveler's checks.

Banking hours nationwide are Monday to Thursday from 9:30am to 3pm and Friday from 9:30am to 4pm.

You can get a better rate for traveler's checks at **Fexco Pacific/Western Union** offices at Nadi Airport and in Nadi Town and Suva. See the "Fast Facts: Nadi" section, in chapter 5, for specific currency exchange locations.

Credit Cards

American Express, MasterCard, and Visa are widely accepted by the hotels, car-rental firms, travel and tour companies, large stores, and most restaurants. Don't count on using a Diners Club card outside the hotels, and leave your Discover card at home.

Credit Card Add-Ons

Many Fiji businesses add 3% to 5% to your bill if you use a credit card, while others may offer a similar discount for cash payments. Credit card issuers frown on the add-ons, but the locals do it anyway. Always ask if an add-on or discount will be assessed. I found it less expensive to pay my bank a 1% fee to withdraw cash from an ATM than to pay the local add-on plus my credit card company's 3% international-transaction fee.

Beware of hidden credit-card fees while traveling. Check with your credit or debit card issuer to see what fees, if any, will be charged for overseas transactions. Recent reform legislation in the U.S., for example, has curbed some exploitative lending practices. But many banks have responded by increasing fees in other areas, including fees for customers who use credit and debit cards while out of the country—even if those charges were made in U.S. dollars. Fees can amount to 3% or more of the purchase price. Check with your bank before departing to avoid any surprise charges on your statement.

STAYING HEALTHY

Fiji poses no major health problems for most travelers, although it's a good idea to have your tetanus, hepatitis-A, and hepatitis-B vaccinations up-to-date.

If you have a chronic condition, check with your doctor before visiting the islands.

Fiji's main islands have drug stores that carry over-the-counter and **prescription medications.** Most medications can be purchased without a local prescription, but bring your own medications (in your carry-on luggage), in their original containers. Carry the generic name of medicines, because local pharmacies primarily carry medications manufactured in Australia, New Zealand, and the U.K.

Cuts, scratches, and all open sores should be treated promptly in the Tropics to avoid infection. I carry a tube of antibacterial ointment and a small package of adhesive bandages such as Band-Aids.

Don't forget **sunglasses** and an extra pair of **contact lenses** or **prescription glasses,** though you can easily replace your contacts and prescription lenses in Nadi, Lautoka, and Suva.

Regional Health Concerns

Among minor illnesses, Fiji has the common cold and occasional outbreaks of influenza and conjunctivitis (pink eye).

TROPICAL ILLNESSES Fiji has plenty of mosquitoes, but they do not carry deadly endemic diseases such as malaria. From time to time, the islands will experience an outbreak of **dengue fever,** a viral disease borne by the *Adës aegypti* mosquito, which lives indoors and bites only during daylight hours. Dengue seldom is fatal in adults, but you should take extra precautions to keep children from being bitten by mosquitoes if the disease is present during your visit. (Other precautions should be taken if you are traveling with **children;** see "Specialized Travel Resources," below.)

BUGS, BITES & OTHER HEALTH CONCERNS   Living among the friendly Fijians are some of the world's friendliest creatures, including the likes of ants, roaches, geckos, crabs, and other insects.

Ants are omnipresent here, so don't leave crumbs or dirty dishes lying around your room. A few beaches and swampy areas also have invisible **sand flies**—the dreaded "no-see-ums" or "no-nos"—which bite the ankles around daybreak and dusk. (I am oblivious to mosquito bites, but sand flies make me scratch to the bone!)

I always apply insect repellent at dusk, when mosquitoes and sand flies are most active. The most effective repellents contain a high percentage of "DEET" (N,N-Diethyl-m-Toluamide). Insect repellent is widely available in most drug stores and groceries in Fiji.

I also light a mosquito coil in my non-air-conditioned rooms at dusk in order to keep the pests from flying in, and I start another one at bedtime. Grocery stores throughout the islands carry these inexpensive coils. I have found the Fish brand coils, made by the appropriately named Blood Protection Company, to work best.

SUN EXPOSURE   I don't have to remind you, but I will: The tropical sun in the islands can be brutal, even on what seems like an overcast day. Accordingly, it's important to use sunscreen whenever you're outdoors, especially at midday. This is particularly true for children. I also wear a hat or sun visor to shade my ample nose.

If You Get Sick

Hospitals and clinics are widespread in Fiji, but the quality is not up to Western standards. You can get a broken bone set and a coral scrape tended, but treating more serious ailments likely will be beyond the capability of the local hospital.

I list hospitals, emergency numbers, and some of the country's best doctors under the "Fast Facts" sections in the destination chapters. Elsewhere, doctors are listed in the local Yellow Pages, under "Medical Practitioners." Your hotel or resort staff will either have a doctor on call or can refer you to one.

Even if you have health insurance, you may have to pay all medical costs up front and be reimbursed later. The American Medicare and Medicaid programs do not provide coverage for medical costs outside the U.S. Before leaving home, find out what medical services your health insurance covers. To protect yourself, consider buying medical travel insurance.

For information on traveler's insurance, trip cancelation insurance, and medical insurance while traveling, please visit **www.frommers.com/tips**.

Multitudes of Animals

Don't bother complaining to me about the multitude of dogs, chickens, pigs, and squawking myna birds running loose out here, even in the finest restaurants. They are as much a part of life as the islanders themselves. And don't be frightened by those little **geckos** (lizards) crawling around the rafters of even the most expensive bungalows. They're harmless to us humans but lethal to insects.

BE CAREFUL IN THE water

Most of Fiji's marine creatures are harmless to humans, but you need to avoid some. Always **seek local advice** before snorkeling or swimming in a lagoon away from the hotel beaches. Many diving operators conduct snorkeling tours; if you don't know what you're doing, go with them.

Wash and apply a good antiseptic or antibacterial ointment to all **coral cuts and scrapes** as soon as possible.

Because coral cannot grow in fresh water, the flow of rivers and streams into the lagoon creates narrow channels known as **passes** through the reef. Currents can be very strong in the passes, so stay in the protected, shallow water of the inner lagoons.

Sharks are curious beasts that are attracted by bright objects such as watches and knives, so be careful what you wear in the water. Don't swim in areas where sewage or edible wastes are dumped, and never swim alone if you have any suspicion that sharks might be present. If you do see a shark, don't splash in the water or urinate. Calmly retreat and get out of the water as quickly as you can, without creating a disturbance.

Those round things on the rocks and reefs that look like pincushions are **sea urchins,** and their calcium spikes can be more painful than needles. A sea-urchin puncture can result in burning, aching, swelling, and discoloration (black or purple) around the area where the spines entered your skin. The best thing to do is to pull any protruding spines out. The body will absorb the spines within 24 hours to 3 weeks, or the remainder of the spines will work themselves out. In the meantime, take aspirin or other pain killers. Contrary to popular advice, do not urinate or pour vinegar on the embedded spines—this will not help.

Jellyfish stings can hurt like the devil but are seldom life-threatening. You need to get any visible tentacles off your body right away, but not with your hands, unless you are wearing gloves. Use a stick or anything else that is handy. Then rinse the sting with salt- or fresh water, and apply ice to prevent swelling and to help control the pain. If you can find it at an island grocery store, Adolph's Meat Tenderizer is a great antidote.

The **stone fish** is so named because it looks like a piece of stone or coral as it lies buried in the sand on the lagoon bottom with only its back and 13 venomous spikes sticking out. Its venom can cause paralysis and even death. You'll know by the intense pain if you're stuck. Serum is available, so get to a hospital at once. **Sea snakes, cone shells, crown-of-thorns starfish, moray eels, lionfish,** and **demon stingers** also can be painful, if not deadly. The last thing any of these creatures wants to do is to tangle with a human, so keep your hands to yourself.

CRIME & SAFETY

While international terrorism is still a threat throughout the world, Fiji is among the planet's safest destinations. Security procedures are in effect at Nadi and Nausori airports, but once you're on the outer islands, don't expect to see a metal detector or to have anyone inspect your carry-on.

Although its military coups brought Fiji to the world's attention and caused great consternation on the part of the New Zealand and Australian governments, I have seen little impact of the takeover during my recent visits. From a traveler's point of view, everything was working normally and peacefully.

Some parts of Viti Levu had a very serious crime problem before the December 2006 coup, especially with robberies and home invasions. Say what you may about military governments, this one greatly reduced that problem. Street crimes against tourists have been infrequent, especially in busy areas such as Martintar, in Nadi, and Victoria Parade, the main drag in Suva. Nevertheless, friends of mine who live here don't stroll off the busy streets after dark, especially in Suva, and they keep a sharp eye on their personal belongings everywhere. You should stay alert wherever you are, especially after dusk.

Don't leave valuable items in your hotel room, in your rental car, or unattended anywhere.

Women should not wander alone on deserted beaches any time, as some island men may consider such behavior to be an invitation for instant amorous activity.

When heading outdoors, keep in mind that injuries often occur when people fail to follow instructions. Hike only in designated areas, swim and snorkel only where you see other people swimming and snorkeling, follow the marine charts if piloting your own boat, carry rain gear, and wear a life jacket when canoeing or rafting. Mountain weather can be fickle at any time. Watch out for sudden storms that can leave you drenched and send bolts of lightning your way.

> ### Healthy Travels to You
>
> The following government websites offer up-to-date health-related travel advice.
> o **Australia:** www.dfat.gov.au/travel
> o **Canada:** www.hc-sc.gc.ca/index_e.html
> o **U.K.:** www.dh.gov.uk/en/index.htm
> o **U.S.:** www.cdc.gov/travel

SPECIALIZED TRAVEL RESOURCES

In addition to the Fiji-specific resources listed below, please visit Frommers.com for other specialized travel resources.

LGBT Travelers

Although homosexuality is officially frowned upon by local laws and by some local religious leaders, an old Fiji custom makes this a relatively friendly destination for gay men with one proviso: **Stay away from gay prostitutes.**

In the Pacific islands, many families with a shortage of female offspring literally rear young boys as girls, or at least relegate them to female chores around the home and village. Some of them grow up to live a heterosexual existence; others choose a homosexual or bisexual lifestyle and, often appearing publicly in women's attire, actively seek the company of tourists. Some dance the female parts in traditional island night shows. You'll see them throughout Fiji; many hold jobs in hotels and restaurants.

On the other hand, women were not considered equal in this respect in ancient times; thus, "choosing" lesbianism was discouraged.

Travelers with Disabilities

Most disabilities shouldn't stop anyone from traveling, even in Fiji, where ramps, handles, accessible toilets, automatic opening doors, telephones at convenient heights, and other helpful aids such as those found in Western countries are appearing but are not yet universal.

Some hotels provide rooms specially equipped for people with disabilities. Such improvements are ongoing; inquire when making a reservation whether such rooms are available.

The major international airlines make special arrangements for travelers with disabilities. Be sure to tell them of your needs when you reserve. Although most local airlines use small planes that are not equipped for those with disabilities, their staffs go out of their way to help everyone get in and out of the craft.

Family Travel

Fijians adore infants and young children, but childhood does not last as long here as it does in Western societies. As soon as they are capable, children are put to work, first caring for their younger siblings and cousins and helping out with household chores, later tending the village gardens. It's only as teenagers—and then only if they leave their villages for town—that they cannot find jobs and thus know unemployment in the Western sense. Accordingly, few towns and villages have children's facilities, such as playgrounds, outside of school property.

On the other hand, the Fijians invariably love children and are extraordinarily good at babysitting. The hotels can take care of this for you.

The larger hotels in Fiji cater to Australian and New Zealander families, with ample activities to keep everyone occupied. **Jean-Michel Cousteau Fiji Islands Resort** in Savusavu (see p. 214) is one of the top family resorts in all of the South Pacific islands, and several others have excellent kids programs. See "The Best Family Resorts," in chapter 1.

Some resorts do not accept children at all; I point those out in the establishment listings, but you should ask to make sure. Even if they are able to accommodate young visitors, check whether the hotel can provide cribs and other needs, and if they have children's menus.

To locate accommodations, restaurants, and attractions that are particularly kid-friendly, look for the "Kids" icon throughout this guide.

Disposable diapers, cotton swabs (known as Buds, not Q-Tips), and baby food are sold in many main-town stores, but you should take along a supply of such items as children's aspirin, a thermometer, adhesive bandages (plasters), and special medications. Make sure your children's vaccinations are up-to-date before you leave home. If your children are very small, perhaps you should discuss your travel plans with your family doctor.

Remember to protect youngsters with ample sunscreen.

Other tips: Some tropical plants and animals may resemble rocks or vegetation, so teach your youngsters to avoid touching or brushing up against rocks, seaweed, and other objects. If your children are prone to swimmer's ear, use vinegar or preventive drops before they go swimming in freshwater streams or lakes. Having them shower soon after swimming or suffering cuts or abrasions will help reduce the chance of infection.

Rascals in Paradise, One Daniel Burnham Court, Ste. 105-C, San Francisco, CA 94107 (© **415/921-7000;** fax 415/921-7050; www.rascalsinparadise.com), specializes in organizing tours for families with kids, including visits with local families and children.

Women Travelers

Fiji is relatively safe for women traveling alone, but don't let the charm of warm nights and smiling faces lull you into any less caution than you would exercise at home. *Do not* wander alone on deserted beaches. In the old days this was an invitation for sex. If that's what you want today, then that's what you're likely to get. Otherwise, it could result in your being raped.

And don't ever hitchhike alone, either.

Senior Travel

Nevertheless, mention the fact that you're a senior when you first make your travel reservations. All major airlines and many chain hotels offer discounts for seniors.

Elderhostel, 75 Federal St., Boston, MA 02110-1941 (© **877/426-8056;** www.elderhostel.org), occasionally has study programs to Fiji for those ages 55 and older (and a spouse or companion of any age) in the United States and in more than 80 countries. Most include airfare and accommodations in university dorms or modest inns, meals, and tuition.

Student Travel

Fiji has one of the most developed backpacker industries in the world, with numerous resorts beckoning young people out to see the world without spending a fortune. It seems like every flight I'm on to Fiji is half full of people under 25 in search of sun, sand, and suds, especially in the **Yasawa Islands,** their party destination of choice (see chapter 6).

On the other hand, you won't find student discounts here per se.

If you're going on to New Zealand and Australia, you'd be wise to get an **international student ID card** from the **International Student Travel Confederation** (**ISTC;** www.istc.org), which offers savings on plane tickets.

Single Travelers

Having traveled alone through the South Pacific islands for more years than I care to admit, I can tell you Fiji is a great place to be unattached. After all, this is the land of smiles and genuine warmth toward strangers. The attitude soon infects visitors: All I've ever had to do to meet my fellow travelers is wander into a hotel bar, order a beer, and ask the persons next to me where they are from and what they have done on their vacations.

Leave Fido at Home

Don't even think about bringing your pet to Fiji. Fido will be quarantined until you are ready to fly home.

And with its backpacker industry, Fiji seems to be crawling with young singles at all times.

If you're single, you will have a wonderful time in Fiji.

RESPONSIBLE TOURISM

Climate change and rising sea levels resulting from global warming are having a noticeable impact on all the South Pacific islands. Fijians I have known for more than 30 years tell me the seasons are now unpredictable (it's more likely to rain in the dry season, and vice versa), and the tides are higher than ever (in some places the lagoons lap directly on shore at high tide rather than on the beach). Indeed, most islanders don't want to hear any corporate-induced spin about the lack of evidence of global warming and its consequences. They know it's true from firsthand experience.

On the other hand, they are contributing to the problem. Buses, ancient taxis, and other vehicles spew clouds of sooty exhaust fumes into the air. Fiji has clean-air laws, but many owners are too poor to do the necessary maintenance and repairs to their vehicles. Because strictly enforcing the law would deny them their means of transportation, some officials look the other way. I wish we visitors could fight back, perhaps by refusing to ride in polluting vehicles, but I've never seen a green bus or taxi in Fiji.

Fiji also has been slack in allowing some resort owners to remove parts of the reef to create marinas and swimming holes, despite its laws protecting the lagoons, reefs, and sea life. To the Fijians, lagoons are not just places where you swim around and look at beautiful corals and sea life; they are major sources of food. Protecting their lagoons and reefs is a matter of survival.

Most small offshore resorts have instituted eco-friendly practices, if for no other reason than to save money. Diesel-powered generators are very expensive to operate, especially when fuel must be transported by boat to remote islands, so installing solar or even wind devices can be cost effective. Composting and recycling are now widespread among the smaller resorts. Many have also instituted marine reserves to protect the lagoons in front of their properties.

We visitors can help by practicing **responsible tourism,** which means being careful with the environments we explore, and respecting the communities we visit. We can also choose to stay in properties which minimize their impact on the environment.

SPECIAL INTEREST & ESCORTED TRIPS

Special Interest Trips

Although outdoor activities take first place in Fiji (see "The Active Traveler," below), you can also spend your time learning a new craft, exploring the reefs as part of a conservation project, or helping to build a new home for the under privileged.

BIRD-WATCHING   Avid bird-watchers are likely to see terns, boobies, herons, petrols, noddies, and many other seabirds throughout the islands. Land birds, on the other hand, live in the bush away from settlements and the accompanying cats, dogs, and rats, so you will need to head into the bush for the best watching.

GENERAL RESOURCES FOR responsible travel

In addition to the resources for Fiji listed above, the following websites provide valuable wide-ranging information on sustainable travel.

- **Responsible Travel** (www.responsibletravel.com) is a great source of sustainable travel ideas; the site is run by a spokesperson for ethical tourism in the travel industry. **Sustainable Travel International** (www.sustainabletravelinternational.org) promotes ethical tourism practices, and manages an extensive directory of sustainable properties and tour operators around the world.
- **Carbonfund** (www.carbonfund.org), **TerraPass** (www.terrapass.org), and **Cool Climate** (http://coolclimate.berkeley.edu) provide info on "carbon offsetting," or offsetting the greenhouse gas emitted during flights.
- **Greenhotels** (www.greenhotels.com) recommends green-rated member hotels around the world that fulfill the company's stringent environmental requirements. **Environmentally Friendly Hotels** (www.environmentallyfriendlyhotels.com) offers more green accommodation ratings.
- **Volunteer International** (www.volunteerinternational.org) has a list of questions to help you determine the intentions and the nature of a volunteer program. For general info on volunteer travel, visit **www.volunteerabroad.org** and **www.idealist.org**.

With 26 endemic species of land birds, Fiji has more diversity than any other South Pacific island country. Many are on display in **Kula Eco Park** (© 650 0505; www.fijiwild.com), on Fiji's Coral Coast (see p. 148).

Taveuni island is best for bird-watching in Fiji, with more than 100 species including the rare orange dove, which lives high on Des Veoux Peak. See chapter 14.

Savusavu on Vanua Levu is also good, especially the nearby Waisali Rainforest Reserve. **Daku Resort** in Savusavu (© 885 0046; www.dakuresort.com) hosts bird-watching tours run by veteran Fiji watcher Robin Mercer. See p. 217.

A few companies have bird-watching tours to Fiji, including the U.K.-based **Bird Quest** (© 44/1254-826317; www.birdquest.co.uk) and **Birdwatching Breaks** (© 44/1381-610495; www.birdwatchingbreaks.com).

ACADEMIC TRIPS In addition to bird-watching, **Daku Resort** in Savusavu (© 885 0046; www.dakuresort.com), hosts weeklong courses in writing, sketching, painting, quilting, gospel singing, and yoga. The courses are organized by creative writing teacher Delia Rothnie-Jones (she and her husband John own the resort). They have special package rates for the courses and will help you arrange air transportation to Fiji as well. I could be teaching all about travel writing. See p. 217.

ECO-TRAVEL TOURS The **Oceanic Society** (© 800/326-7491; www.oceanic-society.org), an award-winning organization based in California, has natural history and ecotourism expeditions to Fiji. A marine naturalist accompanies its annual 11-day snorkeling trip to the colorful, pristine reefs off Namena and Taveuni islands in northern Fiji (see chapters 13 and 14, respectively). The trip includes village visits and bird-watching excursions.

Formerly known as Tui Tai Adventure Cruises, the environmentally and culturally friendly **Active Fiji** (www.activefiji.com) uses a 42m (140-ft.) sailing schooner to explore out-of-the-way islands in northern Fiji. The boat goes to Fijian villages and carries mountain bikes as well as snorkeling and diving gear. See p. 211.

VOLUNTEER & WORKING TRIPS Seacology (© 510/559-3505; www. seacology.org), a California-based organization dedicated to preserving island cultures and environments, has an annual trip to Jean-Michel Cousteau Fiji Islands Resort.

Based in London but with an office in the U.S., the nonprofit **Greenforce** (© 0207/470-8888 in London, 740/416-4016 in the U.S.; www.greenforce.org) sends expeditions to help survey Fiji's coral reefs for the World Conservation Society. They'll even teach you to dive while you're there. The trips last from 6 to 10 weeks. Check the website for prices.

Famous for former President Jimmy Carter's efforts to build houses for the underprivileged, **Habitat for Humanity** (www.habitat.org) has an office in Suva (© 331 2012) which hosts annual 2-week volunteer projects.

Escorted General Interest Tours

Escorted tours are structured group tours, with a group leader (I prefer the old-fashion term "tour guide"). The price usually includes everything from airfare to hotels, meals, tours, admission costs, and local transportation.

Escorted tours are not a big part of the business in Fiji, where it's easy to find your way around and book local tours and activities. Most of the travel agents I mention under "Getting to Fiji," above, will have someone meet and greet you at the airport upon arrival, take you to your hotel, and make sure you get on any prearranged tours and activities; but you will not have a tour guide.

Some tour companies add a short stopover in Fiji to their escorted tours of Australia and New Zealand, but these may not include a guide for the island portion. Leaders in this add-on feature include **Tauck Tours** (© 800/788-7885; www. tauck.com), **Qantas Vacations** (© 800/641-8772; www.qantasvacations.com), **Australia Escorted Tours** (© 888/333-6607; www.australia-escorted-tours. com), and **Abercrombie & Kent** (© 800/652-7986; www.abercrombiekent. com), which adds Fiji to its high-end escorted tours. Otherwise, I recommend getting a travel agent to track down an escorted tour.

Despite the fact that escorted tours require big deposits and predetermine hotels, restaurants, and itineraries, many people derive security and peace of mind from the structure they offer. Escorted tours let travelers sit back and enjoy the trip without having to drive or worry about details. They're particularly convenient for people with limited mobility, and they can be a great way to make new friends.

On the downside, you'll have little opportunity for serendipitous interactions with locals. The tours can be jam-packed with activities, leaving little room for individual sightseeing, whim, or adventure—plus they often focus on the heavily touristed sites, so you miss out on many a lesser-known gem.

THE ACTIVE TRAVELER

Fiji is a dream for active travelers who are into diving, snorkeling, swimming, boating, and other water sports. You can also play golf and tennis, or hike into the jungle-clad mountainous interiors of the islands. Kayaking is popular everywhere, and Fiji has river rafting. Good biking can be had along the many roads skirting colorful lagoons. Here's a brief rundown of my favorite active pursuits.

Biking

Bicycles are one of my favorite means of getting around. Most of the coastal roads are relatively flat and fabulously scenic. It's simple and inexpensive to rent bikes, and many hotels and resorts provide either rental or complimentary bikes for their guests to use.

Active Fiji (www.activefiji.com), also known as Tui Tai Adventure Cruises, carries mountain bikes on its eco-cruises. See p. 211.

Diving & Snorkeling

Fiji is famous among divers as being the "Soft Coral Capital of the World" because of its enormous number and variety of colorful corals, which attract a host of fish: More than 35 species of angelfish and butterfly fish swim in these waters.

All but a few resorts in Fiji have dive operations on-site, as I point out in the following chapters. Most of them have equipment for rent, but ask before coming out here what they have available. Preferably bring your own, including a spare mask.

Even the heavily visited **Mamanuca Islands** off Nadi have their share of good sites, including the **Pinnacle,** a coral head ("bommie" in this part of the world) rising 18m (60 ft.) from the lagoon floor, and a W-shaped protrusion from the outer reef. A drawback for some divers is that they don't have the Mamanuca sites all to themselves. See chapter 6.

In Beqa Lagoon, the soft corals of **Frigate Passage** seem like cascades falling over one another, and **Side Streets** has unusual orange coral. The nearby southern coast of Viti Levu has mostly hard corals, but you can go **shark diving** off Pacific Harbour; that is, the dive masters attract sharks by feeding them. See chapter 8.

South of Viti Levu, **Kadavu** island is skirted by the **Great Astrolabe Reef,** known for its steep outside walls dotted with both soft and hard corals. The Astrolabe attracts Fiji's largest concentration of manta rays. See chapter 9.

The reefs off **Rakiraki and northern Viti Levu** offer many tunnels and canyons plus golden soft corals growing on the sides of coral pinnacles. This is also the best place for wreck diving. See chapter 11.

In the **Lomaiviti Group** east of Viti Levu, Ovalau Island and the historic town of Levuka aren't beach destinations, but good dive sites are nearby and near Levuka harbor, and soft coral spots are off nearby Wakaya Island, home of the ultra-deluxe Wakaya Club. See chapter 12.

Off Savusavu, the barrier reef around Namenalala Island is officially the **Namena Marine Protected Reserve.** Both hard and soft corals attract an enormous number of small fish and their predators. See chapter 13.

Fiji's best and most famous site for soft corals is **Somosomo Strait** between Vanua Levu and Taveuni in northern Fiji, home of the **Great White Wall** and its **Rainbow**

The best way to dive a lot of reefs in Fiji, especially in Bligh Water between Viti Levu and Vanua Levu—Its famous E6 and Mount Mutiny rise some 1,000m (3,000 ft.) from the bottom—is on a live-aboard dive boat. The *NAI'A* (© 888/510-1593 in North America, or 345 0382 in Fiji; www.naia.com.fj), is a 36m (120-ft.) motor-sailing yacht which carries up to 18 persons in nine staterooms. It's the favorite of every diver I know who lives in Fiji. Rates start at US$3,140 per person double occupancy for a 7-day diving cruise.

Reef (see chapter 14). The Great White Wall is covered from between 23 and 60m (75–200 ft.) deep with pale lavender corals, which appear almost snow-white underwater. Near Qamea and Matagi, off Taveuni, are the appropriately named **Purple Wall,** a straight drop from 9 to 24m (30–80 ft.), and **Mariah's Cove,** a small wall as colorful as the Rainbow Reef.

Just in case, the **Fiji Recompression Chamber Facility** (© 336 2172) is in Suva near Colonial War Memorial Hospital.

And remember, you will need at least 12 hours—longer after multiple dives—between your last dive and flying, so plan accordingly.

Golf & Tennis

Denarau Golf & Racquet Club is a modern complex with an 18-hole resort course and 10 tennis courts near Nadi. Nearby is the **Nadi Airport Golf Club,** where veteran PGA pro Vijay Singh took his first swings. See chapter 5.

Malololailai Island, home of Plantation Island Resort and Musket Cove Resort & Spa, has a flat 9 holes (see chapter 6).

Vijay Singh had a hand in designing the spectacular **Natadola Bay Championship Golf Course,** where 14 of the 18 holes have ocean views, and one even plays along Viti Levu's most beautiful beach. It's Fiji's best. See chapter 7.

The **Naviti Resort** has a course on the Coral Coast (see chapter 7).

Also picturesque are the links at **The Pearl Championship Golf Course & Country Club,** in Pacific Harbour. See chapter 8.

You can also play at **Koro Sun Resort** in Savusavu (see chapter 13) and at **Taveuni Estates** on Taveuni (see chapter 14).

Hiking

These aren't the Rocky Mountains, nor are there blazed trails out here, but hiking in the islands is a lot of fun.

In Fiji, you can trek into the mountains and stop at—or stay in—native Fijian villages. **Adventure Fiji,** an arm of Fiji's Rosie the Travel Service (www.rosiefiji.com), has guided hikes ranging from 1 to 10 days into the mountains of Viti Levu, with meals and accommodations provided by Fijian villagers. See chapter 5.

On Taveuni island, you can hike a spectacular **Lavena Coastal Walk** to a waterfall or up to **Lake Tagimaucia,** in a crater at an altitude of more than 800m (2,700 ft.). It's home to the rare *tagimaucia* flower. See chapter 14.

Kayaking

All but a few beachfront resorts have canoes, kayaks, small sailboats, sailboards, and other toys for their guests' amusement. Because most of these properties sit beside lagoons, using these crafts is not only fun, it's relatively safe.

Sea kayaking is popular among Fiji's many small islands. **Tamarillo Tropical Expeditions** (② 877/682-5433 in the U.S., 4/2399-855 in New Zealand; www.tamarillo.co.nz) has guided 5- to 9-day kayak expeditions along the shore of Kadavu island. See chapter 9.

River Rafting

Fiji has rivers long enough and swift enough for white-water rafting. The best is the Navua River on Viti Levu, which starts in the mountainous interior and flows swiftly down to a flat delta on the island's south coast. Local companies offer trips using traditional *bilibilis* (bamboo rafts) on the lower, slow-flowing section of the river. The outstanding **Rivers Fiji** (② 800/446-2411; www.riversfiji.com) uses inflatable rafts for white-water trips up in the highlands. See chapter 8.

Surfing

Fiji has some popular surfer-dude hangouts such as **Tavarua Island Resort** (② 805/687-4551 in the U.S.; www.tavarua.com), in the Mamanuca Islands near the main pass through the Great Sea Reef (see chapter 6).

Its most famous surfing spots are **Frigate Passage** in the Beqa Lagoon and at **Cape Washington** on Kadavu (see chapters 8 and 9, respectively).

All the best are reef breaks; that is, the surf crashes out on coral reefs instead of on sandy beaches. These are no places for beginners, as you could suffer serious injury by landing on a razor-sharp coral reef—or as one of my island friends puts it, "You'll become hamburger in a hurry."

STAYING CONNECTED

Mobile Phones

Mobile phones are prevalent throughout Fiji. With a few exceptions, most notably the western side of the Yasawa Islands, coverage is excellent.

It's G3 technology here, so you likely will be able to log on using your Blackberry or iPhone, provided it uses the Global System for Mobiles (GSM) technology, the standard in Fiji.

Of the American firms, only AT&T Wireless and T-Mobile use this quasi-universal system; Verizon does not (you will need a special Verizon "world phone" in Fiji). In Canada, Microcell and some Rogers customers are GSM. Europeans, Australians, and New Zealanders use GSM. Call your wireless company to see if your phone is GSM.

If you have a GSM device, you may be able to use it in Fiji if (1) it transmits and receives in the 900 mHz band, and (2) your home provider has a roaming agreement with **Vodafone Fiji** (② 672 6226; www.vodafone.com.fj) or **Digicel Fiji** (② 708 8004; www.digicelfiji.com), the two local providers. Call your wireless operator and ask if it has roaming in Fiji, and if so, ask that "international roaming" be activated on your account.

Be sure to ask how much it will cost to use your phone in Fiji, for your home provider may extract a per-minute fee that could seem exorbitant.

A less-expensive alternative for regular phones may be to buy a prepaid local SIM card (the removable computer chip that stores your and your provider's information), *if* your phone transmits and receives on the 900 mHz GMS band and has been "unlocked" from its original SIM card.

The Travel Insider (www.thetravelinsider.info) has an excellent explanation of all this as well as a phone unlocking service. Click on "Road Warrior Resources."

Both Vodafone Fiji and Digicel Fiji sell prepaid SIM cards at outlets all over Fiji. You will pay about F$5 for the card itself plus prepaid "top-up" cards to cover the cost of your calls, which run about F50¢ a minute during the day, F30¢ on nights and weekends. Most incoming calls are free.

Although it's generally more expensive, Vodafone Fiji rents mobile phones and GSM-compatible SIM cards (for unlocked 900 mHz phones) at its desk in the arrivals concourse at Nadi airport, which is staffed daily from 5am to 11pm and for major international flights. Phones cost F$6 a day to rent, while SIM cards are F$2 per day, plus F95¢ per minute for outgoing calls to land lines, F50¢ to other mobile phones. Incoming calls are free. Vodafone will charge the rental and calls to your credit card, so you don't have to worry about how many minutes you have left on your prepaid card.

Internet & E-Mail

The Internet is as much a part of life in Fiji as it is anywhere else these days so you will have little difficulty getting online.

High-speed access is prevalent, but many ADSL systems operate at 512 kilobits per second. That's a snail's pace compared to the 3 megabits per second or more in most Western countries.

Most hotels and resorts have computers from which guests can send and receive e-mail and surf the Web, and many have wireless Internet connections (WiFi). I point these out in the hotel listings in this book.

Cybercafes are widespread in Nadi and Suva, and in Savusavu. See the "Fast Facts" sections in chapters 5, 10, and 13.

You can find wireless hot spots at some coffee shops in Nadi and Suva. See the "Fast Facts" in chapters 5 and 10.

No international Internet service provider has a local dial-up number in Fiji.

Newspapers & Magazines

Two national newspapers are published in English: the *Fiji Times* (www.fijitimes. com) and the *Fiji Sun* (www.sun.com.fj). Both appear daily and carry a few major stories from overseas. The military government censors local news in both.

The international editions of *Time* and the leading Australian and New Zealand daily newspapers are available at some bookstores and hotel shops. Published monthly in Suva, the excellent *Islands Business Magazine* (www.islandsbusiness. com) covers South Pacific regional news.

Radio & Tv

The Fijian government operates two nationwide AM radio networks with programming in Fijian and Hindi. Several private stations operate on the FM band in Suva and Nadi.

One of them retransmits the news from BBC around the clock. The country has two over-the-air TV channels: Fiji One and Mai TV. Fiji One has local news and weather at 6pm daily. The schedules are carried in the local newspapers. Many hotels have Sky TV, a pay system with the BBC, sports, and a few other channels.

Telephones

Land-line telephone service is provided throughout the country by **Telecom Fiji Limited,** or **TFL** (✆ **112 233;** www.tfl.com.fj). Although calls are relatively expensive, it's a modern system.

TO CALL FIJI To call into Fiji, first dial the international access code (011 from the U.S.; 00 from the U.K., Ireland, or New Zealand; or 0011 from Australia), then Fiji's country code **679,** and the local number (Fiji has no area codes).

TO CALL INTERNATIONALLY FROM WITHIN FIJI To make an international call from within Fiji, first dial **00,** then the country code (U.S. or Canada 1, U.K. 44, Ireland 353, Australia 61, New Zealand 64), then the area code and phone number. Calls to most countries cost about F60¢ a minute when dialed directly. Frequent TFL promotions cut the price by 20% or more on nights and weekends.

LOCAL ACCESS NUMBERS You cannot use a credit card to make calls in Fiji, but several international long-distance carriers have local access numbers their customers can call to access their international networks and use their company cards: **AT&T USA** (✆ 004/890-1001); **AT&T Canada** (✆ 004/890-1009); **Australia Telstra** (✆ 004/890-6101); **Australia Octopus** (✆ 004/890-6102); **Bell South** (✆ 004/890-1008); **BT** (✆ 004/890-4401); **BT Prepaid** (✆ 004/890-4402); **MCI** (✆ 004/890-1002); **New Zealand Telecom** (✆ 004/890-6401); **Sprint** (✆ 004/890-1003); **Teleglobe Canada** (✆ 004/890-1005); and **Verizon** (✆ 004/890-1007). These numbers can be dialed toll-free from any land-line phone.

TO CALL WITHIN FIJI No prefix or area code is required for domestic long-distance calls, so dial the local number.

DIRECTORY ASSISTANCE Dial ✆ **011** for domestic information, ✆ **022** for international numbers. (On the Web you can look up local numbers at **www.whitepages.com.fj** and **www.yellowpages.com.fj.**)

OPERATOR ASSISTANCE Dial ✆ **010** for operator assistance in making a call.

TOLL-FREE NUMBERS Local numbers beginning with **0800** are toll-free within Fiji, but calling a 1-800 number in the U.S. or Canada from Fiji is not toll-free. In fact, it costs the same as an overseas call.

PAY PHONES These are located at all post offices and in many other locations (look for Fijian war spears sticking out from plastic booths). You can make local, domestic long-distance ("trunk"), or international calls without operator assistance from any of them. They accept only prepaid Fiji Telecom **Telecards,** not coins. Post offices and many shops (including the gift shops in the Nadi Airport terminal) sell Telecards in denominations up to F$50. Scratch the tape off the back of the card to reveal your personal identification number (PIN), which you must enter prior to placing a call.

Skype—Voice over Internet protocol (VOIP)

I use my laptop to call internationally using **Skype** (www.skype.com), a broadband-based telephone service (in technical terms, **Voice over Internet protocol,** or **VoIP**), which allows you to make free international calls from your laptop or in some cybercafes. Talking worldwide on Skype is free if the people you're calling also have it (that is, computer-to-computer calls). You can also make calls to land-line phones for a fee, which is based on the country you are calling, not where you are calling from. Skype calls to land-line phones in most Western countries cost less than US2¢ per minute. Check Skype's website for details.

TIPS ON ACCOMMODATIONS

As I said in the introduction to this chapter, rare is the Fiji hotel which isn't offering special deals these days. They hesitate to reduce their published rates for fear they would have to raise them when the good times return. Instead they offer discounts such as letting you stay for 7 nights but pay only for 5 nights.

Also, many of them have **local rates** for islanders, which they may extend to visitors if business is slack on a given day.

Most hotels pay travel agents up to 30% of their rates for sending clients their way, and some may give you the benefit of at least part of this commission if you book directly instead of going through an airline or travel agent.

On that last point, the rate ranges quoted in this book are **rack rates,** or published rates; that is, the maximum a property charges for a room. Rack rates are a useful way of comparing whether one hotel is more expensive than another, but they are virtually meaningless because many hotels change their rates daily and sometimes hourly depending on how many people are booked in for a particular night. In fact, you likely will not know how much you will pay for a room until you pick a date and try to book it.

Types of Rooms

My favorite type of hotel accommodates its guests in individual bungalows set in a coconut grove beside a sandy beach and quiet lagoon. If that's not the quintessential definition of the South Seas, then I don't know what is!

Hotels of this style are widespread in Fiji. **Likuliku Lagoon Resort** (p. 127) was the first in Fiji with romantic bungalows actually standing on stilts out over the reef. Others are as basic as camping out. In between, they vary in size, furnishings, and comfort. In all, however, you enjoy your own space and a certain degree of privacy. The bungalows are usually built or accented with thatch and other native materials but they contain most of the modern conveniences.

An increasing number of these accommodations are air-conditioned, which is a definite plus during the humid summer months from November through March. All but a few bungalows have ceiling fans, which usually will keep you comfortable during the rest of the year.

Fiji's major tourist markets for the island countries are Australia and New Zealand. Accordingly, the vast majority of hotels are tailored to Aussie and Kiwi tastes, expectations, and uses of the English language.

The standard Down Under room has a double or queen-size bed and a single bed that also serves as a settee. The room may or may not have a bathtub but always has a shower. There will be tea, instant coffee, sugar, creamer, and an electric jug to heat water. Televisions and telephones are numerous but are not yet universal.

> ### Bring a Face Cloth
>
> All South Pacific hotels and resorts supply bath and hand towels, but many do not have face towels (or wash cloths) in their bathrooms. Just in case, bring your own.

Rooms are known to Fiji reservation desks as "singles" if one person books them, regardless of the number and size of beds they have. Singles are slightly less expensive than other rooms. A unit is a "double" if it has a double bed and is reserved for two persons who intend to sleep together in that bed. On the other hand, a "twin" has two twin beds; it is known as a "shared twin" if two unmarried people book them and don't intend to sleep together. Third and fourth occupants of any room are usually charged a few dollars on top of the double or shared twin rates.

Some hotel rooms have kitchenettes equipped with a small refrigerator (the "fridge"), hot plates (the "cooker"), pots, pans, crockery, silverware, and utensils. Having a kitchenette can result in quite a savings on breakfasts and light meals.

Surfing For Hotel Rooms

Regardless of how many websites I visit when searching for accommodations, I always go to the hotel's site before booking, as many offer their own Internet specials, which often beat the big-site prices.

As noted in "Getting to Fiji," earlier in this chapter, two small agencies in Fiji specialize in discount travel arrangements, including hotel rooms: **Impulse Fiji** (© 253/617-1375 in the U.S., 672 0600 in Fiji; www.impulsefiji.com) and **Sun Vacations** (© 672 4273 in Fiji; www.sunvacationsfiji.com). I would check with their websites as well as your choice of hotels before paying for your room.

A very good independent website for Fiji hotel discount shopping is **www.Travel maxia.com**, where many properties post their specials. You can search for resorts, hotels, bed-and-breakfasts, dive operators, and cruises.

The Australian-based **Whotif.com** (© 300/88 7979 and 866/514-3281 in the U.S.; 0845/458-4567 in the U.K.; www.whotif.com) discounts rooms in Fiji.

Backpackers and other budget travelers can book inexpensive rooms and dorm beds at hostels in most island countries at **www.hostelworld.com**.

Other websites have reviews and comments about accommodations worldwide. The biggest is **TripAdvisor.com.** Anyone can post reviews, including hotel owners themselves and "guests" who have never stayed at a property, so I read them with a proverbial grain of salt.

It's a good idea to **get a confirmation number** and **make a printout** of any online booking transaction.

SUGGESTED FIJI ITINERARIES

4

People often ask me where they should go and what they should do in Fiji. In this chapter, I recommend some options to help you personalize your own visit to Fiji. The end result will depend on what you want to see and do, how much time you have, and how much money you want to spend.

For a majority of its visitors, especially those from nearby Australia and New Zealand, Fiji is one of those "3-S" tropical destinations: sun, sea, and sand. For those relaxing diversions, I think you should choose one resort in your price range and stay there for the better part of your vacation.

You could spend your entire vacation in Nadi or one of the nearby islands, but you will miss what I consider to be the best parts of Fiji. This is a country of more than 300 gorgeous islands, and, in order to get a sense of this diversity, I would try to experience more than one.

By that, I do not mean island hopping in the Mamanuca or Yasawa islands off Nadi. Those islands and their resorts are variations on the same theme, and you would waste valuable time jumping from one similar environment to another.

While Aussies and Kiwis can fly up here for a weekend, the long flights coming and going mean the rest of us burn a whole day getting to Fiji and another day returning home. Consequently, we Northern Hemisphere folks should certainly spend at least a week here, more if possible.

When planning your trip, first find out both the international and domestic airline schedules, and try to book all domestic interisland flights at the same time as your international flights. Do not wait until you arrive in Fiji to take care of this important chore. See the "Getting to Fiji" and "Getting Around Fiji" sections in chapter 3.

And remember the travel agent's classic advice: Never stay at the most luxurious property first. Anything after that will seem inferior, sending you home disappointed.

FIJI'S REGIONS IN BRIEF

First let's review Fiji's regions and the differences among them. I present them here in the order in which they appear in this book.

Everyone starts on **Viti Levu.** Known locally as the "mainland," it is Fiji's largest island. **Suva,** the capital city, lies 197km (122 miles) from Nadi airport, or about halfway around the island. With a few exceptions, Viti Levu does not have the best beaches in Fiji. Where it does have good sands, the reef offshore is more walkable than swimmable, especially at low tide. In other words, plan to look beyond Nadi and Viti Levu for most of the best beaches and all of the best diving

THE NADI AREA   Among the sugar-cane fields, **Nadi International Airport** is located on Viti Levu's dry western side. To locals, the name Nadi applies to this area, which is the focal point of much of Fiji's tourism industry. Many tourists on package deals spend all their time here, and, in fact, there is plenty to do, including day trips out to the Mamanuca Islands. Nadi also is a convenient base from which to explore the nearby areas. Unless I have only a few days to spend in Fiji, however, I make it a stopover on the way to another destination.

A variety of hotels are concentrated between the airport and the predominately Indian-populated **Nadi Town,** whose main industries are tourism and farming. Here you will find numerous handicraft, electronics, and clothing merchants.

None of the airport hotels are on the beach, and even at **Denarau Island,** where the country's major resort development boasts half a dozen large beachfront hotels, coastal mangrove forests make the sand gray, and runoff from the nearby cane fields often causes the lagoon to be murky.

THE MAMANUCA ISLANDS   Beckoning just off Nadi, the Mamanuca Islands are popular among day cruisers. Offshore resorts of various sizes and prices appeal to a broad spectrum of travelers, from swinging singles to quieter couples and families. Generally speaking, this is the driest part of Fiji, which means it is sunny most of the time. Some of the Mamanucas are flat atolls that are so small you can walk around them in 5 minutes. Others are hilly, grassy islands reminiscent of the Virgin Islands in the Caribbean or the Whitsundays in Australia. Because the islands lie relatively close together, most offer excursions to the others. They also are conveniently close to Nadi, so you don't have to spend much extra money or time to get there.

THE YASAWA ISLANDS   A chain of gorgeous and relatively unspoiled islands stretching to the north of the Mamanucas, the hilly Yasawas are blessed with the best collection of beaches in Fiji. Two movie versions of *The Blue Lagoon* were filmed here: the 1949 original and the 1980s remake, starring Brooke Shields as the castaway schoolgirl. Young backpackers turned the Yasawas into one of the country's hottest destinations, but the islands now have resorts to fit every pocketbook. The Yasawas are easy to reach from Nadi by daily high-speed ferry service, and you can visit them on **Blue Lagoon Cruises** or **Captain Cook Cruises** (p. 122).

THE CORAL COAST   The **Queen's Road** runs around the south coast of Viti Levu through the area known as the Coral Coast. This was Fiji's first resort area, developed even before the international airport opened in Nadi in the early 1960s. You'll find big resorts, comfortable small hotels, fire-walking Fijians, and a host of things to see and do, such as a collection of Fiji's native fauna in the excellent **Kula Eco Park.** Most of the beaches along the Coral Coast lead into lagoons that are very shallow, especially at low tide. Many visitors staying on the Coast these days are tourists on package holidays, but it's still a good choice for anyone who wants beachfront resort living while also being able to conveniently explore the country.

PACIFIC HARBOUR & BEQA ISLAND   About 48km (30 miles) west of Suva, Pacific Harbour was developed in the early 1970s as a resort complex with a golf course, private residences, shopping center, cultural center, and a seaside hotel (in other words, a real-estate development). Because this area is on the edge of Viti Levu's rain belt, the project never reached its full potential. Nevertheless, it has the country's best cultural center, most scenic golf course, and excellent deep-sea fishing. It's also the most central location for river rafting on the **Navua River,** kayaking along the coast, gliding on wires through a rainforest canopy, diving in marvelous **Beqa Lagoon** (pronounced *Beng*-ga), and one of the world's top shark dives just off the mainland—all of which make Pacific Harbour the self-anointed "Adventure Capital of Fiji."

A 30-minute boat ride off Pacific Harbour, rugged **Beqa** is best known for its surrounding lagoon. Here you'll also find **Frigate Passage,** one of the world's best surfing spots (but not for novices, as the curling breakers slam onto the reef). Beqa has a bevy of comfortable hotels.

KADAVU ISLAND   Fiji's third-largest island, **Kadavu** lies about 100km (60 miles) south of Viti Levu. It's a long skinny island skirted by the **Great Astrolabe Reef,** another of Fiji's top diving destinations and one of its top kayaking venues. On the north coast, **Long Beach,** at several kilometers in length, lives up to its name. Ashore, its lack of mongooses, iguanas, and other imported predators make it a haven for indigenous wildlife and birds, including the endemic musk parrot, fantail, honeyeater, and whistling dove.

SUVA   The Queen's Road runs between Nadi Airport and **Suva,** Fiji's busy capital and one of the South Pacific's most cosmopolitan cities. Suva city has a population of 86,178, according to the 2007 census, but more than 300,000 are believed to live in the metropolitan area. The country's history is on display at the excellent **Fiji Museum,** Suva's top attraction. Remnants of Fiji's century as a British possession and the presence of so many Indians give downtown Suva a certain air of the colonial "Raj"—as if this were Madras or Bombay, instead of the boundary between Polynesia and Melanesia. On the other hand, Suva has modern high-rise buildings and lives at a fast pace—not surprising because, in many respects, it is the bustling economic center of the South Pacific islands and the home of many regional organizations. The streets are a melting-pot of Indians, Chinese, Fijians, other South Pacific islanders, "Europeans" (a term used in Fiji to mean persons with white skin, regardless of geographic origin), and individuals of mixed race.

RAKIRAKI & NORTHERN VITI LEVU   An alternative to the Queen's Road driving route to Suva, the **King's Road** runs from Lautoka through the "Sugar Belt" of northern Viti Levu, passing through the predominately Indian towns of **Ba** and **Tavua** to **Rakiraki,** a Fijian village near the island's northernmost point and site of one of the country's few remaining colonial-era hotels. Jagged green mountains lend a gorgeous backdrop to the shoreline along the Rakiraki coast. At Viti Levu's northernmost point, **Volivoli Beach** is one of the country's most beautiful. Offshore, **Nananu-I-Ra Island** beckons windsurfers and budget-minded travelers, and the nearby reefs are Fiji's best for wreck diving.

East of Rakiraki, the King's Road hugs deep, mountain-bounded **Viti Levu Bay,** one of the most beautiful parts of Fiji. From the head of the bay, the road then twists through the mountains until it emerges near the inland town of Korovou. A left turn there takes you to Natovi Wharf, where ferries depart for northern Fiji. A right turn leads to Suva.

LEVUKA & OVALAU   East of Viti Levu, in the central Lomaiviti Group of islands, picturesque **Ovalau** is home to the historic town of **Levuka,** which has changed little in appearance since its days as a boisterous whaling port and the first capital of a united Fiji in the mid-1800s. No other place in Fiji has retained its frontier facade as has this living museum. Ovalau is an incredibly beautiful island, but its lack of beaches has deterred major tourism development; consequently, it remains in a time warp and is of interest mainly to those who want fine diving while seeing the way the South Seas used to be.

Within sight of Levuka, **Wakaya Island** is the home of Fiji's top resort, the Wakaya Club, an enclave for Hollywood stars and other well-heeled folks. It's the project of Canadian David Gilmour, who also is responsible for giving us Fiji Water.

SAVUSAVU   Vanua Levu, Taveuni, and their nearby islands are known collectively as "The North" because they lie northeast of Viti Levu and comprise Fiji's Northern Province.

The northern side of **Vanua Levu,** Fiji's second-largest island, is dedicated to sugar cane, and its main town of **Labasa** is like Nadi without the tourists—and without anything for tourists to do should they go there.

But on the south shore, the little town with the singsong name **Savusavu** lies nestled in one of the region's most protected deepwater bays, making it a favorite stop for cruising yachts. Tucked behind a small islet, the town is a throwback to the old days when schooners arrived from Suva to trade cloth and rum for cattle and *copra* (coconut oil).

Southern Vanua Levu has a considerable amount of freehold land; in fact, so many of my compatriots have bought parcels that Fijians now facetiously refer to Savusavu as "Little America." One of them is motivational speaker Anthony Robbins, who owns Namale Fiji Islands Resort & Spa and holds some of his seminars there. Another is environmentalist Jean-Michel Cousteau, son of Jacques Cousteau, who has lent his name to **Jean-Michel Cousteau Fiji Islands Resort,** the finest family resort in all of the South Pacific.

Savusavu also is the homeport of **Adventure Fiji,** which uses the 42m (140-ft.) sailing schooner *Tui Tai* to make 7- and 10-day soft-adventure voyages to Taveuni, Kioa, and Rabi islands in northern Fiji, and to the Lau Group on the eastern side of the archipelago.

TAVEUNI   Fiji's "Garden Isle" of **Taveuni** is another representation of the old South Seas, a land of copra plantations and small Fijian villages tucked away in the bush. Unlike Vanua Levu, Taveuni has some of Fiji's best beaches, especially near **Matei,** at the airstrip on its northern end. Matei is one of my favorite places in Fiji. It has several small hotels and surprisingly good restaurants within walking distance of each other, yet it seems a century removed from modern life. Taveuni is the best place in Fiji to visit a waterfall in **Bouma National Heritage Park** and go for a hike on the **Lavena Coastal Walk** along its wild eastern shore. Offshore lies the **Somosomo Strait,** Fiji's most famous diving destination. Two excellent resorts inhabit lovely **Matagi** and **Qamea** islands off Taveuni's northern coast.

HIGHLIGHTS OF FIJI IN 2 WEEKS

This whirlwind trip whisks you through the highlights of Fiji. The Queen's Road links Nadi, the Coral Coast, and Suva, so you'll make this part of the trip overland. Bus connections are available, but I recommend renting a car in order to have maximum flexibility. Ferries run from Suva to Taveuni and Savusavu, but they take at least 12 hours in each direction, usually overnight, so they are not a viable alternative when time is of the essence.

Note: Pacific Sun no longer flies between Taveuni and Savusavu (a 15-minute flight in the old days). This throws a kink into easily hopping around the islands. The best option is to fly from one to either Nadi or Suva airports on a morning flight, then take an afternoon flight to the other. Still, that eats up a valuable day. An alternative is to take the *Amazing Grace,* a small passenger ferry that takes 1½ hours to cross the Somosomo Strait between Taveuni and Buca Bay on Vanua Levu, plus a 2-hour bus ride between Savusavu and Buca Bay.

Days 1-2: Relaxing in Nadi

Take the first day to recover from your international flight by lounging around the pool, shopping in Nadi Town, or doing some light sightseeing. Spend Day 2 on land-based excursions, such as one to the late Raymond Burr's Garden of the Sleeping Giant (p. 92); Lautoka, Fiji's second-largest city (p. 95); or Viseisei Village, the country's oldest native Fijian village (p. 94). Finish off with some more shopping and dinner in Nadi.

Days 3-4: Exploring the Coral Coast ★

Get up early and drive south to the Coral Coast, along the southern coast of Viti Levu. On the way, stop at the **Momi Guns** (p. 94) for a look at the World War II battery and a gorgeous view across Nadi Bay; the **Kalevu South Pacific Cultural Centre** (p. 146) for a glimpse into Fijian culture; and at **Sigatoka Sand Dunes National Park** (p. 146) for an example of its unique geology. The next day, visit **Kula Eco Park** (p. 148) to meet Fiji's wildlife, and hike to a waterfall with **Adventures in Paradise Fiji** (p. 148). Catch an evening show featuring the **"fire walkers"** from Beqa Island (p. 156).

Day 5: Rafting on the Navua River ★★★

One of my favorite Fiji excursions is on the **Navua River,** which carves a dramatic gorge through Viti Levu's mountainous interior before spilling into a flood plain west of Suva. The usual trip takes you upriver on a fast speedboat but brings you back on a *bilibili* (bamboo raft). Alternately, you can ride an inflatable boat over white waters with the excellent **Rivers Fiji** (p. 65).

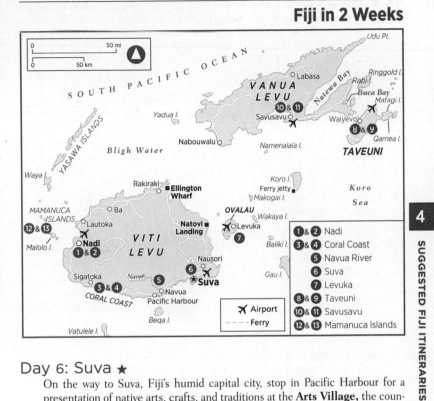

Fiji in 2 Weeks

① & ② Nadi
③ & ④ Coral Coast
⑤ Navua River
⑥ Suva
⑦ Levuka
⑧ & ⑨ Taveuni
⑩ & ⑪ Savusavu
⑫ & ⑬ Mamanuca Islands

✈ Airport
---- Ferry

Day 6: Suva ★

On the way to Suva, Fiji's humid capital city, stop in Pacific Harbour for a presentation of native arts, crafts, and traditions at the **Arts Village,** the country's best cultural center (p. 159). Once in Suva, take a walking tour of downtown, ending at the **Fiji Museum** (p. 177). Be sure to have a Fijian lunch at the **Old Mill Cottage** (p. 188) next to the U.S. Embassy.

Day 7: A Trip Back in Time to Levuka

A day trip from Suva to **Levuka** always highlights a visit to Fiji. The country's original capital, the old town has retained its 19th-century appearance, and the backdrop of sheer cliffs makes it one of the South Pacific's most beautiful towns. Get **Ovalau Watersports** (p. 204) to organize a morning walking tour and an afternoon excursion to Ovalau. Either catch the late afternoon flight back to Suva or plan an overnight at the charming **Levuka Homestay** (p. 205).

Days 8-9: Exploring Taveuni ★★★

If you slept on Ovalau, take the early morning Air Fiji flight back to Nausori Airport near Suva. You can connect from there to **Taveuni,** Fiji's third-largest island. Famous for world-class diving on the nearby **Great White Wall** and its **Rainbow Reef,** Taveuni also is a hiker's paradise. Stay near the airport, from there it's an easy trip to the waterfalls in **Bouma National Heritage Park** and the scenic **Lavena Coastal Walk** (p. 224). The next day, hike to the mountain-top **Lake Tagimaucia** to catch a glimpse of the rare flower of the same name.

Days 10-11: Savusavu: "Little America" ★★

Most of Day 10 will be devoted to flying, as you will have to retreat to Nadi or Suva on the morning flight, and then wait for the afternoon flight to Savusavu. An adventurous alternative is the *Amazing Grace* **bus-ferry** (p. 208) across the Somosomo Strait to Buca Bay. Although it is rapidly developing, **Savusavu** still recalls its days as a 19th-century copra port. Stroll along the harbor, have lunch at the **Surf 'n' Turf** (p. 219), and visit the famous **Savusavu Hot Springs** (p. 211), where Fijians still cook their evening meals. Stop by **Rock 'n Downunder Divers** (p. 213) to arrange an excursion to a Fijian village and the **Waisali Rainforest Reserve** (p. 211). If you're traveling with children, stay at **Jean-Michel Cousteau Fiji Islands Resort** (p. 214), one of the South Pacific's top family resorts.

Days 12-13: An Island Retreat

Spending at least 1 night on a small island in the Mamanucas or Yasawas is an essential ingredient to fully experience Fiji; whether it's in one of Fiji's first over-water bungalows at **Likuliku Lagoon Resort** (p. 127), at the raucous **Beachcomber Island Resort** (p. 130), the family-oriented **Plantation Island Resort** (p. 126), a quiet couples-only hideaway such as **Matamanoa Island Resort** (p. 129), the charming Navutu Stars Resort in the Yasawas, or one of the dormitories dotting the islands. They all have much better beaches than you'll find on Viti Levu, and the stopover will give you a chance to rest up for your trip home.

Day 14: Last-Minute Shopping in Nadi

If your homeward flight departs late at night, you can stay in the islands for an extra day. Otherwise spend your last day catching up on shopping or any excursions you might have missed in and around Nadi.

AROUND VITI LEVU IN 1 WEEK

This trip will expose you to Fiji's diversity by taking you all the way around Viti Levu from Nadi to Coral Coast, Pacific Harbour, Suva, and Rakiraki. The most convenient means of traveling the island is by car, which allows maximum flexibility and lets you get off the beaten path. You can also ride the **Feejee Experience** (p. 49), a backpacker-oriented bus that circles the island daily with stops at attractions and inexpensive accommodations. Public buses also circle Viti Levu via the Queen's and King's roads, but you will have to change buses in Suva and Lautoka.

Days 1-2: Exploring the Coral Coast ★

From Nadi, drive south to the Coral Coast, stopping at the **Momi Guns** (p. 94) for a look at the World War II battery and a gorgeous view across Nadi Bay; at the **Kalevu South Pacific Cultural Centre** (p. 146) for a glimpse

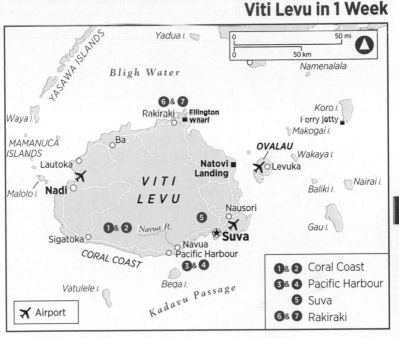

into Fijian culture; and at **Sigatoka Sand Dunes National Park** (p. 146) for an example of its more interesting geology. On Day 2, visit **Kula Eco Park** (p. 148) to meet Fiji's interesting wildlife, and hike to a waterfall with **Adventures in Paradise Fiji** (p. 148). Catch an evening show featuring the "fire walkers" from Beqa Island (p. 156).

Days 3-4: Rafting the Navua River ★★★
Pacific Harbour is the most convenient base from which to go rafting on the **Navua River,** either on a bilibili or over white waters in the gorges with the excellent **Rivers Fiji** (p. 65). On Day 4, visit the cultural center at the **Arts Village** (p. 159), and go flying through a rainforest canopy with **ZIP Fiji** (p. 160).

Day 5: Strolling Around Suva ★
Once in Suva, take a walking tour of downtown, ending at the excellent **Fiji Museum** (p. 177). The lunchtime Fijian fare at the **Old Mill Cottage,** next to the U.S. Embassy (p. 188), is among the country's best.

Days 6-7: Rakiraki
You'll spend at least half of Day 6 driving or riding via the King's Road from Suva to Rakiraki, on the northern tip of Viti Levu. The road follows the **Wainbuka**

River most of the way through the mountains and emerges on the north shore at picturesque **Viti Levu Bay.** Once in Rakiraki spend the morning exploring nearby **Vaileka,** the area's predominately Indian commercial center, and the afternoon at **Volivoli Beach,** one of Fiji's best and home to the inexpensive **Volivoli Beach Resort** (p. 195). Rakiraki itself is a small Fijian village where you can stay at the **Tanoa Rakiraki Hotel** (p. 195), Fiji's last remaining colonial-era accommodations. On Day 7, head back to Nadi. The central mountains will be off to your left as you pass through the **Yaqara Cattle Ranch,** home of the famous Fiji Water, and the predominately Indian towns of **Tavua** and **Ba.** See chapter 11.

SAVUSAVU & TAVEUNI IN 1 WEEK

Venturing to Savusavu and Taveuni islands in northern Fiji means paying for additional airfares, but this is my favorite part of the country. Children will love it up here, too, particularly at Savusavu's **Jean-Michel Cousteau Fiji Islands Resort** (p. 214), the best Fiji has to offer for children. Both Savusavu and Taveuni have other fine resorts and hotels, but tourism is minor in "The North," which is much more reminiscent of the Old South Seas than is Viti Levu. The country's best diving and snorkeling is up here, but this also is a fine place to explore the great outdoors ashore. ***Note:*** Remember when planning that Pacific Sun does not fly between Savusavu and Taveuni.

Day 1: Exploring Savusavu

Take a morning flight from Nadi to Savusavu's little airstrip, on the southern side of Vanua Levu. Check in or leave your bags at your hotel and spend the rest of the morning and early afternoon seeing the scenery, examining the **hot springs,** and shopping for the orb of your dreams at **J. Hunter Pearls** (p. 213) in Savusavu town.

Day 2: Waisali Rainforest Reserve

While most Fiji activities are at or near the seaside, spend this day in the jungle interior at **Waisali Rainforest Reserve** (p. 211), a national forest with a waterfall up in Vanua Levu's central mountains.

Day 3: Boat Tour of Savusavu Bay

The bay at Savusavu is so large the U.S. navy made plans to hide the Pacific fleet there in case of a hurricane. Spend Day 3 exploring it on a boat tour organized by your hotel or **Rock 'n Downunder Divers** (p. 211).

Day 4: Straddling the 180° Meridian

Today will be devoted to flying unless you take the *Amazing Grace* bus-ferry (p. 208) across the Somosomo Strait to Taveuni. If you took the ferry, you will have time to settle into your hotel, hire a taxi and ride through **Somosomo** and **Waiyevo** villages to **Wairiki,** where the **180th meridian** passes through Fiji (p. 222). Although the international date line technically detours from the 180° longitude line to bypass Fiji, you can stand under a sign at the meridian, one

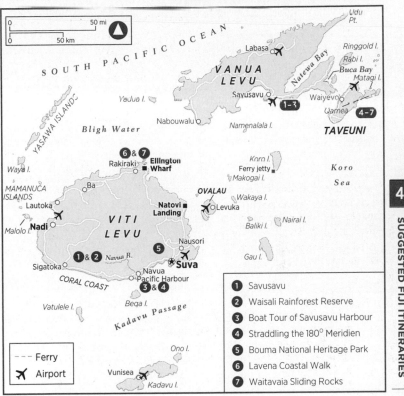

Legend:
1. Savusavu
2. Waisali Rainforest Reserve
3. Boat Tour of Savusavu Harbour
4. Straddling the 180° Meridien
5. Bouma National Heritage Park
6. Lavena Coastal Walk
7. Waitavaia Sliding Rocks

--- Ferry
✈ Airport

foot in today, the other in "yesterday." On the way back, stop for a swim at **Prince Charles Beach,** which holds a place among Fiji's best (p. 226).

Day 5: Bouma National Heritage Park ★★★

Spend most of today in **Bouma National Heritage Park** (p. 222), Fiji's best national park. You will not need a guide for the short walk up to Bouma Falls, but you will on the longer **Vidawa Rainforest Walk,** which has great views of the islands off northern Taveuni. Retire for a sunset drink at **Tramontu Bar & Grill,** on a clifftop high above the Somosomo Strait (p. 232).

Day 6: Lavena Coastal Walk ★★★

Plan on more hiking today, this time along the beautiful **Lavena Coastal Walk** on Taveuni's wild east coast. Be prepared to swim the last few yards to reach **Wainibau Falls.** If this is a Friday night, graze the buffet of Fijian foods at **Vunibokoi Restaurant** (p. 232).

Day 7: Waitavaia Sliding Rocks

You'll need to catch the afternoon flight back to Nadi, but can spend the morning cascading down the **Waitavaia Sliding Rocks** (p. 226) near Waiyevo village.

FIJI FOR FAMILIES

Although it's not in the same league as Florida or other places with attractions such as Disney World, Fiji is a fine place for families with children. My cousin Virginia Silverman and her then 9-year-old daughter, Eve, joined me for 10 days in Savusavu and Taveuni during one of my recent trips, and Eve had a blast while learning a lot in the process (read their reports in chapter 13). Many Australian and New Zealand families take their annual holidays in Fiji, usually at one resort equipped with a children's program (see "The Best Family Resorts," in chapter 1). Or you can take your youngsters on the following 2-week educational tour around Fiji.

Day 1: Recovering in Nadi

Spend your first day in Nadi recovering from your flight and getting acclimated to the heat and humidity. Kids will love frolicking in the pools at the **Radisson Resort Fiji Denarau Island** (p. 102) or the less expensive **Raffle's Gateway Hotel** opposite the airport (p. 108).

Days 2-3: Coral Coast: Culture & Wildlife ★★

On Day 2, move to the Coral Coast, stopping on the way at the **Kalevu South Pacific Cultural Centre** (p. 146) for a demonstration of traditional Fijian ways. Across the Queen's Road, **Shangri-La's Fijian Resort** (p. 149) is well equipped for families, as is the more convenient **Outrigger on the Lagoon Fiji** (p. 150), which has a fine swimming pool complex. On Day 3, go across the road to **Kula Eco Park** (p. 148), where the kids can touch tame iguanas and admire Fiji birds and other wildlife. It's a bit of a hike, but you can take them to a Fijian village and either a cave or waterfall with **Adventures in Paradise Fiji** (p. 148). At night they will be mesmerized by a Fijian *meke* dance, especially if a fire-walking demonstration is part of it.

Days 4-5: Pacific Harbour: River Rafting & Jungle Canopy Rides ★

Moving on to Pacific Harbour, take the kids to the **Arts Village Cultural Centre** (p. 156), where they can ride a boat while learning about Fijian culture. That afternoon they can glide through a rainforest canopy with **ZIP Fiji** (p. 160). You'll need all of Day 5 to take them on a bilibili rafting trip on the Navua River with **Discover Fiji Tours** (p. 161). (**Note:** Kids must be 5 or older to go river rafting or canopy riding.) With a fine pool and beach, the **Pearl South Pacific** (p. 162) is primarily aimed at couples, but is also a lodging option for families.

Day 6: Suva: The Fiji Museum ★★★

Most children I know aren't particularly excited to tour new cities, but Fiji's capital does have the excellent **Fiji Museum** (p. 177), where kids can gape at actual war clubs the ancients used in real-life combat.

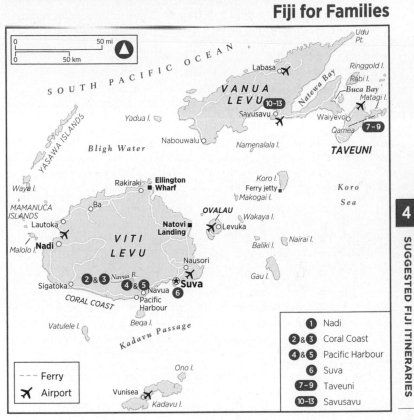

Days 7–9: Taveuni: Waterfalls & Rock Slides ★★★

Take the morning flight from Nausori airport to Taveuni, where several outdoor adventures await. Spend the first afternoon cascading down the **Waitavaia Sliding Rocks** (p. 226), where your kids may pick up a few slight bruises but will have a grand time. On the morning of Day 8, take them to **Bouma National Heritage Park** (p. 222), where a short walk leads to a swimming hole beneath Bouma Falls. Fijian children love it here, so yours could make some local friends. The park also has the guided **Vidawa Rainforest Walk,** which leads to historic hill fortifications and great views. On Day 9, take them on a horseback riding excursion at **Maravu Plantation Beach Resort & Spa** (p. 228).

Days 10–13: Savusavu: Environmental Education ★★★

On the morning of Day 10, either fly back to Nadi to connect to an afternoon flight to Savusavu, or take the 4½-hour trip across the Somosomo Strait on the *Amazing Grace* (p. 208). It's a long trip by boat and bus, but your kids likely will have Fijian children as fellow passengers. Assuming your broker agrees, check into **Jean-Michel Cousteau Fiji Islands Resort** (p. 214), whose Bula Club is the finest children's program I've ever seen. It's both educational and fun for the youngsters, who are almost guaranteed to become friends with their assigned Fijian "buddy." Off campus, take them to **Waisali Rainforest Reserve** (p. 211), where gravel pathways lead to a waterfall.

Day 14: Back to Nadi

Flights back to Australia and New Zealand depart Nadi during the day, but those for North America and Europe leave just before midnight. Accordingly, fly back to Nadi today and spend your spare time lounging at a resort pool (see "Day 1," above).

CRUISING IN FIJI

Large cruise ships frequently visit Suva and Lautoka, usually from Sydney, Australia, but the country has three fine small-vessel operations based here all the time. **Captain Cook Cruises** sails in the Mamanuca and Yasawa islands, while **Blue Lagoon Cruises,** primarily plies the Yasawas. See "Cruising Through the Islands," in chapter 6. Based at Savusavu, **Active Fiji** (p. 211) sends the luxurious schooner *Tui Tai* on soft-adventure cruises through the seldom-explored islands of northern Fiji. This 2-week itinerary allows you to make cruises on both sides of the country, but I based it on their usual operations. Needless to say, check their sailing schedules to see when they're going during the time you want to be here.

Day 1: Savusavu

Arrive at Nadi and take a flight to **Active Fiji's** homeport in Savusavu (p. 211). Kill the morning shopping for black pearls.

Days 2-8: Adventure Cruise on the *Tui Tai* ★★★

The typical 1-week cruise on the 42m (140-ft.) schooner *Tui Tai* will take you to Taveuni for a visit to **Bouma Falls** (p. 222), and then to the seldom visited islands of Kioa and Rabi. The boat carries dive equipment, snorkeling gear, and kayaks for exploring the reefs and shoreline.

Days 9-10: Relaxing in the Mamanuca Islands

After the *Tui Tai* cruise, fly back to Nadi and catch a ferry from Denarau Island to a resort in the Mamanuca Islands (see chapter 6), where you can relax for 2 days prior to being picked up by Captain Cook Cruises. (Blue Lagoon Cruises does not pick passengers up in the islands, so you will have to find your way to Lautoka if that is your choice.) I normally would suggest finishing your visit in an overwater bungalow at **Likuliku Lagoon Resort** (p. 127).

Days 11-13: A Yasawa Island Cruise ★★★

Either **Blue Lagoon Cruises** or **Captain Cook Cruises** (p. 122) will take you through the gorgeous Yasawa Islands, stopping during the day for snorkeling, beach picnics, and visits to Fijian villages. A cruise is the best way to see several of the islands in a minimum amount of time.

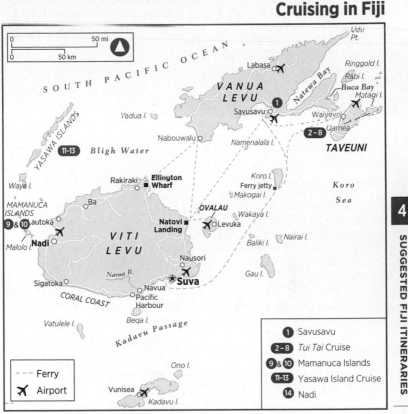

Day 14: Departing from Nadi

Blue Lagoon Cruises will drop you at Lautoka in time to catch a flight back to Australia or New Zealand. The rest of us can kill time waiting for our night flight by shopping in Nadi Town (p. 100) or lounging by the pool at **Raffle's Gateway Hotel,** opposite the airport (p. 108).

DIVING IN FIJI

One could spend months in Fiji diving all its marvelous sites, and you will still miss a few. Not being a diver myself, I cannot speak from personal experience, but I've talked to hundreds of divers—and traveled with two of them—so I have a reasonably good idea of where you will find the best waters. This 2-week itinerary starts out with an exhilarating shark dive off Pacific Harbour and ends at the famous White Wall in the Somosomo Strait off Taveuni. **Note:** I built in the 12 hours or more you will need between diving and flying.

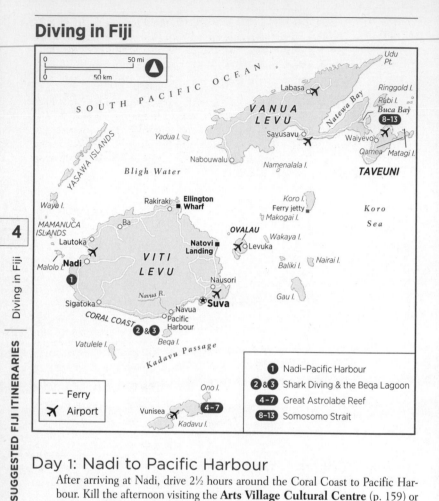

Day 1: Nadi to Pacific Harbour

After arriving at Nadi, drive 2½ hours around the Coral Coast to Pacific Harbour. Kill the afternoon visiting the **Arts Village Cultural Centre** (p. 159) or flying through the jungle canopy with **ZIP Fiji** (p. 160).

Days 2-3: Shark Diving & the Beqa Lagoon ★★★

Day 2 will test your mettle right away during a shark dive off Pacific Harbour with **Beqa Adventure Divers** (p. 161), whose masters will draw the attention of tiger, bull, and other sharks by feeding them, while you watch from behind a coral wall. Day 3 is spent out in the **Beqa Lagoon,** perhaps seeing the colorful walls of **Frigate Passage.** See chapter 8.

Days 4-7: The Great Astrolabe Reef

Day 4 is devoted to driving from Pacific Harbour to Suva's Nausori Airport, flying to Vunisea on **Kadavu Island,** and taking a boat to your new dive base from which to explore the **Great Astrolabe Reef,** skirting Kadavu's eastern and southern coasts. The eco-friendly **Matava—The Astrolabe Hideaway**

(p. 171) is the closest resort to the so-called Manta Pass, which draws Fiji's largest congregation of manta rays. That will take Day 5, while Days 6 and 7 can be spent diving the colorful passage between Kadavu and nearby Ono Island. See chapter 9.

Days 8–13: The Somosomo Strait ★★★

Assuming Pacific Sun is punctual on Day 8, fly back to Nausori Airport at midday and connect from there to Taveuni. I have more fun staying near the airstrip at Matei, but the modest **Garden Island Resort** (p. 230) is nearest the **Great White Wall** and **Rainbow Reef**, which are on the reefs out in the Somosomo Strait. Spend the next few days here exploring Fiji's best collection of colorful soft corals. See chapter 14.

Day 14: Back to Nadi & Home

Your last day will be spent flying back to Nadi and connecting to your flight back home.

THE NADI AREA

You won't see much of the real Fiji if you spend your entire vacation in Nadi, but this area has more to keep you busy than any other part of the country. That's because the international airport and a dry climate combine to make it the country's main tourist center, with the multitude of activities that entails. The lagoon off Nadi is usually murky from mangrove forests and runoff coming from the area's sugar-cane fields, however, so this is not the ideal place in Fiji for a beach vacation. On the other hand, it is the most convenient base from which to explore the rest of the country, and a vacation here means you don't have to spend extra money to get elsewhere in Fiji.

Despite the cloudy waters, many visitors spend their entire holidays on pancake-flat **Denarau Island,** the country's largest tourist development with several resorts, a golf-and-tennis center, and a shopping complex at **Port Denarau,** the marina from whence shuttles and cruises depart to the Mamanuca and Yasawa islands. In a matter of seconds, the short bridge from the mainland onto Denarau whisks you from the Third World into the First World.

By "Nadi" the locals mean the entire area around the international airport. It's the fastest-growing part of Fiji. New homes, stores, shopping centers, and office buildings are popping up along the 9km (5½ miles) of traffic-heavy Queen's Road between the airport and **Nadi Town,** a farming community stocked with handicraft, souvenir, and other stores as well as some of the country's better restaurants.

Rather than fight for parking spaces in town, many locals now do their shopping in **Namaka,** a rapidly developing commercial strip between Nadi Town and the airport. **Martintar,** the liveliest Queen's Road suburb, is the one place you can stay and walk from your hotel to restaurants and bars. From Martintar, a paved road leads to **Wailoaloa Beach,** a 1.5km-long (1-mile) stretch of grayish sand, where a development known as **Newtown Beach** has several inexpensive hotels and hostels.

From Nadi, it's an easy 33km (20-mile) side trip to **Lautoka,** Fiji's second-largest city. Lautoka offers a genteel contrast to tourist-oriented Nadi Town.

GETTING AROUND THE NADI AREA

Between the Airport & Nadi Town

All of Fiji's major international and local **car-rental** firms have offices in the international arrival concourse of Nadi International Airport. See "Getting Around Fiji," in chapter 3.

Westside Motorbike Rentals (© 672 6402; www.motorbikerentalsfiji.com) in Namaka, Martintar, Denarau Island, and Sigatoka rents scooters for F$79 including helmets and third-party insurance. However, in my opinion, riding scooters in Fiji is not for novices.

Taxis gather outside the arrival concourse at the airport and are stationed at the larger hotels. Ask the reception desk to call one, or contact **Ruwai Levu** (© 672 3202), one of the more reliable companies whose cabs are radio dispatched. The aggressive drivers will find you in Nadi Town. See the taxi fare chart in "Getting Around Fiji," in chapter 3, p. 51.

I often ride the **local buses** that ply the Queen's Road between the markets in Nadi Town and Lautoka frequently during daylight, every 30 minutes after dark. Tell the driver where you're going; he'll tell you how much to pay when you board. Fares vary according to the length of the trip. No more than F65¢ will take you anywhere between the airport and Nadi Town.

Getting Around Denarau Island

Westbus (© 672 2917) operates a public bus service between Nadi Town and Denarau Island. Its white-and-blue buses depart Nadi Market approximately every 30 minutes between 8am and 5pm daily. The express bus takes less than 30 minutes to reach the resorts, while the local bus stops in the villages along the way and thus takes longer. One-way fare is F$1.10 on either.

On the island, the open-air, thatch-roofed **Bula Bus** shuttles between the resorts and Port Denarau daily from 7am to 11:30pm. A 1-day Bula Pass costs F$6 for adults. Children under 12 ride free. You can buy passes on the bus or at the hotel gift shops. The Bula Bus stops at the front porticos of all the Denarau Island resorts.

A free alternative is the **Denarau Island Courtesy Shuttle,** a cream-and-blue minivan that runs between the resorts and Port Denarau daily from 8am to 9pm. It stops at the front door of the Radisson Resort Fiji Denarau Island but runs along the road in front of the other hotels. Except at the Radisson, you must hail it on the main road.

Taxi fare is F$5 between the resorts and Port Denarau, F$12 from the resorts to Nadi Town. Don't let the drivers rip you off.

The resorts have free **parking** for their guests. Everyone gets up to 2 hours free parking in the public lot at Port Denarau, after which you pay F$3 an hour. Don't lose your parking ticket.

Nadi Bay

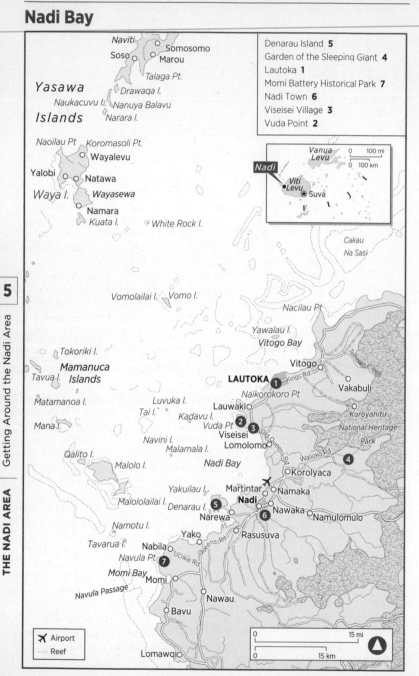

Denarau Island **5**
Garden of the Sleeping Giant **4**
Lautoka **1**
Momi Battery Historical Park **7**
Nadi Town **6**
Viseisei Village **3**
Vuda Point **2**

Naviti
Somosomo
Soso
Marou
Talaga Pt.
Yasawa
Drawaqa I.
Naukacuvu I.
Nanuya Balavu
Islands
Narara I.

Naoilau Pt
Koromasoli Pt.
Wayalevu
Yalobi
Natawa
Waya I.
Wayasewa
Namara
Kuata I.
White Rock I.

Vanua Levu
Nadi
Viti Levu
Suva
F

0   100 mi
0   100 km

Cakau
Na Sasi

Vomolailai I.
Vomo I.

Nacilau Pt
Yawalau I.
Vitogo Bay

Tokoriki I.
Mamanuca
Vitogo
Kings Rd
Islands
Tavua I.
LAUTOKA
Vakabuli
Matamanoa I.
Naikorokoro Pt
Luvuka I.
Lauwaki
Koroyanitu
Tai I.
Kadavu I.
Vuda Pt
National Heritage Park
Mana I.
Viseisei
Navini I.
Lomolomo
Qalito I.
Malamala I.
Wailoko Rd
Malolo I.
Nadi Bay
Korolyaca
Yakuilau I.
Martintar
MaloloIailai I.
Namaka
Denarau I.
Nadi
Namtou I.
Narewa
Nawaka
Namulomulo
Tavarua I.
Yako
Rasusuva
Nabila
Uciwai Rd
Navula Pt
Momi Bay
Momi
Navula Passage
Nawau
Bavu

✈ Airport
---- Reef

0   15 mi
0   15 km

Lomawqi

Adrenalin Watersports (© 675 1288; www.adrenalinfiji.com), which provides water-based activities at all the resorts, rents bicycles for F$15 an hour or F$40 a day. Book at the company's beach shacks and activity desks.

[FastFACTS] NADI

The following facts apply specifically to Nadi and Lautoka. For more information, see chapter 15.

Bookstores The best bookstore is in the departures area of Nadi International Airport; it's open 24/7. Hotel boutiques are also good places to buy magazines and books. Bookshops in town are actually stationery stores.

Currency Exchange ANZ Bank, Westpac Bank, and **Colonial National Bank** have offices with cash machines in Namaka and on the Queen's Road in Nadi Town. ANZ and Westpac have ATMs at the Port Denarau marina on Denarau Island, and ANZ's airport office is open 24 hours a day. You may get a better rate for currency and traveler's checks at the **Fexco Pacific/Western Union** offices at the airport and on the Queen's Road in Nadi Town.

Drugstores There are drugstores on the Queen's Road in Nadi Town, but **United Discount Chemists/ Budget Pharmacy** (© 670 0064) is the most well-stocked. It has a branch in Namaka (© 672 2533), and it operates **Denarau Pharmacy** (© 675 0780) in the Port Denarau complex.

Emergencies & Police The emergency phone number for **police** is © 917. Dial © 911 for **fire** and **ambulance.** The Fiji **police** have stations at Nadi Town (© 670 0222) and at the airport terminal (© 672 2222).

Eyeglasses For optical needs, try **Eyesite,** on the Queen's Road near the bridge in Nadi Town (© 670 7178).

Healthcare The government-operated **Lautoka Hospital** (© 666 3337) is the region's main facility. There is a **government medical clinic** (© 670 0362) in Nadi Town. **Dr. Ram Raju,** 2 Lodhia St., Nadi Town (© 670 0240 or 992 0444 mobile), has treated many visitors, including me. His residence and after-hours practice are on the Denarau Road (© 670 1769).The private **Namaka Medical Center** (© 672 2228) is open 24 hours a day and has doctors on call. Ask your hotel staff to recommend a **dentist** in private practice.

Internet Access All hotels and hostels have computers for their guests to access the Internet, and many have Wi-Fi. See the hotel listing below. Internet kiosks are in the Nadi

Airport terminal, and the very fine **Bulaccino,** on the Queen's Road in Nadi Town, has access (see "Where to Dine in Nadi," below).

Laundry & Dry Cleaning Flagstaff Laundry & Dry Cleaning (© 672 2161), on Northern Press Road in Martintar, has 1-day laundry and dry-cleaning service.

Mail The **Nadi Town post office,** on Hospital Road near the south end of the market, is open Monday to Friday 8am to 4pm, Saturday 8am to noon. It has a well-stocked stationery store in the lobby. A small airport branch is across the main entry road from the terminal (go through the gates and turn left). It is open Monday to Friday 8am to 4pm, Saturday 8am to noon.

Visitor Information You can get brochures and other information from the tour companies in the arrivals concourse at Nadi Airport. Other so-called Tourist Information Centres are really travel agents or tour operators.

Water The tap water is safe to drink except in periods of heavy rain.

EXPLORING THE NADI AREA

You can easily waste time driving around this area without seeing much of anything, so I recommend a half-day guided sightseeing tour with a reputable company. Round-trip bus transportation from Nadi area hotels is included in the price of the tours and outings; that is, a bus will pick you up within 30 minutes or so of the scheduled departure time for Nadi area trips, 1 hour or more for those on the Coral Coast. Children 11 years old and under pay half fare on most activities. Most hotel and hostel activity desks, or the reception-desk staffs, will make reservations or arrangements for all activities.

Nadi Town

Along the banks of the muddy Nadi River, the actual town of Nadi earns its livelihood by selling supplies to sugar-cane farmers and souvenirs to tourists. The Queen's Road passes through town as **Main Street,** an 8-block-long commercial strip lined with stores of every description. The biggest and best are on the north end of town near the river (see "Shopping in Nadi," below). Many shop owners will beckon you to come into their stores and have a look.

By contrast, the teeming **Nadi Market,** on Hospital Road inland, has a multitude of vendors purveying fresh local produce. It's not as large as the markets in Suva and Lautoka, but it's a fascinating glimpse into how Fijians—and Third World people in general, for that matter—buy their fruits and vegetables.

The town's other prime attraction is the **Sri Siva Subrahmaniya Swami Temple** (© 670 0016), on the south end of Main Street; the local Hindu community erected it in 1994. Artisans from India carved the images of the Hindu gods adorning the colorful building, itself dedicated to Lord Muruga, the mythical general said to have defeated evil. The temple is open daily from 8am to 5pm. Admission is F$3.50. **Note:** You must wear modest dress and remove your shoes when entering the temple; photography is not permitted inside.

Denarau Island

Only a muddy mangrove creek separates **Denarau Island,** about 7km (4⅓ miles) west of Nadi Town, from the mainland. Denarau is home to Fiji's largest real estate development, a huge project officially known in its entirety as **Denarau Island Resort Fiji** (www.denarau.com). To my mind—and that of many local folks—it's a generic tropical resort development bearing little resemblance to the rest of Fiji.

Denarau includes several resort hotels, a 150-unit timeshare complex, and numerous homes and condos (see "Where to Stay in Nadi," below).

As much as Denarau could be in Hawaii, Florida, or Australia's Gold Coast, it is still the place for play in Nadi. All the resorts have watersports and other activities

---

⚠️ **Beware of Unofficial "Tourist Information Centres"**

When you see "Tourist Information Centre" in Nadi or elsewhere, it is most likely a travel agent or tour operator, whose staff will invariably steer you to its own products. The only official, non-profit tourist information source is Tourism Fiji (see p. 239).

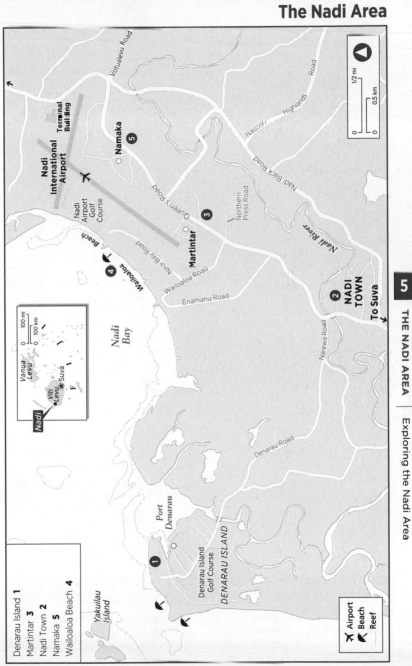

Denarau Island **1**
Martintar **3**
Nadi Town **2**
Namaka **5**
Wailoaloa Beach **4**

Nadi Town

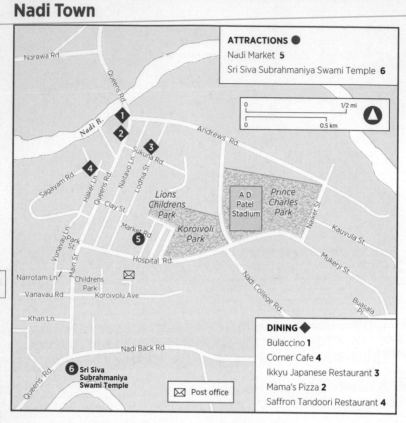

ATTRACTIONS ●
Nadi Market **5**
Sri Siva Subrahmaniya Swami Temple **6**

DINING ◆
Bulaccino **1**
Corner Cafe **4**
Ikkyu Japanese Restaurant **3**
Mama's Pizza **2**
Saffron Tandoori Restaurant **4**

✉ Post office

that their guests and outsiders alike can use, and the **Denarau Golf & Racquet Club** has an 18-hole golf course as well as top-flight tennis courts (see "Boating, Golf, Hiking & Other Outdoor Activities," below).

Except for those paying extra to fly, everyone else heading out to the islands departs from **Port Denarau** (www.portdenarau.com.fj), a modern shopping center and marina where most of the area's shuttle boats and cruises are based (see chapter 6). The shopping center has a number of retail outlets, two banks (with ATMs) and a money exchange, an ice-cream parlor, a Budget Rent A Car office, and several good restaurants, including Fiji's first Hard Rock Cafe (see "Where to Dine in Nadi," below).

Attractions North of Nadi

My favorite half-day tour goes north of Nadi Airport to the **Garden of the Sleeping Giant ★**. In 1977, the late Raymond Burr, star of TV's *Perry Mason* and *Ironside*, started this lovely, 20-hectare (50-acre) orchid range north of the airport to house his private collection of tropical orchids (he once also owned Naitoba, a small island in the Lau Group). It sits at the base of "Sleeping Giant Mountain," whose profile

Denarau Island

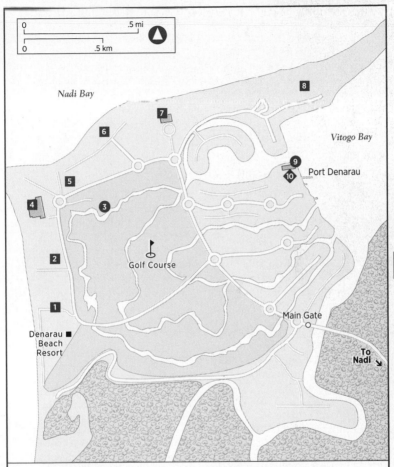

ATTRACTIONS ●
Port Denarau **9**
Denarau Golf & Racquet Club **3**

DINING ◆
Cardo's Steakhouse &
  Cocktail Bar **10**
Hard Rock Cafe **10**
Indigo **10**
Lulu Cafe, Bar & Restaurant **10**

ACCOMMODATIONS ■
Fiji Beach Resort & Spa Managed
  by Hilton **8**
Radisson Resort Denarau Island **2**
Sheraton Denarau Villas **5**
Sheraton Fiji Resort **4**
Sofitel Fiji Resort & Spa **7**
Westin Denarau Island
  Resort & Spa **6**
WorldMark Denarau Island Fiji **1**

5

forms the outline of a man fast asleep. There's much more here than orchids, however, and the guides will describe a variety of local plants and their uses.

You can get here on your own by rental car or taxi. Look for the sign at Wailoko Road off the Queen's Road between Nadi and Lautoka. It's open Monday to Saturday from 9am to 5pm. Entrance fees are F$12 for adults, F$6 for children, including guided tour and a fruit drink.

From there the tour stops at historic **Viseisei Village,** on the Queen's Road about halfway between Nadi and Lautoka. One legend says that the first Fijians settled here. Today it's a typical, fairly prosperous Fijian village, with some modern houses and some shacks of concrete block and tin, a small handicraft shop, and the usual road humps that bring traffic to a crawl.

Coral Sun Fiji (✆ **672 3105;** www.coralsunfiji.com) charges about F$90 for its afternoon "Orchids and Chiefly Village" tour.

An Attraction South of Nadi

Installed during World War II to protect the main pass through the Great Sea Reef, the concrete bunkers and naval guns in **Momi Battery Historical Park** are now under the care of the National Trust of Fiji (✆ **628 4356;** www.nationaltrust.org. fj), which operates the country's national parks and historical sites. The drive to the park is worth it just for the splendid view over the lagoon and western coast of Viti Levu. It's open daily from 9am to 5pm. Admission is F$3 for adults, F$1 for students. Turn west off the Queen's Road 16km (10 miles) south of Nadi Town toward **Momi Bay.** The road toward the coast is paved, as it leads to an on-again, off-again resort project being developed on Momi Bay. Turn right at the signpost beside the school and follow a rough dirt track another 4km (2½ miles) to the park. *Note:* The park does not have toilets or drinking water.

💬 The Dreaded Degei

Viseisei village between Nadi and Lautoka reputedly is where the great canoe *Kaunitoni* came out of the west and deposited the first Fijians some 3,000 years ago. From there, as the legend goes, they dispersed all over the islands. The yarn is encouraged by the local district name Vuda, which means "our origin" in Fijian, and Viseisei, which means "to scatter."

Although it's clear today that the Fijians did indeed migrate from the west, no one knows for sure whether they landed first at Viseisei; like all Pacific Islanders, the Fijians had no written language until the missionaries arrived in the mid–19th century.

The most common story has the great chiefs Lutunasobasoba and Degei arriving in the *Kaunitoni* on the northwest coast of Viti Levu. From there, they moved inland along the Nakauvadra Range in Northern Viti Levu. Lutunasobasoba died on this trip, but Degei lived on to become a combination man, ancestor, and spirit—and an angry spirit at that: He is blamed for causing wars and a great flood that washed the Fijians to all parts of the islands.

The dreaded Degei supposedly still inhabits a mysterious cave in the mountains above Rakiraki.

Lautoka

Fiji's second-largest city, **Lautoka** has broad avenues, green parks, and a row of towering royal palms marching along the middle of **Vitogo Parade,** the main drag running from the harbor along the eastern side of downtown.

Tourism may rule Nadi, but other than cruise ships putting into port for a day, sugar is king in Lautoka. The **Fiji Sugar Corporation**'s huge mill was built in 1903 and is one of the largest crushing operations in the Southern Hemisphere. At the industrial port, you'll also see a mountain of wood chips ready for export; the chips are a prime product of the country's pine plantations.

The stores along Vitogo Parade mark the boundary of Lautoka's business district; behind them are several blocks of shops and the lively **Lautoka Market,** which doubles as the bus station and is second in size only to Suva's Municipal Market. Handicraft stalls at the front of the market offer a variety of goods, especially when cruise ships are in port. Shady residential streets trail off beyond the playing fields of **Churchill Park** on the other side of Vitogo Parade. The Hare Krishnas have their most important temple in the South Pacific on Tavewa Avenue.

GETTING TO LAUTOKA

Local **buses** leave the market in Nadi Town every half-hour for the Lautoka Market from Monday to Saturday between 6am and 8pm. The fare is no more than F$5, depending on where you get on. The one-way **taxi** fare to Lautoka is about F$35 from Nadi. **Rosie the Travel Service** has a half-day Lautoka excursion from Nadi; book at any hotel activity desk.

When **driving** from Nadi, you will come to two traffic circles on the outskirts of Lautoka. Take the second exit off the first one and the first exit off the second. That will take you directly to the post office and the southern end of Vitogo Parade.

WHERE TO STAY & DINE IN LAUTOKA

The southern end of downtown gives way to a large park and picturesque promenade along the harbor. Beside it are Lautoka's best digs, the moderately priced **Waterfront Hotel** (© 666 4777; www.tanoahotels.com), which primarily attracts business travelers.

I usually stop for breakfast or lunch at the **Chilli Tree Café** (© 655 1824), a modern coffee shop at Tukani and Nede streets; it is open Monday to Saturday 7:30am to 4pm.

Even if I don't eat at **Jolly Good** (© 666 9980), an inexpensive cafeteria at Naviti and Vakabale streets, I often stop for a cold drink and a rest at its shady outdoor tables. It's operated by a family who split time between here and New Zealand. Opening hours are daily from 8am to 9pm.

For Indian fare, you can't beat the inexpensive curries at the extraordinarily clean **Ganga Vegetarian Restaurant,** 58 Naviti St. (© 666 0591), beside the big Jack's of Fiji store. It's open Monday through Saturday from 7am to 6:30pm.

Flightseeing & Sky Diving

Island Hoppers Fiji (© 672 0410; www.helicopters.com.fj) and **Pacific Islands Seaplanes** (© 672 5643; www.fijiseaplanes.com) both offer sightseeing flights over Denarau Island, Nadi Bay, the Mamanucas, and Vuda Point north of Nadi between Viseisei village and Lautoka. Call them or inquire at any hotel activities desk for prices and reservations.

I've never had the courage to put my life in someone's hands while falling to Denarau Island from 3,000m (10,000 ft.) up in the air, but you can with **Skydive Fiji** (ⓒ **672 8166;** www.skydivefiji.com.fj). You'll pay at least F$350 for a tandem flight.

EXPLORING VITI LEVU FROM NADI

Although I wouldn't spend my entire vacation in Nadi, it does make a good base from which to explore Fiji. In fact, you can make day trips from Nadi to other parts of Viti Levu. Most Coral Coast and Pacific Harbour attractions provide transportation from the Nadi area hotels, so you will not need a rental car.

Rafting on the Navua River

The best of these excursions onto the water—in fact, it's one of Fiji's top experiences—is a full-day rafting trip on the **Navua River,** between Pacific Harbour and Suva on Viti Levu's south coast. The tour visits a Fijian village that puts on a *yaqona* (kava) welcoming ceremony, a lunch of local-style foods, and a traditional dance show. Be sure to opt for the variation of this tour that includes a ride down the river on a *bilibili* (bamboo raft). See "River Rafting & Kayaking," in chapter 8, for details and prices.

Excursions to the Coral Coast

Other fine outdoor excursions are the jet boat rides offered by **Sigatoka River Safari** (ⓒ **0800 650 1721**; www.sigatokariver.com), which are more interesting and educational than the jet boat rides at Denarau Island. Also good are the waterfall and cave tours offered by **Adventures in Paradise Fiji** (ⓒ **652 0833;** www.adventuresinparadisefiji.com), on the Coral Coast.

Less exciting are rides on the **Coral Coast Railway Co.** (ⓒ **652 0434**), based outside Shangri-La's Fijian Resort. I'm most fond of the trip to lovely Natadola Beach, where you swim (bring your own towel) and have a barbecue lunch. Another Coral Coast tour visits the town of Sigatoka and the meandering river and fertile valley of the same name.

For animal lovers, the best attraction on the Coral Coast is **Kula Eco Park** (ⓒ **650 0505;** www.fijiwild.com).

It's far to go compared to the Mamanuca Islands just off Nadi (see chapter 6), but **Robinson Crusoe Island** (ⓒ **628 1999;** www.robinsoncrusoeislandfiji.com), on an islet off Natadola Beach, offers a day trip from Nadi including bus transportation to its jetty, a jungle river cruise (on the mainland), snorkeling trips, lunch and an island dance show for F$119. You will pay extra for waterskiing, tube rides, hair braiding and massages.

For details see "What to See & Do on the Coral Coast," in chapter 7.

Day Trips to Suva

Full-day guided tours go from Nadi to Suva, picking up guests at the Coral Coast hotels in between. From Nadi you'll spend a total of 8 hours riding in the bus for 4

Exploring Viti Levu from Nadi

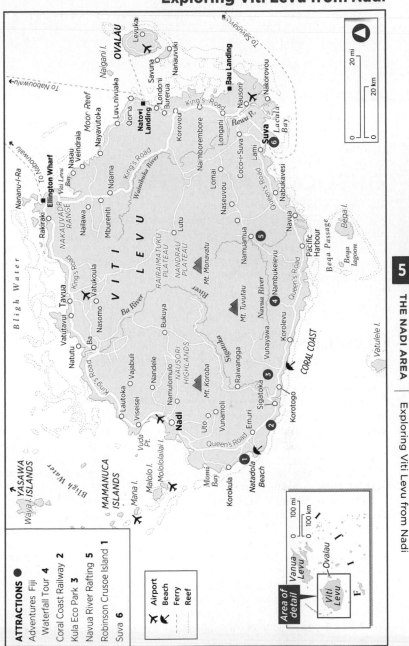

ATTRACTIONS ●
Adventures Fiji
Waterfall Tour **4**
Coral Coast Railway **2**
Kula Eco Park **3**
Navua River Rafting **5**
Robinson Crusoe Island **1**
Suva **6**

✈ Airport
🏖 Beach
--- Ferry
····· Reef

hours in Suva, half of which can easily be spent in the **Fiji Museum** (p. 177); so think about staying overnight and riding the Fiji Express back to Nadi the next day. You'll pay about F$100 per person from Nadi, less from the Coral Coast hotels, including admission to the museum. See chapter 10.

OUTDOOR ACTIVITIES

The Nadi area offers a host of sporting and outdoor activities to suit almost every interest. Most of these excursions take place near Nadi, but some—such as white-water rafting on the Navua River (see "River Rafting & Kayaking" in "Pacific Harbour & Beqa Island," chapter 8)—require a boat trip to the Mamanuca Islands or a bus ride to other locations on Viti Levu.

    Adrenalin Watersports (ⓒ 675 1288; www.adrenalinfiji.com) provides diving, jet-skiing, wakeboarding, sailing, parasailing, game fishing, and other watersports at all of the resorts on Denarau Island. Book at the beach shacks or at Adrenalin activities desks in the resort lobbies.

Fishing ★★

The Denarau Island hotels and all the resorts in the Mamanucas offer sportfishing as a pay-extra activity for their guests. On Denarau Island, both Adrenalin Watersports and **South Sea Cruises** (ⓒ 675 0050; www.ssc.com.fj) have fleets of fishing boats that ply the waters off the Mamanucas for wahoo, giant trevally, mahimahi, tuna, and other game fish.

Golf & Tennis

The 18-hole, 7,150-yard, par-72 links at the **Denarau Golf & Racquet Club ★★** (ⓒ 675 9710) occupy most of Denarau Island, with the clubhouse opposite the Sheraton Fiji Resort. Its somewhat shopworn restaurant and bar serve breakfast, lunch, and dinner at moderate prices. It also has locker rooms with showers. Greens fees for 18 holes are F$110. The course is open daily from 7am to dark, and lessons are available.

    The club's six Wimbledon-standard grass tennis courts are open daily from 7am to dark, and its four all-weather courts stay open until 10pm. Fees are F$25 per person per hour on grass, or F$28 per hour on the hard courts. Lessons are available, and proper tennis attire is required.

    The **Novotel Nadi Hotel** (ⓒ 672 2000) has a 9-hole executive course, and the hotel tour desks can arrange for you to play at the 18-hole **Nadi Airport Golf Club** (ⓒ 672 2148) near Newtown Beach, behind the airport. The latter is a 5,882-yard, par-70 course that isn't particularly challenging or well kept, but the setting, on the shores of Nadi Bay, is attractive.

Hiking

In addition to Adventures in Paradise's waterfall hikes on the Coral Coast (see earlier in this chapter), **Adventure Fiji** (© **672 2935** or 672 2755; www.rosiefiji.com), a branch of Rosie Holidays, takes trekkers (as hikers are known in these parts) on 1-day walks some 600m (2,000 ft.) up into the Nausori Highlands above Nadi. I found this hike to be fascinating but strenuous; in fact, you have to be between 10 and 45 years old to sign up. Wear high-traction walking shoes that you don't mind getting wet, because the sandy trail goes into and out of steep valleys and crosses streams. Most of this walk is through grasslands with no shade, so wear sunscreen. We had a long midday break in a Fijian village, where we shared a local-style lunch sitting cross-legged in a simple Fijian home. The cost is about F$85 per person. The company also has 4-, 6-, and 10-day hikes across the Sigatoka Valley and Nausori Highlands, ranging from about F$828 to F$2,000, including transfers, guide, accommodations, and meals provided by Fijian villagers along the way.

I have never been up there, nor do I know anyone who has, but in the mountains 15km (9 miles) east of Lautoka is the **Koroyanitu National Heritage Park,** an ecotourism project operated by Ambaca (pronounced Am-*bar*-tha) village and funded by the Native Land Trust Board, the South Pacific Regional Environment Programme, and the New Zealand government. The park includes native forests, grasslands, waterfalls, and magnificent mountain vistas. Admission is F$8. Before you set out call the **Ambaca Visitor Center** (© **666 6644** and dial 1234 after the second beep) to make sure the village has someone on hand to show you around.

Jet Boats

For a thrill-a-minute carnival ride afloat, **Adrenalin Jet Fiji** (© **675 1258;** www.adrenalinfiji.com) will take you twisting and turning through the mangrove-lined creeks behind Denarau Island. Heart-stopping 360-degree turns are guaranteed to get the heart pumping and the clothes wet. The half-hour rides depart every 30 minutes daily from Port Denarau. A shuttle connects the nearby Sheratons; scheduled pickups are arranged from other Nadi area hotels, so call for reservations. The price is about F$80 for adults; children 14 and under ride for half-fare, and kids 5 and under ride for free. Although it takes a full day, the rides offered by **Sigatoka River Safari** (© **0800 650 1721**; www.sigatokariver.com) are much more scenic and educational. See p. 96.

See p. 96.

Where "V. Singh" Started Swinging

The Nadi Airport Golf Club plays second fiddle to the manicured links at the Denarau Golf & Racquet Club these days, but it was here that one V. Singh won the Grade A Open Championship in 1981. That would be Vijay Singh, one of the world's top professional golfers. Before he started playing, the Fiji native served as caddy for his father, who was club president. Vijay Singh now lives in Florida and is seldom seen around Fiji.

Scuba Diving & Snorkeling

Nadi Bay usually is too murky for good snorkeling, and serious divers head elsewhere in Fiji (see "The Active Traveler," in chapter 3). You can go diving near the Great Sea Reef and the Mamanuca Islands with **Adrenalin Watersports** (© **675 1288;** www.adrenalinfiji.com), which is based on Denarau Island.

SHOPPING

Haggling is not considered to be polite when dealing with Fijians, and the better stores now have fixed prices. Bargaining is still acceptable, however, when dealing with Indo-Fijian merchants in many small shops. They will start high, you will start low, and somewhere in between you will find a mutually agreeable price. I usually knock 40% off the asking price as an initial counteroffer and then suffer the merchants' indignant snickers, secure in the knowledge that they aren't about to kick me out of the store when the fun has just begun.

To avoid the hassles of bargaining, visit **Jack's of Fiji** (Fiji's largest merchant), **Prouds,** and **Tappoo,** all of which have branches on the Queen's Road in Nadi Town, at Port Denarau, and in Sigatoka, Suva, and the shopping arcades of the larger hotels. In Nadi Town, the upstairs rooms of Jack's of Fiji are filled with clothing and leather goods. Tappoo carries a broad range of merchandise, including electronics, cameras, and sporting goods. Prouds concentrates on perfumes, watches, and jewelry including black and gold orbs from Savusavu's **J. Hunter Pearls** (see p. 213).

In addition to being the shove-off point for cruises and transfers to the islands, **Port Denarau** is the shopping place on Denarau Island. The modern mall—"This looks just like home," I overheard an American tourist remark to her husband—has a Jack's of Fiji branch, a surf shop, two banks and a currency exchange, the best deli and wine store in Fiji, an ice-cream parlor, and several restaurants (see "Where to Dine in Nadi," later in this chapter).

"Duty-Free" Shopping

Fiji has the most developed shopping industry in the South Pacific, as will be very obvious when you walk along the main thoroughfare in Nadi Town. The Fiji government charges an import tax on merchandise brought into the country; so, despite their claims to the contrary, the stores aren't "duty-free." I have found much better

5

Shopping

THE NADI AREA

> ### Beware of Men Wielding Swords
>
> Fijians are extremely friendly people, but beware of so-called **sword sellers.** These are Fijian men who carry bags under their arms and approach you on the street. "Where you from, 'Stralia? States?" will be their opening line, followed by, "What's your name?" If you respond, they will quickly inscribe your name on a sloppily carved wooden sword. They expect you to buy the sword, whether you want it or not. They are numerous in Nadi, and they may even come up to you in Suva, though government efforts to discourage the practice have been more successful there. The easiest way to avoid this scam is to not tell any stranger your name and walk away as soon as you see the bag.

prices and selections on the Internet and at large-volume dealers such as Best Buy and Circuit City in the United States, so shop around at home first so that you can compare the prices in Fiji. Also the models offered in the duty-free shops here are seldom the latest editions.

You should have no problems buying watches, cameras, and electronic gear from large merchants such as Prouds and Tappoo, but get receipts that accurately describe your purchases from small stores. Make sure all guarantee and warranty cards are properly completed and stamped by the merchant. Examine all items before making payment. If you later find that the item is not what you expected, return to the shop immediately with the item and your receipt. As a general rule, purchases are not returnable and deposits are not refundable. Always pay for your duty-free purchases by credit card. That way, if something goes wrong after you're back home, you can solicit help from the financial institution that issued the card.

If you missed anything, you'll get one last chance at the huge shops in the departure lounge at Nadi Airport.

Handicrafts

Fijians produce a wide variety of handicrafts, such as carved *tanoa* (kava) bowls, war clubs, and cannibal forks; woven baskets and mats; pottery (which has seen a renaissance of late); and *masi* (tapa) cloth. Be careful when buying souvenirs and some woodcarvings, however, for many of today's items are machine-made, and many smaller items are imported from Asia. Look at the lines on wood carvings; if they are straight, the item likely was made by machine, not by hand. Only with masi can you be sure of getting a genuine Fijian handicraft.

The larger shops sell some very fine face masks and *nguzunguzus* (pronounced noo-zoo-noo-zoos), the inlaid canoe prows carved in the Solomon Islands, and some primitive art from Papua New Guinea. (Although you will see plenty hanging in the shops, the Fijians never carved masks in the old days.)

The largest and best-stocked shop on Queen's Road is **Jack's of Fiji** ★★ (© **670 0744**). It has a wide selection of handicrafts, jewelry, T-shirts, clothing, and paintings by local artists. The prices are reasonable and the staff is helpful rather than pushy. Jack's has other outlets including the shopping arcades of most major resorts.

Other places to look are **Nadi Handicraft Center** (© **670 2357**) and **Nad's Handicrafts** (© **670 3588**). Nadi Handicraft Center has an upstairs room carrying clothing, leather goods, jewelry, and black pearls. Nad's usually has a good selection of Fijian pottery. **Nadi Handicraft Market** (no phone) is a collection of stalls on the Queen's Road near the south end of Nadi Town. The best are operated by Fijian women who sell baskets and other goods woven of *pandanus*, a palm whose supple leaves are more durable than those of the coconut tree.

VAT Refunds

The Fiji government imposes a 12.5% Value Added Tax (VAT) on every purchase. The VAT is included in the price, so you will not be aware of it, like you would sales taxes charged in the United States. Visitors can claim a **VAT refund** when they leave the country of 10%—not the full 12.5%—on up to F$500 spent per day. The merchant must fill out a VAT form at the time of purchase. Take the VAT form and your original receipts to a refund desk when you depart at Nadi International Airport.

WHERE TO STAY

Most Nadi area hotels are on or near the Queen's Road, either near the airport or in **Martintar,** a suburban area halfway between the airport and Nadi Town. An advantage of Martintar is that you can safely walk from your hotel to grocery stores, a pharmacy, restaurants, and bars. Only the resorts on **Denarau Island** and beside **Wailoaloa Beach** actually sit beside a beach. Even if they do, runoff from the mountains, hills, cane fields, and coastal mangrove swamps perpetually leaves Nadi Bay less than clear and its beaches more gray than white.

This area has a host of backpacker hostels, all of them in fierce competition with each other. The **Fiji Backpackers Association** (www.fiji-backpacking.com) is an organization of reputable hostel owners.

On Denarau Island

You timeshare owners can exchange your intervals at **WorldMark Denarau Island Fiji** (© 800/860-6142 or 675 0442; www.worldmarkbywyndham.com), a 175-unit complex on the beach next to the Radisson Resort Fiji Denarau Island. Formerly known as TrendWest Fiji, it has a huge rectangular pool with swim-up bar, a spa and fitness center, and the Seafront Restaurant (see "Where to Dine in Nadi," below).

Fiji Beach Resort & Spa Managed by Hilton   Extending for what seems like a kilometer along the northeastern point of Denarau Island, this resort was experiencing financial difficulties during my most recent visit, and I'm not sure Hilton will be managing by the time you arrive. Two-story buildings house the accommodations, which are two-bedroom, two-bathroom condos designed so that one bedroom and bathroom can be rented as a standard room. The remaining bedroom, bathroom, kitchen, and living area are known as "villas." High-tech prevails, including big flatscreen TVs and PlayStations in each unit. Sliding doors separate the bedrooms from the bathrooms, which have both showers and soaking tubs. Each villa has a gas barbecue grill on its balcony, most of which look out to a long, rectangular beachside pool divided into seven separate areas. The main restaurant is out by the pool, but the star here is **Lépicier,** a coffee shop–deli with superb, freshly baked breads and pastries.

P.O. Box 11185, Nadi Airport. © **800/HILTONS** (445-8667) or 675 8000. Fax 675 6801. www.fiji beachresortbyhilton.com. 225 units. F$485–F$675. AE, DC, MC, V. **Amenities:** 2 restaurants; 1 bar; babysitting; bikes; children's programs; health club; Jacuzzi; 7 pools; room service; smoke-free rooms; spa; watersports equipment/rentals. *In room:* A/C, TV, fridge, hair dryer, Internet (ADSL, F$30/hr.), kitchen (in 1-bedroom units).

Radisson Resort Fiji Denarau Island ★★★ ☺   A large and artistically designed swimming pool complex helps make this Denarau Island's top resort for families. The four pools are designed like lagoons—some sand-surrounded, others with waterfalls and green islands. Decorated in calming colors, the guest units have white porcelain-tiled floors, practical for back-and-forth activity between the pool, beach, and hotel rooms. Each room has a furnished patio or balcony where you can enjoy night views of the Southern Hemisphere skies. Families and large parties should consider renting the condolike suites, which offer both full kitchens and washers and dryers. Spa-goers can request specialized wellness menus in addition to the offerings of the hotel's restaurants, which feature a pizza kitchen as well as island and traditional Western fare.

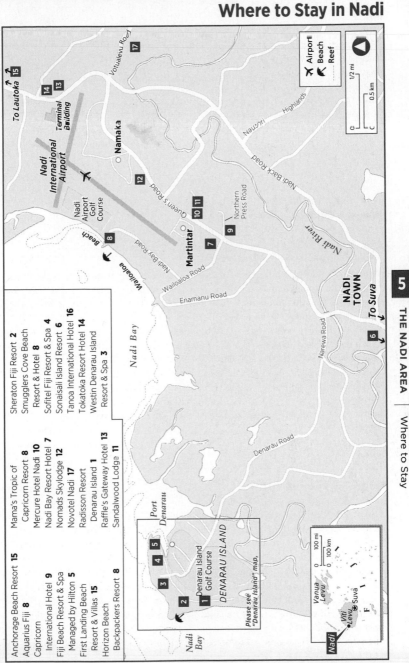

Anchorage Beach Resort **15**
Aquarius Fiji **8**
Capricorn
International Hotel **9**
Fiji Beach Resort & Spa
Managed by Hilton **5**
First Landing Beach
Resort & Villas **15**
Horizon Beach
Backpackers Resort **8**

Mama's Tropic of
Capricorn Resort **8**
Mercure Hotel Nadi **10**
Nadi Bay Resort Hotel **7**
Nomads Skylodge **12**
Novotel Nadi **17**
Radisson Resort
Denarau Island **1**
Raffle's Gateway Hotel **13**
Sandalwood Lodge **11**

Sheraton Fiji Resort **2**
Smugglers Cove Beach
Resort & Hotel **8**
Sofitel Fiji Resort & Spa **4**
Sonaisali Island Resort **6**
Tanoa International Hotel **16**
Tokatoka Resort Hotel **14**
Westin Denarau Island
Resort & Spa **3**

5

THE NADI AREA | Where to Stay

103

If you're making last-minute plans, contact **Impulse Fiji**, P.O. Box 10000, Nadi Airport (© **253/617-1375** In the U.S.; 672 3952; fax 672 5064; www.impulse fiji.com), which sells "unused" hotel rooms at reduced rates. It saves you the trouble of asking the front desk for a discount on rooms that would otherwise go unused. You can also get discounts on airline tickets and hotel rooms if you book in advance on the company's website.

P.O. Box 9347, Nadi Airport. © **800/395-7046** or 675 1264. Fax 675 1117. www.radisson.com/fiji. 270 units. F$180–F$500. AE, DC, MC, V. **Amenities:** 3 restaurants; 3 bars; babysitting; bikes; children's programs; health club; Jacuzzi; 4 pools; room service; smoke-free rooms; spa; watersports equipment/rentals; Wi-Fi (in lobby; free first 3 days). *In room:* A/C, TV, fridge, hair dryer, Internet (free first 3 days), kitchen (in suites).

Sheraton Fiji Resort ★★   This 1987-vintage hotel underwent a thorough renovation in 2008, which trimmed its public areas in teak and mahogany; consequently it now looks less like a generic tropical resort and more like it belongs in Fiji. Nevertheless, it still lacks the overall Fijian-charm of its nearby sister, the Westin Denarau Island Resort & Spa (see below). In two-story buildings flanking the central complex, the rooms here are among the largest on Denarau Island, and most have ocean views from their private terraces or balconies. The food choices (none of them inexpensive) include fine dining in the swanky Ports O' Call. Guests can swim, snorkel, and sunbathe on a private island across the lagoon.

The resort also manages the 184 adjacent condos known as the **Sheraton Denarau Villas,** built around a courtyard with two swimming pools. The beach has been eroded away, but guests can play in the sand at the Sheraton. The guest quarters come in various sizes, ranging from single rooms to three-bedroom apartments, and are appointed with full kitchens and washers and dryers.

P.O. Box 9761, Nadi. © **800/325-3535** or 675 0777. Fax 675 0818. www.sheraton.com/fiji. 292 hotel units, 184 condos. US$330–US$535 double; US$435–US$1,065 condo. AE, DC, MC, V. **Amenities:** 4 restaurants; 3 bars; babysitting; bikes; children's programs; concierge; executive or concierge-level rooms; health club; Jacuzzi; pool; room service; smoke-free rooms; spa; watersports equipment/rentals; Wi-Fi (in lobby; F$35/day). *In room:* A/C, TV, fridge, hair dryer, Internet (F$35/day), kitchen (in villas).

Sofitel Fiji Resort & Spa ★★   One of Fiji's largest outdoor swimming pools and some of its best big-hotel dining highlight this French-accented luxury resort. The central building sports a gleaming open-air lobby overlooking the pool and beach. The spacious guest quarters are in three-story buildings lined up along the beach. Furnished and equipped in European style, they range from oceanview rooms to presidential suites. Terrific for couples are the "junior suites" with romantic Jacuzzis hidden behind louvered windows on their balconies. Under the direction of European chefs, the central kitchen provides excellent fare for three food outlets, including La Parisienne Café and "V," a fine-dining seafood restaurant. The Sofitel lacks the Fijian charm of the Westin Denarau Island Resort & Spa, and the pool isn't as spectacular as the Radisson Fiji Denarau Island's.

Private Mail Bag 396, Nadi Airport. © **800/763-4835** or 675 1111. Fax 675 1122. www.sofitelfiji.com.fj. 296 units. F$430–F$2,000. AE, DC, MC, V. **Amenities:** 3 restaurants; 5 bars; babysitting; bikes; children's programs; concierge; executive or concierge-level rooms; health club; Jacuzzi; pool; room service; smoke-free rooms; spa; watersports equipment/rentals. *In room:* A/C, TV, hair dryer, kitchen (in suites), minibar, Wi-Fi (F$18/hr.).

The Westin Denarau Island Resort & Spa ★★★   Built in 1972 as the Regent of Fiji, and more recently known as the Sheraton Royal Denarau Resort, this venerable property still maintains more Fijian charm than any other large hotel here. Covered by a peaked wooden roof and laden with artifacts, the dark, breezy foyer opens to an irregularly shaped pool and the gray-sand beach. The rooms are in a series of two-story, motel-style blocks grouped in "villages" surrounded by thick, lush tropical gardens and linked by covered walkways to the central building. All but two of these buildings face the beach. With lots of varnished wood trim, exposed timbers, and masi cloth accents, the spacious units ooze tropical charm. Guests here can use the private island shared with the Sheraton Fiji, while guests there can use the fitness center and attractive Heavenly Spa by Westin here. This is the most tranquil resort on Denarau Island, which makes it more attractive to couples than families.

P.O. Box 9761, Nadi Airport. © **800/325-3535** or 675 0000. Fax 675 0259. www.westin.com. 274 units. US$475–US$600 double; US$1,130 suite. AE, DC, MC, V. **Amenities:** 4 restaurants; 4 bars; babysitting; bikes; children's programs; concierge; executive or concierge-level rooms; health club; Internet; Jacuzzi; pool; room service; smoke-free rooms; spa; watersports equipment/rentals; Wi-Fi (in main bldg.; F$9/ hr.). *In room:* A/C, TV, fridge, hair dryer, Internet (F$9/hr.), minibar.

At Wailoaloa Beach

Wailoaloa Beach, about 3km (2 miles) off the Queen's Road, is a long strip of grayish-brown sand fringing Nadi Bay. Although it was originally built as a tract-housing project, the area known as **Newtown Beach** is now host to both suburban homes and several budget accommodations.

Aquarius Fiji ★   Canadian Terrence Buckley merged these two beachside condos into Fiji's first "flashpacker" budget-priced resort. Although backpackers usually occupy the five downstairs rooms with 2, 6, or 10 bunk beds (each room is air-conditioned and has its own bathroom), the eight spacious rooms upstairs are suitable for anyone searching for an inexpensive beachside stay. The four upstairs rooms facing the bay are particularly attractive, because they have large balconies overlooking the beach and a small outdoor swimming pool. The other upstairs units have smaller balconies facing the mountains. Downstairs, a restaurant, bar, and TV lounge open to the pool.

Check Hotel Websites for Rates & Specials

Resorts in Fiji have been offering substantial discounts during the worldwide economic recession. The practice has been especially widespread on Denarau Island, whose resorts have a glut of rooms to fill. Their rates were so erratic that the resorts were unwilling to tell me what they were; consequently, the amounts quoted here are an educated guess on my part. Be sure to check the hotel websites to see what specials or Internet-only rates they are offering when you plan to visit.

P.O. Box 7, Nadi (Wasawasa Rd., Newtown Beach). ✆ **672 6000.** Fax 672 6001. www.aquariusfiji.com. 8 units, 18 dorm beds. F$105–F$115 double; F$28–F$30 dorm bed. AE, MC, V. **Amenities:** Restaurant; bar; Internet (F$6/hr.); outdoor pool; Wi-Fi (F$6/hr.). *In room:* A/C, fan, no phone.

Horizon Beach Backpackers Resort   Although it's not directly on the beach, this two-story clapboard house is a less expensive alternative to the nearby Aquarius Fiji and Smugglers Cove Beach Resort & Hotel and Mama's Tropic of Capricorn Resort, both next door. The rooms are spacious if not luxurious and have their own bathrooms with hot-water showers. Superior units are air-conditioned, while the others have fans. The dorm beds are in two rooms; the smaller one with eight bunks is air-conditioned. The open-air restaurant serves inexpensive meals, and Fijian musicians perform at night at the bar. Guests here can use the facilities at Smugglers Cove Beach Resort & Hotel, which has the same owners.

P.O. Box 1401, Nadi (Wasawasa Rd., Newtown Beach). ✆ **672 2832.** Fax 672 4578. www.horizonbeach fiji.com. 14 units, 16 dorm beds. F$50–F$155 double; F$15–F$22 dorm bed. Rates include continental breakfast. AE, MC, V. **Amenities:** Restaurant; bar; outdoor pool; Wi-Fi (F$8/hr.). *In room:* A/C (all rooms and 8 dorm beds), fan, no phone.

Mama's Tropic of Capricorn Resort   Owned by a well-traveled Fijian named Mama Salena, this hostel includes a three-story building between the outdoor pool and the beach—meaning that, with the pool not beside the beach, Mama's is not as resorty as Aquarius and Smugglers Cove. The two-story wing includes a mix of air-conditioned and fan-cooled rooms and dorms. One rooftop unit has three walls of louvered windows, making it seem like a bungalow. It has the privilege of sharing the roof with a sunset bar.

P.O. Box 1736, Nadi (Wasawasa Rd., Newtown Beach). ✆ **672 3089.** Fax 672 3050. www.mamasfiji.com. 20 units, 32 dorm beds. F$90 double; F$35 dorm bed. Rates include continental breakfast. AE, MC, V. **Amenities:** Restaurant; 2 bars; outdoor pool Wi-Fi (F$8/hr.). *In room:* A/C (some units), fan, no phone.

Smugglers Cove Beach Resort & Hotel ★★ 🍴   This three-story hotel is larger than Aquarius Fiji, and its medium-size rooms are equipped with amenities found at more expensive hotels. The family suite also has a kitchen, but best are the four rooms on the front of the building with balconies overlooking the swimming pool, the beach, and Nadi Bay. Arranged in four-bed coed cubicles, the 34 beds in the first-floor Pirates Dormitory are often full (overflow heads to the owners' Horizon Beach Backpackers Resort next door). The young guests keep the restaurant and bar—which open to the deck-surrounded pool—busy and sometimes noisy at night. Another plus here is a large, air-conditioned Internet room.

P.O. Box 5401, Nadi (Wasawasa Rd., Newtown Beach). ✆ **672 6578.** Fax 672 8740. www.smugglers beachfiji.com. 22 units, 34 dorm beds. F$115–F$198 double; F$33 dorm bed. Rates include continental breakfast. AE, MC, V. **Amenities:** Restaurant; bar; free Internet; outdoor pool; room service; Wi-Fi (F$8/ hr.). *In room:* A/C, TV, fridge, kitchen (in family suite).

In the Martintar Area

Capricorn International Hotel 🍴   Cleanliness and firm mattresses are trademarks at this budget property, along with its Suva sister, the Capricorn Apartment Hotel (see "Where to Stay in Suva," in chapter 10). Least expensive are the standard rooms, which are entered from the rear and have window walls instead of balconies overlooking a lush tropical courtyard with a pool and a hot tub (they are the highlight here); but I would opt for a unit with a balcony or patio. Six family units have kitchens and two bedrooms. The fan-cooled dorm is an afterthought.

P.O. Box 9043, Nadi Airport. © **672 0088.** Fax 672 0522. www.capricornfiji.com. 68 units, 14 dorm beds. F$100–F$170 double; F$25 dorm bed. Rates include continental breakfast. AE, DC, MC, V. **Amenities:** Restaurant; bar; babysitting; Internet (F$48/hr.); Jacuzzi; outdoor pool; room service; spa; free airport transfers. *In room:* A/C, TV, fridge, kitchen (family units).

Mercure Hotel Nadi This motel sports modern European decor and furniture, thanks to a face-lift when it recently became a Mercure property. The spacious rooms are in two three-story, walk-up buildings flanking a tropical garden surrounding a swimming pool and wooden deck. The rooms have desks, shower-only bathrooms with French-style "bowl" hand basins, and glass doors sliding open to patios or balconies. Some have king-size beds; others have both queen-size and single beds. A few units are equipped for guests with disabilities.

P.O. Box 9178, Nadi Airport. © **800/637-2873** or 672 0272. Fax 672 0187. www.accorhotels.com. 85 units. F$140–F$235 double. AE, DC, MC, V. **Amenities:** Restaurant; bar; babysitting; outdoor pool; room service; spa; tennis court; free airport transfers; Wi-Fi (F$10/hr.). *In room:* A/C, TV, fridge, hair dryer.

Nadi Bay Resort Hotel Although suitable for any cost-conscious traveler, 110 dormitory beds make this Nadi's largest backpacker establishment. It was also the most popular until Smugglers Cove opened on Wailoaloa Beach. Behind its walls you'll find three bars, two sophisticated restaurants serving reasonably priced meals, an air-conditioned TV lounge, and courtyards with two swimming pools. The hotel even has a hair salon, a massage parlor, and a 70-seat theater for watching movies and sporting events on TV. In addition to the dormitories, its five buildings hold standard motel rooms and apartments. The property is directly under Nadi Airport's flight path, however, so jets occasionally roar overhead in the middle of the night. Lower-priced units and dorms are not air-conditioned.

NAP 0359, Nadi Airport. © **672 3599.** Fax 672 0092. www.fijinadibayhotel.com. 42 units (19 with bathroom), 110 dorm beds. F$85–F$165 double; F$30–F$33 dorm bed. Room rates include continental breakfast; dormitory rates do not. AE, MC, V. **Amenities:** 2 restaurants; 3 bars; 2 outdoor pools; free airport transfers; Wi-Fi (in lobby; F$10/hr.). *In room:* A/C (most units), fan, fridge, no phone.

Nomads Skylodge This sprawling, 4.4-hectare (11-acre) property is part of Nomads World, an Australian company specializing in accommodations and tours for backpackers and other budget-minded travelers, although it's expertly managed by Fiji's Tanoa hotels. Thirteen hotel rooms are air-conditioned dormitories, each with four or six bunk beds, private lockers (bring a lock), and its own bathroom but no other amenities such as TVs and phones. One unit has cooking facilities. Imported sand forms a small faux beach by the swimming pool.

P.O. Box 9222, Nadi Airport. © **672 2200.** Fax 671 4330. www.nomadsskylodge.com. 53 units, 27 dorm beds. F$78–F$153 double; F$30–F$35 dorm bed. AE, MC, V. **Amenities:** Restaurant; bar; outdoor pool; free airport transfers; Wi-Fi (F$8/hr.). *In room:* A/C, fan, fridge.

Sandalwood Lodge ★ 🖉 "Clean and comfortable at a sensible price" is the appropriate motto at John and Ana Birch's establishment, which is now managed by their charming daughter, Angela. I have long considered the Sandalwood to be Nadi's best value—provided you don't need a restaurant on the premises. Quietly situated about 270m (900 ft.) off the Queen's Road behind the Mercure Hotel Nadi, the New Zealand–style motel consists of three two-story buildings flanking a nicely landscaped lawn with a rock-bordered pool. Units in the Orchid Wing are somewhat larger than the others and have queen-size beds instead of doubles. Every unit has a kitchen and sofa bed.

P.O. Box 9454, Nadi Airport. ✆ **672 2044.** Fax 672 0103. www.sandalwoodfiji.com. 34 units. F$108–F$117 double. AE, MC, V. **Amenities:** Babysitting; outdoor pool; free airport transfers. *In room:* A/C, TV, fan, kitchen.

Near the Airport

Novotel Nadi   Fondly remembered in these parts as the Fiji Mocambo, this sprawling hotel atop a hill received a much-needed face-lift after being taken over by Accor Hotels a few years ago. It's a fitting competitor to the nearby Tanoa International Hotel (see below). Most rooms have excellent views across the cane fields to the mountains; the best are on the top floor, where their peaked ceilings give them the feel of bungalows. You can practice your swing at the hotel's 9-hole executive golf course.

P.O. Box 11133, Nadi Airport. ✆ **800/942-5050** or 672 2000. Fax 672 0324. www.novotel.com. 125 units. F$201–F$276 double. AE, DC, MC, V. **Amenities:** Restaurant; bar; babysitting; golf course; health club; outdoor pool; room service; 2 tennis courts; free airport transfers; Wi-Fi (F$10/hr.). *In room:* A/C, TV, fridge, hair dryer, Internet (F$36/day).

Raffle's Gateway Hotel ☺   This older but very well-maintained property (no connection whatsoever to Singapore's famous Raffles Hotel) is my favorite place to wait for a flight at the airport just across Queen's Road. As at the slipping Tokatoka Resort Hotel next door (see below), you can whisk yourself down a water slide into a figure-8 swimming pool, the larger of two here. All units sport attractive tropical furniture and shower-only bathrooms. The best have sitting areas and patios or balconies next to the large pool. The tiny, least expensive "standard" rooms can barely hold their double beds and are devoid of most amenities. The roadside main building houses an open-air, 24-hour coffee shop and an air-conditioned nighttime restaurant.

P.O. Box 9891, Nadi Airport. ✆ **672 2444.** Fax 672 0620. www.rafflesgateway.com. 93 units. F$98–F$210 double. AE, DC, MC, V. **Amenities:** 2 restaurants; bar; babysitting; Internet (F$20/hr.); Jacuzzi; 2 outdoor pools; room service; tennis court; free airport transfers; Wi-Fi (F$20/hr.). *In room:* A/C, TV, fridge, hair dryer.

Tanoa International Hotel ★   This motel is the top place to stay near the airport. The bright public areas open onto a lush garden with a waterfall splashing into a modest size swimming pool. Shingle-covered walkways lead to medium-size, motel-style rooms in two-story blocks. The Tanoa was built in the 1970s as a TraveLodge, so its rooms are somewhat smaller than the Novotel Nadi's. Most have a double and a single bed, combination tub-and-shower bathrooms, and balconies or patios. Superior rooms have king-size beds, large desks, sofas, and walk-in showers. Dignitaries often take the two luxurious one-bedroom suites. The open-air restaurant by the pool is open 24 hours.

P.O. Box 9203, Nadi Airport. ✆ **800/835-7742** or 672 0277. Fax 672 0191. www.tanoahotels.com. 135 units. F$220–F$280 double; F$350–F$500 suite. AE, DC, MC, V. **Amenities:** Restaurant; bar; babysitting; executive or concierge-level rooms; health club; Jacuzzi; outdoor pool; room service; spa; tennis court; free airport transfers; Wi-Fi (throughout; F$9/hr.). *In room:* A/C, TV, fridge, hair dryer.

Tokatoka Resort Hotel   The highlight at this complex, at the edge of sugar-cane fields across the Queen's Road from the airport, is an unusual swimming pool–restaurant-bar at the rear of the property. Unfortunately, the resort has had ownership problems of late and has been on rocky financial footing. If you can't get into the Raffle's Gateway next door, you'll find Nadi's most varied mix of accommodations here, from hotel rooms to apartments to two-bedroom bungalows, many of them equipped with cooking facilities.

P.O. Box 9305, Nadi Airport. ℂ **672 0222.** Fax 672 0400. www.tokatokaresortfiji.com. 112 units. F$189–F$395 double. AE, MC, V. **Amenities:** Restaurant; bar; babysitting; Jacuzzi; outdoor pool; room service; spa; free airport transfers; Wi-Fi (in Internet cafe; F$10/hr.). *In room:* A/C, fans, TV, fridge, kitchen (some units).

Resorts Near Nadi

The three resorts below are beside Nadi Bay within 30 minutes of the airport. The lagoon off each is so shallow it can turn into a mud flat at low tide, but they all have removed enough of the reef to make marinas and swimming holes, and imported enough sand to make you think you're on a fine beach. You can base your Fiji vacation here and not have to pay extra for transportation, but, to my mind, these resorts are best for lagoonside layovers. Getting into Nadi Town will require a rental vehicle or taxi.

SOUTH OF NADI

Sonaisali Island Resort   You drive through cane fields and ride a boat across a narrow muddy channel to this modern resort set on a flat, 42-hectare (105-acre) island. The lagoon is very shallow here at low tide, so imported sand held in place by a seawall serves as the main beach. You can also frolic in an attractive rock-lined pool with a swim-up bar. The tropically attired guest quarters include spacious hotel rooms, but the top choice are the airy duplex bungalows out in the lush gardens—some of the largest bures on Viti Levu. Beachfront spa bures have small Jacuzzi tubs on their front porches (these are *duplex* units, however, so don't expect the ultimate in privacy). Three of the units have two bedrooms each and are attractive to families.

P.O. Box 2544, Nadi (Sonaisali Island, 20 min. south of Nadi Town). ℂ **670 6011.** Fax 670 6092. www.sonaisali.com. 123 units. F$495 double; F$582–F$819 bungalow. Rates include full breakfast. AE, DC, MC, V. **Amenities:** 2 restaurants; 4 bars; babysitting; children's center; health club; Internet (in business center; F$20/hr.); Jacuzzi; outdoor pool; room service; spa; tennis court; watersports equipment/rentals. *In room:* A/C, fan, TV, fridge, hair dryer.

NORTH OF NADI

The two resorts below are on the paved Vuda Point Road, which runs from the Queen's Road west to Vuda Point, the promontory where the first legendary Fijians came ashore some 2,500 years ago. Today, this is where modern Fiji's oil is imported, so the landmarks are large petroleum storage tanks. This also is home to **Vuda Point Marina,** the best mainland stop for cruising yachts.

Anchorage Beach Resort   Originally a motel with a gorgeous view of Nadi Bay from atop Vuda Point, Anchorage now includes a block of hotel rooms, a few duplex cottages, a massage bure, and a poolside restaurant and bar down by the lagoon. The resort has a bit of beach, and more white sand for sunning is held in place by a stone wall. The best views are from the original units atop the hill, but the spacious bungalows climbing the hill above the beach are the most luxurious accommodations here. The hotel rooms down there are rather typical except for their Jacuzzi tubs. The resort runs its own day trips from its marina to **Beachcomber Island Resort** (p. 130), with whom it shares owners. Note that trains hauling sugar cane run on narrow gauge tracks between the restaurant and hotel rooms during the harvest season from June through November.

P.O. Box 10314, Nadi Airport (on Vuna Point Rd. 13km/8 miles north of Nadi Airport). © **666 2099.** Fax 666 5571. www.anchoragefiji.com. 50 units. F$193–F$410 double. AE, MC, V. **Amenities:** Restaurant; bar; Internet (computer in lobby; F$20/hr.); outdoor pool; watersports equipment/rentals. *In room:* A/C, fans, TV, fridge, hair dryer.

First Landing Beach Resort & Villas   The creation of American Jim Dunn and Australian George Stock, this little resort sits beachside near where the first Fijians came ashore 3 millennia ago. Vuda Point Marina and its restaurant are next door. The grounds here are festooned with coconut palms and other tropical plants. A partially shaded outdoor swimming pool is an attractive option, and Jim and George have dredged the shallow reef to create a swimming hole and small islet offshore. The duplex guest bungalows are comfortably furnished with both king-size and single beds, and their bathrooms have whirlpool tubs. The bures also boast charming screened porches, and four beachside bures also have decks. The resort also has three two-bedroom, two-bathroom villas with their own pools.

P.O. Box 348, Lautoka (at Vuda Point, 15km/9 miles north of Nadi Airport). © **666 6171.** Fax 666 8882. www.firstlandingfiji.com. 39 units. F$325–F$820 double. Rates include full breakfast. AE, DC, MC, V. **Amenities:** Restaurant; bar; babysitting; Internet (computer in boutique; F$20/hr.); outdoor pool; room service; spa; watersports equipment/rentals. *In room:* A/C, fans, fridge, kitchen (in villas).

WHERE TO DINE

On Denarau Island

You will pay a relatively high price to dine in them, but all of the Denarau Island resorts have restaurants, most either on or near the beach. Fiji's best breads and pastries are at **Lépicier,** a coffee shop cum deli in the Fiji Beach Resort & Spa Managed by Hilton (© **675 8000;** daily 8am to 10pm).

The shopping/dining complex at **Port Denarau** (www.portdenarau.com.fj) has a score of restaurants, including all of those I recommend below. Also here is a branch of **Mama's Pizza** (© **675 0533;** daily 9am–11pm), which has the same menu as the Nadi Town outlet (see below). Both **Amalfi Italian Restaurant** (© **675 0200;** www.amalfifiji.com) and **Chefs Restaurant & Bar** (© **675 0197;** www.chefsfiji.com) make a stab at fine dining, but romance at the outdoor tables is often compromised by rock bands which play on the dock after dark.

Biloccino Coffee Lounge (© **675 0065;** daily 8:30am–7:30pm) has decent java but should not be confused with the terrific **Bulaccino in Nadi Town** (see below).

Cardo's Steakhouse & Cocktail Bar ★★ ☞ BARBECUE/GRILL/SEAFOOD   Owner Cardo is known throughout Fiji for providing quality chargrilled steaks and fish, and they're his best offerings here, taken at a multitude of tables on the large deck beside the marina waterway—which can be problematic if it's raining, and deafening when bands play at night. I usually chill over a cold brew after a cruise to the islands. Lunch specials, such as a chargrilled chicken salad, are posted on a blackboard. I ignore the Chinese part of the menu. All in all, Cardo's is the best value on Denarau Island.

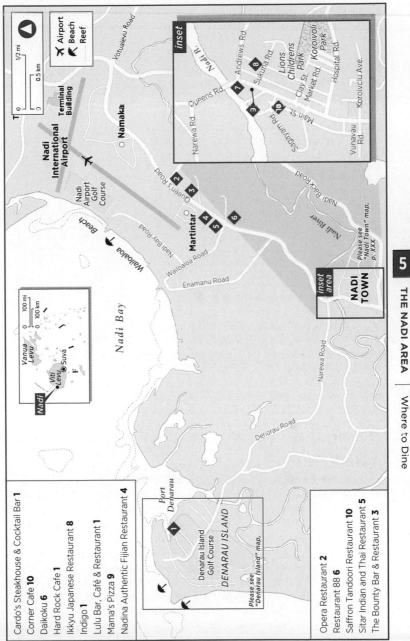

Where to Dine in Nadi

Cardo's Steakhouse & Cocktail Bar **1**
Corner Cafe **10**
Daikoku **6**
Hard Rock Cafe **1**
Ikkyu Japanese Restaurant **8**
Indigo **1**
Lulu Bar, Café & Restaurant **1**
Mama's Pizza **9**
Nadina Authentic Fijian Restaurant **4**

Opera Restaurant **2**
Restaurant 88 **6**
Saffron Tandoori Restaurant **10**
Sitar Indian and Thai Restaurant **5**
The Bounty Bar & Restaurant **3**

Port Denarau. © **675 0900.** Reservations recommended. Breakfast F$4.50–F$10; burgers and sandwiches F$6–F$8; main courses F$22–F$52. AE, MC, V. Daily 7am–10:30pm.

Hard Rock Cafe Fiji AMERICAN/INTERNATIONAL   I am tempted to wear my earplugs to Fiji's first franchise of the famous chain because it's just like the others: loud, hip, relatively expensive, and adorned with autographed rock-'n'-roll memorabilia. In fact, you could be in a Hard Rock in Berlin or Beirut, New York or New Orleans. The menu offers the usual selection of nachos, blackened chicken pasta, huge burgers, and grilled steaks and fish. Unlike many restaurants in Fiji, where you'll get poor imitations, everything here is up to international standards. The fajitas really taste like Mexican fare, for example, and the pulled pork barbecue sandwiches could be from South Carolina.   ·

Port Denarau. © **675 0032.** www.hardrockcafe.com. Reservations recommended. Burgers and sandwiches F$15–F$28; main courses F$23–F$48. AE, MC, V. Daily 11am–10pm.

Indigo ★★★ 🌶 INDIAN/ASIAN   This excellent restaurant with mostly outdoor tables serves some of the country's best and most authentic Indian cuisine. The top (and most expensive) offering is mangrove crab masala, but I prefer the Goan pork curry (an import from Goa, the former Portuguese colony now part of India). The butter chicken is excellent, too. The Asian side of the menu features Thai-style crab and Rendang curry. Vegetarians can choose from among at least eight dishes.

Port Denarau. © **675 0026.** Reservations recommended. Main courses F$13–F$56. AE, MC, V. Daily 11am–10pm.

Lulu Bar, Café & Restaurant ★★ 🌶 AMERICAN/INTERNATIONAL   This hip, open-air cafe is opposite the Port Denarau piers, making it a great stop for breakfast before boarding the shuttle boats to the islands. The creation of Leyla and Mike Dennis (Leyla is American; Mike was born in Fiji to an American mother and New Zealander father), it also offers grab-and-go sandwiches any time and a wide ranging menu of sandwiches, burgers, tapas, and main courses from lunch onward. My cardiologist would have heartily approved of my very good and very healthy dinner of seared tuna served with fresh local fruits seasoned and sautéed as if they were potatoes. The grilled items are very good, including the bacon at breakfast.

Port Denarau. © **672 5858.** Reservations not accepted. Breakfast F$8–F$15; sandwiches F$7–F$17; main courses F$18–F$25. AE, MC, V. Daily 7am–10pm; bar later.

In Nadi Town

Bulaccino ★★★ 🌶 COFFEEHOUSE/DELI/BAKERY   This urbane establishment beside the Nadi River is my favorite place in all of Fiji for breakfast and lunch. Bulaccino's freshly roasted coffee is rich and steamy, the pastries—including the best bagels in Fiji—are fresh from **Nutmeg & Tulips** bakery next door, and the lunchtime offerings are among the finest I've had in Fiji: I am absolutely in love with the warm roasted chicken over a salad of mescaline greens with a lemony dressing. Grilled swordfish with Italian salsa, yellowfin tuna with wasabi mayonnaise, and vegetarian ratatouille are winners, too. You can dine at tables in the air-conditioned shop or under ceiling fans out on a deck overlooking the muddy river. I have only one problem: This exceptional restaurant is not open for dinner.

Queen's Rd. (at Nadi River bridge). © **672 8638.** www.coffee.com.fj. Reservations not accepted. Breakfast F$6.50–F$17; lunch F$11–F$18. MC, V. Mon–Fri 7:30am–4:30pm; Sat–Sun 8am–3pm.

Corner Cafe INTERNATIONAL   Sharing quarters in Jack's Handicrafts with Saffron Tandoori Restaurant (see below), is a fine place to stop for a civilized lunch while shopping in Nadi Town. The menu is limited to hot dogs and hamburgers, sandwiches and salads, pizzas and pastas, and stir-fried dishes. There's usually a lunch special of three small courses. You can also order from the adjacent Saffron's menu (see below).

Sagayam Rd. at Haker Lane (in Jack's of Fiji building). © **670 3131.** www.chefsfiji.com. Most items F$6-F$15. AE, DC, MC, V. Daily 10am-4pm and 5:30-9:30pm.

Ikkyu Japanese Restaurant JAPANESE   This little restaurant on a Nadi Town backstreet looks like a house, and it is in fact the home of Chef Takafuji Shimizu, who immigrated here from Japan. He serves either on an enclosed veranda or in a Japanese dining room, where you sit on the floor. Takafuji prepares sushi, sashimi, tempura, udon noodles and miso in the traditional Japanese ways. Teriyaki-style tuna is my favorite. Make sure Takafuji is here and cooking when you call for reservations. His is very good home cooking but not the professional quality at Daikoku (see below).

Sakuna Rd. at Lodhia St., Nadi Town. © **670 2722.** Reservations recommended. Sushi and sashimi F$3-F$22; main courses F$13-F$17. No credit cards. Mon-Sat 11:30am-2pm and 6-9:30pm; Sun 6-9:30pm.

Mama's Pizza ITALIAN   If you need a tomato sauce fix, follow the aroma of garlic to Robin O'Donnell's establishment. Her wood-fired pizzas range from a small plain model to a large deluxe version with all the toppings. Just remember that this is Nadi, not New York or Naples, so adjust your expectations accordingly. She also has spaghetti with tomato-and-meat sauce, lasagna, and fresh salads. Two other locations of Mama's Pizzas are at Port Denarau (© **675 0533**) and in the Colonial Plaza shopping mall on the Queen's Road north of Martintar (© **672 0922**).

Queen's Rd., opposite Mobil Station. © **670 0221.** Pizzas F$8-28; pastas F$10-F$12. MC, V. Daily 10am-11pm.

Saffron Tandoori Restaurant ★★ NORTHERN INDIAN/VEGETAR-IAN   Sharing a dining room with the Corner Cafe (see above), this restaurant serves some of Fiji's best Tandoori cooking—chicken and lamb baked in a clay oven in the style of northern India and Pakistan. The menu also features a number of vegetarian and other dishes from around the subcontinent. You'll be greeted with a complimentary basket of crispy *papadam* chips (made from an Indian flatbread) with dipping sauce. The Punjabi chicken *tikka* is great, although I'm addicted to the smooth butter chicken curry.

Sagayam Rd. at Haker Lane (in Jack's of Fiji building). © **670 3131.** www.chefsfiji.com. Reservations accepted. Main courses F$12-F$53. AE, DC, MC, V. Daily 10am-4pm and 5:30-9:30pm.

In Martintar

The suburban version of **Mama's Pizza** resides in the rear of the Colonial Plaza shopping center on the Queen's Road between Martintar and Namaka (© **672 0922**). It has the same menu, prices, and hours as its Nadi Town mama (see above).

The local **McDonald's** is on the Queen's Road at Emananu Road, between Nadi Town and Martintar.

The Bounty Bar & Restaurant BARBECUE/GRILL   Once among the best restaurants in Nadi, this informal pub is now primarily a civilized drinking establishment, especially during happy hour (5–8pm) and on weekend evenings. The best menu items are the grilled steaks and large burgers.

Queen's Rd., Martintar. ☏ **672 0840.** www.bountyfiji.com. Reservations accepted. Main courses F$16–F$33. AE, MC, V. Daily 7:30am–11pm.

Daikoku ★★ JAPANESE   There are two dining areas at this authentic restaurant, which was prefabricated in Japan and reconstructed here. Downstairs is the sushi bar, which uses only the freshest salmon, tuna, shrimp, and lobster, but I'm a devotee of the upstairs teppanyaki room, where the chef will stir-fry vegetables, shrimp, chicken, or extraordinarily tender beef as you watch. You can also order sukiyaki, udon, and other traditional Japanese dishes. Fiji's best Nipponese cuisine is here.

Queen's Rd., Martintar (at Northern Press Rd.). ☏ **672 3622.** www.daikokufiji.com. Reservations recommended. Sushi and sashimi F$6–F$29; main courses F$12–F$29. AE, DC, MC, V. Daily noon–2pm and 6–9:30pm.

Nadina Authentic Fijian Restaurant ★★★ PACIFIC RIM   Nadi lacked a really good Fijian restaurant until proprietor Amy Suvan opened this one in a small wooden cottage with wraparound porch and a traditional *bure* in the front yard. Amy's chef excels in traditional fare such as *kokoda* (raw fish marinated in lime juice and served with fresh vegetables) and *kovu walu* (Spanish mackerel steamed with coconut milk in banana leaves). Nadina is the only place I know that regularly serves *miti,* the crunchy young shoots of the wood fern—delicious served with coconut milk. Some ordinarily bland Fijian dishes are spiced up for those with worldly tastes, and you can get a good curry here, too. Amy does not accept credit cards, nor does she serve alcohol, but you can bring your own from the big Airpointe supermarket across the road or from the bottle shop at the nearby Mercure Hotel Nadi.

Queen's Rd., Martintar (opposite Capricorn International Hotel). ☏ **672 7313.** Reservations recommended. Main courses F$17–F$68. No credit cards. Daily 7am–10pm.

Opera Restaurant INDIAN   The only Martintar restaurant open after 10pm, this inexpensive family-run establishment serves good home-cooked curries accompanied by hot-off-the-griddle *roti* (pancake-like Indian bread). A few specials such as garlic prawns are offered daily, but I stick to the chicken, shrimp, and vegetarian curries, all cooked to order in the Fiji style. They are ordinarily very spicy so ask the cook to turn down the heat. There is a dining room but I prefer to sit at white plastic tables outside despite the traffic noise from the Queen's Road.

Queen's Rd., Martintar (opposite Rosie Tours bldg.). ☏ **672 1022.** Reservations accepted. Main courses F$7–F$20. No credit cards. Daily 9:30am–11pm.

Restaurant 88 ★ ASIAN   This large upstairs room was a garment factory until émigrés from Singapore converted it into this restaurant. A wall-size photo of the Singapore waterfront attests to their origins, as do their Singaporean-influenced Chinese dishes and choices from nearby countries in Southeast Asia. Peking ducks hanging in the glassed-in kitchen become very good meals here, and the Thai fired chicken in curry and coconut sauce is excellent. The service is attentive and efficient, but this is no place for romance since the room is large and the overhead lights not always dim.

Northern Press Rd., Martintar. ✆ **672 6688.** Reservations accepted. Main courses F$12–F$70. MC, V. Mon–Sat 11am–3pm and 6–10pm; Sun 9am–2pm and 6–10pm.

Sitar Indian and Thai Restaurant ★★★ INDIAN/THAI Part of a small Australian chain of restaurants founded by a family originally from Bangladesh, Sitar combines authentic cooking from the subcontinent with the ambience of an Aussie pub. There is an air-conditioned dining room, but most tables—including some chest-high models designed more for drinking than eating—are under pavilions or umbrellas out on a large patio. Both the Indian and Thai cuisine are exceptional here, especially the chicken tikka from the Tandoori oven. All ingredients are fresh, and the chefs use only canola oil and no MSG. A lively, open-air bar with a big sports TV makes this a good place to slake a thirst as well as satisfy an appetite. Bands make music on weekend evenings.

Queen's Rd., Martintar (at Wailoaloa Rd.). ✆ **672 7722.** www.sitar.com.au. Reservations accepted. Main courses F$12–F$24. AE, MC, V. Daily 11am–5pm and 5:30–10pm.

Special Dining Experiences

For a scenic dining experience, you can sail out on Nadi Bay with **Captain Cook Cruises** (✆ **670 1823;** www.captaincook.com.au). While you dine on rather ordinary Australian fare, Fijians serenade you with island music. The boat departs from Port Denarau Tuesday and Saturday at noon for lunch, daily at 5:30pm for dinner. The lunch cruises cost F$59 for adults, while dinner cruises are F$99, or F$133 including lobster. Children 3 to 15 pay half fare on either cruise, while those 2 and under eat for free. Reservations are required.

　First Landing Beach Resort & Villas (✆ **666 6171;** see "Where to Stay in Nadi," earlier in this chapter) offers dinner excursions by boat from Denarau Island to its pleasant outdoor dining area near Vuda Point for F$110 to F$149 per person. The higher price includes lobster as the main course, instead of fish or steak. *Note:* You must make reservations.

ISLAND NIGHTS IN NADI

The large hotels usually have something going on every night. This might be a special meal followed by a Fijian dance show, and the large hotels also frequently offer live entertainment in their bars during the cocktail hour. Check with the hotel activities desk to see what's happening.

　With several pubs, Martintar is Nadi's most civilized nightlife center, with several of its restaurants providing live music, especially on weekend nights. See "Where to Dine in Nadi," above. Among them, **Sitar Indian and Thai Restaurant** (✆ **672 6622)** is the most pleasant, with plentiful outdoor tables, live music, and a sports TV over its bar. The **Bounty Bar & Restaurant** (✆ **672 0840)** draws many expatriates and has live music on weekend nights. Across the Queen's Road, the outdoor tables at **Ed's Bar** (✆ **672 4650)** are popular with locals.

　Out on Denarau Island, bands play every evening except Sunday along the outdoor patio surrounding the restaurants at Port Denarau.

THE MAMANUCA & YASAWA ISLANDS

The Great Sea Reef off northwest Viti Levu encloses a huge lagoon where usually calm waters surround the nearby Mamanuca and Yasawa island groups with speckled shades of yellow, green, and blue. With ample sunshine and some of Fiji's best beaches, these little islands are great places to escape from the hustle of modern civilization.

The **Mamanuca Group,** as it's officially known, consists of small flat atolls and hilly islands ranging from 8 to 32km (5–20 miles) west of Nadi. Day cruises have made the Mamanucas a destination since the dawn of Fiji's modern tourism in the early 1960s; these islands are home to some of the country's oldest offshore resorts, which are still very popular among Australians and New Zealanders on 1- or 2-week holidays.

The Mamanucas generally are divided into two sections. To the north are a group of flat, tiny sand islands that barely break the lagoon's surface. Three of them are within virtual hailing distance, including **Tai Island,** better known for the rollicking Beachcomber Island Resort; **Elevuka,** home to family-oriented Treasure Island Resort; and **Kadavu,** shared by a nature preserve and Bounty Island Resort.

To the south, a row of hilly islands begins with **Malololailai,** which is nearly joined to the larger **Malolo.** Each has three resorts. Next to Malolo lie tiny **Wadigi Island,** a favorite getaway for celebrities, and **Qalito Island,** which is better known as Castaway for its lone hotel, Castaway Island Resort. Beyond them, **Mana Island** has one of the group's larger resorts as well as low-budget properties, all sharing a great beach. The Mamanucas end to the west with **Matamanoa** and **Tokoriki** islands, both with resorts, and the beautiful, uninhabited **Monuriki,** where Tom Hanks starred in the movie *Castaway.*

North of the Mamanucas, the **Yasawa Islands** stretch as much as 100km (62 miles) from Nadi. Lt. Charles Wilkes, commander of the

U.S. exploring expedition that charted Fiji in 1840, described the Yasawa Islands as "a string of blue beads lying along the horizon."

For the most part, Fijians still live in small villages huddled among the curving coconut palms beside lagoons with excellent snorkeling and some of the country's most awesomely beautiful beaches. But the Yasawas are changing rapidly, with more than two dozen small resorts spanning all price ranges. Particularly prolific are the low-budget establishments aimed at young backpackers, who now see a bit of beach time in the Yasawas as an essential part of their Fiji experience. In fact, rather than tour around Fiji, many backpackers today simply head for the Yasawas.

While accommodations are spread throughout the Yasawa chain, the largest concentration is on the shores of the so-called **Blue Lagoon,** a lovely baylike body of water nearly enclosed by **Matacawalevu, Nacula, Nanuya Lailai, Tavewa,** and **Nanuya Levu** islands.

GETTING TO THE ISLANDS

While a few run their own transfer boats, the Mamanuca and Yasawa resorts arrange third-party transfers for their guests. All of them require reservations, and most leave from the Port Denarau marina.

By Plane & Helicopter

The quickest, easiest, and most expensive way to the islands is via seaplane or helicopter. **Pacific Island Seaplanes** (© 672 5643; www.fijiseaplanes.com) and **Turtle Airways** (© 672 1888; www.turtleairways.com) provide seaplane service to the islands. Their flights are on a charter basis arranged by the resorts, which will also quote you prices. Turtle Airways has been charging F$220 each way to the Yasawas, which makes flying one or both ways a viable alternative to the long rides on the *Yasawa Flyer* (see "By Shuttle Boat," below).

Island Hoppers (© 672 0140; www.helicopters.com.fj) flies its helicopters between Nadi airport and most of the moderate and expensive resorts. Expect to pay about F$360 per person each way to the Mamanucas.

Only Malololailai and Mana islands have airstrips in the Mamanucas, both served by **Pacific Sun** (© 672 0888). See "Getting Around Fiji," in chapter 3. There is an airstrip on Yasawa Island, but it's a private affair for Yasawa Island Resort and Spa.

By Shuttle Boat

Most folks take one of the fast, air-conditioned catamarans providing daily shuttle service from Port Denarau to and from the islands. Only a few offshore resorts have piers, so be prepared to get your feet wet wading ashore.

TO THE MAMANUCA ISLANDS

The **Malolo Cat** (© 675 0205) runs daily between Port Denarau and Malololailai, home to Musket Cove, Plantation Island, and Lomani resorts. One-way fare is about F$60.

Most travelers take one of three fast catamarans operated between Port Denarau and the islands by **South Sea Cruises** (© 675 0500; www.ssc.com.fj). The *Tiger IV* and the *Cheetah* depart for most of the Mamanuca resorts three times daily,

The Mamanuca & Yasawa Islands

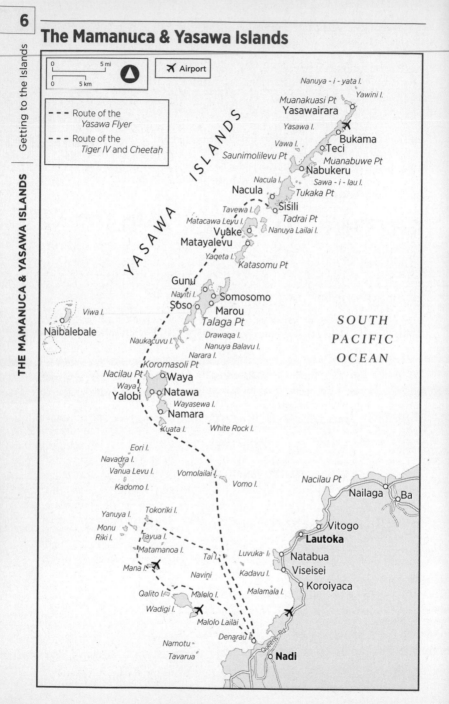

✈ **Airport**

0   5 mi
0   5 km

- - - Route of the
      Yasawa Flyer
- - - Route of the
      Tiger IV and *Cheetah*

Nanuya - i - yata I.

Yawini I.

Muanakuasi Pt

Yasawairara

Yasawa I.

Bukama

Vawa I.

Teci

Saunimolilevu Pt

Muanabuwe Pt

Nabukeru

Nacula I.

Sawa - i - lau I.

Nacula

Tukaka Pt

Sisili

Tavewa I.

Matacawa Levu I.

Tadrai Pt

Vuake

Nanuya Lailai I.

Matayalevu

Yaqeta I.

Katasomu Pt

Gunu

Naviti I.

Somosomo

Soso

Marou

Talaga Pt

Viwa I.

Drawaqa I.

SOUTH

PACIFIC

OCEAN

Naibalebale

Nanuya Balavu I.

Naukacuvu I.

Narara I.

Koromasoli Pt

Nacilau Pt

Waya

Waya I.

Natawa

Yalobi

Wayasewa I.

Namara

Kuata I.

White Rock I.

Eori I.

Navadra I.

Vanua Levu I.

Vomolailai I.

Kadomo I.

Vomo I.

Nacilau Pt

Nailaga

Ba

Vitogo

Lautoka

Yanuya I.

Tokoriki I.

Monu

Tayua I.

Natabua

Riki I.

Luvuka I.

Matamanoa I.

Tai I.

Viseisei

Kadavu I.

Mana I.

Navini

Koroiyaca

Malamala I.

Qalito I.

Malolo I.

Wadigi I.

Malolo Lailai

Namotu

Denarau I.

Tavarua

Nadi

Queens Rd

Take a Big Boat

Some inexpensive properties may offer to take you to the islands in their own small craft for less money than you would pay on the *Tiger IV,* the *Cheetah,* or the *Yasawa Flyer.* These rides take at least an hour to the Mamanucas, several hours to the Yasawas. Treasure Island Resort, Bounty Island Resort, Octopus Resort, and a few others provide their own alternative transfers in seaworthy boats (see the "Where to Stay" sections, below). Others can be small, poorly equipped, and perhaps lacking covers to protect you from the elements. One of them sank a few years ago, fortunately without any loss of life. Take my advice and board one of the fast catamarans.

usually 9am, 12:15pm, and 3:15pm. The *Tiger IV* normally serves the islands as far as Mana, while the *Cheetah* goes as far as Matamanoa and Tokoriki islands. One-way fares are about F$140. For a bit extra, you can ride up in the captain's lounge and have someone bring you refreshments.

SeaFiji (© 672 5961; www.seafiji.net) provides 24-hour water-taxi service to the Mamanuca Islands from Port Denarau.

TO THE YASAWA ISLANDS

Often packed with young travelers, the bright yellow **Yasawa Flyer** (© 675 0500; www.ssc.com.fj)—or "The Yellow Boat," as it is known in the islands—makes one voyage daily to the Yasawas, northbound in the morning, southbound in the afternoon. Departing from Port Denarau at 8:30am, it goes as far north as Nacula Island, a 4½-hour voyage from Port Denarau, and returns to Port Denarau at 5:30pm via the same route. Round-trip fares range from F$111 to F$138 per person, depending on the distance from Port Denarau. The Yasawa resorts dispatch boats as small as skiffs to retrieve their guests from the *Yasawa Flyer* when it stops near them. You will wade ashore when you get to your hotel.

If you don't already have rooms reserved, a tour desk on the *Yasawa Flyer* will do it for you.

The *Yasawa Flyer* is operated by **Awesome Adventures Fiji** (© 670 5006; www.awesomefiji.com), which has a myriad of transportation-and-accommodation packages to the Yasawas. For example, its "Bula Pass" allows unlimited rides for 7, 14, and 21 days. These cost F$391, F$535, and F$628 per person, respectively. A "Bula Combo Pass" adds accommodations. These range from about F$871 to F$2,228 for a double room, or from F$781 to F$1,928 for a dorm bed. Most backpacker-oriented establishments include meals, but you will pay extra for them at the more upscale resorts.

DAY TRIPS FROM NADI

Even if you're laying over in Fiji for just a short time, you should get out to the islands for a day from Nadi or the Coral Coast. Most of the trips mentioned below depart from the Port Denarau marina on Denarau Island. Bus transportation from the Nadi or Coral Coast hotels to the marina is included in their prices (you'll pay more from the Coral Coast). Children pay half fare on all the day trips.

Sand Between My Toes

Nothing relaxes me more than digging my toes into the sand at one of Fiji's small get-away-from-it-all resorts. If I have a day to spare in Nadi, I head out to Beachcomber Island Resort, where the floor of the bar and dining room is nothing but sand. And with all those young folks running around out on the beach, I feel like I'm 25 again.

TO THE MAMANUCA ISLANDS

My favorite day-trip provider is **Beachcomber Day Cruises** ★★★ (℡ 666 1500; www.beachcomberfiji.com), which goes to youth-oriented Beachcomber Island Resort (see "Resorts in the Mamanuca Islands," below). Despite the advent of so many inexpensive properties elsewhere, Beachcomber still is a most popular stop for young people seeking sand, sun, and suds—but beware if you have fundamentalist eyes: Young European women have been known to drop their tops at Beachcomber. You'll pay F$105 for bus transportation, the cruise, and an all-you-can-eat buffet lunch on Beachcomber Island. Swimming is free, but snorkeling gear, scuba diving, and other activities cost extra.

Storck Cruises (℡ 925 5336; www.storckcruises.com) uses the comfortable, double-decker *Oolala* to cruise to Savala, a private sand islet off Lautoka, which is a wildlife sanctuary. The island's only human inhabitants will be you and your fellow passengers, who can go snorkeling over protected reefs. The F$169 price includes lunch and snorkel gear.

You will have more options on **Malololailai Island,** home of Plantation Island, Musket Cove, and Lomani resorts. You can visit them on a day cruise via the *Malololo Cat* (℡ 672 0744) for about F$60 round-trip, or fly over on **Pacific Sun** (℡ 672 0888) for about F$116 round-trip. You can hang out at the two resorts, shop at Georgie Czukelter's **Art Gallery** (no phone) on the hill above Musket Cove, and dine at **Anandas Restaurant and Bar** (℡ 672 2333) by the airstrip. You can book at the restaurant to play the island's short 9-hole **golf course;** fees are F$20.

Adrenalin Watersports (℡ 675 1288; www.adrenalinfiji.com) has jet-ski safaris from Port Denarau to Bounty Island Resort for F$85 adults, F$45 for kids 6 to 15.

You can sightsee through the Mamanucas on the *Tiger IV* (see "Getting to the Islands," above). The half-day sightseeing-only voyage costs about F$90. I prefer taking the morning voyage, getting off at **South Sea Island, Malolo Island Resort, Castaway Island Resort, Mana Island Resort,** or **Bounty Island** (see "Resorts in the Mamanuca Islands," below, before making your decision). These sailings include a buffet lunch, swimming, and sunbathing. Depending on where you spend the day, these cost between F$135 and F$180.

TO THE YASAWA ISLANDS

You can ride the *Yasawa Flyer* (℡ 675 0500; www.ssc.com.fj) on its daily voyages to the Yasawas and get off at Wayalailai, Octopus, or Botaira resorts, have lunch, and catch the Yellow Boat back in the afternoon. These excursions range from F$130 to F$190, depending on how far you go and whether you have lobster for lunch. See "Where to Stay in Yasawa Islands," below, for descriptions of the resorts.

SAILING THROUGH THE ISLANDS

I hesitate to use such a well-worn cliché as "reef-strewn," but that's the most precise way to describe Fiji's waters—so strewn, in fact, that the government does not allow you to charter a "bareboat" yacht (without a skipper). It's just too dangerous. You can rent both boat and skipper or local guide for extended cruises through the islands. The marina at **Musket Cove Island Resort & Marina** (see "Resorts in the Mamanuca Islands," below) is a mecca for cruising yachts, some of whose skippers take charters for a living. Contact the resort for details.

On the other hand, you can easily get out on the lagoons under sail for a day. Most interesting to my mind is the **MV Seaspray** ★★ (ⓒ **675 0500;** www.ssc.com.fj), a 25m (83-ft.) schooner that starred in the 1960s TV series *Adventures in Paradise,* based on James A. Michener's short stories. Based at Mana Island, it sails through the outer Mamanucas and stops for swimming and snorkeling at the same beach on rocky **Monuriki Island** upon which Tom Hanks filmed the movie *Castaway.* (Hanks, by the way, did *not* live on the islet all by himself during production). The cruises range from F$150 to F$195, depending on where you board, including morning tea, lunch, beer, wine, and soft drinks. You pay more to come out from Port Denarau to Mana on the *Tiger IV,* less from the Mamanuca resorts.

The **Whale's Tale** (ⓒ **672 2455;** funcruises@connect.com.fj), a luxury, 30m (100-ft.) auxiliary sailboat, takes no more than 12 guests on day cruises from Port Denarau through the Mamanucas. The F$180 per-person cost includes a continental breakfast with champagne on departure; a buffet lunch prepared on board; and all beverages, including beer, wine, liquor, and sunset cocktails. The *Whale's Tale* is also available for charters ranging from 1 day in the Mamanucas to 3 days and 2 nights in the Yasawas. Rates vary according to the length of the trip.

Captain Cook Cruises (ⓒ **670 1823;** www.captaincook.com.fj) uses the *Ra Marama,* a 33m (110-ft.) square-rigged brigantine built in Singapore during the 1950s and once the official yacht of Fiji's colonial governors-general, for the 1-hour sail out to Tivua Island, an uninhabited 1.6-hectare (4-acre) islet in the Mamanucas. A traditional Fijian welcoming ceremony greets you at the island, where you can swim, snorkel, and canoe over 200 hectares (500 acres) of surrounding coral gardens (or see the colors from a glass-bottom boat). Lunch and drinks are included in the F$139 charge.

💬 Drop-Dead Good Looks

The late actor Gardner McKay, who sailed around on the MV *Seaspray* while starring as Capt. Adam Troy, walked away from the boob tube after the popular TV series *Adventures in Paradise* bit the dust in the 1960s. At first he opted for real dust—as in riding across the Sahara Desert with the Egyptian Camel Corps. He went on to crew on yachts in the Caribbean and hike the Amazonian jungles before settling down as a novelist, poet, playwright, and newspaper drama critic. Despite his drop-dead good looks, he never acted again.

Captain Cook Cruises also sends its tall-ship *Spirit of the Pacific* on 3- and 4-day **Fiji Windjammer Barefoot Cruises** (℃ 670 1823; www.fijisailingsafari.com.fj) to the Yasawas. It sails during daylight, with stops for snorkeling and visits to a Fijian village. At night it deposits you ashore at its Barefoot Lodge on Drawaqa Island, where you stay in clean but basic bures. The units do not have bathrooms, so you will share facilities. Safaris start at F$599 per person double-occupancy including meals.

CRUISING THROUGH THE ISLANDS

The Australian-based **Captain Cook Cruises** (℃ 670 1823; www.captaincook. com.fj) uses the 120-passenger MV *Reef Escape* for most of its 3- to 7-night cruises from Port Denarau to the Mamanucas and Yasawas. The *Reef Escape* has a swimming pool, spa, and sauna.

Blue Lagoon Cruises (℃ 666 1622; www.bluelagooncruises.com) began in the 1950s when Captain Trevor Withers—who had worked on the original 1949 *Blue Lagoon* movie starring Jean Simmons—converted an American crash vessel and began running trips to the islands. His successors sold the company to Fijian interests, who have taken it down from its former lofty perch as the best cruise experience in the South Pacific islands.

In fact, Blue Lagoon Cruises recently cancelled some cruises at the last minute because it did not have enough passengers to make each voyage profitable. This nearsighted, inexcusable practice is enough for me to recommend Captain Cook Cruises instead.

Most voyages on both lines range from 3 to 7 nights through the Yasawas, with Captain Cook Cruises also venturing off into northern Fiji (see chapters 13 and 14). Trips explore the islands, stopping in little bays for snorkeling, picnics, or *lovo* feasts (featuring food cooked underground in a freshly dug pit oven) on sandy beaches, and visits with the Yasawans in their villages. The ships anchor in peaceful coves at night, and even when they cruise from island to island, the water is usually so calm that only incurable landlubbers get seasick.

Fares can start at A$700 per person double occupancy depending on the discount, the length of the voyage, the season, and the cabin's location. Diving cruises cost more. All meals, activities, and taxes are included. Singles and children staying in their parents' cabins pay supplements. Check the websites for details.

Island Pickups by Captain Cook Cruises

Captain Cook Cruises will pick up its passengers from some Mamanuca resorts at the beginning of each trip, which Blue Lagoon Cruises does not. The ships always return directly to Port Denarau at the end. In other words, you can stay at one of the resorts and depart on your Captain Cook cruise directly from there.

MAMANUCA ISLAND RESORTS

The **Mamanuca Hotel Association,** Private Mail Bag, Nadi Airport (℃ **670 0144;** fax 670 2336; www.fijiresorts.com), has information about most of the resorts.

They all have watersports and scuba dive operators on premises. **Subsurface Fiji Diving and Watersports** (℃ **666 6738;** www.subsurfacefiji.com), a PADI five-star operation, staffs more than a dozen of the resorts, while **Awesome Adventures Fiji** (℃ **670 5006;** www.awesomefiji.com) is at Mana Island Resort.

Also here is **South Sea Island** (℃ **675 0500,** www.ssc.com.fj), which like Beachcomber Island Resort (see below) occupies a tiny islet. It has dormitory accommodations and is included in the Awesome Adventures packages (see "Getting to the Island," above), but it is primarily a day-trip destination.

Near the main pass through the Great Sea Reef, the American-operated **Tavarua Island Resort** (℃ **805/687-4551** in the U.S., or 670 6513; www.tavarua.com) caters to anyone but is still Fiji's best-known surf camp. Tavarua has an outdoor pool, so "surfing widows" (or widowers) can enjoy reasonable luxuries while their other halves are out riding the waves.

Another small islet off Lautoka is home to the 10-unit **Navini Island Resort** (℃ **666 2188;** www.navinifiji.com.fj), which does its own transfers rather than rely on the *Tiger IV.* It's on a small sand islet.

The resorts are organized by the islands on which they reside, in alphabetical order. Consult the map to see which resorts are closest to Viti Levu.

Eluvuka (Treasure) Island

This tiny atoll-like islet is nearly surrounded by a white-sand beach (a stroll of 15 min. or less brings you back to your starting point). The name Eluvuka is seldom used, since locals call it simply "Treasure" because it is completely occupied by this one resort.

Treasure Island Resort ☺ This venerable resort is geared to couples and families rather than to the sometimes-raucous singles who frequent its neighbor, Beachcomber Island Resort (see later in this chapter). Pathways through tropical shrubs pass playgrounds for both adults and children, a sea turtle breeding pool, and a minigolf course—all of which, along with the air-conditioned kids' center, makes this a good choice for families. For those wishing to start one, the resort has a glass-wall wedding chapel with a lagoon view. Treasure's 33 duplex bungalows hold 66 bright rooms. An on-going program is upgrading them to have outdoor showers. All face the beach and have both a queen-size and single bed, and a porch facing the lagoon. An airy beachside building housing the restaurant and bar opens to two swimming pools, one an attractive, partially shaded infinity model. Guests pay extra for motorized activities and to visit Beachcomber Island Resort.

P.O. Box 2210, Lautoka. ℃ **672 7002** or 666 1599. Fax 672 1444. www.treasure.com.fj. 67 units. F$570–F$775 double. AE, MC, V. **Amenities:** Restaurant; bar; babysitting; children's center; 2 outdoor pools; room service; spa; tennis court; watersports equipment/rentals; Wi-Fi (F$8/hour). *In room:* A/C, ceiling fan, fridge, hair dryer.

Where to Stay in the Mamanuca Islands

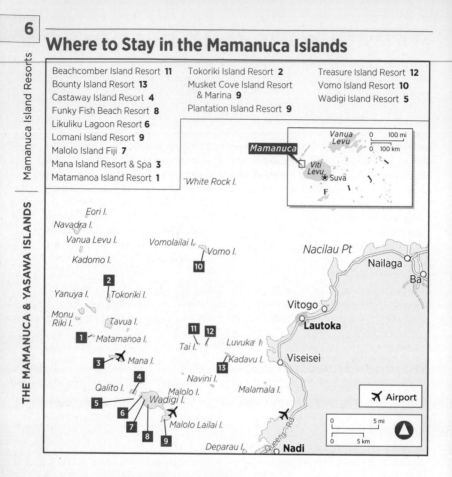

Beachcomber Island Resort **11**
Bounty Island Resort **13**
Castaway Island Resort **4**
Funky Fish Beach Resort **8**
Likuliku Lagoon Resort **6**
Lomani Island Resort **9**
Malolo Island Fiji **7**
Mana Island Resort & Spa **3**
Matamanoa Island Resort **1**

Tokoriki Island Resort **2**
Musket Cove Island Resort & Marina **9**
Plantation Island Resort **9**

Treasure Island Resort **12**
Vomo Island Resort **10**
Wadigi Island Resort **5**

Kadavu (Bounty) Island

Not to be confused with the larger Kadavu Island south of Viti Levu (see chapter 9), this one is near Treasure Island and Beachcomber Island resorts. It's a flat, 19-hectare (48-acre) island, of which more than half is a nature preserve with birdlife, a sea turtle nursery, the remains of an ancient Fijian village, and a house built for the BBC TV series "Celebrity Love Island," which filmed here a few years ago.

Bounty Island Resort   While Beachcomber Island continues to be the most popular Mamanuca resort among young, budget-minded travelers, you can get away from the crowds without paying a fortune at this no-frills hotel. A main building with a restaurant and bar opens to a swimming pool beside a very good beach. The 22 beachside bungalows are rather simple, but they all have bathrooms and are clean and comfortable. Half of them are air-conditioned and all have electric fans and screened, louvered windows to take advantage of the prevailing southeast trade winds. One of the three dormitories is air-conditioned, which attracts backpackers enjoying their last few days in the islands. There may be some construction going on, for the owners have announced plans to upgrade the property, including 60 units with kitchens.

P.O. Box 2210, Lautoka. © **628 3387** or 628 3390. Fax 666 6955. www.fiji-bounty.com. 22 units, 72 dorm beds. F$170–F$180 double; F$84–F$89 dorm bed. MC, V. **Amenities:** Restaurant; bar; Internet (F$8/hour); outdoor pool; watersports equipment/rentals. *In room:* A/C (11 units), ceiling fan, fridge, no phone.

Malololailai Island

The closest island to Nadi, boomerang-shape Malololailai faces a shallow bay. This is the one island in the Mamanucas where you can stay at one resort and wander over to another for dinner or drinks. As I noted under "Seeing the Islands on Day Trips from Nadi," above, you can also browse Georgie Czukelter's **Art Gallery,** shop for groceries and have dinner at **Anandas Restaurant and Bar** (© **672 2333**) near the airport, and play a short 9-hole golf course. The dirt airstrip divides the island into two, with Musket Cove Island Resort & Marina on one end, and Lomani Island Resort and Plantation Island Resort on the other. Lomani and Plantation resorts share one of Fiji's best beaches (shallow though the lagoon may be at low tide), while scores of cruising yachts put into Musket Cove from April into October.

Lomani Island Resort ★   This small boutique hotel is next door to Plantation Island Resort and shares its long, picturesque beach. The main building formerly was a private residence but now houses a comfy guest lounge, restaurant, and bar in an innlike atmosphere. Serving good international fare, the dining room opens to a 35m-long (115-ft.) pool—plenty of room to swim your laps. You can also dine poolside or by the beach. The best units here are five individual bungalows privately situated on the far end of the property. Built in 2010, they have outdoor showers and beachside porches. Of the other units, my choice would be a Hibiscus suite, which are all in duplex buildings. The Deluxe Suites are in two-story motel-like buildings, but they do have separate bedrooms, which the Hibiscus Suites do not. Guests here have full use of Plantation Island's facilities, but guests there can only use the spa and dine here. This is the most intimate resort on Malololailai Island.

P.O. Box 9732, Nadi Airport. © **666 8212.** Fax 666 8523. www.lomaniisland.com. 12 units. F$630–F$740 double. Rates include full breakfast. AE, MC, V. **Amenities:** Restaurant; bar; outdoor pool; room service; spa; watersports equipment/rentals; Wi-Fi (F$75/week). *In room:* A/C, ceiling fan, TV/DVD, fridge, hair dryer.

Musket Cove Island Resort & Marina   Founded in 1977, this retreat has grown to include Fiji's most popular marina for cruising yachties from June to September. They congregate at an open-air bar under a thatched roof out on a tiny man-made island reached by the marina's pontoons. The pleasant bar and restaurant open to two swimming pools, one with a real yacht protruding from its side, as if it has run aground. Although a broad mud bank appears here at low tide, a dredged area provides a swimmable beach area. Accommodations range from charming one-room bures for couples to luxury villas with living rooms, full kitchens, master bedrooms downstairs, and two bedrooms upstairs, each with its own private bathroom. Musket Cove also manages Armstrong Villas at Musket Cove, a group of two-bedroom condo bungalows on a man-made island; the units have kitchens and phones. Check the website and consult with the reservationist when booking your unit to make sure you'll have the in-room amenities you desire.

Private Mail Bag, Nadi Airport. © **666 2215.** Fax 666 2633. www.musketcovefiji.com. 55 units. F$495–F$604 bungalow; F$742 villa. AE, MC, V. **Amenities:** 2 restaurants; 2 bars; bikes; babysitting; 2 outdoor pools; spa; watersports equipment/rentals; Wi-Fi (in main building; F$5/hour). *In room:* A/C (in villas only), ceiling fan, fridge, hair dryer, kitchen (in villas only), MP3 docking station, no phone (in bungalows).

Plantation Island Resort ☺ The oldest, largest, and most diverse of the Mamanuca resorts, Plantation primarily attracts Australian couples and families, plus day-trippers from Nadi. Like Mana Island Resort & Spa (see below), it has a Club Med–style atmosphere of nonstop activity. The resort has several types of accommodations: duplex bures suitable for singles or couples, two-bedroom bungalows for families, and motel-style rooms. Some are next to the beach, others surround a swimming pool, and the rest are removed from the resort action. A large central building beside the beach has a bar, dance floor, lounge area, restaurant, and coffee shop. A children's playroom with a full-time babysitter makes this another good choice for families.

P.O. Box 9176, Nadi Airport. © **666 9333.** Fax 666 9200. www.plantationisland.com. 192 units. F$281–F$404 double; F$465–F$606 bungalow. AE, DC, MC, V. **Amenities:** 2 restaurants; 2 bars; babysitting; children's center; 3 outdoor pools; tennis courts; watersports equipment/rentals; Wi-Fi (F$13/hour). *In room:* A/C, ceiling fan, fridge.

Malolo Island

Joined at low tide to its smaller sister, Malololailai (Little Malolo), this island is one of the largest of the Mamanucas. Malolo is hilly with a serrated coastline dotted with beaches. Fijians live in traditional villages on the eastern side, while the west coast is occupied by resorts in all price ranges. You can hike into the hills but not from one resort to the other to have a meal or drink.

You likely will see advertisements in Fiji for inexpensive **Walu Beach Resort** (© **665 1777;** www.walubeach.com), on Malolo's western side, which began life as a time share operation but ran into trouble with its Fijian landowners. I went through it during my most recent visit to Fiji, and I found it to be falling apart. Until it gets new owners with a ton of cash for repairs, I would stay elsewhere.

Funky Fish Beach Resort Former New Zealand All Black Rugby star and coach of the Fijian and Italian national teams Brad Johnstone decided he was tired of cold weather and so, with his wife, Rosemary, created this "flashpacker" resort—flashpackers being backpackers looking for more than cheap hostels. They put their main building with casual, sand-floor restaurant and bar up on a hill to take advantage of a fine sea view. The outdoor pool and accommodations are down beside the beach. They do have a regular dorm (the coed, 12-bunk "Octopussy Lodge"), but they also have five "Thorny Oyster" private dorm rooms with ceiling fans. Each of their 10

Ask About Meal Plans

Except on Malololailai Island, where you can walk among Musket Cove, Plantation, and Lomani resorts, you will have no choice but to dine in your resort's or hostel's restaurant. Be sure to ask if it has meal packages available, which usually are less expensive than paying separately for each meal.

"Rock Lobster" bures has a bedroom and private bathroom with outdoor shower. Atop the heap, each of the "Grand Grouper" units has two bedrooms and a private bathroom, also with outdoor shower. Although its guest rooms are spacious enough for families, the resort has no children's program.

P.O. Box 11053, Nadi Airport. ℭ **651 3180.** Fax 651 6180. www.funkyfishresort.com. 17 units (12 with bathroom), 12 dorm beds. F$101–F$317 bungalow; F$99 dorm room; F$35 dorm bed. MC, V. **Amenities:** Restaurant; bar; Internet (F34¢/min.); watersports equipment/rentals. *In room:* Ceiling fan, fridge (2 units), no phone.

Likuliku Lagoon Resort ★★★

Opened in 2007, this exquisitely designed resort is the first in Fiji to have overwater bungalows—romantic cottages built on stilts over the lagoon. Beside a half-moon, beach-fringed bay on the northwestern corner of Malolo Island, Likuliku shows intricate Fijian touches throughout, with *magimagi* (sennit, or coconut rope) lashing the log beams under the natural thatched roofs of its buildings. It was built and is owned by the Fiji-bred Whitten family, who made sure it reflects their country's indigenous culture. The 10 overwater bures have glass fish-viewing floor panels flanking their coffee tables, and more glass behind the sinks in their airy bathrooms. Each unit has a deck with steps leading down into the lagoon, which can be very shallow at low tide. The overwaters are close to a reef edge, however, so you can easily reach deep water at all tides. The split-level bungalows ashore all face the beach and are identical except for plunge pools set in the front decks of the deluxe models. Overlooking the sea and a large swimming pool, the restaurant serves very good (and sometimes exotic) Pacific Rim fare. The service is attentive, efficient, and friendly; in fact, I know several veteran staffers who came here from other top-end Fijian resorts. You can pamper yourself in Likuliku's full-service adults-only spa. To my mind the only drawback is that the beach in front of the resort becomes a broad sand flat at low tide. You won't have to walk across it to get ashore, for a long pier (with its own bar) reaches deep water.

P.O. Box 10044, Nadi Airport. ℭ **672 4275** or 666 3344. Fax 664 0014. www.likulikulagoon.com. 45 units. F$1,444–F$2,426 bungalow. Rates include all meals and nonmotorized water sports. AE, DC, MC, V. Children 16 and under not accepted. **Amenities:** Restaurant; 2 bars; health club; Jacuzzi; outdoor pool; room service; spa; watersports equipment/rentals; free Wi-Fi. *In room:* A/C, ceiling fan, TV/DVD (in overwater and deluxe units), hair dryer, minibar, MP3 docking station.

Malolo Island Fiji ★ ☺

Although it draws mostly couples, this resort is a good choice for families with children. Among adults, it's notable for having an outdoor spa and one of the better beachside restaurant and bars in Fiji. Casual- and fine-dining restaurants (the latter with views of the treetops from its big second-story balcony) occupy a building at the base of a hill at the rear of the property. They overlook two swimming pools, one especially suited for children because it has a walk-in sand bottom under a tarp to provide shade, the other good for grown-ups as it sports a swim-up bar. The guest bungalows are spread out in an old-growth forest which provides shade and a bit of privacy. All smartly renovated in 2009, most of the bungalows are duplexes. Of these, two have been joined into one-bedroom family units, 18 have separate bedrooms, and the others are studios. In addition, an upstairs family unit can sleep eight persons. Malolo is around a headland from its sister Likuliku Lagoon Resort (see above), and it's possible to have dinner over there. Like Likuliku, Malolo has a pier, so you don't have to wade ashore from the *Tiger IV.*

P.O. Box 10044, Nadi Airport. © **666 9192.** Fax 666 9197. www.maloloisland.com. 47 units. F$595–F$1,120 double. AE, DC, MC, V. **Amenities:** 3 restaurants; 3 bars; babysitting; children's center; Internet (computers in gift shop; free); Jacuzzi; 2 outdoor pools; spa; watersports equipment/rentals; Wi-Fi (in reception; free). *In room:* A/C, ceiling fan, fridge, hair dryer, no phone.

Mana Island

A long, rectangular island, Mana is half occupied by Mana Island Resort and half by Fijians, who operate backpacker-oriented accommodations. All of them share one of Fiji's best beaches, which runs along the island's southern side. A barrier reef offshore creates a safe lagoon for water sports. The lagoon on the north side lacks a beach but is very good for windsurfing.

The backpacker lodges include **Mana Island Lodge** (© **620 7030;** manalodge2@yahoo.com), on the beach about 180m (600 ft.) south of Mana Island Resort. Accommodation in simple bungalows (with coldwater showers) cost F$180 to F$250, and dorm beds are F$60, including meals.

Next door is **Ratu Kini Backpackers** (© **672 1959;** www.ratukini.com), offering dormitories for F$55 per person and units with bathrooms for F$155, including meals. Ratu Kini's restaurant virtually hangs over the beach.

CHOOSING YOUR offshore RESORT

Fiji has one of the world's finest collections of offshore resorts—small establishments with islands all to themselves. They invariably have lovely beach settings and modern facilities, and are excellent places to get away from it all. The major drawback of any offshore resort, of course, is that you've done just that. You won't see much of Fiji while you're basking in the sun on a tiny rock some 40km (25 miles) at sea. Consider them for what they have to offer but not as bases from which to explore the country.

You can check your e-mail, but you're unlikely to have a television in your bungalow at most of Fiji's offshore resorts, and you may not get a telephone, either. If you must be in touch with the world every minute of every day, stay on the mainland of Viti Levu. Come out here with one goal in mind: relaxation.

Although the Mamanuca and Yasawas have more offshore resorts than anywhere else in Fiji, others are on Vatulele Island, off the Coral Coast; Beqa Island,

off Pacific Harbour; Wakaya Island, near old capital of Levuka; Toberua Island, off Suva; Namenalala Island, off Savusavu; and Qamea and Matagi islands, off Taveuni. If you decide to stay at one of them, I suggest you read all my descriptions before making your choice.

Pay attention to what I say about the resorts' styles. For example, if you like a large establishment with lively, Club Med–like ambience, you might prefer Mana Island and Plantation Island resorts. Many other resorts offer peace, quiet, and few fellow guests—and no children. In other words, choosing carefully could mean the difference between a miserable week or a slice of heaven.

In most cases, you'll have no place to dine other than your resort's restaurants. Be sure to inquire about meal plans, if food is not already included in the rates. All but a few of the island resorts provide free snorkeling gear, kayaks, and other nonmotorized watersports equipment. They charge extra for scuba diving and other motorized sports.

Guests at these accommodations cannot use Mana Island Resort's watersports facilities, but both hostels have their own dive shops. Facilities are much more basic than at Funky Fish Beach Resort, Beachcomber Island Resort, and Bounty Island Resort.

Mana Island Resort & Spa ☺   One of the largest off Nadi, this lively resort occupies more than half of Mana Island and attracts Australian and New Zealand couples and families. It's also a popular day-trip destination from Nadi (see "Seeing the Islands on Day Trips from Nadi," earlier in this chapter). Seaplanes, planes, and helicopters also land here. In other words, you'll have a *lot* of company on Mana. Accommodations include varied bungalows, town houses, and hotel rooms. Least expensive are the few original "island" bures, which have been upgraded and air-conditioned (they have outdoor showers, too). Situated by themselves on the beach north of the airstrip, seven honeymoon bures feature Jacuzzis and butler service. Six executive beachfront bures have their own hot tubs. Least charming are town house–style oceanfront suites featuring mezzanine bedrooms and two bathrooms, one with claw-foot tub. A good children's program makes Mana a fine family choice.

P.O. Box 610, Lautoka. ℂ **665 0423.** Fax 665 0788. www.manafiji.com. 160 units. F$320–F$900 double. AE, DC, MC, V. **Amenities:** 2 restaurants; 3 bars; babysitting; children's center; Jacuzzi; outdoor pool; spa; 2 tennis courts; watersports equipment/rentals. *In room:* A/C, ceiling fan, fridge, Wi-Fi (F$20/day).

Matamanoa Island

A small rocky island with two steep hills, Matamanoa is the westernmost—and thus the most remote—of the Mamanuca resorts. The island terminates on its southwestern corner in a small flat point with a beach of deep, white sand, one of Fiji's best. The beach is exposed to the prevailing winds, so the lagoon can be a bit choppy at times. The reef shelf falls away steeply, however, resulting in great snorkeling even at low tide. For scuba divers, this is the closest of all Mamanuca resorts to sites on the Great Sea Reef.

Matamanoa Island Resort ★★ ◆   This intimate, adults-oriented complex (no kids 15 and under) sits beside the great beach. A horizon-edge pool and a central building with bar and open-air dining room overlook the beach and lagoon. Each of the rectangular beachfront bungalows has a porch overlooking the lagoon, and they are all furnished in a minimalist fashion to maximize their interior space. The 13 motel rooms are much smaller and do not face the beach. Because this well-managed resort is one of the better values in the Mamanucas, Australian, American, and European couples keep it busy year-round; book as early as possible.

P.O. Box 9729, Nadi Airport. ℂ **666 0511.** Fax 666 0069. www.matamanoa.com. 33 units. F$425 double room; F$685 bungalow. Rates include full breakfast. AE, MC, V. Children 16 and under not accepted. **Amenities:** Restaurant; bar; health club; outdoor pool; spa; tennis court; watersports equipment/rentals; Wi-Fi (F$15/day). *In room:* A/C, ceiling fan, fridge, hair dryer.

Qalito (Castaway) Island

Off the northwestern corner of Malolo, Qalito is usually referred to as Castaway because of its resident resort. Its northern point is flanked by a very good beach.

Castaway Island Resort ★★ ☺   Built in the mid-1960s of logs and thatch, Castaway maintains its rustic, Fijian-style charm despite many improvements over the years. The central activities building, perched on the point, has a thatch-covered roof, and the ceilings of it and the guest bures are lined with genuine masi cloth.

Although the bures sit relatively close together in a coconut grove, their roofs sweep low enough to provide some privacy. Located upstairs at the beachside watersports shack, the Sundowner Bar appropriately faces west toward the Great Sea Reef. Guests have wood-fired pizzas there or dine in

> **Impressions**
>
> *Every resort seemed to have a platoon of insanely friendly Fijians.*
> —Scott L. Malcolmson, *Tuturani,* 1990

the central building, usually at umbrella tables on a stone beachside patio. This is a very good family resort, with a nurse on duty and the staff providing a wide range of activities, from learning Fijian to sack races. Consequently, couples seeking a quiet romantic retreat should look elsewhere during school holiday periods. Australian restaurateur Geoff Shaw owns both this resort and the Outrigger on the Lagoon Fiji on the Coral Coast (p. 142), and the two often have attractive joint packages, including helicopter transfers between them.

Private Mail Bag, Nadi Airport. *℡* **800/773-2107** or 666 1233. Fax 666 5753. www.castawayfiji.com. 66 units. F$805–F$1,085 bungalow. AE, DC, MC, V. **Amenities:** 2 restaurants; 3 bars; babysitting; children's center; health club; Jacuzzi; outdoor pool; tennis court; watersports equipment/rentals; Wi-Fi (in main bldg; F$20/hour). *In room:* A/C, ceiling fan, fridge, hair dryer, no phone.

Tai (Beachcomber) Island

One of the founders of modern tourism in Fiji, the late Dan Costello bought an old Colonial Sugar Refining Company tugboat in 1963, converted it into a day cruiser, and started carrying tourists on day trips out to a tiny piece of sand and coconut palms known as Tai Island, which he renamed Beachcomber Island. The visitors liked it so much that some of them didn't want to leave. Some of their grandchildren still love it.

Beachcomber Island Resort ★★ 🏺 Although the Yasawa Islands have stolen some of its thunder, Beachcomber still attracts the young, young-at-heart, and other like-minded souls in search of fun, members of the opposite sex, and a relatively inexpensive vacation (considering that all-you-can-eat meals are included in the rates). The youngest-at-heart cram into the coed dormitories. If you want more room, you can have or share a semiprivate lodge. And if you want your own charming bure, you can have that, too—just don't expect luxury. Rates also include a wide range of activities, though you pay extra for sailboats, canoes, windsurfing, scuba diving, water-skiing, and fishing trips.

P.O. Box 364, Lautoka. *℡* **800/521-7242** or 666 1500. Fax 666 4496. www.beachcomberfiji.com. 36 units, 102 dorm beds. F$479–F$529 double bure; F$365 double lodge; F$119 dorm bed. Rates include all meals. AE, MC, V. **Amenities:** Restaurant; bar; watersports equipment/rentals; Wi-Fi (in main bldg.; F$16/hour). *In room:* Ceiling fan, fridge, no phone.

Tokoriki Island

At the end of the line for the ferry shuttles from Port Denarau, Tokoriki is another hilly island with two good beaches. *Heads up:* Tokoriki sporadically has a problem with seaweed creating an unpleasant odor, although the resort has learned to remove it from the beach before the stench starts.

Also on Tokoriki is **Amunuca Island Resort** (*℡* **664 0087;** www.amunuca. com), an eclectic property which has had financial problems of late. I much prefer its neighbor:

Tokoriki Island Resort This adults-only property sits beside a wide beach stretching 1.5km (1 mile) on Tokoriki's northern side. Although it doesn't have deep sand, once you get past rock shelves along the shoreline, the bottom slopes gradually into a safe lagoon with colorful coral gardens protected by a barrier reef. The resort itself sits on a flat shelf of land backed by a steep hill (a 4km/2½-mile hiking trail leads up to the ridgeline). Lined up along the beach, most of the spacious units have separate sleeping and living areas equipped with wet-bars, and both indoor and outdoor showers. Best are the luxurious Sunset Pool units, which have outdoor showers plus daybeds under thatched roofs next to their own plunge pools. Three more tree-house-like units also have their own pools, but they are not directly on the beach. A central thatch-topped bar divides the one-room central building into lounge and main restaurant (the latter opening to a lily pond). There should be a small Japanese restaurant by the time you arrive. Except for scuba diving, there are no motorized water sports here.

P.O. Box 10547, Nadi Airport. © **666 1999.** Fax 666 5295. www.tokoriki.com. 34 units. F$784–F$1,078 bungalow. AE, MC, V. No children 12 and under accepted. **Amenities:** 2 restaurants; bar; Internet (in business center; F$1/minute); 2 outdoor pools; spa; tennis court; watersports equipment/rentals. *In room:* A/C, ceiling hair dryer, minibar.

Vomo Island

An unusual clump of land, Vomo features a steep, 165m-high (550-ft.) hill on one end and a perfectly flat, 80-hectare (200-acre) shelf surrounded by a reef edged by brilliantly colorful corals on the other. Offshore, **Vomolailai (Little Vomo)** is a rocky islet with its own little beach. Vomo is the northernmost of the Mamanuca Islands and is almost on the border with the Yasawa Islands.

Vomo Fiji Island Resort This upmarket resort occupies all of Vomo Island. The restaurant is adjacent to the beach, a deck-surrounded pool, and a stylish bar. Some

Keeping You Entertained

Don't worry about staying busy at the offshore resorts in the Mamanucas and Yasawas. The range of activities depends on the resort, and you can participate in as much or as little as you like.

Not surprisingly, most resort activities center around, on, and in the ocean. In addition to snorkeling, kayaking, and fishing, most resorts offer PADI-certified scuba classes. Snorkeling itself offers incredible glimpses of electric blue starfish, zebra-striped fish, and underwater plant life.

Cultural activities include village visits and church services. Many resorts partner with local villages, providing jobs for the villagers and money for

their families. The visits usually include a stop at a school where children will sing and teachers explain the children's daily activities. Toward the end of the visit and depending on the village, women lay out homemade wares for tourists to purchase. Worship services are always at a Methodist church, the predominate religion here. *Remember:* Female visitors must wear clothing that covers shoulders and knees, and no one wears a hat in a Fijian village.

Most resorts have a Fijian *meke* night when the resort staff performs traditional Fijian song and dance, and guests are asked to join in later in the show.

of the luxurious guest bungalows climb the hill to provide views of the reef and sea, although I prefer those along a fine stretch of beach. Some of the beach bures are in duplex buildings, so ask for a self-standing one if you don't want next-door neighbors. Honeymooners, take note: About half of the duplex units interconnect, making them popular choices for well-heeled families with young children, especially during Australian school holidays, likewise the two-bedroom, two-bathroom Royal Deluxe Villa. All of the well-equipped units have sitting areas with sofas, and their large bathrooms have both showers and two-person Jacuzzis. Vomo is served by the *Yasawa Flyer* as well as by seaplane and helicopter.

P.O. Box 5650, Lautoka. © **666 7955.** Fax 666 7997. www.vomofiji.com. 29 units. F$1,975–F$2,275 bungalow; F$5,350–F$9,000 villa. Rates include meals, soft drinks during meals, and nonmotorized water sports. AE, MC, V. **Amenities:** Restaurant; bar; babysitting; bikes; children's programs; golf course (9-hole pitch-and-putt); health club; Jacuzzi; outdoor pool; room service; spa; tennis court; watersports equipment/rentals; Wi-Fi. *In room:* A/C, ceiling fan, hair dryer, minibar, MP3 docking station, Wi-Fi.

Wadigi Island

Off Malolo's northwestern side, 1.2-hectare (3-acre) Wadigi (Wah-*ding*-ee) appears like a single hill precipitously protruding from the colorful lagoon. It and its two beaches are owned by Australians Jim and Tracey Johnston, who allow no one to set foot on Wadigi without advance permission, making it one of the best places in Fiji to get away from it all—as certain celebrities can testify.

Wadigi Island Resort ★★★ Staying with the Johnstons on Wadigi is more like having your own private island than staying at a resort. Jim and Tracey live here, and, in a way, you'll be their guests (although they and the staff will leave you absolutely alone if that's your desire). You will stay in a villa built on top of the island with spectacular views of the nearby islands and reefs, from the rooms as well as from an infinity-edge swimming pool. A central lounge and three bedrooms are like separate bungalows linked by walkways (the bedrooms can be rented separately or all together, thus giving you the entire island). A short walk downhill leads to the dining room and bar, or you can be served excellent fare in your room, by the pool, down by the beach, or wherever else you can imagine. Every unit has a satellite-fed TV with DVD player (you actors can watch yourselves from an extensive movie library) and a large veranda with daybed. The honeymoon unit comes equipped with an outdoor shower and two king-size beds that can be pushed together to form one humongous bed. This outstanding choice is the most private retreat in Fiji.

P.O. Box 10134, Nadi Airport. © **672 0901.** www.wadigi.com. 3 units. US$1,920 double. Rates include all meals, beverages, and activities except scuba diving, surfing, and sport fishing. AE, MC, V. Minimum stay 3 nights. **Amenities:** Restaurant; bar; outdoor pool; room service; watersports equipment/rentals; Wi-Fi. *In room:* A/C, ceiling fan, TV/DVD, hair dryer, Internet, movie library, minibar, MP3 docking station, no phone, Wi-Fi.

YASAWA ISLAND RESORTS

Once quiet, sleepy, and devoid of most tourists except a few backpackers and well-heeled guests at Turtle Island and Yasawa Island Resort and Spa, this gorgeous chain of islands has seen an explosion of accommodations in recent years, many of them owned by villagers and aimed at backpackers and other cost-conscious travelers. In fact, the Yasawas are the hottest destination in Fiji for budget-minded travelers.

Where to Stay in the Yasawa Islands

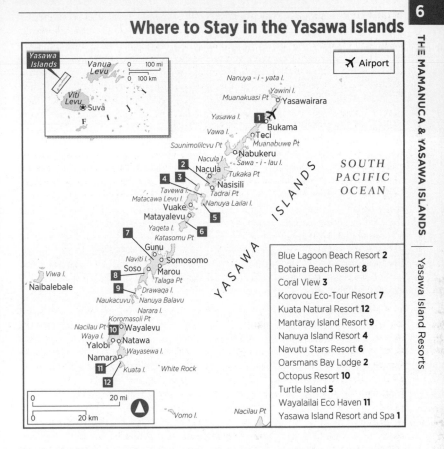

Blue Lagoon Beach Resort **2**
Botaira Beach Resort **8**
Coral View **3**
Korovou Eco-Tour Resort **7**
Kuata Natural Resort **12**
Mantaray Island Resort **9**
Nanuya Island Resort **4**
Navutu Stars Resort **6**
Oarsmans Bay Lodge **2**
Octopus Resort **10**
Turtle Island **5**
Wayalailai Eco Haven **11**
Yasawa Island Resort and Spa **1**

The chain is about 50km (30 miles) long, so it is no quick boat ride from bottom to top. From Port Denarau, the relatively speedy *Yasawa Flyer* takes 4½ hours to go halfway up the chain to the Blue Lagoon area, which has the largest number of resorts and hostels (see "Getting to the Islands," at the beginning of this chapter). Many visitors get off and spend a few nights on different islands as they advance up from the south. See "How to Travel in the Yasawa Islands," below, for more advice.

The sand on the Yasawa beaches gets finer and whiter as you go north.

Most of the resorts and hostels have kayaks, snorkel gear, and other equipment for their guests to use (some free, some for a fee), and some also have sailboats and other toys.

Based on Nanuya Lailai Island in the Blue Lagoon area, **West Side Water Sports** (© 666 1462; www.fiji-dive.com) provides daily dive trips for all of the northern Yasawa retreats and teaches introductory and PADI certification courses. **Reef Safari** (© 675 0950; www.reefsafari.com.fj) does the same from its base at Mantaray Island Resort in the southern Yasawas.

We have organized the islands below in the order in which you will come to them on the *Yasawa Flyer,* that is, from south to north.

Kuata & Wayasewa Islands

Kuata and Wayasewa (also known as Waya Lailai, or Little Waya) are the southern-most of the Yasawas. I include them together because two resorts, one on each island, face each other across a narrow strait and are operated by the same Fijian clan. Among the Yasawas, I think Wayasewa is second only to its big sister, Waya Island, in physical beauty. Its rocky outcrops and jagged mountains give it a majestic splendor.

Kuata Natural Resort   On the northern tip of Kuata and appealing primarily to young backpackers on low budgets, this hostel sits by a good beach bordered on one end by a black skull-shaped outcrop. The view across the strait to another outcrop rising above Wayasewa is one of the better vistas in the Yasawas. Accommodations are in basic bungalows and dorms facing the beach. The bungalows have bathrooms with cold-water showers and contain either a double or two single beds. Buffet-style meals are served in a central building and beachside pavilion with thatch roof. The lagoon offers good snorkeling along the edges of the strait. You can get a massage in a cave here but you cannot get on the Internet.

P.O. Box 3623, Lautoka. ℂ **666 6426** or 625 3573. naturalresort@yahoo.com. 17 bungalows (all with bathrooms), 35 dorm beds. F$80 per person in bungalow; F$65 per person dorm bed. Rates include all meals. No credit cards. **Amenities:** Restaurant; bar; watersports equipment/rentals. *In room:* Ceiling fans, no phone.

Wayalailai Eco Haven   Perched on a flat shelf at the base of a rocky mountain and above a good beach beside the strait, this is one of the better Fijian-owned resorts. Older local-style bures are being replaced by larger cottages with thatch roofs and their own bathrooms (cold water showers). The best have porches espying the lagoon and the black rocks of Kuata Island across the strait. A few motel-style rooms are less expensive. Providing buffet meals, the dining room also has the view from its large deck. An on-site dive shop serves guests here and at Kuata Natural Resort across the strait.

P.O. Box 6353, Lautoka. ℂ **603 0215.** wayalailai@connect.com.fj. 8 bungalows; 23 dorm beds. F$160–F$200 double in bungalow; F$65 per person dorm bed. Rates include all meals. No credit cards. **Amenities:** Restaurant; bar; Internet (F$10/hour); watersports equipment/rentals. *In room:* Ceiling fan, no phone.

Waya Island

Waya is one of the most beautiful islands in Fiji. You can see the jagged outline of Mount Batinareba soaring over Yalobi Bay from as far away as the Viti Levu mainland. Trails over the mountains link Waya's four Fijian villages and make it the best place in the Yasawas for hiking.

Octopus Resort ★★ 🔥   Beside a long, half-moon shaped beach of deep white sand skirting Likuliku Bay, this lively resort has broad appeal for singles and families alike. A mix of accommodations include dorms, bungalow-style rooms with shared facilities, deluxe hotel-style rooms, older Fijian-style bures, and four luxurious bungalows with large outdoor showers. The leafy Fijian bures are small but charming, and most will eventually also have outdoor showers; those with porches directly facing the beach are better choices than the garden units. The motel-style rooms are the only units here with TVs and DVD players, but you can rent them and watch movies in your own quarters. With activities including the likes of scuba diving, snorkeling in turquoise waters, movies under the stars, and massages by the beach, Octopus is one of the few Yasawa resorts with a swimming pool. Meals are served in a sand-floor dining room which opens to the pool on one side and a well-used volleyball court on the other. Octopus runs its own boat to Vuda Point twice a day, so you don't necessarily have to take the *Yasawa Flyer* to get here. New Zealander owner Nick Wood also has an interest in Blue Lagoon Beach Resort on Nacula Island (see below).

P.O. Box 1861, Lautoka. ℂ **666 6337** or 603 0071. Fax 666 6210. www.octopusresort.com. 14 units (11 with bathrooms), 20 dorm beds. US$89–F$249 double; US$20–US$35 dorm bed. MC, V. **Amenities:** Restaurant; bar; babysitting; Internet (laptops in office, F$24/hour); outdoor pool; watersports rentals. *In room:* A/C (7 units), ceiling fan, TV/DVD (3 units), movie library, fridge (7 units), no phone.

Naviti & Islands

About halfway up the chain, Naviti is one of the largest and highest of the Yasawas. Soso, an important Fijian village, is on the east coast, while three resorts sit beside little bays on the western side.

The basic **White Sandy Beach Resort** (ℂ **666 6644**) is attractive primarily to travelers who can't get space at Korovou Eco-Tour Resort next door (see below).

Botaira Beach Resort ★★ ☀ This is the finest Fijian-owned resort I've ever seen. Proprietors Alumita and Jeremaia Sovatobua worked at the Warwick Resort & Spa on the Coral Coast for 17 years, and they put that experience to very good use in designing, building, and operating this establishment. Their main building opens to a deck hanging over one of Fiji's best white-sand beaches. The lagoon here is speckled with colorful corals, making for great snorkeling right off the beach at high tide or from a floating pontoon at shallow times. With lots of Fijian charm, the bamboo-clad, thatch-roof bungalows are among the largest in the Yasawas and come equipped with queen bed, bathroom (usually with hot-water showers), screened louvered windows on three sides, and front porches. Most face the beach, but four garden units have outdoor showers. Alumita oversees a large garden that provides the ingredients for Western- and Fijian-style meals and supplies pineapples to nearby villages. This is not a luxurious resort, but it has a lot of Fijian charm. Your mobile phone will not work here, nor will you be able to log on the Internet.

P.O. Box 911, Lautoka. ℂ **603 0200.** www.botaira.com. 11 units. F$443 double. Rates include meals and afternoon tea. MC, V. **Amenities:** Restaurant; bar; watersports equipment/rentals. *In room:* Ceiling fan, no phone.

Korovou Eco-Tour Resort The most advanced inexpensive resort in the Yasawas, Korovou has both an outdoor swimming pool and an air-conditioned building housing half a dozen laptops connected to a wireless network. The relatively small bungalows are comfortable, and each has a front porch and a bathroom with hot-water shower. The standard bungalows are built of wood, while the somewhat larger deluxe models have stone walls. The main building has a big deck extending over a good beach, but the lagoon gets so shallow at low tide that the owners have built a concrete walkway to deep water.

P.O. Box 6627, Lautoka. ℂ **665 2812** or 603 0049. Fax 665 1001. www.korovouecoresort.com.fj. 11 units; 24 dorm beds. F$200–F$250 double; F$80 dorm bed. Rates include meals. MC, V. **Amenities:** Restaurant; bar; outdoor pool; watersports equipment/rentals; Wi-Fi (F30¢/minute). *In room:* Ceiling fan, fridge (4 units), no phone.

📎 TRAVELING IN THE yasawa islands

You might think you're a time traveler to the 1980s as you lounge on the top deck of the *Yasawa Flyer,* listening to a strange mix of hair bands and Paul Simon (if you don't know the lyrics to "You Can Call Me Al" before heading to Fiji, you can be sure you'll have them down pat by the time you depart). Even with these songs running through your head, you'll be inspired to burst into song, belting out "Bali Ha'i" as you sail past tall, skinny mountains shooting out of tropical waters, scenery straight out of *South Pacific.* Travelers immediately pull out cameras to the sounds of oohs and ahhs as they get a first glimpse of breathtaking tropical islands bordered by white-sand beaches giving way to a patchwork quilt of variegated blue water.

For someone who wants to escape from it all, the Yasawa Islands are the place to do it. In the fast-paced modern world, where Blackberries and iPhones buzz constantly and people are linked-in 24/7, the Yasawas are a stark contrast. While many resorts provide Internet access and some have phones, there's very little reason to bother logging on, as connection speed is slow, computers are in offices tucked away from the ocean, and mobile phones don't work on the western sides of most islands.

Some hostels sell **phone cards** for more than their face value. That's illegal but almost impossible to enforce because these little islands are far removed. You should stock up on phone cards while in Nadi. You will also need **cash,** both to pay the inexpensive

hostels, which don't accept credit cards, and for putting down deposits on room keys, snorkel gear, and other returnable items.

A convivial atmosphere usually prevails on the *Yasawa Flyer,* and your fellow travelers can be valuable tour guides by suggesting things to do and warning you against some resorts and recommending others based on their own experiences.

Because you'll find a swarm of young backpackers throughout the Yasawas, the atmosphere everywhere is casual. A swimsuit and a *sulu* (sarong) are entirely appropriate for traveling within the Yasawas. There's plenty of time to lay out when you reach your resort. On your way there, though, keep your hat and sun block close by. You don't want to be burned to a crisp before the adventure has even begun.

The *Yasawa Flyer* has **restrooms** on board, and a **concession stand** sells beer, soda, and ice cream. If you're prone to seasickness, take your own medicine before boarding. Staff members announce resort stops about 15 minutes before arrival time, and you can follow along with a schedule, which is usually on time. The resorts and the cruise company handle luggage, which you won't be able to access while traveling.

When you **arrive at your resort or hostel,** the staff will orient you and often serve a fresh, tropical drink. Meals are served during set hours, either buffet style or by waitstaff. The better resorts serve a variety of dishes, including vegetarian fare; but if you have strict

Nanuya Balavu Island

South of Naviti, you can swim with the manta rays that gather near the smaller islands of **Nanuya Balavu** and **Drawaqa** between March and November.

dietary restrictions, notify the resort, which can likely accommodate. Depending on the resort, guests will pay a mandatory per diem food charge, which includes breakfast, lunch, and dinner. Others charge a la carte for lunch and dinner but usually include a continental breakfast with the room fee.

Yaqona (welcoming) ceremonies are held each night for guests who have arrived earlier that day. If you're uncomfortable participating, simply forgo the ceremony of introductions and lots of clapping.

Tropical escapes conjure up images of calm, still waters, but the South Seas can be surprisingly choppy. Keep that in mind when deciding where to stay. If you're looking for a steady stream of ocean swimming and laying out, choose a resort such as Nanuya, where waters are calm and beach chairs are comfy. **Navutu Stars** doesn't have the best beach, but it has a saltwater swimming pool that gives a great view of an inlet that can be crossed on foot at low tide. **Mantaray Island Resort,** while more of a budget place, has another great beach, but the sand is a bit pebbly.

Travelers hitting only the higher-end places don't need to worry about packing shampoo, soap, and towels. Even **Octopus Resort**—a combination budget/midrange property—provides plush towels, soap, shampoo, and lotions. Bring your own **beach towel,** as they are a big part of vacationing in the Yasawas. Some resorts don't provide lounge chairs, and a towel is all you have between your body and the sand.

Tap water at the mild- to upper-range resorts is purified, and guests don't need to worry about drinking it. But think twice about drinking unpurified water at the inexpensive places, as it can cause diarrhea and general malaise. Stock up on bottled water before leaving Nadi, or avoid the low-budget places altogether.

Postal service on the islands is nearly nonexistent. Wait and mail your postcards from Nadi.

There is no **electrical system** in the Yasawas, and while midrange and upscale resorts generate power round-the-clock, the inexpensive resorts shut theirs off during the day and overnight. You'll want to pack a flashlight regardless of the resort.

The resorts are self-contained, and while you will be able to buy **personal supplies,** it's best to prepare in advance and pack what you need, rather than expecting to find necessities here. You'll definitely pay a premium for them. In fact, all prices in the Yasawas are a little higher than on Viti Levu because most supplies must be shipped to and from the resorts, including fuel. Similarly, you won't find much to buy for friends back home; purchase your souvenirs on the mainland.

If you have only a week in the Yasawas, spend it on one island. Otherwise you'll waste valuable time planning, packing, riding the boat, and unpacking instead of using it to really enjoy all that these beautiful islands offer.

—Valerie Haeder

Mantaray Island Resort ★   Set beside an attractive but pebbly beach strewn with pumicelike rocks, Mantaray is primarily a backpacker's hangout, although its quality scuba-dive operation attracts others. The 32-bed dorm room clusters four beds to a group, affording quite a lot of privacy in an otherwise open area. The simple but comfortable bungalows—many standing on stilts—are bare-bones, with only a bed with mosquito netting and a chair. The newer "Jungle" models have bathrooms with hot-water showers. Snacks are served at a beachside bar, while meals are served in a breezy lodge set atop a ridge with one of the best views the Yasawas can offer.

P.O. Box 42, Port Denarau. ☎ **664 0520.** www.mantarayisland.com. 15 units (5 with bathrooms), 32 dorm beds. F$135–F$235; F$49 dorm bed. MC, V. **Amenities:** Restaurant; 2 bars; watersports equipment/rentals; Wi-Fi (in office; F$12/hour). *In room:* Ceiling fan, no phone.

Yaqeta Island

Navutu Stars Resort ★★   Owned and operated by a young Italian couple, Manfredi de Lucia and Maddalena Morandi, Navutu Stars provides a relaxing Fijian atmosphere with laid-back Mediterranean elegance. Guests receive individualized, focused yet discreet attention. The beach here isn't as welcoming as at other Yasawa resorts, but a saltwater swimming pool gives a great view of an inlet that can be crossed on foot at low tide. Six of the nine spacious bures are beachfront. They all are exquisitely decorated, painted a stark white but with bedding and cushions providing splashes of color. Two grand bures have soaking tubs set in their floors (careful you don't fall into them at night). Dinner is a gastronomic delight of Italian and Fijian dishes (don't miss the homemade fish ravioli in garlic butter sauce).

P.O. Box 1838 Lautoka. ☎ **664 0553.** Fax 666 0807. www.navutustarsfiji.com. 9 units. F$252–F$892 double. MC, V. **Amenities:** Restaurant; bar; Internet (after 5pm); outdoor pool; watersports equipment/rentals; Wi-Fi. *In room:* Ceiling fan, hair dryer, minibar, no phone.

Nanuya Levu Island

San Franciscan Richard Evanson graduated from Harvard Business School, made a bundle in cable television, got divorced, ran away to Fiji, and in 1972 bought Nanuya Levu Island. Growing lonely and bored, he decided to build Turtle Island (see below) on his hilly, 180-hectare (450-acre) retreat. He had completed three bures by 1980, when a Hollywood producer leased the entire island as a set for a second version of *The Blue Lagoon,* starring the then-teenage Brooke Shields. Clocks were set ahead 1 hour to maximize daylight, and except during daylight saving time, the resort still operates on "Turtle Time," an hour ahead of the rest of Fiji. The movie's most familiar scenes were shot on Devil's Beach, one of Nanuya Levu's 14 gorgeous little stretches of sand wedged between rocky headlands.

✎ A Package Deal Worth Your Money

Awesome Adventures Fiji (☎ **670 5006;** www.awesomefiji.com) has packages including transportation on the *Yasawa Flyer* and accommodations at several Yasawa Islands resorts and hostels, which are thoroughly inspected for cleanliness and safety. Frankly, several Yasawa hostels are operated by Fijian families and can be very basic. I like to recommend Fijian-owned businesses whenever possible, but I would stick to those approved by Awesome Adventures Fiji. The packages are easily arranged at any Nadi area hotel or hostel, but because the choices are many and complicated, check the website or pick up a current Awesome Adventures Fiji brochure at the airport tour offices or at many hotel activities desks.

Turtle Island ★★★ Enjoying one of the most picturesque settings of any resort in Fiji, this venerable little getaway nestles beside an idyllic, half-moon-shaped beach and looks out on a nearly landlocked body of water. Supplied by the resort's own garden, the kitchen serves excellent meals dinner-party fashion in the open-air dining room or out on the beach (sand flies have bitten me here, so use insect repellent at dusk). If you don't want company, you can dine alone on the beach or on a pontoon floating on the lagoon. The beach turns into a sandbar at low tide, but you can swim and snorkel off a long pier. A dozen of the superluxe, widely spaced bungalows have two-person spa tubs embedded in the floors of their enormous bedrooms or bathrooms. In a few bungalows, the front porch has a lily pond on one side and a queen-size day bed under a roof on the other. The most private of all sits on a headland with a 360-degree view of the lagoon and surrounding islands. Unlike more modern units at many other resorts, all of them ooze Fijian charm; for example, bedposts and writing desks are made of tree limbs. Every unit has its own kayaks and a hammock strung between shade trees by the beach. Only couples and singles are accepted here, except during certain family weeks in July and at Christmas. Instead of a phone in your bungalow, you will have a two-way radio to call for room service.

P.O. Box 9317, Nadi Airport. 🕐 **800/225-4347** or 672 2921. Fax 672 0007. www.turtlefiji.com. 14 units. US$2,000–US$3,000 per couple. Rates include meals, drinks, all activities including game fishing and 1 scuba dive per day. 6-night stay required. AE, MC, V. Children 15 and under not accepted except during family weeks in July and at Christmas. **Amenities:** Restaurant; bar; free Internet; Jacuzzi (in 12 units); room service; watersports equipment/rentals. *In room:* A/C, ceiling fans, TV/DVD, hair dryer, movie library, minibar, MP3 docking station, no phone.

Nanuya Lailai Island

Sitting next to the Blue Lagoon, Nanuya Lailai Island has a fantastic beach on its southern and eastern sides, a long stretch of white sand wrapping around a narrow point. Nanuya Island Resort sits on the western end of the beach, and Blue Lagoon Cruises expeditions lets its passengers enjoy the sand and sea here.

Nanuya Island Resort ★★ This moderately priced resort offers any number of activities from kayaking to diving to caving to snorkeling. The lagoon is shallow at low tide, but you can follow a sandy path out to deep water for swimming and snorkeling. With a natural thatch roof constructed in the Fijian fashion, the central restaurant-bar-lounge complex stands on a sandy point at the northern end of Nanuya Lailai's great beach. Three larger deluxe guest bungalows are down by the beach. They have tin roofs and two rooms inside. With natural thatch roofs, a majority of the bungalows are nestled in the wooded hills, requiring a steep climb but offering stunning views of the ocean from their porches. Every unit has an open-air if not completely outdoor shower. No children under 7 years old are accepted here.

P.O. Box 7136, Lautoka. 🕐 **666 7633.** Fax 666 1462. www.nanuyafiji.com. 12 units. F$285–F$440 double. MC, V. No children under 7 years old. **Amenities:** Restaurant; bar; massage; watersports equipment/rentals. *In room:* Fridge, no phone.

Tavewa Island

Before the coming of the *Yasawa Flyer* and the phenomenal growth it spurred, Tavewa was a favorite backpacker hangout. Two of its hostels, **David's Place** (🕐 **672 1820**) and **Kingfisher Lodge** (🕐 **672 2921**) are still around but off the radar scopes. Travelers still stay at **Otto & Fanny's Place** (© **620 1250** or 672 0952; www.ottoandfanny.com), which also has been around since the 1980s.

Coral View   Sprawling across a large beachside lawn, Coral View is the most popular Yasawa resort with backpackers, with as many as 70 of them in residence—and likely imbibing at the lively bar, which despite local law often stays open all night. The beach is rocky and the lagoon is shallow, but you can soak up a lot of rays in lawn loungers and hammocks. The 15 square bungalows are simple, but they all have bathrooms (if not always hot-water showers). The dorms can be a bit cramped, but two more spacious models are due to open by the end of 2010. Advance bookings are always a good idea here.

P.O. Box 3764, Lautoka. © **666 2648** or 925 8341. Fax 665 2777. www.coral.com.fj. 15 units, 40 dorm beds. F$210 double; F$65 dorm bed. Rates include meals. MC, V. **Amenities:** Restaurant; bar; Internet (in office; F$20/hour); watersports equipment/rentals. *In room:* Ceiling fan, no phone.

Nacula Island

On the northeastern edge of the Blue Lagoon area, Nacula possesses Fiji's finest beach, a dreamy, world-class stretch of deep white sand bordering Nalova Bay, a lagoon deep enough for swimming at all tides. Blue Lagoon Beach Resort and Oarsmans Bay Lodge share this magnificent setting.

During the coup of 2000, villagers from Nacula invaded Turtle Island (see above) and held its guests hostage for a few days. I later talked to a "hostage" who said it was more like an enforced party, with lots of kava drinking and Fijian music! As a result, Turtle owner Richard Evanson designed and built two little resorts—Oarsmans Bay (see below) and Safe Landing—for the villagers to eventually operate on their own. While Oarsmans Bay sits by Nalova Bay's terrific beach, **Safe Landing Resort** (© **623 2984**; www.safelandingfiji.com) sits on a promontory flanked by beaches. It has struggled of late, however, and was like a ghost town when I stopped by during my recent visit.

Also on Nacula is **Nabua Lodge** (© **666 9173;** www.nabualodge-yasawa.com), where many backpackers stay while awaiting a vacancy at Coral View on nearby Tavewa. Half its 10 bures are made of thatch, while the others are newer and have their own bathrooms.

Blue Lagoon Beach Resort ★★★ 🍴   This is not one of the most luxurious resorts in Fiji, but it is one of my favorites. Not only does it sit beside the best beach in the country, it was designed and built by Chris and Kylie Hogan, who spent several years managing Octopus Resort (see above). Here they have reconstituted a small version of Octopus, complete with a sand-floor dining room and a volleyball court. They also have a variety of accommodations, from dormitories to beachfront bungalows for couples and families. All but one of the bures has both natural thatch on their rooftops and lining their ceilings, which adds charm. The one family unit has a small separate bedroom with bunk beds. All of them have outdoor showers. Even the dorms are in two bungalows here, with seven beds each. All in all, there is extraordinary value here.

Nalova Bay, Nacula Island © **666 6337** or 603 0223. Fax 603 0224. www.bluelagoonbeachresort. fj. 8 units, 14 dorm beds. F$189–F$449 bungalow; F$40 dorm bed. Rates include afternoon tea, transfers to the *Yasawa Flyer.* MC, V. **Amenities:** Restaurant; bar; babysitting; Internet (laptop in office; F$24/hour); watersports equipment/rentals. *In room:* A/C (in family unit), ceiling fan, fridge (in family unit), no phone.

> ### 💬 Running Away to a Famous Cave
>
> In the 1980 version of the *Blue Lagoon* movie, actress Brooke Shields runs away to a cave on **Sawa-i-Lau Island,** a small rocky islet between Nacula and Yasawa Islands. Carved out of limestone by rainwater, the cave has a hole at the top, which lets in light, and you can swim underwater into a smaller, dark cave. The resorts often run trips to Sawa-i-Lau, and some cruise ships stop here.

Oarsmans Bay Lodge   Although designed and built by Richard Evanson, owner of Turtle Island (see above), this Fijian-owned resort has suffered under inept management for the past several years. It's a good choice if you need to wait for a vacancy at Blue Lagoon Beach Resort next door, as you can walk over there for libation and fine meals. Although the tin-roof guest bungalows here are a bit cramped and in need of refurbishment, they are nicely appointed with wooden cabinets, full-length mirrors, reading lights over their double beds, screened louvered windows, and bathrooms with solar-heated showers.

P.O. Box 9317, Nadi Airport. 🕐 **672 2921.** Fax 672 0007. www.fijibudget.com. 6 units, 13 dorm beds. F$132–F$265; F$23 dorm bed; F$25 per person campsite; F$36 per person campsite with tent rental. MC, V. **Amenities:** Restaurant; bar; watersports equipment,rentals. *In room:* No phone.

Yasawa Island

Long, skinny Yasawa Island stretches from the Blue Lagoon area all the way to the top of the chain. Its north end forms a hook bordered by a long beach, one of Fiji's best. Big black rocks break the beach in two parts and separate two Fijian villages. It's worth taking a Blue Lagoon Cruise just to see this beach, because that's the only way you can get there.

Yasawa Island Resort and Spa ★★★   This luxurious resort sits in a small indention among steep cliffs about midway up Yasawa Island. The Great Sea Reef is far enough offshore here that surf can slap against shelves of black rock just off a terrific beach of deep white sand. Or you can dip in a saltwater swimming pool. Most of the large, air-conditioned guest bures are long, 93 sq. m (1,000 sq. ft.) rectangular models with thatched roofs over white stucco walls. A door leads from the bathroom, which has an indoor shower, to an outdoor shower and a private sunbathing patio. A few other one- and two-bedroom models are less appealing but are better arranged for families and have fine views from the side of the hill backing the property. Best of all is the remote, extremely private Lomolagi honeymoon bure, which has its own beach and pool. This is the only Yasawa resort with an airstrip.

P.O. Box 10128, Nadi Airport. 🕐 **672 2266.** Fax 672 4456. www.yasawa.com. 18 units. US$890–US$1,800 double. Rates include all meals and nonmotorized water sports, but no drinks. AE, DC, MC, V. Children 11 and under not accepted except in Jan, mid-June to mid-July, Dec. **Amenities:** Restaurant; bar; free Internet (in main bldg.); Jacuzzi; outdoor pool; room service; spa; tennis courts; watersports equipment/rentals. *In room:* A/C, ceiling fan, hair dryer, minibar, MP3 docking station, no phone.

THE CORAL COAST

7

Long before big jets began bringing visitors to Fiji, many affluent local residents built cottages on the dry southwestern shore of Viti Levu as sunny retreats from the rain and high humidity of Suva. When visitors started arriving in big numbers during the early 1960s, resorts sprang up among the cottages, and promoters gave a new, more appealing name to the 70km (43-mile) stretch of beaches and reef on either side of the town of Sigatoka: the Coral Coast.

The appellation was apt, for coral reefs jut out like wide shelves from the white beaches that run between mountain ridges all along this picturesque coastline. In most spots, the lagoon just reaches snorkeling depth at high tide, and when the water retreats, you can put on your reef sandals or a pair of old sneakers and walk out nearly to the surf pounding on the outer edge of the shelf.

Frankly, the Coral Coast is now overshadowed by other parts of Fiji. Its large hotels cater primarily to meetings, groups, and families from Australia and New Zealand on 1-week holidays. Nevertheless, it has dramatic scenery and some of the country's better historical sites, and it's a central location from which to see both the Suva and Nadi sides of Viti Levu. Pacific Harbour's river rafting and other adventures are relatively close at hand.

The Coral Coast is divided into three natural regions. Its only town, **Sigatoka** serves as both commercial and administrative headquarters. A primarily Indian settlement, it earns its living trading with farmers in the **Sigatoka Valley,** Fiji's breadbasket.

The area west of Sigatoka is dominated by the great Natadola Beach, with its InterContinental Golf Resort & Spa, and by Shangri-La's Fijian Resort & Spa, the country's largest hotel. Across the road are the Coral Coast Railway and the Kalevu South Pacific Cultural Centre.

East of Sigatoka, the central area is anchored by the village of **Korotogo,** where several hotels, restaurants, and the Kula Eco Park are grouped around the Outrigger on the Lagoon Fiji, another major hotel. Some smaller properties are on Sunset Strip, a dead-end section of the highway that was rerouted inland around the Outrigger.

To the far east, more resorts and hotels are dispersed on either side of **Korolevu** village.

GETTING TO & AROUND THE CORAL COAST

The Coral Coast doesn't have an airport, so you must get here from Nadi International Airport by taxi, bus, or rental car along the Queen's Road (see "Getting Around Fiji" in chapter 3).

The drive from Nadi to Natadola Beach takes about 45 minutes. After a sharp right turn at the south end of Nadi Town, the highway runs well inland, first through sugarcane fields undulating in the wind and then past acre after acre of pine trees planted in orderly rows, part of Fiji's national forestry program. The blue-green mountains lie off to the left; the deep-blue sea occasionally comes into view off to the right.

Because the Coral Coast essentially is a strip running for 70km (43 miles), a rental car is by far the easiest way to get around. The large hotels have taxis waiting outside their main entrances as well as Avis and Thrifty car-rental desks in their lobbies. Local firms are **Coastal Rental Cars** (✆ **652 0228**) and **Michael's Beach Rental** (✆ **997 6232** or 652 0584).

Express buses between Nadi and Suva stop at Shangri-La's Fijian Resort & Spa, the Outrigger on the Lagoon Fiji, Rydge's Hideaway Resort, the Naviti Resort, and the Warwick Fiji Resort & Spa. Local buses will stop for anyone who flags them down.

See "Getting Around Nadi," in chapter 5, for more information.

[FastFACTS] THE CORAL COAST

The following information applies to the Coral Coast. If you don't see an item here, see "Fast Facts: Fiji," in chapter 15, and "Fast Facts: Nadi," in chapter 5.

Camera & Film **Caines Photofast** (✆ **650 0877**) has a shop on Market Road in Sigatoka where you can burn your digital photos to CD. Most hotel boutiques sell film and provide 1-day processing.

Currency Exchange **ANZ Bank, Westpac Bank,** and **Colonial National Bank** all have branches with ATMs on the riverfront in Sigatoka. The Outrigger on the Lagoon Fiji, the Warwick Fiji Resort & Spa, and the Naviti resorts have ATMs in their lobbies (see "Where to Stay on the Coral Coast," below).

Drugstores **Patel Pharmacy** (✆ **650 0213**) is on Market Road in Sigatoka.

Healthcare The government-run **Sigatoka Hospital** (✆ **650 0455**) can handle minor problems.

Police The **Fiji Police** has posts at Sigatoka (✆ **650 0222**) and at Korolevu (**653 0322**).

Post Office Post offices are on the Queen's Road in Sigatoka and Korolevu.

The Coral Coast

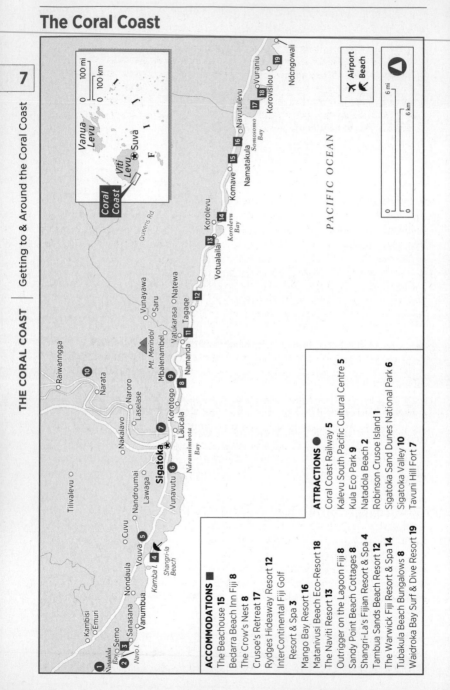

ACCOMMODATIONS ■

The Beachouse **15**
Bedarra Beach Inn Fiji **8**
The Crow's Nest **8**
Crusoe's Retreat **17**
Rydges Hideaway Resort **12**
InterContinental Fiji Golf
  Resort & Spa **3**
Mango Bay Resort **16**
Matanivusi Beach Eco-Resort **18**
The Naviti Resort **13**
Outrigger on the Lagoon Fiji **8**
Sandy Point Beach Cottages **8**
Shangri-La's Fijian Resort & Spa **4**
Tambua Sands Beach Resort **12**
The Warwick Fiji Resort & Spa **14**
Tubakula Beach Bungalows **8**
Waidroka Bay Surf & Dive Resort **19**

ATTRACTIONS ●

Coral Coast Railway **5**
Kalevu South Pacific Cultural Centre **5**
Kula Eco Park **9**
Natadola Beach **2**
Robinson Crusoe Island **1**
Sigatoka Sand Dunes National Park **6**
Sigatoka Valley **10**
Tavuni Hill Fort **7**

EXPLORING THE CORAL COAST

Hotel reception or tour desks can make reservations for most of the Nadi activities and Mamanuca Islands day cruises mentioned in chapters 5 and 6, respectively. You will likely pay slightly more for Nadi-based activities than if you were staying on the west coast. On the other hand, you are closer to such activities as the rafting trips on the Navua River (see chapter 8). You also can easily take advantage of the golf, fishing, and diving at Pacific Harbour and see the sights in Suva.

I have organized the attractions below from west to east; that is, in the order in which you will come to them from Nadi.

Natadola Beach ★★★

Off the Queen's Road 35km (22 miles) south of Nadi, the paved Maro Road runs westward through grasslands (this is the driest part of Viti Levu) to the exceptional **Natadola Beach ★★★**. Its deep white sand curves for nearly a kilometer (.6 mile) along the half-moon shape of Natadola Bay. A gap in the reef allows some surf to break on beach, especially on the south end, where stands the luxury-laden **InterContinental Fiji Golf Resort & Spa** (see "Where to Stay on the Coral Coast," below) and the spectacular links at **Natadola Bay Championship Golf Course** (see "Golfing," below). You can also get to Natadola via the Coral Coast Railway train from Shangri-La's Fijian Resort & Spa (see below).

Golfing at Natadola Beach ★★★

Fiji's golf scene took a giant leap forward with the 2009 opening of **Natadola Bay Championship Golf Course** (© 673 3500; www.natadolaby.com), on Maro Road near the InterContinental Fiji Golf Resort & Spa. Initially designed by Fiji native Vijay Singh, who eventually backed out of the project, the 18 holes extend from the hilltop clubhouse down to the beach and back. Bring extra balls, for you will be playing along the beach. The club house contains a bar, restaurant, and pro shop. The course is open daily except Christmas from 7am to 6:30pm. Greens fees are F$135 for InterContinental guests, F$179 for everyone else, including a cart. Rental clubs are available.

Robinson Crusoe Island

On Likuri, a small islet north of Natadola Beach, the backpacker-oriented **Robinson Crusoe Island** (© 628 1999; www.robinsoncrusoeislandfiji.com) has a lovely beach, a swimming pool, restaurant, bar, small *bures* (bungalows), and two dorms. It's an alternative to making the trek from the Coral Coast to Nadi for day trips to the Mamanuca and Yasawa islands, or a relaxing stop on the low-budget trail around Viti Levu. Snorkeling, water-skiing, tube rides, hair braiding, and massages are available to overnight guests and day-trippers alike. Rates range from F$89 per person in dorms to F$126 per person in bures, double occupancy, including all meals.

Coral Coast Railway ★

Based on the Queen's Road outside Shangri-La's Fijian Resort & Spa, the **Coral Coast Railway Co.** (🕿 **652 0434**) uses the restored sugar-cane locomotive *Fijian Princess* for tours on narrow-gauge railroads through the cane fields, across bridges, and along the coast. The best destination is lovely Natadola Beach, where you swim (bring your own towel) and have a barbecue lunch at the beach for F$79 per person. They run Tuesday, Thursday, and Saturday from the station at Shangri-La's Fijian resort, departing at 10am and returning at 4pm.

On other days, the locomotive makes trips east to Sigatoka. A half-day version (F$38) takes you to Sigatoka town for shopping and sightseeing, but you can stay on for an all-day "Ratu's Scenic Inland" tours into the Sigatoka Valley (F$100). The latter includes a visit to a Fijian village and kindergarten.

Children pay half fare, and all fares are somewhat more expensive if you are staying at a Nadi area hotel.

Kalevu South Pacific Cultural Centre

Part of a project known as Gecko's Resort, on the Queen's Road opposite Shangri-La's Fijian Resort & Spa, **Kalevu South Pacific Cultural Centre** (🕿 **652 0200**) is not nearly as good as Arts Village Cultural Centre in Pacific Harbour (see chapter 8), but it does have cultural exhibits about indigenous islander life in Fiji, Samoa, Kiribati (in the central Pacific), and New Zealand. You can take a 1-hour tour of the grounds exhibits for F$20. Call to see if it's still operating. The center is open daily from 9am to 3pm. You can also get refreshments here at Gecko's Restaurant (see "Where to Dine on the Coral Coast," later).

Sigatoka Sand Dunes National Park ★

The pine forests on either side of the Queen's Road soon give way to rolling fields of mission grass before the sea emerges at a viewpoint above Shangri-La's Fijian Resort & Spa on Yanuca Island. After you pass the resort, watch on the right for the visitor center for **Sigatoka Sand Dunes National Park** (🕿 **652 0243**; www.national trust.org.fj). Fiji's first national park protects high sand hills, which extend for several miles along the coast. About two-thirds of them are stabilized with grass, but some along the shore are still shifting sand (the surf crashing on them is dangerous). Ancient burial grounds and pieces of pottery dating from 5 B.C. to A.D. 240 have been found among the dunes, but be warned: Removing them is against the law. Exhibits in the visitor center explain the dunes and their history. Rangers are on duty daily from 8am to 4:30pm. Admission to the visitor center is free, but adults pay F$8, students F$3 to visit the actual dunes. Call ahead for a free guided tour. ***Note:*** You *must* go to the visitor center before visiting the dunes.

Sigatoka Town

About 3km (2 miles) from the sand dunes visitor center, the Queen's Road enters **Sigatoka** (pop. 2,000), the commercial center of the Coral Coast. This quiet, predominantly Indo-Fijian town is perched along the west bank of the **Sigatoka River,** Fiji's longest waterway. The broad, muddy river lies on one side of the main street; on the other is a row of stores. The river is crossed by the Melrose Bridge, built in 1997 and named in honor of Fiji's winning the Melrose Cup at the Hong Kong Sevens rugby matches. The old bridge it replaced is now for pedestrians only.

Sigatoka Valley

From Sigatoka, you can go inland along the west bank of the meandering river, flanked on both sides by a patchwork of flat green fields of vegetables that give the **Sigatoka Valley** its nickname: "Fiji's Salad Bowl." The pavement ends about 1km (½ mile) from the town; after that, the road surface is poorly graded and covered with loose stones.

The residents of **Lawai** village (1.5km/1 mile from town) offer Fijian handicrafts for sale. Two kilometers (1¼ miles) farther on, a small dirt track branches off to the left and runs down a hill to **Nakabuta,** the "Pottery Village," where the residents make and sell authentic Fijian pottery. This art has seen a renaissance of late, and you will find Nakabuta-made bowls, plates, and other items in handicraft shops elsewhere. Tour buses from Nadi and the Coral Coast stop there most days.

Unless you're subject to vertigo, you can look forward to driving past Nakabuta: The road climbs steeply along a narrow ridge, commanding panoramic views across the winding Sigatoka Valley with its quiltlike fields to the right and much smaller, more rugged ravine to the left. It then winds its way down to the valley floor and the **Sigatoka Agricultural Research Station,** on whose shady grounds some tour groups stop for picnic lunches. The road climbs into the interior and eventually to Ba on the northwest coast; it intersects the **Nausori Highlands Road** leading back to Nadi, but it can be rough or even washed out during periods of heavy rain. Unless you have a four-wheel-drive vehicle or are on an organized tour with a guide, I would turn around at the research station and head back to Sigatoka.

Jet Boat Tours ★★★

A much better alternative to driving up the Sigatoka Valley is to ride up the river itself in a jet boat operated by **Sigatoka River Safari** (✆ **0800 650 1721** in Fiji. sigatokariver.com). Much more scenic and culturally interesting than Adrenalin Jet Fiji in Nadi (p. 99), these half-day tours are not just thrill rides, for they stop for 2 hours in a Fijian village for a kava welcoming ceremony and a look at local life. The safaris cost F$210 for adults, F$99 for children 4 to 15. Add F$20 for departures from Nadi.

Tavuni Hill Fort

A dirt road runs from Queen's Road at the eastern end of the Sigatoka River bridge inland 5km (3 miles) to the **Tavuni Hill Fort,** built by an exiled Tongan chief as a safe haven from the ferocious Fijian hill tribes living up the valley. Those highlanders constantly fought wars with the coastal Fijians, and they were the last to give up cannibalism and convert to Christianity. When they rebelled against the Deed of Cession to Great Britain in 1875, the colonial administration sent a force of 1,000 men up the Sigatoka River. They destroyed all the hill forts lining the river, including Tavuni. Part of the fort has been restored as a Fiji Heritage Project. The visitor center (© 650 0818) has exhibits explaining the history, and park rangers will lead 30-minute tours if you ask. The fort is open to the public Monday to Saturday 8am to 4pm. Admission is F$12 for adults and F$6 for children.

Kula Eco Park ★★

Off the Queen's Road opposite the Outrigger on the Lagoon Fiji, **Kula Eco Park** (© 650 0505; www.fijiwild.com) is Fiji's only wildlife park. Along the banks of a stream in a tropical forest, it has a fine collection of rainbow-feathered tropical birds and an aquarium stocked with examples of local sea life. Allow 2 hours here, as this is one of the South Pacific's best places to view local flora and fauna in a natural setting. Children will love it. It's open daily 10am to 4pm. Admission is F$20 for adults, F$10 for children 11 and under.

Waterfall & Cave Tours ★★

You won't soon forget the waterfall and cave tours offered by **Adventures in Paradise Fiji** (© 652 0833; www.adventuresinparadisefiji.com), near the Outrigger on the Lagoon Fiji. The waterfall tour goes to Biausevu village in the Korolevu Valley. A tour bus takes you to the village, where you'll be welcomed at a traditional *yaqona* (kava) ceremony. Then comes a 30-minute hike along a rocky stream to the falls, which plunge straight over a cliff into a swimming hole. The sometimes slippery trail fords the stream seven times, so wear canvas or reef shoes or a pair of strap-on sandals. Wear a bathing suit and bring a towel if you want to take a very cool and refreshing dip after the sweaty hike. You'll be treated to a barbecue lunch.

On the other excursion, you'll spend 45 minutes inside the Naihehe Cave, which was used as a fortress by Fiji's last cannibal tribe. After a picnic lunch, you'll return via a *bilibili* (bamboo) raft on the Sigatoka River (the cave is a 35-min. drive up the Sigatoka Valley).

The tours cost F$119 per person. Add F$20 from Nadi. They run on alternate days and can be booked at any hotel activities desk.

Shopping on the Coral Coast

In Sigatoka Town, you can do some serious hunting at **Sigatoka Indigenous Women's Handicraft Centre** (no phone), in a tin-roof shack on the main street beside the river. Operated by local women, it has carvings, shell jewelry, *masi* (bark) cloth, and other items made in Fiji. Jack's of Fiji and Tappoo both have large stores across the street.

Prices at relaxed, "browse-in-peace" **Baravi Handicrafts ★★** (© 652 0364) in Vatukarasa village, 13km (8 miles) east of Sigatoka, are somewhat lower than you'll find at the larger stores, and it has a snack bar that sells tea and excellent coffee made from Fijian-grown beans (you will be offered a freebie cup). The shop buys woodcarvings and pottery directly from village artisans. It's open Monday to Saturday 7:30am to 6pm, Sunday 8:30am to 5pm. Vatukarasa is the only village on the Queen's Road which still has traditional Fijian bures built of thatch.

WHERE TO STAY

Most hotels have abundant sports facilities, including diving, and those that don't will arrange activities for you. Outsiders are welcome to use the facilities at most resorts—for a fee, of course.

The InterContinental Fiji Golf Resort & Spa and the Shangri-La's Fijian Resort & Spa are west of Sigatoka town, but most other accommodations are in two areas: Near **Korotogo,** a small village about 8km (5 miles) east of Sigatoka, and spread out on either side of **Korolevu,** another village some 30km (19 miles) east of Sigatoka. The greatest concentration is at Korolevu, where the Outrigger on the Lagoon Fiji and several other hotels are within walking distance of each other, as are restaurants on **Sunset Strip,** which leaves the Queen's Road at a traffic circle and skirts the lagoon until it dead-ends at the Outrigger. In other words, you can easily walk among the Korotogo hotels and restaurants. Elsewhere you will need transportation to go out to dinner or visit another resort.

I have organized the accommodations below by area, from west to east.

West of Sigatoka

InterContinental Fiji Golf Resort & Spa ★★★ ☺ This luxurious, state-of-the art resort opened in 2009 on the south end of Natadola Beach, where the sands end and a low-tide mud flat begins. Reception, a lounge bar, and a buffet-style restaurant are in the main building which opens to the deep white sands. From there the resort extends southward to the accommodations (12 units per building), two swimming pools, both casual- and fine-dining restaurants, an excellent spa, and a large children's center. Adding to the family appeal is a shallow 110m (300 ft.) long pool wrapping halfway around the casual restaurant. An infinity-edge pool on the sea side of the restaurant is reserved for adults. The spacious units are especially appealing to romantic couples, as their large balconies or patios are equipped with day beds, oval-shaped "Cleopatra" soaking tubs, and privacy curtains. The hotel units are designed for indoor-outdoor living, but the air-conditioners inside automatically shut off when the sliding doors open, thus making this a problematic proposition during the hot months of December through February. Larger and more luxurious Club InterContinental suites stand on a hillside overlooking the sea. Guests staying up there have butler service and their own restaurant and outside pool. Some club units even have private plunge pools. Except for its friendly Fijian staff, this fine establishment could be anywhere in the world. The resort manages the nearby Natadola Bay Championship Golf Course (see "Golfing on the Coral Coast," above).

Private Mail Bag, Nadi Airport (Natadola Beach). ⓒ **888/424-6835** or 763 3300. Fax 673 3499. www. intercontinental.com. 271 units. F$450–F$925 double. AE, MC, V. **Amenities:** 3 restaurants; 4 bars; babysitting; children's center; concierge; executive or concierge-level rooms; golf course; health club; Jacuzzi; 2 outdoor pools; room service; spa; watersports equipment/rentals; Wi-Fi (in main bldg.; F$30/day). In room: A/C, ceiling fan, TV/DVD, hair dryer, Internet (F$30/day), minibar, MP3 docking station.

Shangri-La's Fijian Resort & Spa ★★★ ☺ Fiji's largest hotel, "The Fijian" occupies all 42 hectares (105 acres) of flat Yanuca Island, which is bordered by a crystal clear lagoon and a coral-colored sand beach. There are a host of watersports activities here, including diving, or you can play tennis or knock around the 9-hole golf course. There's a very good children's program, too. Covered walkways wander through thick tropical foliage to link the hotel blocks to three main restaurant-and-bar buildings, both adjacent to swimming pools. The spacious rooms and suites occupy two- and three-story buildings, all on the shore of the island. Each room has a view of the lagoon and sea from its own private balcony or patio. The suites have separate bedrooms and two bathroom sinks. While the Fijian draws many families, its Ocean Premier units on one end of the sprawling property are reserved exclusively for couples. Away from the throngs at the end of the island, **CHI, the Spa Village** is a knockout, with bungalowlike treatment rooms where you can spend the night after being pampered. The half-dozen luxurious Premier Ocean bures—between the spa and the resort's glass-walled wedding chapel—are great for honeymooners.

Private Mail Bag (NAPO 353), Nadi Airport (Yanuca Island). (℃ **866/565-5050** or 652 0155. Fax 652 0402. www.shangri-la.com. 442 units. F$440–F$580 double; F$650–F$800 suite; F$1,150 bungalow. AE, DC, MC, V. **Amenities:** 4 restaurants; 4 bars; babysitting; bikes; children's center; concierge; executive or concierge-level rooms; golf course; health club; Jacuzzi; 3 outdoor pools; room service; spa; tennis courts; watersports equipment/rentals; Wi-Fi (at pool areas; F$30/day). *In room:* A/C, ceiling fan, TV, TV/DVD (in bures), fridge, hair dryer, Internet (F$30/day).

Near Korotogo

Bedarra Beach Inn Fiji ★ ✦ This comfortable inn began life as a private home with bedrooms on either end of a two-story central hall, which opened to a veranda overlooking a swimming pool and the lagoon. The beach is across a dead-end road known as Sunset Strip, which was the main drag before the Queen's Road was diverted around the Outrigger on the Lagoon Fiji, a short walk from here. Today, a bar, lounge furniture, and potted palms occupy the great hall, and two restaurants have taken over the verandas (see "Where to Dine on the Coral Coast," below). Upstairs, four rooms open to another veranda wrapping around the house. Inside, guests can opt for two-bedroom family rooms capable of sleeping up to four persons. To the side of the house, a two-story motel block holds 16 air-conditioned rooms, all sporting large bathrooms with walk-in showers.

P.O. Box 1213, Sigatoka (Sunset Strip). (℃ **650 0476.** Fax 652 0166. www.bedarrafiji.com. 24 units. F$145–F$180 double. AE, MC, V. **Amenities:** 2 restaurants; bar; babysitting; laundry service; outdoor pool. *In room:* A/C, fridge, no phone.

The Crow's Nest Although it's getting a bit long in the tooth, this hotel enjoys a convenient location on Sunset Strip within walking distance of restaurants and the Outrigger on the Lagoon Fiji. Accommodations are in two rows of duplex buildings, the first sitting in a coconut grove across the road from the beach. Behind is a second row up on a terraced hillside. The outdoor pool, bar, and pedestrian restaurant are even higher up, which gives them fine views over the lagoon to the sea. The split-level units have queen-size beds on their mezzanine level and two single beds down in the lounge area. Executive units add a kitchen, which makes them money-saving options for families or two couples sharing a room. All have balconies.

P.O. Box 270, Sigatoka (Sunset Strip). (℃ **650 0230.** Fax 650 0513. 25 units. F$99–F$145 double. AE, MC, V. **Amenities:** Restaurant; bar; outdoor pool; watersports equipment/rentals; free Wi-Fi. *In room:* A/C, ceiling fan, hair dryer, no phone.

Outrigger on the Lagoon Fiji ★★ ☺ This fine lagoonside resort compensates for Mother Nature having robbed its beach of most of the sand with one of the most attractive swimming pools in Fiji. You can still go kayaking, *spy boarding* (riding face-down on a board with a plastic window for fish-viewing), and snorkeling at high tide, but the gorgeous pool is the center of attention here. In a way, the Outrigger is two hotels in one. A majority of the accommodations are hotel rooms in five-story hillside buildings at the rear of the property. They all have balconies, with spectacular views from the upper floor units. In a coconut grove down by the lagoon, a stand of thatched-roof guest bungalows and restaurants resembles a traditional Fijian village. Hotel rooms in the Reef Wing, a three-story lagoonside building (and the last remnant of the Reef Resort which once stood here), are smaller than their hillside counterparts and better suited to couples than families. You'll have more charm in the comfortable guest bures, which have masi-lined peaked ceilings. The beachfront bungalows are the pick of the litter. A few others are joined as family units. Australian restaurateur Geoff Shaw, who owns both this resort and Castaway Island Resort (see "Resorts in the Mamanuca Islands," in chapter 6), sees to it that everyone is well-fed in Ivi (an intimate fine-dining restaurant with outstanding food; reservations required), a large open-air, buffet-style dining room, and a midday pizza restaurant by the pool. The wedding chapel and full-service spa sits high on a hill with stunning lagoon and sea views.

P.O. Box 173, Sigatoka (Queen's Rd.). ✆ **800/688-7444** or 650 0044. Fax 652 0074. www.outrigger. com. 254 units. F$370–F$863 double; F$575–F$925. suite AE, DC, MC, V. **Amenities:** 4 restaurants; 5 bars; babysitting; children's center; health club; Jacuzzi; outdoor pool; room service; spa; 2 tennis courts; watersports equipment/rentals; Wi-Fi (in reception and pool areas; F$30/hour). *In room:* A/C, ceiling fan, TV, fridge, hair dryer.

Sandy Point Beach Cottages ✦

These five cottages occupy a coconut grove across a usually dry stream bed from the Outrigger. There is a sandy point at the mouth of the stream, but a breakwater runs in front of the property. The spacious cottages date from the 1960s, and they could use a coat of paint. They are popular with local families, who recognize them to be very reasonably priced temporary vacation homes. One family unit is larger, but the others are one large room with a lou-vered divider separating living and sleeping areas. Each has a veranda across the front and a carport to one side. Owners Bob and Coral Kennedy live here, and guests can use the swimming pool between their home and the lagoon. Bob is descended from an Irishman who came to Fiji in 1870, and he is a font of information about the country. He's also a techie, which explains the small forest of satellite dishes here. They feed a dozen TV channels to each cottage's TV.

P.O. Box 23, Sigatoka (Queens' Rd.). ✆ **650 0125.** Fax 650 0147. www.sandypointfiji.com. 5 units. F$90–F$160. MC, V. **Amenities:** Outdoor pool; free Wi-Fi (in office). *In room:* Ceiling fans, TV, kitchen, no phone.

Tubakula Beach Bungalows

While most backpackers head for the Beachouse or Mango Bay Resort near Korolevu, a few opt for brief stays at this simple, staid property (whose name is pronounced *Toomb*-a-koola) because it is within walking distance of the Outrigger on the Lagoon Fiji, the restaurants on Sunset Strip, and Kula Eco Park. The dorms are in European-style houses; no more than four beds are in any one room. The A-frame bungalows have kitchens, but I think cost-conscious families will be happier at Sandy Point Beach Cottages.

P.O. Box 2, Sigatoka (Queen's Rd.). ✆ **650 0097.** Fax 650 0201. www.fiji4less.com.fj. 27 bungalows, 24 dorm beds. F$126–F$180 bungalow; F$28 dorm bed. AE, MC, V. **Amenities:** Restaurant; bar; outdoor pool; Internet (F$30/hour). *In room:* Kitchen, no phone.

Between Korotogo & Korolevu

Rydges Hideaway Resort   Owned by an Australian hotel chain, this lively, all-bungalow resort occupies a narrow strip of land between the Queen's Road and the lagoon. It's long enough so that families, singles, and couples don't get in each other's way or disturb each other's sleep—or lack thereof, given lively nightlife in the central bar and restaurant. For optimum peace and quiet, choose a duplex "deluxe villa" on the far western end of the property. They have dual indoor showers as well as outdoor showers. Older A-frame bungalows are much closer to the action. Other units are in modern, duplex bungalows with tropical furnishings and shower-only bathrooms. A few larger family units here can sleep up to five persons. The main building opens to a beachside pool with a waterfall and a water slide. As has happened at the Outrigger on the Lagoon Fiji (see above), most of the beach is obscured at high tide, but you can follow a trail out on the reef and observe a coral restoration project.

P.O. Box 233, Sigatoka (Queen's Rd.). © **650 0177.** Fax 652 0025. www.hideawayfiji.com. 112 units. F$199–F$540 double. Rates include full breakfast buffet. AE, MC, V. **Amenities:** Restaurant; bar; children's programs; minigolf course; health club; outdoor pool; tennis court; watersports equipment/rentals; Wi-Fi (F$20/day). In room: A/C, ceiling fan, fridge, hair dryer.

Tambua Sands Beach Resort   This sedate, all-bungalow hotel sits in a narrow, 6.8-hectare (17-acre) grove of coconut palms beside a somewhat better white-sand beach than fronts the nearby Hideaway Resort. The bungalows have high-peaked ceilings with tin roofs, and their front porches all face the lagoon (those closest to the beach cost slightly more than the "oceanview" units). Each has both a queen-size and single bed. A wooden footbridge crosses a stream flowing through the grounds and connects the bungalows with a swimming pool and plantation-style central building. The low-ceiling, open-air restaurant and bar are somewhat dark, but they do look out to the pool and the sea.

P.O. Box 177, Sigatoka (Queen's Rd.). © **650 0399.** Fax 650 0265. www.tambuasandsfiji.com. 25 units. F$125–F$135 double. AE, MC, V. **Amenities:** Restaurant; bar; babysitting; Internet (in lobby; F25¢/minute); outdoor pool; watersports equipment/rentals. In room: Ceiling fan, fridge, no phone.

Near Korolevu

The Beachouse ★   Andrew Waldken-Brown, a European who was born in Fiji, and his Australian wife, Jessica, have turned his family's old vacation retreat—beside one of the finest beaches on the Coral Coast—into this excellent backpacker resort. The British TV show *Love Island* took over the premises a few years ago and built a charming South Seas stage set and swimming pool, which now serves as lounge, bar, and dining room providing inexpensive meals. Each dorm is screened and has its own ceiling fan, and all beds have reading lights. The upstairs is aimed at couples, with partitions separating roomettes, but the walls don't reach the ceiling; the accommodations also have ceiling fans and mosquito-netted double beds. More private for couples are the bungalowlike garden units, each of which has a double bed. All guests, including the campers who pitch their tents on the spacious lawn, share clean toilets and a modern communal kitchen. Although it lacks bures with bathrooms, the Beachouse is more intimate than the rocking Mango Bay Resort (see below). It's directly on the Queen's Road, which means easy bus connections.

P.O. Box 68, Korolevu (Queen's Rd.). © **0800/653 0530** toll-free in Fiji, or 653 0500. www.fijibeachouse.com. 12 units (none with bathroom), 48 dorm beds. F$110 double; F$35 dorm bed; F$25 (per person) camping. MC, V. **Amenities:** Restaurant; bar; bikes; outdoor pool; watersports equipment; free Wi-Fi. *In room:* Fan, no phone.

Crusoe's Retreat   Only the foot shaped swimming pool reminds me of when this low-key resort was known as Man Friday. It's still one of the Coral Coast's oldest hotels, but much has been done in recent years to improve it, including installation of bathrooms with "his-and-her" shower heads and sinks. It's a rough but scenic 4km (2½-mile) ride along a dirt road and a steep downhill descent to reach the resort. In fact, you'll have to climb uphill to guest units nos. 12 through 29. They have stunning views, but I prefer those down near the beach, especially the thatch-encased "seaside luxury" bungalows. They're not that luxurious by modern standards, but they are much more charming than the other A-frame units here—and they have air-conditioners and outdoor showers. The skimpy beach in front of the resort is augmented by sand held in place by a rock wall; it's much better in front of Namaqmaqua, the adjoining Fijian village. Crusoe's has what appears to be a grass tennis court, but don't bother bringing your racket.

P.O. Box 20, Korolevu (Somosomo Bay). ✆ **650 0185.** Fax 650 0666. www.crusoesretreat.com. 29 units. F$234–F$401 double. AE, MC, V. **Amenities:** Restaurant; bar; babysitting; Internet (computer in boutique; F20¢/minute); outdoor pool; watersports equipment/rentals. *In room:* A/C (seaside units only), ceiling fan, fridge, hair dryer.

Mango Bay Resort   This beachside resort is popular among 25- to 30-year-olds, although its small bungalows and African–influenced safari cabins appeal to travelers of any age who don't mind a lot of bustle or a poolside bar that can rock past midnight. Fortunately it's all spread out over several acres of lawn and palm trees, so the noise shouldn't seriously interfere with sleeping. Mango Bay is an eco-friendly place, so none of the natural thatched-roof units or dorms have air-conditioners. The tents have wood floors and walls, front porches, and both double and single beds. The more expensive dorm has double beds separated by dividers, while the other has over-and-under bunk beds. The units are not screened, but every bed here has its own mosquito net.

P.O. Box 1720, Sigatoka (Queen's Rd.). ✆ **653 0069.** Fax 653 0138. www.mangobayresortfiji.com. 20 units, 70 dorm beds. F$195–F$275 double; F$36–F$45 dorm bed. Rates include continental breakfast. AE, MC, V. No children 11 and under accepted. **Amenities:** Restaurant; 2 bars; outdoor pool; watersports equipment/rentals; Wi-Fi (in reception; F$10/hour). *In room:* Ceiling fan, no phone.

Matanivusi Beach Eco-Resort   Brian McDonald moved from Australia's Gold Coast to Suva in 1996 to work as a librarian, but he and wife Donna really came here to satisfy their love of surfing. In 2005, they opened this little resort strictly as a surf camp. After upgrading it, they now cater to folks who share their passion for riding the waves and to their family and friends who do not. Like Waidroka Bay Surf & Dive Resort (see below), Matanivusi is closer to the breaks at Frigate Passage than either Pacific Harbour or Beqa Island. Unlike Waidroka, the McDonalds have a beach in front of their main building, which houses a satellite-fed TV lounge as well as restaurant and bar. A pierlike pathway leads across a wetland to their four spacious guest bungalows. They stand on posts rather than concrete slabs in order to minimize their impact on the environment. Surfing trips to the nearby breaks are included in the rates; you'll pay extra for Frigates Passage.

P.O. Box 316, Pacific Harbour (3km/2 miles south of Vunaniu Village). ✆ **992 3230** or 360 9479. www.surfingfiji.com. 4 units. F$400 per person. Rates include meals, surfing, and snorkeling. MC, V. **Amenities:**

Restaurant; bar; babysitting; free Internet (in office); Jacuzzi; outdoor pool; watersports equipment/ rentals. *In room:* Ceiling fan, no phone.

The Naviti Resort   A sister of the Warwick Fiji Resort & Spa (see below), this sprawling resort attracts mainly Australians and New Zealanders lured by its extensive activities and optional all-inclusive rates, which include all the beer and booze you can drink. The resort sits on 15 hectares (38 acres) of coconut palms waving in the trade wind beside a beach and dredged lagoon (you can wade to two islets). Or you can lounge beside two swimming pools, one with a shaded swim-up bar. Double-deck covered walkways lead from the central complex to two- and three-story concrete block buildings, two of them constructed in 2005. The older wings hold some of Fiji's largest hotel rooms (bathrooms have both tubs and walk-in showers). The two-room suites on the ends of the older buildings are especially spacious. The best units here, however, are 16 beachside bungalows, ranging from studios to two-bedrooms. Tall shingle roofs cover a coffee shop, a candlelit restaurant for fine dining, and a large lounge where a band plays most evenings. A fine Chinese restaurant looks out on an unchallenging 9-hole golf course.

P.O. Box 29, Korolevu (Queen's Rd.). ✆ **800/203-3232** or 653 0444. Fax 653 0099. www.navitiresort. com.fj. 224 units. F$335–F$615 double; F$510–F$710 bungalow. Rates include breakfast. All-inclusive rates available. AE, DC, MC, V. **Amenities:** 3 restaurants; 3 bars; babysitting; bikes; children's center; 9-hole golf course; health club; Jacuzzi; 2 outdoor pools; room service; spa; tennis courts; watersports equipment/rentals; Wi-Fi (F$10/hour). *In room:* A/C, TV, fridge, hair dryer.

Waidroka Bay Surf & Dive Resort   The easternmost of the Coral Coast resorts, this little lagoonside retreat has more in common with those at Pacific Harbour, which is much closer to here than is Korotogo. The lagoon here has no beach, so owners Boris and Karin Kaz—a German-Israeli couple who relocated here from New York City—specialize in diving, snorkeling, fishing, and surfing. The guest bungalows flank their spacious, Mediterranean-style main building with a restaurant, bar, and large front porch opening to a swimming pool (with its own bar) set on a grassy lawn beside the palm-fringed lagoon. Guest quarters are either in bungalows (some have two bedrooms) or in a motel-like building. Waidroka is 4km (2½ miles) south of the Queen's Road via a dirt track that literally climbs over a mountain before descending through a development of modest vacation homes.

P.O. Box 323, Pacific Harbour (Waidroka Bay). ✆ **330 4605.** Fax 330 4383. www.waidroka.com. 11 units. F$200–F$320 double. MC, V. **Amenities:** Restaurant; 2 bars; outdoor pool; watersports equipment/ rentals; Wi-Fi (in main bldg; F$45/stay). *In room:* Ceiling fan, no phone.

The Warwick Fiji Resort & Spa ★★   Sitting on a palm-dotted beach with a bit more sand than you'll find at the Outrigger or the Hideaway, this complex reflects distinctive architecture from its origins as the Hyatt Regency Fiji. A sweeping roof supported by wood beams covers a wide reception and lobby area bordered on either end by huge carved murals depicting Captain James Cook's discovery of Fiji in 1779. A curving staircase descends from the center of the lobby into a large square well, giving access to the dining and recreation areas on the lagoon level. The medium-size guest rooms are in two wings—appropriately dubbed "Nadi" and "Suva"—flanking the central building. They are smaller than at The Warwick's sister, The Naviti Resort, which makes it less attractive to families than to couples. Each room has its own balcony or patio with a view of the sea or the tropical gardens surrounding the complex. The most expensive units are suites that directly face the lagoon from the ends of the buildings. Guests staying in Warwick Club rooms have access to one of Fiji's better executive-level lounges. Under a thatched roof on a tiny island offshore, the sand-floored Wicked Walu is the choice dining spot here. Guests can take a free shuttle to the Naviti and use its golf course and other facilities.

P.O. Box 100, Korolevu (Queen's Rd.). © **800/203-3232** or 653 0555. Fax 653 0010. www.warwickfiji. com. 250 units. F$410–F$579 double; F$790 suite. Rates include full breakfast. All-inclusive rates available. AE, DC, MC, V. **Amenities:** 5 restaurants; 5 bars; babysitting; bikes; children's programs; concierge; executive rooms; health club; Jacuzzi; 2 outdoor pools; room service; spa; tennis courts; watersports equipment/rentals; Wi-Fi (F$30/day). *In room:* A/C, ceiling fan, TV, VCR (in club rooms), fridge, hair dryer

WHERE TO DINE

In Sigatoka Town next to Jack's of Fiji, Roshni and Jean-Pierre Gerber's clean **Le Cafe Town** (© **652 0668**) offers inexpensive sandwiches, salads, curries, spaghetti, pizzas, fish and chips, and other snacks. Credit cards are not accepted. Le Cafe Town is open Monday to Friday from 9am to 5pm, Saturday 9am to 2pm. The Gerbers—she's from Fiji, he's Swiss, and both are chefs—also serve dinners at Le Cafe in Korotogo (see below).

Many Coral Coast hotels have special nights, such as meke feasts of Fijian foods cooked in a lovo, served buffet style and followed by traditional dancing.

As with the hotels above, I have organized the restaurants by location.

West of Sigatoka

Gecko's Restaurant PACIFIC RIM   Occupying the veranda of one of the Western-style buildings at the Kalevu South Pacific Cultural Centre, this open-air restaurant offers a more affordable—but not nearly as good—alternative to the dining rooms at Shangri-La's Fijian Resort & Spa across the Queen's Road. You can have a breakfast of omelets and other egg dishes all day here. Lunch features a choice of sandwiches, burgers, fish and chips, curry, stir-fries, and other local favorites. Dinner sees a wide-ranging menu.

Queen's Rd., in Kalevu South Pacific Museum opposite Shangri-La's Fijian Resort & Spa. © **652 0200.** Reservations accepted. Breakfast F$15; lunch F$10–F$16; main courses F$10–F$55. MC, V. Daily 8am–9:30pm.

Near Korotogo

Beachside Cafe & Restaurant PACIFIC RIM   Indian curries are the most numerous offerings at this open-air restaurant under a tin roof next to a convenience store—although I picked a decent version of garlic prawns off the daily specials board. Fish and chips and stir-fried vegetables also appear. The Bula Bar has full service and billiards tables, although I prefer to imbibe at Le Cafe next door (see below).

Sunset Strip, Korotogo, west of the Outrigger on the Lagoon Fiji. © **652 0584.** Main courses F$10–F$19. No credit cards. Daily 8am–10pm.

Le Cafe INTERNATIONAL   In addition to running Le Cafe Town in Sigatoka, Roshni and Jean-Pierre Gerber turn their attention to this little establishment, where they oversee the production of fish and chips, curries, pastas, and some reasonably good pizzas. The nightly specials board features the likes of fresh fish filet with lemon butter sauce, pepper or garlic steak, garlic prawns, and local lobster with Mornay sauce. Even if you don't dine here, the thatched-top bar out front is a great place for a sunset cocktail during happy hour from 5 to 8pm daily.

Sunset Strip, Korotogo, west of the Outrigger on the Lagoon Fiji. © **652 0877**. Reservations accepted. Pizzas F$13–F$17; main courses F$15–F$20. No credit cards. Daily 11am–10pm.

Ocean Terrace Restaurant/EbbTide Cafe ★ INTERNATIONAL   Occupying the veranda overlooking the swimming pool at the Bedarra Beach Inn Fiji (see "Where to Stay on the Coral Coast," earlier in this chapter), this is one restaurant with two names. During the day it's known as the Ebb Tide Cafe, serving breakfast and a lunchtime menu of salads, sandwiches, burgers, a few main courses, and 12-inch pizzas with a limited selection of toppings. At night it turns into the romantic Ocean Terrace Restaurant, where the chef takes flight with his own versions of chicken and seafood curries, Fijian dishes such as *kokoda* (marinated raw fish) and *ika vakalolo* (Spanish mackerel steamed with coconut milk), and Western fare such as reef fish with a creamy lemon and coriander sauce.

Sunset Strip, Korotogo, in Bedarra Beach Inn Fiji. © **650 0476**. Reservations accepted. Breakfast F$7–F$18; sandwiches and burgers F$15; pizzas F$22; main courses F$25–F$29. AE, MC, V. Daily 7am–3pm and 6–9pm.

Near Korolevu

Vilisite's Seafood Restaurant ★ 🍴 SEAFOOD/INDIAN/CHINESE   Vilisite (sounds like "Felicity"), a friendly Fijian who lived in Australia, owns one of the few nonhotel establishments in Fiji where you can dine right by the lagoon's edge. Come in time for a sunset drink and bring a camera, for the westward view from Vilisite's veranda belongs on a postcard. Her cuisine is predominately fresh local seafood—fish, shrimp, lobster, octopus—in curry, garlic and butter, or coconut milk (the Fijian way). She offers a choice of five full seafood meals at dinner, or you can choose from chop suey, curry, shrimp, or fish and chips from a blackboard menu. Vilisite will arrange rides for dinner parties of four or more from as far away as the Outrigger on the Lagoon Fiji, but be sure to ask about the cost. You won't soon forget the view.

Queen's Rd., Korolevu, btw. the Warwick and the Naviti. © **653 0054**. Reservations recommended. Full dinners F$25–F$50; other main courses F$10–F$48. MC, V. Daily 7am–9pm.

NIGHTLIFE ON THE CORAL COAST

Coral Coast nightlife centers around the hotels and whatever Fijian meke shows they are sponsoring.

The **Fijian fire walkers** from Beqa, an island off the south coast (remember, it's pronounced M-*bengga*, not *Beck*-a) parade across the steaming stones to the incantations of "witch doctors" at least once a week at **Rydges Hideaway Resort** (© **650 0177**), **Outrigger on the Lagoon Fiji** (© **650 0044**), and the **Warwick Fiji Resort & Spa** (© **653 0010**). Call them or ask at your hotel for the schedule.

A RESORT ON VATULELE ISLAND

A flat, raised coral atoll 48km (30 miles) south of Viti Levu, **Vatulele Island** is known for its unusual red shrimp—that is, they're red while alive, not just after being cooked. The only way to see them, however, is to stay at Vatulele Island Resort, which is accessible only from Nadi Airport.

Vatulele Island Resort ★★★ This luxury resort resides beside a gorgeous, 1km (½ mile) –long beach of brilliantly white sand fronting a lagoon deep enough for swimming and snorkeling at all tides. In a blend of Santa Fe and Fijian native architectural styles, the bungalows and main building have thick adobe walls supporting Fijian thatch roofs. During the day you can take a picnic lunch out on a tiny nearby islet known for good reason as "Nookie Island." Seemingly vast distances and thick native forest separate the spacious *bures*. Most of these are L-shaped and have a lounge and raised sleeping areas under one roof, plus another roof covering a large bathroom. Air-conditioners blow down over their beds, but these big units were not designed to be cooled by anything other than ocean breezes. At the far end of the property, the private, exquisitely designed Pink House is a delight for honeymooners, with its own private beach, plunge pool, and a unique two-person, face-to-face bathtub in the middle of its large bathroom. Celebrity guests often opt for the terrific views from The Point, a two-story villa sitting on a headland; it also has its own private pool.

P.O. Box 11368, Nadi Airport (Vatulele Island, 50km/31 miles south of Viti Levu, a 30-min. flight from Nadi). © **672 0300.** Fax 672 0062. www.vatulele.com. 19 units. US$924–US$2,079 bungalow. Rates include meals, drinks, and all activities except sportfishing and scuba diving. 4-night minimum stay required. AE, DC, MC, V. Children 11 and under not accepted. **Amenities:** Restaurant; bar; room service; tennis court. *In room:* Minibar, no phone.

PACIFIC HARBOUR & BEQA ISLAND

8

Pacific Harbour was begun in the early 1970s as a recreation-oriented, luxury residential community and resort (translated: a real-estate development). Given the heat, humidity, and amount of rain it gets, Pacific Harbour is not the place to come for a typical beach vacation, although you can swim at all tides off 3km (2 miles) of deep, grayish sand. On the other hand, it does have an excellent golf course, fine deep-sea fishing, fabulous scuba diving both out in the **Beqa Lagoon** and along the coast (this is one place in Fiji where you can go on shark-feeding dives), and outstanding white-water rafting trips on the nearby **Navua River.** Local promoters are correct when they describe Pacific Harbour as "The Adventure Capital of Fiji."

It's also my favorite place to experience Fijian culture without visiting a village. Formerly known as the Pacific Harbour Cultural Centre & Market Place but now called the **Arts Village,** this shopping center on the Queen's Road serves tourists and residents of the housing development. Although going through the throes of new ownership, it consists of colonial-style clapboard buildings joined by covered walkways leading to restaurants, a grocery store, boutiques, handicraft shops, a fancy swimming pool complex, and the country's best cultural center (see below).

Offshore, rugged **Beqa Island** is nearly cut in two by Malumu Bay, making it one of Fiji's more scenic spots. Most of Fiji's famous fire walkers come from Dakuibeqa, Naceva, and Ruka villages on Beqa. The island is surrounded by the beautiful **Beqa Lagoon,** where more than a dozen dive sites feature both soft and hard corals. Among them is **Frigate Passage,** which has a 48m (158-ft.) wall for divers but is even better known among surfers for its powerful left-handed surf break over a relatively smooth coral reef.

A number of expatriates have built homes here, and they have their own tourist information websites at **www.pacificharbour-fiji.com** and **www.pacificcoast fiji.com.**

GETTING TO & AROUND PACIFIC HARBOUR

Pacific Harbour is on the Queen's Road, 30km (18 miles) west of Suva. The express buses between Nadi and Suva stop at the Pearl South Pacific Resort, where you'll also find taxis waiting in the parking lot. See "Getting Around Fiji" in chapter 3 for more information. **Thrifty Car Rental** has an office here (© **345 0655**) and a desk in the lobby of The Pearl South Pacific resort (© **368 0013**).

No regular ferry service runs between Pacific Harbour and Beqa Island; the resorts out there arrange transfers for their guests, either by boat from Pacific Harbour or by seaplane from Nadi.

THE ARTS VILLAGE ★

Still referred to locally by its original name, the Pacific Harbour Cultural Center, the centerpiece of the **Arts Village Cultural Centre** (© **345 0065**), on the Queen's Road, is a lakeside Fijian village, complete with thatched roofs over the grand chief's *bure* (bungalow) and the tallest traditional temple in Fiji. There are fire-walking shows, boat trips around the outskirts, and tours into the village for visits with Fijians working at carving, weaving, boat building, and other crafts. All are worth doing, so call ahead to see what's going on. Prices range from F$25 for a boat tour to F$80 for a village tour including a *lovo* lunch. Children ages 6 to 16 are charged half price. The tours usually run Wednesday through Saturday from 10:45am to 3:30pm.

OUTDOOR ACTIVITIES

Fishing

The waters off southern Viti Levu are renowned for their big game fish, especially when the tuna and mahimahi are running from January to May, and when big wahoo pass by in June and July. The women's world records for wahoo and trevally were set here. **Xtasea Charters** (© **992 7124** or 992 7131; www.xtaseacharters.com) can tailor excursions—from going for big ones offshore to trolling for smaller but exciting catch inshore. Up to six persons can be accommodated on each trip. Call for prices and reservations, which are essential.

Golf

Robert Trent Jones, Jr., designed the scenic 18-hole, par-72 **The Pearl Championship Fiji Golf Course** (© **368 0644**), on the north side of the Queen's Road, which is now operated by The Pearl South Pacific hotel (see p. 162). Some of its fairways cross lakes; others cut their way through narrow valleys surrounded by jungle-clad hills. Greens fees are F$47, and the pro shop has equipment for rent. The clubhouse restaurant is open daily from 9am to 5pm.

Pacific Harbour

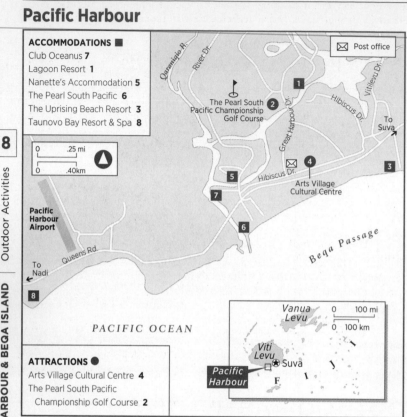

ACCOMMODATIONS ■
Club Oceanus **7**
Lagoon Resort **1**
Nanette's Accommodation **5**
The Pearl South Pacific **6**
The Uprising Beach Resort **3**
Taunovo Bay Resort & Spa **8**

☒ Post office

The Pearl South Pacific Championship Golf Course

To Suva

Arts Village Cultural Centre

Pacific Harbour Airport

To Nadi

Queens Rd.

Beqa Passage

PACIFIC OCEAN

ATTRACTIONS ●
Arts Village Cultural Centre **4**
The Pearl South Pacific
  Championship Golf Course **2**

Vanua Levu

Viti Levu

☐ ★ Suva

Pacific Harbour

0 100 mi
0 100 km

Jet Skiing

An adventurous way to see Beqa lagoon is on a 60km (37-mile) excursion led by **Jetski Safari** (© 345 0933; www.jetski-safari.com). Depending on weather conditions, you may speed across Beqa Passage and explore Beqa Island's picturesque Malumu Bay. The boats also stop for snorkeling on a tiny sand islet in the lagoon. Up to three persons can ride on each boat (realistically, two adults and one child) for about F$300 per craft, but call well in advance for reservations and prices.

Jungle Canopy Rides ★★

ZIP Fiji (© 930 0545; www.zip-fiji.com) has strung wires in a rainforest between Pacific Harbour and Suva; you are strapped into a harness and ride from platform to platform high up in the jungle canopy, sometimes as fast as 50kph (30 mph). Some wires are 200m (650 ft.) long and 30m (98 ft.) up in the trees. The rides cost F$125 per adult; children under 13 are charged half price. Reservations are required.

River Rafting & Kayaking ★★★

The South Pacific's best white-water rafting is with **Rivers Fiji ★★★** (© **800/446-2411** in the U.S., or 345 0147; fax 345 0148; www.riversfiji.com). This American-owned outfit uses inflatable rafts and kayaks for trips through the Upper Navua River Gorge, the "Grand Canyon of Fiji" and an official conservation area. I have met experienced rafters who say the Navua Gorge was one of their top experiences. The adventures cost about US$200 per person. It also has inflatable kayaking trips—"funyacking," it calls them—on the 'Luva River, another picturesque waterway up in the Namosi Highlands, for about US$150 per person. They also have 6-day multisport trips that include kayaking down the 'Luva, sea kayaking in the Beqa Lagoon, and white-water rafting the Navua Gorge. Reservations are essential.

Videos and brochures often feature tourists lazily floating down a Fijian river on a raft made of bamboo poles lashed together. In the old days, mountain-dwelling Fijians really did use *bilibilis*—flimsy bamboo rafts—to float their crops downriver to market. They would discard the rafts and walk home. **Discover Fiji Tours** (© **345 0180;** www.discoverfijitours.com) takes you upriver by motorized canoe and usually brings you back on a bilibili (ask if the bilibili ride is included before you sign up). These 7-hour trips cost about F$135 per person from Pacific Harbour, more from Nadi and the Coral Coast. Reservations and a minimum of three passengers are required.

The Navua River is a scenic delight as it cuts its way through the foothills. Depending on how much it has rained recently, you'll have a few gentle rapids to negotiate, and you'll stop for dips in waterfalls that tumble right into the river. Wear swimsuits and sandals, but bring a sarong to wear in the Fijian village, where you'll be welcomed at a *yaqona* (kava) ceremony.

Scuba Diving ★★★

In addition to its close proximity to the Beqa Lagoon, Pacific Harbour is famous for its **shark-feeding dives,** especially over the nearby Shark Reef Marine Reserve. You're almost guaranteed to come close to seven species of sharks, including large bull and tiger sharks. That's more than any other shark dive in the world. You go down about 90 feet and watch from behind a manmade coral wall while the dive master does the feeding. Only experienced divers need apply for these exciting excursions.

Beqa Adventure Divers (© **345 0911;** www.fijisharkdive.com) pioneered the shark-feeding dives and charges F$200, plus a F$20 contribution to maintain the marine reserve. San Francisco–based **Aqua-Trek** (© **800/541-4334** in the U.S., or 345 0324; fax 345 0324; www.aquatrek.com) also has shark-feeding dives among its repertoire.

Both companies also dive in Beqa Lagoon, and Aqua-Trek teaches resort diving and a full range of PADI courses.

WHERE TO STAY IN PACIFIC HARBOUR

A riverside option for divers and fishers is **Club Oceanus** (© **345 0498;** www. cluboceanus.com), which has 10 units in a motel-style building, an open-air restaurant, a swimming pool, and a bar frequented by local expatriate residents. Owners Brad Cupit and Rob Krause, who also operate Xtasea Charters (see "Fishing," above), are upgrading the rooms. Rates are F$155 double for a much more comfortable renovated unit, F$95 for a standard room.

Bed-and-breakfast aficionados will find a friendly home at **Nanette's Accommodation,** 108 River Dr. (© **345 2041** or 331 6316; www.nanettes.com.fj), where Australian expatriate Nanette MacAdam rents rooms in her villa in the Pacific Harbour housing development. She lives out here but also owns Nanette's Homestay Suva (see p. 186). The villa has a full kitchen and swimming pool. Rooms cost F$150 double, or you can have the whole house for F$600 a night. No children under 13 need apply.

You may hear about **Taunovo Bay Resort & Spa** (© **999 2227;** www.taunovo bay.com), which opened to much fanfare in 2008. The developers were building, selling, and then renting 450-sq.-m (4,700-sq.-ft.) four-bedroom luxury villas with their own plunge pools. They couldn't sell enough of them, however, and by the end of 2009 they were unable to pay the resort staff. Forget it.

Lagoon Resort   Divers and ardent golfers who don't need a beachside location will find a base at this comfortable hotel about 2km (1¼ miles) inland beside the Qaraniqio River and near The Pearl South Pacific Championship Golf Course. Beqa Adventure Divers depart on their shark dives from the hotel's dock. The production crew of the movie *Anaconda* stayed here and left behind the *Bloody Mary,* the rickety boat that played a leading role (it's now part of the bar). The spacious accommodations range from standard rooms to suites. Although lacking in Fijian charm, all have niceties such as Italian marble bathrooms.

P.O. Box 11, Pacific Harbour. © **345 0100.** Fax 345 0270. www.lagoonresort.com. 21 units. F$190–F$350 double. MC, V. **Amenities:** Restaurant; bar; outdoor pool; Wi-Fi (F$5/day). *In room:* A/C, TV/DVD, fridge, hair dryer.

The Pearl South Pacific ★★   This three-story resort is so cool, sexy, and stylish that it would be more at home in New York or Sydney—or even Suva—than here beside this long beach of deep, gray sand. Jazz music permeates the public areas, from the lobby bar before a waterfall wall to the oversize day-bed loungers, where you can stretch out while enjoying a drink or reading a book. Most units are standard hotel rooms, but some have been transformed into luxurious, one-bedroom "Penthouse Suites," each with hardwood floors, its own decor, and butler service. Dining choices include an informal restaurant, a fine-dining outlet, and a bar out by the beach and swimming pool, where Sunday jazz brunches draw crowds of well-heeled locals.

P.O. Box 144, Deuba. © **345 0022.** Fax 345 0262. www.thepearlsouthpacific.com. 78 units. F$310–F$377 double; F$582–F$660 suite. Rates include continental breakfast. AE, MC, V. **Amenities:** 4 restaurants; 4 bars; golf course; health club; Jacuzzi; outdoor pool; room service; spa; 3 tennis courts; watersports equipment/rentals; Wi-Fi (in lobby; F$16/hour). *In room:* A/C, TV, fridge, hair dryer.

The Uprising Beach Resort ★ 🔥 This "flashpacker" resort shares Pacific Harbour's long beach with The Pearl South Pacific. The 12 surprisingly spacious guest bungalows have both queen-size and single beds plus sitting areas, wet bars, and small front porches. You must go outside to reach their outdoor showers and cramped bathrooms, however, so a Fijian *sulu* (sarong) will come in handy. (A dozen larger bungalows were on the drawing board; you won't have to go outside in those.) Consisting of one large, fan-cooled room with over-and-under bunk beds, the 24-bed dorm is quietly situated at the rear of the property. The central building with bar and inexpensive restaurant opens to an outdoor pool and the beach. Young guests and imbibing locals can keep the bar rocking until 1am, so I would avoid huts nos. 1, 2, 3, 7, 8, and 9, which are closest to the action. You can camp here and share the dorm's facilities, but bring your own tent. A full range of outdoor activities includes horseback riding and "horse-boarding" (you and your boogie board are pulled over the lagoon by a horse trotting along the beach).

P.O. Box 416, Pacific Harbour. ✆ **345 2200.** Fax 345 2059. www.uprisingbeachresort.com. 12 units, 24 dorm beds, 20 tent sites. F$160–F$180 double; F$35 dorm bed; F$15 (per person) camping. MC, V. **Amenities:** Restaurant; 2 bars; outdoor pool; watersports equipment/rentals; Wi-Fi (in main bldg.; free). *In room:* Ceiling fan, kitchen.

WHERE TO STAY ON OR NEAR BEQA ISLAND

Batiluva Beach Resort ★ On the north shore of lovely, cliff-edged Yanuca Island, this little American-owned surf camp is rustic, but it sits beside one of Fiji's great beaches, a half moon of white sand extending all the way to coral heads out in the lagoon. Some of Yanuca's cliffs rise directly behind the property, creating the most idyllic setting of any hotel in Fiji. The snorkeling is so good that resorts in Pacific Harbour bring their guests out here on day trips. As is the case with hard-core surf camps, the accommodations are basic, with two rooms and two dorms with four bunk beds apiece, all in buildings which from the outside resemble barns. Everyone shares toilets and cold-water showers straight from a rainwater storage tank. Featuring fresh fish and tropical lobster, meals are served in a central building, housing furniture that was showing serious wear and tear during my visit.

P.O. Box 149, Pacific Harbour. ✆ **992 0021** or 345 0384. www.batiluva.com. 2 units (both with shared bathrooms), 8 dorm beds. F$200 per person. Rates include meals, kayaks, snorkel gear, fishing, 1 surfing trip to Frigates Passage. MC, V. **Amenities:** Restaurant; bar; watersports equipment/rentals. *In room:* Fan, no phone.

Beqa Lagoon Resort ★ On the island's north shore, this is the oldest hotel on Beqa but it has been upgraded in recent years to include an attractive spa and half a dozen lagoonside bungalows with jetted plunge pools recessed into their front porches, which overlook each unit's private lagoonside yard. These are excellent choices for diving honeymooners. Other units come in a conglomeration of styles, from bungalows beside a man-made lily pond to two-bedroom, two-bathroom units in a two-story building. The latter are good for families or groups. Many units feature antique Indian and Asian furniture, a bit of a juxtaposition here in tropical Fiji. The central building's restaurant opens to an attractive swimming pool on one side, the

Beqa Island

ACCOMMODATIONS ■
Batiluva Beach Resort **1**
Beqa Lagoon Resort **4**
Lalati Resort & Spa **5**
Lawaki Beach House **3**
Royal Davui Island Fiji **2**

Vanua Levu

Viti Levu ⭐ Suva

Beqa Island **F**

0 — 100 mi
0 — 100 km

0 — 3 mi
0 — 3 km

······ Reef

Beqa Passage

Nanuki I.

1 *Yanuca I.*

Beqa Lagoon

Waisomo ○ *Malumu Bay*

Raviravi ○

4 *Beqa I.* Lalati ○ **5** ○ *Suliyaga*

Vaga Bay ○ Rukua Dakuni ○

Frigate Passage

3 Dakuibeqa ○

○ Naceva *Moturiki I.*

2 *Royal Davui I.*

Beqa Barrier Reef

beach on the other. Although much of the lagoon gets shallow at low tide, you can still go scuba diving off the beach.

P.O. Box 112, Deuba. ℂ **800/592-3454** or 330 4042. Fax 330 4028. www.beqalagoonresort.com. 25 units. F$438–F$585 bungalow. AE, MC, V. **Amenities:** Restaurant; bar; babysitting; Internet (in office; F$1/minute); Jacuzzi; outdoor pool; spa; watersports equipment/rentals. *In room:* A/C, ceiling fan, fridge, no phone.

Lalati Resort & Spa ★★ Another fine destination for honeymooners who like to dive, this pleasant little resort sits near the mouth of narrow Malumu Bay, which nearly slices Beqa in two. As a result, it enjoys one of the most picturesque views of any Fiji resort. A jagged peak gives way to the azure Beqa Lagoon, while Viti Levu's southern coast lines the horizon (the lights of Suva can illuminate the sky at night). All buildings have tin roofs and ship-plank siding, lending a South Seas plantation ambience to the property. Bathrooms in the spacious guest bures open to both living rooms and bedrooms, and two larger honeymoon bures (one by the beach, one on a hillside) have Jacuzzis and outdoor showers. A swimming pool fronts the full-service spa, which has an air-conditioned lounge with TV and DVD player. The beach ranges from almost nonexistent at high tide to a broad mud flat when the tide is out. On the other hand, you can snorkel in deep water anytime from the resort's long pier, or kayak to a lovely white-sand beach nearby.

P.O. Box 166, Deuba. ✆ **347 2033.** Fax 347 2034. www.lalati-fiji.com. 7 units. US$310 per person. Rates include all meals and nonmotorized watersports equipment. AE, MC, V. Children under 12 not accepted. **Amenities:** Restaurant; bar; Internet (F$50 per visit); Jacuzzi; outdoor pool; room service; spa; watersports equipment/rentals. *In room:* Ceiling fan, TV/DVD (in honeymoon units), fridge, hair dryer, no phone.

Lawaki Beach House ★★ 🏅

For travelers on tight budgets, this is as good a place to get away from it all as Fiji has to offer. You will not get away from your hosts, Semisi (Sam) and Christine Tawake. Sam grew up on Beqa and met Christine when he was in the Fiji army and she was vacationing here from her native Switzerland. Later, while on UN peace-keeping duty in Lebanon, Sam spent his vacations visiting Christine at her home. They married and lived for 9 years in Switzerland (Sam is the only Fijian I know who speaks English with a German accent!) before returning to Fiji in 1998. They now live here, and although you will have your own bungalow or dorm, staying here is like visiting them. A homestay, in other words. Their two individual bungalows are simply furnished, but they have hot-water showers in their bathrooms. Sam and Christine serve meals on their sand-floored veranda. Although the lagoon is shallow at low tide, a fine beach fronts their property.

P.O. Box 250, Navua. ✆ **992 1621** or 368 4088. www.lawakibeachhousefiji.com. 2 units; 5 dorm beds. F$99 per person. Rates include all meals. No credit cards. **Amenities:** Restaurant; bar; Internet (F$6/hour); watersports equipment/rentals. *In room:* No phone.

Royal Davui Island Fiji ★★

On a rocky, 3.2-hectare (8-acre) islet off Beqa's southwestern coast, Royal Davui provides competition for Fiji's other top-end, luxury resorts. The island has no flat land, however, so all but one of the bungalows sit up on the hillside. The trade-off for not being able to step from your bure onto the beach is that you will have a wonderful view. (Westward-facing units espy the sunset but can become uncomfortably warm in the afternoon sun during the austral summer, when I prefer one looking east toward Beqa.) Designed to fit among the rocks and old-growth forest, these spacious units have living rooms and bedrooms in separate buildings. Each has a private plunge pool off the living room balcony, while their bedroom balconies hold two lounge chairs. Bathrooms have whirlpool tubs as well as showers. Part of each bathroom roof retracts to let in fresh air or sunshine. A walkway leads from the four-level reception building up to the open-air restaurant and bar. Guests can dine under the shade of a huge banyan tree (a remote, private space for honeymooners is facetiously dubbed "the fertilizer table"). This is an excellent choice for well-heeled divers and fishers.

P.O. Box 3171, Lami. ✆ **330 7090.** Fax 331 1500. www.royaldavui.com. 16 units. US$940–US$1,515 double. AE, MC, V. Rates include meals and nonmotorized watersports equipment. **Amenities:** Restaurant; bar; Jacuzzi; outdoor pool; room service; spa; watersports equipment/rentals; Wi-Fi (in restaurant; free). *In room:* A/C (in bedroom), ceiling fan, hair dryer, minibar.

WHERE TO DINE IN PACIFIC HARBOUR

Pacific Harbour's best pies are at **Perkins' Pizza,** facing the Queen's Road in the Arts Village (© **345 2244**). Sandwiches, burgers, and pasta also are on hand. Pizzas range from F$19 to F$25; everything else, F$6 to F$12. No credit cards. Open daily from 9:30am to 9pm.

Oasis Restaurant ★ PACIFIC RIM   Owned by English expatriate Monica Vine, this airy dining room with widely spaced tables makes an excellent pit stop if you're driving between Nadi and Suva. The house specialty is vinegary London-style fish and chips. You can get tasty burgers, sandwiches, salads, curries, omelets, and English-style breakfasts all day. Evening sees the likes of pan-fried mahimahi, perhaps caught by one of the charter boat skippers having a cold one at the corner bar. Monica will let you use her computer with Internet access for F20¢ per minute.

Queen's Rd., in Arts Village. © **345 0617.** Reservations accepted. Breakfast F$8–F$20; snacks, sandwiches, and lunch F$9–F$15; main courses F$16–F$36. MC, V. Mon–Sat 9:30am–2:30pm and 6–9:30pm; Sun 10am–2:30pm and 6–9:30pm.

The Waters Edge Bar & Grill PACIFIC RIM   Ex–New Yorker Renee Lange operates this open-air restaurant beside the big lily pond at the front of the Arts Village. She provides breakfast all day plus sandwiches, burgers, pizza and pasta, and blackboard dinner specials on weekend nights, when she may have live jazz music.

Queen's Rd., in Arts Village. © **345 0146.** Reservations accepted. Sandwiches and burgers F$7.50–F$16; pizza and pasta F$18–F$28; main courses F$8–F$24. No credit cards. Mon–Thurs 8:30am–3pm; Fri–Sat 8:30am–9pm.

KADAVU

No other Fiji island is as rich in wildlife as is rugged **Kadavu,** about 100km (62 miles) south of Viti Levu. No cane toads, no iguanas, no mongooses, and no myna birds live on Kadavu to destroy the native flora and fauna in its hills and valleys. As a result, bird-watchers stand a good chance of seeing the endemic Kadavu musk (or shining) parrot, the Kadavu fantail, the Kadavu honeyeater, and the Kadavu whistling dove.

What you will not see on Fiji's least-developed large island is modern civilization. Kadavu has only two dirt roads, and they really don't go anywhere. The island's 10,000 or so residents, all of them Fijians, live in 70 small villages scattered along the serrated coastline. With tourism in its infancy on Kadavu, most villagers make their livings the old-fashioned way, by fishing and subsistence farming. Consequently, this is an excellent place to visit a village and experience relatively unchanged Fijian culture.

The country's fourth-largest island, skinny Kadavu is about 60km (37 miles) long by just 14km (8½ miles) wide—and that's at its widest point. Several bays, including **Galoa Harbour** and **Namalata Bay,** almost cut it into pieces. The Kadavu airstrip and **Vunisea,** the government administrative center, are on the narrow Namalata Isthmus between them. Vunisea has a post office, a school, an infirmary, and a few small shops, but it doesn't qualify as a town. The area around Vunisea saw its heyday in the 19th century, when whalers and other ships would anchor behind the protection afforded by **Galoa Island.**

When I first flew down to Kadavu, I was startled to see much of the north coast skirted by several kilometers of **Long Beach,** the longest uninterrupted strip of white sand in Fiji. Around a corner I could see **Matana Beach,** another jewel.

But Kadavu is best known for the **Great Astrolabe Reef,** which forms a barrier along its eastern and southern sides and encloses its neighbor, **Ono Island,** and several other small dry landmasses to the north. Named for French admiral Dumont d'Urville, who nearly lost his ship, the *Astrolabe,* on it in 1827, the reef is today one of Fiji's most famous scuba dive destinations. The lagoon and mangrove forests along the coast also make Kadavu popular with sea kayakers.

Capt. William Bligh was the first European known to have sighted Kadavu. Although he sailed his longboat between Viti Levu and Vanua Levu after the mutiny on HMS *Bounty* in 1789, Bligh caught sight of Kadavu in 1792 as skipper of HMS *Providence*. Despite the stain of mutiny on his reputation, Bligh went on to a distinguished career including a term as governor of New South Wales colony in Australia.

Compared to Viti Levu, I found the weather to be cooler down here, thanks in large part to the southeast trade winds that blow strongly during much of the year.

GETTING TO & AROUND KADAVU

Pacific Sun (② 800/294-4864 in the U.S., or 672 0888; www.pacificsun.com.fj) flies to Kadavu daily from Nadi and Suva. The flights usually arrive and depart about midday, but they can be late. The airstrip is at **Vunisea,** about midway along the island. See "Getting Around Fiji," in chapter 3.

Small ships haul supplies and passengers from Suva to Kadavu weekly, but the service is unreliable and anything but punctual. Fly instead.

A public transportation system is nonexistent. Consequently, there is no "Exploring Kadavu" section in this chapter because it cannot be done.

You will have to ride a boat to the resorts—10 minutes to Dive Kadavu/Matana Beach Resort, 30 minutes to Papageno Resort, 45 minutes or more to Matava—Fiji's Premier Eco Adventure Resort, and 1½ hours or more to the eastern end (see "Where to Stay & Dine on Kadavu," below). Transfers usually are in small, open speedboats, so bring sun protection and light rain gear with you. No piers or wharfs have been built at the Vunisea airstrip or at the resorts, so you will get your feet wet wading ashore both coming and going.

Local boats land on both sides of the Namalata Isthmus, at the government wharf on the north, and at Galoa Harbour on the south. Really adventurous souls can hitch a ride or pay the owners for water taxi service, but it's an unreliable way to get around and most of the boats lack safety equipment.

OUTDOOR ACTIVITIES

The **Great Astrolabe Reef,** the world's fourth-longest barrier reef, skirts the eastern and southern sides of Kadavu and extends to the north around Ono and other islets. Much coral inside the Great Astrolabe is bleached (the northern reef is closed off even to live-aboard dive boats), but its outside slopes have plentiful hard corals and sea life, including a veritable herd of manta rays that gathers at the so-called Manta Pass on the south coast. In other words, the Great Astrolabe is best for hard corals and abundant sea life. It also is exposed to the usually strong southeast trade winds, which can make for rough boat rides and strong swells on the outer reef.

Kadavu

ACCOMMODATIONS

Dive Kadavu/Matana Beach Resort **1**
Koromakawa Resort **6**
Matava—Fiji's Premier Eco Adventure Resort **3**
Papageno Resort **2**
Tiliva Resort **4**
Waisalima Beach Resort & Drive Center **5**

------ Reef
✈ Airport

Ferry Route ↑
To Suva

North Astrolabe Reef
d'Urville Channel

Dravuni I.

Yaukuvelevu I.

Buliya I.

Naqara ○ **6**
Ono I.
Vabea ○
Ono Channel

Kadavu Passage

Daku Bay Gasele
Rakiraki ○
Lomanikoro ○ **4**
Daku ○
Kavala ○ Tiliva **5**

Sosa Bay
Soso ○ Kadavu
3 ○
Molaniki
Nacomoto Matava

Numalata Bay Vunisea ○
Namara ○

Yakita Nalotu
Naqalotu ○○○ Tavuki ○ ○Wailevu
Lomati
Galoa I.

Nagigia I.
○ Davigele
Burelevu ○ Muani
Matanuku I.

PACIFIC
OCEAN

0 ─── 10 mi
0 ─── 10 km

On the other hand, the **Namalata Reefs** and **King Kong Reef** off the usually protected north shore are known for colorful soft corals, and advanced divers can explore the 71m (235-ft.) *Pacific Voyager,* a tanker deliberately sunk in 1994 to form an artificial reef.

Diving here is handled by the resorts, which have their own operations (see "Where to Stay & Dine on Kadavu," below).

Kadavu is not Fiji's best **snorkeling** destination, as most of the lagoons are shallow close to shore, and the good coral is too far out for a safe swim. Exceptions are a colorful reef just off Dive Kadavu/Matana Beach Resort and around Waya Island off Matava—Fiji's Premier Eco Adventure Resort. You will need to pay your resort for a snorkeling excursion, or go along on a dive expedition to see the best coral and sea life.

Kadavu's many quiet bays, protected lagoons, and mangrove forests make it Fiji's top **kayaking** destination. The resorts have kayaks for their guests to use, and they will organize overnight paddling trips. Longer excursions are best arranged in advance. **Tamarillo Tropical Expeditions** (© **877/682-5433** in the U.S., or

A post office and rudimentary hospital are in Vunisea, but Kadavu does not have a bank. Some but not all of the accommodations accept MasterCard and Visa credit cards, so bring sufficient Fijian currency if yours does not (see "Where to Stay & Dine on Kadavu" below for details).

4/2399 855 in New Zealand; www.tamarillo.co.nz) offers guided 5- to 9-day Kadavu kayak expeditions. You paddle all day and stay in villages or resorts at night.

The resorts also organize **sport- and deep-sea fishing,** which is very good both in the lagoon and offshore. Marlin, sailfish, and wahoo are among the abundant fish in these waters.

9 WHERE TO STAY & DINE

Other accommodations here include **Tiliva Resort** (📞 333 7127; www.tiliva resortfiji.com), on the far northeastern end of Kadavu facing Ono Island. It's the creation of Kim Yabaki, a native of Tiliva village who spent 20 years in the British army, and his Irish wife, Barbara. Their guests stay in large, chalet-style bungalows on a hillside overlooking their 7.2 hectares (18 acres), a beach, and the Ono Passage. Each unit has a kitchen, and the Yabakis have a restaurant and bar. Rates range from F$475 to F$580 for a double, including all meals and airport transfers. Credit cards are accepted only if you book through Tiliva's website.

On Ono Island, **Mai Dive!** (📞 603 0842; www.maidive.com) caters to divers, kayakers, and other adventurers. Accommodation is in a modern beachside bungalow and a two-bedroom lodge. Most guests buy 7-day packages starting at F$1,493 per person, including meals.

Formerly known as Nagigia Island Resort, **Naninya Island Fiji** (📞 603 0454; www.naninya.com), off Kadavu's western end near Cape Washington, is close to the famous King Kong Breaks, making it one of Fiji's top surfing destinations. Two of the 10 bungalows have toilets and outdoor cold-water showers; everyone else shares showers and toilets.

Note: You must ride in a small boat to and from all Kadavu resorts, so be sure to ask if the transfers are included in the rates you are quoted.

Dive Kadavu/Matana Beach Resort ★ 🐚 Home of Dive Kadavu, which dates back to 1987, this low-key resort sits beside Matana Beach, one of Fiji's best. The lagoon is deep enough for swimming and snorkeling over nearby coral heads at all tides, and the view westward along Kadavu's northern coast is spectacular. A hillside main building contains a charming restaurant, bar, lounge, and library crammed with more than 2,000 books. Two private honeymoon bures also are on the hillside, while the others are beside the beach. Unit no. 3 has a living room, two bedrooms, one bathroom, and an expansive veranda. Units 5 and 6 share a building and can interconnect, making them popular with families and dive groups. Others are typical one-room bungalows, which may fall short of today's standards of luxury but are spacious and comfortable. In addition to diving and snorkeling, activities include fishing, waterfall hikes, village visits, and kayak excursions. It's a 10-minute boat ride from here to the Vunisea airstrip.

P.O. Box 8, Vunisea, Kadavu. © **368 3502.** www.divekadavu.com or www.matanabeachresort.com. 10 units. US$155 per person. Rates include meals and use of kayaks. 3-night minimum stay required. MC, V. **Amenities:** Restaurant; 2 bars; Internet (laptop in office; F$15/15 min.); free airport transfers (with 3-night stay); watersports equipment/rentals. *In room:* Ceiling fans, no phone.

Koromakawa Resort ★★
On the northeastern coast of Ono Island, this remote property consists of a beachfront cottage owned by retired Americans Spencer and Karin Kissler, who reside in their own home here. With a spacious living room, two bedrooms, and a large bathroom, the comfortably furnished cottage can accommodate two couples or a family, making this a great get-away-from-it-all escape for everyone. With so few guests in residence, the Kisslers and their Fijian staff render individualized service, including fine meals tailored to your liking. Except for scuba diving, their rates include activities, all meals, soft drinks, and alcoholic beverages—as long as you don't over-indulge at the bar. Spencer is a PADI instructor and accompanies each dive to the nearby Great Astrolabe Reef. Other activities include snorkeling (with manta rays when they are around), fishing, hiking, and private island escapes. Solar panels and wind generators provide the electricity, which stays on all night.

P.O. Box 3763, Samabula, Suva (on Ono Island). ©/fax **603 0782.** www.koromakawa.com.fj. 1 unit. US$250 per person. Rates include meals, some alcoholic beverages, all activities except scuba diving. MC, V. **Amenities:** Restaurant; bar; babysitting; smoke-free rooms; free airport transfers; Wi-Fi (in main house; free). *In room:* Ceiling fans, fridge, no phone.

Matava—Fiji's Premier Eco Adventure Resort ★★★
On the edge of a lush, rainforested valley on Kadavu's southern side, this award-winning resort is the most environmentally friendly hotel in Fiji. Although the staff will crank up a small generator to charge your camera batteries, only 12-volt solar power passes through the wires here. Consequently, your electric razor and hair dryer will be useless. Made predominately of thatch, the spacious and charming accommodations don't have fans, much less air-conditioners, but the prevailing trade winds usually make them unnecessary. They have propane water heaters for their showers. The honeymoon and another unit are up the hillside, giving them terrific views from their large decks. Others are down near the lagoon, which turns into a massive sand flat at low tide. There is excellent snorkeling off a small, picturesque beach on Waya Island, a rocky outcrop a few hundred yards offshore. Other activities include terrific diving, sea kayaking, hiking to nearby Kadavu Koro village, sailing, and deep-sea fishing. A spa and Internet access were on the drawing board.

P.O. Box 63, Vunisea, Kadavu. © **333 6222.** www.matava.com. 12 units. F$300–F$350 per person, double occupancy. Rates include all meals. MC, V. **Amenities:** Restaurant; bar; smoke-free rooms; free airport transfers; watersports equipment/rentals. *In room:* No phone.

Papageno Resort
Beside a long, white beach on Kadavu's north shore, this eclectic resort is loaded with museum-quality South Pacific art collected by owner Anneliese Schimmelpfennig of Laguna Beach, California. It also is environmentally friendly, with organic gardens providing food, and both solar panels and a small hydroelectric dam generating electricity. Ms. Schimmelpfennig's art-laden three bedroom, three-bathroom house serves as the Royal Bure. Next are five Ocean View

Bures and five Garden Bures with queen-size beds and two twins. Least expensive are four Garden Rooms in a motel-like building. A beachside building houses a bar and activities room. As lovely as the beach is, the lagoon turns into a sand bank at low tide, so hikes to a nearby Fijian village and waterfall, snorkeling, and trips to visit manta rays swimming out by the reefs take place away from the resort. It does have its own PADI dive base.

P.O. Box 60, Vunisea, Kadavu. ✆ **866/862-0754** or 600 3128. Fax 600 3127. www.papagenoecoresort. com. 15 units. US$220–US$290 double. Rates include meals. AE, MC, V. **Amenities:** Restaurant; 2 bars; free airport transfers; watersports equipment/rentals. *In room:* Ceiling fans, fridge, no phone.

Waisalima Beach Resort & Dive Centre   This eco-friendly resort sits in a beachside coconut grove at Kavala Bay on the eastern tip of Kadavu, giving quick access to dive sites on the Great Astrolabe Reef. As at Matava, solar cells provide most of the power, so forget using your hair dryer or turning on a ceiling fan. Simply furnished and built in the leafy Fijian fashion, all of the bures are beachfront. Six have their own bathrooms while three smaller models share facilities. Produce from the resort's gardens and freshly caught fish provide the ingredients for hearty Western and Fijian meals served buffet style. This is a somewhat rustic but friendly retreat.

c/o Naleca Post Office, Kavala Bay, Kadavu. ✆/fax **738 9236.** www.waisalima.com. 9 units (6 with bathroom). F$260–F$350 double. Rates include meals. 4-night minimum stay required. MC, V. **Amenities:** Restaurant; bar; Internet (F$20/hour); free airport transfers; watersports equipment/rentals. *In room:* No phone.

SUVA

Neither the likelihood of frequent showers nor an occasional deluge should discourage you from visiting Suva, Fiji's vibrant, sophisticated capital city. Grab your umbrella and wander along its broad avenues lined with grand colonial buildings and orderly parks left over from the British Empire. Its streets will be crowded with Fijians, Indians, Chinese, Europeans, Polynesians, and people of various other ancestries.

Suva sprawls over a hilly, 26-sq.-km (10-sq.-mile) peninsula jutting like a thumb from southeastern Viti Levu. To the east lies windswept **Laucala Bay** and to the west, Suva's busy harbor and the suburbs of **Lami Town** and **Walu Bay.**

Jungle-draped mountains rise to heights of more than 1,200m (4,000 ft.) on the mainland to the north, high enough to condense moisture from the prevailing southeast trade winds and create the damp climate cloaking the city in lush green foliage year-round.

Suva was a typical Fijian village in 1870, when the Polynesia Company sent a group of Australians to settle land it acquired in exchange for paying Chief Cakobau's foreign debts. The Aussies established a camp on the flat, swampy, mosquito-infested banks of **Nubukalou Creek,** on the western shore of the peninsula. When they failed to grow first cotton and then sugar, speculators convinced the new British colonial administration to move the capital from Levuka, which they did in 1882.

The commercial heart of the city still resides in the narrow, twisting streets near Nubukalou Creek, although you will find most of the sites, office buildings, interesting restaurants, and lively nightspots along broad **Victoria Parade,** the historic main drag where the British built their imposing colonial administrative center.

High-rise buildings are springing up all over downtown, a testament to Suva's position as the thriving commercial and diplomatic hub of the South Pacific islands and headquarters for several regional organizations.

As a result of the 2006 coup, the governments of Australia, New Zealand, and some other nations still caution against travel to Suva. Personally, the only sign of the coup I have seen during my visits was the army's having turned the old Grand Pacific Hotel, on Victoria Parade, into a makeshift barracks. No soldiers were in evidence elsewhere, and even at the old hotel they were dressed in civvies.

Too many visitors spend only a day in Suva, which is hardly enough time to do justice to this fascinating city. You can easily spend 2 or 3 days walking its streets, seeing its sights, and poking your head into its multitude of shops.

GETTING TO & AROUND SUVA

Getting to Suva

Suva is served by **Nausori Airport,** 19km (12 miles) northeast of downtown near the Rewa River town of Nausori. **Express buses** operated by **Nausori Taxi & Bus Service** (© 347 7583 in Nausori, or 330 4178 in Suva) are scheduled to depart the airport for downtown Monday to Friday at 8:30am, 9:30am, 11:30am, 2:30pm, 5pm, and 6:30pm. The fare is F$10 each way. That having been said, I always take one of several **taxis** waiting at the terminal, whose fares to downtown Suva officially are F$27. Allow at least 30 minutes for the taxi ride during midday, an hour during morning and evening rush hours.

Express buses leave **Nadi airport** daily for Suva, a ride of approximately 4 hours on the Queen's Road.

I never drive away from Nadi in my **rental car** (p. 46) without a good map of Suva, whose streets can seem like a confusing maze, especially at night.

See "Getting Around Fiji," in chapter 3, for more information.

Getting around Suva

Hundreds of **taxis** prowl Suva's streets. Some have meters, but don't count on it. As a rule of thumb, F$2 to F$3.50 will get you to the sites of interest, but plan on F$7 to F$9 to the Raintree Lodge. If the taxi has a meter, make sure the driver drops the flag. The main **taxi stand** (© 331 2266) is on Central Street, behind the Air Pacific office in the CML Building on Victoria Parade, and on Victoria Parade at Sukuna Park (no phone). I have been very satisfied with **Black Arrow Taxis** (© 330 0541 or 330 0139) and **Nausori Taxi & Bus Service** (© 347 7583 in Nausori, or 330 4178 in Suva), which is based at the Holiday Inn Suva parking lot. Taxis also gather at the Suva Municipal Market.

Although usually crowded, local **buses** fan out from the municipal market from before daybreak to midnight Monday to Saturday (they have limited schedules on Sun). The fares vary but should be no more than F$2 (US$1.30/70p) to most destinations in and around Suva. ***Word to the wise:*** If you're going to ride the bus for the fun of it, do it in Nadi, where you won't get lost and aren't as likely to be robbed.

See "Getting Around Fiji," in chapter 3, for the phone numbers of the **car-rental** firms.

Tickets are required to **park** on downtown streets Monday to Friday from 8am to 4:30pm, Saturday from 8am to 12:30pm. Buy the tickets at the silver machines in every block, and display them on your dashboard. On-street parking fees are F20¢ per 15 minutes.

> ### Impressions
>
> *The English, with a mania for wrong decisions in Fiji, built their capital at Suva, smack in the middle of the heaviest rainfall . . . Yet Suva is a superb tropical city.*
>
> —James A. Michener, *Return to Paradise*, 1951

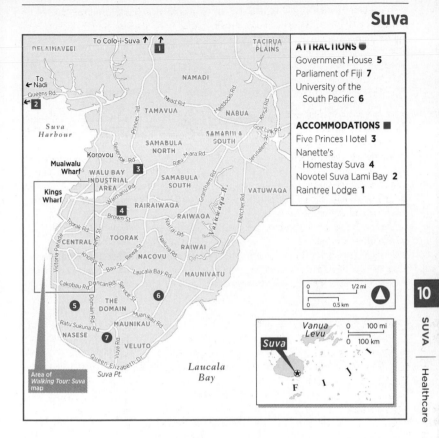

[FastFACTS] SUVA

The following facts apply to Suva. If you don't see an item here, see "Fast Facts: Fiji," in Chapter 15.

Currency Exchange **ANZ Bank, Westpac Bank,** and **Colonial National Bank** have offices with ATMs on Victoria Parade, south of the Fiji Visitors Bureau. ANZ has a walk-up currency exchange window that is open Monday to Friday from 9am to 6pm, Saturday from 9am to 1pm.

Drugstores **City Center Pharmacy,** in the MHCC building, Thomson Street at Nubukalou Creek (© **311 0844**), is open daily from 9am to 9pm.

Emergencies & Police The emergency phone number for **police** is © **917.** For **fire** and **ambulance** dial © **911.** Fiji Police's **central station** (© **331 1222**) is on Joske Street, between Pratt and Gordon streets.

Eyeglasses Dr. Guy Hawley, an American eye specialist, practices at **Asgar & Co. Ltd.,** Queensland Insurance Centre, Victoria Parade (© **330 0433**).

Healthcare Most expatriate residents go to the **Suva Private Hospital,** 120 Amy St. (© **331 3355**). It's open 24 hours a day.

Colonial War Memorial Hospital, at the end of Ratu Mara Road at Brown Street (☎ **331 3444**), is the public hospital (but go to Suva Private Hospital if at all possible).

Internet Access Suva has dozens of Internet cafes and wireless hotspots, many of them on Victoria Parade. Operated by Fiji's major Internet service provider, **Connect Internet Cafe** (☎ **330 0777**), in the General Post Office building, has high-speed broadband access for F$3 an hour, Wi-Fi for F$6 an hour. It's open Monday to Friday 8am to 7pm, Saturday 8am to 4pm. You can print your e-mails, scan documents, and burn CDs here. The country's overseas phone company, **Fiji International Telecommunications Ltd. (FINTEL),** has broadband access at its headquarters (☎ **330 1655**). It's open Monday to Friday from 8:30am to 5pm, Saturday 9am to 5pm, and charges F$3 for an hour. The **Esquires Coffee House**

branches have Wi-Fi hotspots (see "Where to Dine in Suva," below).

Mail Fiji Post's General Post Office is on Thomson Street at Edward Street (Mon–Fri 8am–4:30pm, Sat 9am–noon).

Restrooms Sukuna Park, on Victoria Parade, has attended (and reasonably clean) public restrooms, on the side next to McDonald's. You must pay F80¢ to use the toilets, or F$1.30 for a shower. Restrooms are open Monday to Saturday 8am to 3:45pm. That having been said, I usually pop into McDonald's next door.

Safety Although the situation has improved in recent years, street crime is a problem in Suva, so be alert at all times. Do not wander off Victoria Parade after dark; take a taxi. The busy blocks along Victoria Parade between the Fiji Visitors Bureau and the Holiday Inn Suva are relatively safe during the evenings (a local wag says the many prostitutes on

the main drag keep the robbers away!), but always protect valuables from pickpockets. See "Safety," under "Fast Facts: Fiji," in chapter 15.

Telephone & Fax The easiest way to make international calls is with a Phone Card from any public phone. You can also make them, send faxes, and surf the 'net at **Fiji International Telecommunications Ltd.** (FINTEL; ☎ **331 2933**), on Victoria Parade (see "Internet Access," above).

Visitor Information It's not a visitor information office per se, but the friendly staff of the **Fiji Public Services Commission** (☎ **132 777;** ask for GIRC) government information center, in a restored colonial house at the corner of Thomson and Scott streets, will do their best to help. It's open Monday to Thursday 8am to 4:30pm, Friday 8am to 4pm, Saturday 8am to noon.

Water The tap water in Suva is safe to drink.

EXPLORING SUVA

Although you could easily spend several days poking around the capital, most visitors come here for only a day, usually on one of the guided tours from Nadi or the Coral Coast. That's enough time to see the city's highlights, particularly if you make the walking tour described below.

Sitting on a ridge about 1km (½ mile) southeast of downtown, the **Parliament of Fiji,** Battery Road off Vuya Road (☎ **330 5811**), is a modern shingle-covered replica of a traditional Fijian roof. Parliament has not convened since the 2006 coup, and it is unlikely to meet again until after general elections in 2014, at the earliest.

The Top Attractions

Fiji Museum ★★★   You'll see a marvelous collection of war clubs, cannibal forks, *tanoa* bowls, shell jewelry, and other relics in this excellent museum. Although some artifacts were damaged by Suva's humidity while they were hidden away during World War II, much remains. Later additions include the rudder and other relics of HMS *Bounty*, burned and sunk at Pitcairn Island by Fletcher Christian and the other mutineers in 1789 but recovered in the 1950s by the famed *National Geographic* photographer Luis Marden. Don't miss the *masi* (bark) cloth and Indian art exhibits in the air-conditioned upstairs galleries. The gift shop is worth a browse.

In Thurston Gardens, Ratu Cakobau Rd., off Victoria Parade. ⓒ **331 5944.** www.fijimuseum.org.fj. Admission F$7 adults, F$5 students with IDs. Guided tours by donation. Mon–Thurs and Sat 9am–4:30pm; Fri 9:30am–4pm.

Suva Municipal Market ★★★   A vast array of tropical produce is offered for sale at Suva's main supplier of food, the largest and most lively market in Fiji. If they aren't too busy, the merchants will appreciate your interest and answer your questions about the names and uses of the various fruits and vegetables. The market teems on Saturday morning, when it seems the entire population of Suva shows up to shop and select TV programs for the weekend's viewing: A telling sight about urban life in the modern South Pacific is that of a Fijian carrying home in one hand a bunch of taro roots tied together with *pandanus* (palm leaves), and, in the other, a collection of rented videocassettes stuffed into a plastic bag.

Usher St. at Rodwell Rd. The bus station is behind the market on Rodwell Rd. No phone. Free admission. Mon–Fri 5am–6pm; Sat 5am–1pm.

WALKING TOUR: SUVA

START:	**The Triangle.**
FINISH:	**Government House.**
TIME:	**2½ hours.**
BEST TIME:	**Early morning or late afternoon.**
WORST TIME:	**Midday, or Saturday afternoon and Sunday, when the market and shops are closed and downtown is deserted.**

Begin at the four-way intersection of Victoria Parade, Renwick Road, and Thomson and Central streets. This little island in the middle of heavy traffic is called:

1 The Triangle

The modern center of Suva, in the late 1800s this spot was a lagoon fed by a stream that flowed along what is now Pratt Street. A marker in the park commemorates Suva's becoming the capital, the arrival of Fiji's first missionaries, the first public land sales, and Fiji becoming a colony.

From the Triangle, head north on Thomson Street, bearing right between the government information center's ancient house and the old Garrick Hotel (now the Sichuan Pavilion Restaurant), whose wrought-iron balconies recall a more genteel (but non-air-conditioned) era. Continue on Thomson Street past the modern Morris Hedstrom City Center (MHCC) to:

2 Nubukalou Creek

The Polynesia Company's settlers made camp beside this stream and presumably drank from it. A sign on the bridge warns against eating fish from it today—with good reason, as you will see and smell.

Cross the bridge, looking up at the new Tappoo skyscraper, and head down narrow:

3 Cumming Street

This area, also on reclaimed land, was home of the Suva market until the 1940s. Cumming Street was lined with saloons, *yaqona* (kava) grog shops, and curry houses known as lodges. It became a tourist-oriented shopping mecca when World War II Allied servicemen created a market for curios. When import taxes were lifted from electronic equipment and cameras in the 1960s, Cumming Street merchants quickly added the plethora of duty-free items. This area is reemerging with construction of the huge Morris Hedstrom City Centre and Tappoo department store buildings.

Return to Thomson Street, turn right, and then left on Usher Street. Follow Usher Street past the intersection at Rodwell Road and Scott Street to the:

4 Suva Municipal Market

This market is a beehive of activity, especially on Saturday mornings (see "The Top Attractions," above). Big ships from overseas and small boats from the other islands dock at Princes Wharf and Kings Wharf beyond the market on Usher Street.

Head south along wide Stinson Parade, back across Nubukalou Creek and along the edge of Suva's waterfront to Edward Street and the gray tin roofs of the:

5 Municipal Curio and Handicraft Centre

In yet another bit of cultural diversity, you can haggle over the price of handicrafts at stalls run by Indians. (Don't try to haggle at those operated by Fijians, who sell by set prices and may be offended if you try to bargain.)

Continue on Stinson Parade past Central Street. The gray concrete building on the corner is JJ's on the Park hotel. When you get there, cut diagonally under the palms and flame trees across:

6 Sukuna Park

This shady waterfront park is named for Ratu Sir Lala Sukuna, founding father of independent Fiji. It's a favorite brown-bag lunch spot for Suva's office workers. On the west side is the harbor and on the east, Victoria Parade. For many years only a row of flame trees separated this broad avenue from the harbor, but the shallows have been filled and the land has been extended into the harbor by the width of a city block. The large auditorium that stands south of the park is the Suva Civic Centre.

Head south on the seaward side of Victoria Parade and pass the cream-colored colonial-style headquarters of FINTEL, the country's electronic link to the world. You'll come to the:

Walking Tour: Suva

1 The Triangle
2 Nubukalou Creek
3 Cumming Street
4 Suva Municipal Market
5 Municipal Curio and Handicraft Centre
6 Sukuna Park
7 Old Town Hall
8 Suva City Library
9 Native Land Trust Board Building
10 Government Buildings
11 Albert Park
12 Grand Pacific Hotel
13 Thurston Gardens
14 Fiji Museum
15 Government House

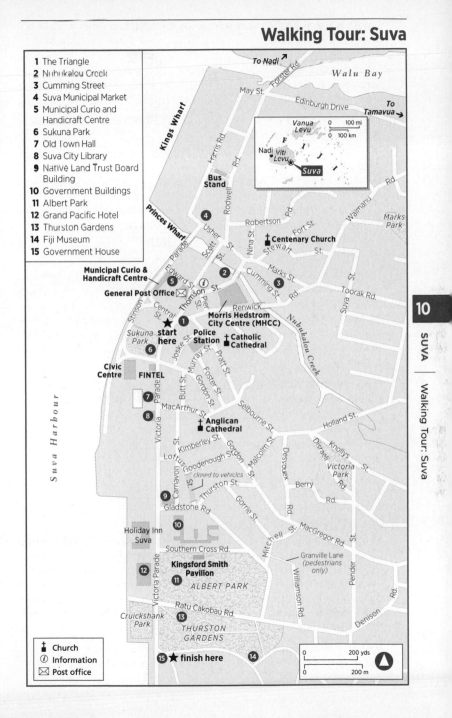

7 Old Town Hall

A picturesque Victorian-era building, it features an intricate, ornamental wrought-iron portico. Built as an auditorium in the early 1900s and named Queen Victoria Memorial Hall, this lovely structure was later used as the Suva Town Hall (city offices are now in the modern Suva City Hall adjacent to the Civic Centre on the waterfront). The stage still stands at the rear of the Chinese restaurant.

Continue south on Victoria Parade until you come to the:

8 Suva City Carnegie Library

The U.S. industrialist and philanthropist Andrew Carnegie gave Fiji the money to build this structure. The central portion of the colonnaded building opened in 1909, with an initial collection of 4,200 books. The wings were added in 1929. (See "Fast Facts: Suva," above, for the library's hours.)

Keep going along Victoria Parade, past Loftus Street, to the corner of Gladstone Road, the locale for the:

9 Native Land Trust Board Building

This site is known locally as Naiqaqi ("The Crusher") because a sugar-crushing mill sat here during Suva's brief and unsuccessful career as a cane-growing region in the 1870s (see box, "My Word!," below). Ratu Sir Lala Sukuna, who prepared his people for independence (see "Looking Back at Fiji," in chapter 2), served as chairman of the Native Land Trust Board, which collects and distributes rents on the 80% of the country that is owned by the Fijians.

Across Gladstone Road you can't miss the imposing gray edifice and clock tower of the:

10 Government Buildings

Erected between 1937 and 1939 (although they look older), these British-style gray stone buildings house the High Court, the prime minister's office, and several government ministries. Parliament met here until 1987, when Colonel Rabuka and his gang marched in and arrested its leaders. (If it ever meets again, Parliament will convene in its complex on Ratu Sukuna Road in the Muanikau suburb.) The clock tower is known as "Fiji's Big Ben." When it works, it chimes every 15 minutes from 6am to midnight.

Walk past the large open field on the south side of the building; this is:

11 Albert Park

This park is named for Queen Victoria's consort, Prince Albert. The pavilion opposite the Government Buildings, however, is named for Charles Kingsford Smith, the Australian aviator and first person to fly across the Pacific. Smith was unaware that a row of palm trees stretched across the middle of Albert Park, his intended landing place. A local radio operator figured out Smith's predicament, and the colonial governor ordered the trees cut down immediately. The resulting "runway" across Albert Park was barely long enough, but Smith managed to stop his plane with a few feet to spare on June 6, 1928.

Opposite the park on Victoria Parade stands the:

12 Grand Pacific Hotel

Vacant for years, this historic hotel was built in 1914 by the Union Steamship Company to house its transpacific passengers during their stopovers in Fiji. The idea was to make it look like they had never gone ashore: Rooms in the GPH were like first-class staterooms, complete with saltwater bathrooms and plumbing fixtures identical to those on an ocean liner. All rooms were on the second floor, and guests could step out onto a 4.5m-wide (15-ft.) veranda overlooking the harbor and walk completely around the building—as if walking on the ship's deck. When members of the British royal family visited Fiji, they stood atop the wrought-iron portico, the "bow" of the Grand Pacific, and addressed their subjects massed across Victoria Parade in Albert Park.

Continue south on Victoria Parade to the corner of Ratu Cakobau Road, and enter:

13 Thurston Gardens

Originally known as the Botanical Gardens, this cool, English-style park is named for its founder, the amateur botanist Sir John Bates Thurston, who started the gardens in 1881. Henry Marks, scion of a family who owned a local trading company, presented the drinking fountain in 1914. After G. J. Marks, a relative and lord mayor of Suva, was drowned that same year in the sinking of the SS *Empress* in the St. Lawrence River in Canada, the Marks family erected the bandstand in his memory. Children can climb aboard the stationary *Thurston Express,* a narrow-gauge locomotive once used to pull harvested cane to the crushing mill.

Walk to the southeast corner of the gardens, where you will find the:

14 Fiji Museum

At this fascinating museum, you can see relics and artifacts of Fiji's history (see "The Top Attractions," above). After touring the complex, take a break at the museum's cafe, under a lean-to roof on one side of the main building; it serves soft drinks, snacks, and curries.

Backtrack through the gardens to Victoria Parade and head south again until, just past the manicured greens of the Suva Bowling Club on the harbor, you arrive at the big iron gates of:

15 Government House

This is the home of Fiji's president, guarded like Buckingham Palace by spit-and-polish Fijian soldiers clad in starched white *sulus* (sarongs). The original house, built in 1882 as the residence of the colonial governor, was struck by lightning and burned in 1921. The present rambling mansion was completed in 1928 and opened with great fanfare. It is closed to the public, but a colorful military ceremony marks the changing of the guard the first week of each month.

From this point southward, Victoria Parade becomes Queen Elizabeth Drive, which skirts the peninsula to Laucala Bay. With homes and gardens on one side and the lagoon on the other, it's a lovely walk or drive. The manicured residential area in the rolling hills behind Government House is known as the Domain. An enclave of British civil servants in colonial times, it is now home to the Fiji parliament, government officials, diplomats, and affluent private citizens.

Colo-I-Suva Forest Park

At an altitude of 121 to 182m (400–600 ft.), **Colo-I-Suva Forest Park,** on the Prince's Road 11km (6½ miles) from downtown Suva (© **332 0211**), provides a cool, refreshing respite from the heat—if not the humidity—of the city below. You can hike the system of trails through the heavy indigenous forests and stands of mahogany to one of several lovely waterfalls cascading into cool swimming holes. Bring walking shoes with good traction because the trails are covered with gravel or slippery soapstone. The park is open Wednesday to Sunday from 8am to 4pm. Admission is F$5. Take a taxi or the Sawani bus, which leaves Suva Municipal Market every 30 minutes. Do not leave valuables unattended in your vehicle or anywhere else.

SHOPPING IN SUVA

Your walking tour of Suva will give you a good idea of where to shop for handicrafts, cameras, electronic gear, and clothing. Most of the city's top shops historically have been along Victoria Parade and in Cumming Street. That began to change with the 2009 opening of the **Morris Hedstrom City Centre (MHCC),** a large shopping mall on Thomson Street at Nubukalou Creek. You can buy almost everything you need in this modern, three-story building, which is open daily from 9am to 9pm. On the ground level is a Morris Hedstrom grocery store, a pharmacy, and coffee shop. Upstairs are **Jack's of Fiji, Proud's,** and other stores. A very good food court resides on the top floor (see "Where to Dine in Suva," below).

Not to be outdone by "MH," **Tappoo** department stores has put up an even more imposing high-rise building across the creek, at Scott and Usher streets, to house one of its stores and national headquarters.

Jack's of Fiji still has its main Suva store at Thomson and Pier streets, but this branch has a very small handicraft section; here, it's mostly a clothing and accessories outlet.

The best place to look for locally made souvenirs is the **Municipal Curio and Handicraft Centre,** on the ground floor of the Municipal Car Park, Stinson Parade at the waterfront (© **331 3433**). Be careful, however, for some of the work here is mass produced and aimed at cruise-ship passengers who have only a few hours to do their shopping in Fiji. It's open Monday to Thursday 8am to 4:30pm, Friday 8am to 4pm, Saturday 8am to noon, and on Sundays when cruise ships are in port.

📎 **Sword Seller Reprise**

Although the government has chased most of them off the streets, you may still be approached by the sword sellers I warned you about under "Shopping in Nadi," in chapter 5. Avoid them!

Suva has some fine tropical clothing outlets, several of them on Victoria Parade near the Regal Theatre. The resort- and beachwear specialist **Sogo Fiji** is on Victoria Parade, opposite the theater.

Stamp collectors will find colorful first-day covers from Fiji and other South Pacific island countries at the **Philatelic Bureau** (© **330 2022;** www.stampsfiji.com), on the first floor of the General Post Office. It's open Monday to Thursday from 8am to 4pm, Friday to 3:30pm. American Express, MasterCard, and Visa cards are accepted.

WHERE TO STAY

Moderate

Five Princes Hotel ★★★ ⚑   On Princes Road in the high-rent Tamavua neighborhood northwest of downtown, Suva's top boutique hotel occupies a charming, colonial-style house built in 1920. The late Harold Gatty, a legendary Australian aviator who founded the forerunner of Air Pacific, owned it from 1949 until his death in 1963. Present owner Tarei Weeks grew up here, and along with her Dutch-born husband, Roderic Evers, converted it into this excellent hotel in 2005. They enlarged the veranda, upon which you can order breakfast and, with advance notice, dinner. Their six bright rooms are in the main house. They also have two cottages and a two-bedroom villa out in the tropical gardens, which also surround a swimming pool. The villa and one of the cottages have kitchens. The property is atop a ridge, and through the thick garden foliage you can occasionally catch a fine view down over Walu Bay and along Viti Levu's south coast.

5 Prince's Rd. (GPO Box 704, Suva). ⓒ **338 1575.** Fax 338 0490. www.fiveprinceshotel.com. 10 units. F$160 double, F$190–F$310 cottage. AE, MC, V. **Amenities:** Outdoor pool; Wi-Fi (in main house; F$10/day). *In room:* A/C, ceiling fan, TV/DVD, fridge, kitchen (2 units).

Holiday Inn Suva ★   This hotel is the unofficial gathering place for the city's movers and shakers. The waterfront location couldn't be better, for Suva Harbour laps one side (at least when the tide is high), the stately government buildings sit across Victoria Parade on the other, and the business district is a 3-block walk away. Even though it's in the middle of the action, a swimming pool surrounded by a large harbor-side lawn makes it seem like a resort rather than a city hotel. Built as a TraveLodge in the 1970s, the building has been improved over the years, although the air-conditioners still seem to struggle with Suva's humid climate. The *Fiji Times* is delivered to your room daily on request. One room is equipped for guests with disabilities.

501 Victoria Parade (P.O. Box 1357, Suva). ⓒ **800/465-4329** or 330 1600. Fax 330 0251. www.holidayinn.com. 130 units. F$249–F$362 double; F$594 suite. Rates include full breakfast. AE, DC, MC, V. **Amenities:** Restaurant; bar; babysitting; health club; outdoor pool; room service; Wi-Fi (in lobby; F$36/day). *In room:* A/C, TV, hair dryer, Internet (F$36/day).

JJ's on the Park   Downtown Suva's only boutique hotel, JJ's on the Park isn't much to look at from the outside since it occupies the former YWCA Building, a stained concrete structure five stories high on the north side of Sukuna Park. But go inside and you'll find comfortable rooms and suites. Accommodations range from smaller rooms without balconies to suites with two balconies and separate bedrooms. Balcony or not, every unit has a harbor view.

Stinson Parade, north side of Sukuna Park (P.O. Box 12499, Suva). ⓒ **330 5055.** Fax 330 5002. www.jjsfiji.com.fj. 22 units. F$257 double; F$457–F$657 suite. AE, MC, V. No children accepted. **Amenities:** Restaurant; bar; access to nearby health club; room service; Wi-Fi (F$15/day). *In room:* A/C, TV/DVD, fridge, hair dryer.

Novotel Suva Lami Bay   A 10-minute drive west of downtown (longer during rush hours), the former Raffles Tradewinds Hotel & Conference Centre sits beside the picturesque Bay of Islands, Suva's yacht harbor. In fact, international cruising yachts tie up alongside the hotel's bulkhead. Comfortable rooms are in two waterfront wings on either side of the main building. Those on the Suva side are smaller and have angled balconies while those on the Nadi side are somewhat larger and have balconies facing directly to the bay. Minimalist European-style décor maximizes the units' limited space. An attractively appointed lounge, bar, and restaurant open to the bay. Facilities include a small bayside pool and large conference center across the Queen's Road.

Queen's Rd., at Bay of Islands (P.O. Box 3377, Lami Town). © **800/942-5050** in the U.S. or 336 2450. Fax 336 2455. www.novotel.com. 108 units. F$135–F$285 double. AE, MC, V. **Amenities:** Restaurant; bar; outdoor pool; room service; Wi-Fi (in lobby; F$6/day). *In room:* A/C, TV, hair dryer, Internet (F$6/day), minibar.

Quest Serviced Apartments   Occupying the sixth and seventh floors of the high-rise Suva Central building, these modern apartments are more secure than any accommodations in the city, since no one except guests are allowed past the reception desk. They range in size and price—from hotel room–like studios to two-bedroom apartments. They all have kitchenettes with fridges, toasters, and microwaves, and 10 have cook stoves. The larger units have washers and dryers. A few have unfurnished balconies with city views. You can take the elevator down to Suva Central's coffee shop. As the name implies, the apartments have daily cleaning service.

Renwick Rd. at Pratt St., in Suva Central Building (P.O. Box 686, Suva). **331 9119.** Fax 331 9118. www.questsuva.com. 32 units. F$139–F$330 double. AE, MC, V. **Amenities:** Wi-Fi (F$3/hr.). *In room:* A/C, TV, fridge, hair dryer, kitchen (10 units).

Tanoa Plaza Hotel   Even sans balcony, you will have a commanding view over Suva, the harbor, and the south coast of Viti Levu from the top floors of this curving, nine-story building. Best of all are the executive suites on the top floor, which are larger and better appointed than the smallish regular rooms; they also feature narrow balconies, which the standard rooms do not. The neighborhood is quiet and residential, yet the hotel is only a 3-block walk from the shops on Victoria Parade (but you should take a taxi at night). Amenities include a pleasant first-floor restaurant serving breakfast, lunch, and dinner, and the swimming pool on the shady side of the building.

Corner Malcolm and Gordon sts. (P.O. Box 112, Suva). © **331 2300.** Fax 331 1300. www.tanoahotels.com. 60 units. F$169–F$187 double; F$332 suite. AE, DC, MC, V. **Amenities:** Restaurant; bar; babysitting; outdoor pool; room service; Wi-Fi (in lobby; F$11/hr.). *In room:* A/C, TV, fridge, hair dryer, Internet (F$8/hr.).

Inexpensive

Capricorn Apartment Hotel 🎖   Although it's a steep, 2-block walk uphill from Cumming Street, Mulchand Patel's super-clean establishment is popular among Australians and New Zealanders who like to do their own cooking. The three-story, L-shaped building looks out on Suva Harbour and down the mountainous coast. Private balconies off each apartment share the view, as does a pear-shaped swimming pool on the Capricorn's grounds. Tropical furniture adorns all units, and the mattresses are among the firmest in Fiji. Mulchand and his friendly staff make sure these roomy efficiencies are kept spotless. Each unit has an air-conditioner, although

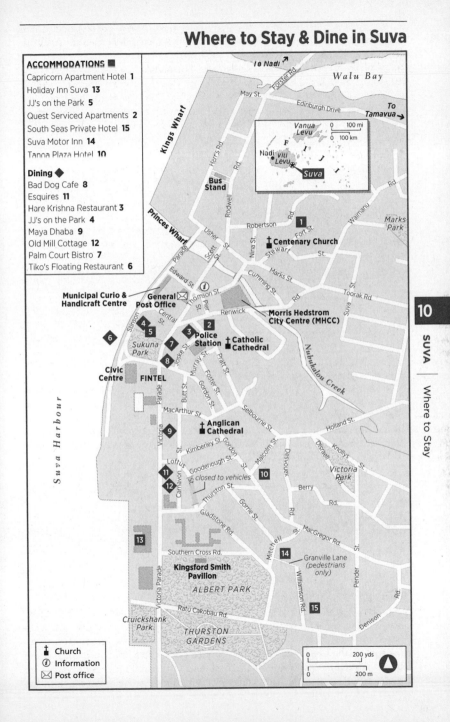

Where to Stay & Dine in Suva

ACCOMMODATIONS ■
Capricorn Apartment Hotel **1**
Holiday Inn Suva **13**
JJ's on the Park **5**
Quest Serviced Apartments **2**
South Seas Private Hotel **15**
Suva Motor Inn **14**
Tanoa Plaza Hotel **10**

Dining ◆
Bad Dog Cafe **8**
Esquires **11**
Hare Krishna Restaurant **3**
JJ's on the Park **4**
Maya Dhaba **9**
Old Mill Cottage **12**
Palm Court Bistro **7**
Tiko's Floating Restaurant **6**

(unscreened) windows on both sides of the building let the cooling trade winds blow through. The reception staff will sell you canned goods from its small on-premises store.

End of Saint Fort St. (P.O. Box 1261, Suva). ℂ **330 3732.** Fax 330 3069. www.capricornfiji.com. 34 units. F$115–F$175 double. AE, DC, MC, V. **Amenities:** Internet (computer in lobby; F20¢/minute); outdoor pool. *In room:* A/C, ceiling fan, TV, kitchen.

Nanette's Homestay Suva 📷 Almost hidden away on a side street behind Colonial War Memorial Hospital, Nanette MacAdam's two-story, white concrete house looks smaller from the road than it is. Upstairs she has a lounge, kitchen, and four breezy rooms, all with private bathrooms. One has its own balcony. Downstairs are three apartments, two of which have two bedrooms, and one of these has two bathrooms. All three have fully modern kitchens. The apartments are popular with overseas workers on assignment to the hospital. Guests are treated to continental breakfast, and they can barbecue on the big veranda off the guest lounge.

56 Extension St. (behind Colonial War Memorial Hospital). ℂ **331 6316.** Fax 331 6902. www.nanettes. com.fj. 7 units. F$99 double; F$145–F$195 apt. Rates include continental breakfast. MC, V. **Amenities:** Wi-Fi. *In room:* A/C, TV (apts only), kitchen (apts only), no phone.

Raintree Lodge Backpackers flock to this rustic lodge beside a nearly round, quarry-turned-lake high in the hills near Colo-I-Suva Forest Park (see above). The climes are cool up here, and although "Raintree" refers to an acacia tree, it can rain a lot in this forest. Except for the vehicles passing on Prince's Road, you'll hear very little except the songs of tropical birds and insects. Built of pine and overlooking the lake, the bungalows are spacious, and their beds have mosquito nets (the windows are screened, too). All have ceiling fans and bathrooms with showers. Dormitories range in size from seven private rooms with double beds to a hall with 21 bunk beds. Their occupants share toilets, hot-water showers, and a kitchen. The lodge is F$8 to F$9 by taxi or F$2 by public express bus from downtown Suva.

Prince's Rd., Colo-I-Suva, opposite police station (P.O. Box 11245, LBE, Suva). ℂ **332 0562.** Fax 332 0113. www.raintreelodge.com. 6 units, 45 dorm beds. F$165–F$220 bungalow; F$65 double dorm room; F$25 dorm bed. AE, MC, V. **Amenities:** Restaurant; bar; Internet (computer in lobby; F10¢/minute); outdoor pool. *In room:* Ceiling fan, TV, DVD (some units), fridge, no phone.

South Seas Private Hotel Many backpackers stay at the Raintree Lodge (see above), but those who opt for the city usually end up at this large barracklike wooden structure with a long sunroom across the front (it can get hot in the afternoons). It's a friendly establishment with dormitories, basic rooms, a rudimentary communal kitchen, a TV lounge, and hand-wash laundry facilities. Bed linen is provided, but bring your own towel or pay a small deposit to use one of theirs. You will have to pay a refundable key deposit, too. Showers have both hot and cold water, and the rooms have fans that operate from 6pm to 6am.

Williamson Rd. off Ratu Cakobau Rd., behind Albert Park (P.O. Box 2086, Government Buildings, Suva). ℂ **331 2296.** Fax 330 8646. www.fiji4less.com. 34 units (1 with bathroom), 42 dorm beds. F$30 dorm bed. MC, V. *In room:* Ceiling fan, no phone.

Suva Motor Inn ★ 🏊 This three-story hotel attracts local business travelers who can't afford the rates elsewhere. It's also a good bet for budget-minded couples and families. Just uphill from Albert Park near the Government Buildings, the L-shaped structure bends around a tropical courtyard with a two-level swimming pool that has a Jacuzzi and a water slide. Opening to this vista is a small restaurant and a bar. Accommodations are in spacious studios and two-bedroom apartments, all with tropical cane-and-wicker furniture. The studios are fully air-conditioned, but only the master bedrooms of the apartments are cooled. Apartments have full kitchens; studios have refrigerators, toasters, coffeemakers, and microwaves. The staff will assist in arranging activities and excursions.

Corner of Mitchell and Gorrie sts. (P.O. Box 2500, Government Buildings, Suva). ℂ **331 3973.** Fax 330 0381. www.hexagonfiji.com. 47 units. F$117 double; F$183 apt. AE, MC, V. **Amenities:** Restaurant; bar; outdoor pool; Wi-Fi (F$10/hr.). *In room:* A/C, TV, fridge, kitchen (apts only).

WHERE TO DINE
Moderate

JJ's on the Park PACIFIC RIM   On the harbor side of JJ's hotel, this lively bistro sports a Southwestern adobe theme, but that's as far it goes: The menu is strictly curries and other regional fare. Best bets are the substantial servings of fish and chips, burgers, salads, steaks, and fish. At dinner check the specials board for the fresh fish of the day. The bar here is a good place to slake a thirst during your walking tour of Suva (p. 177).

In JJ's on the Park, Stinson Parade at Sukuna Park. ℂ **330 5005.** Reservations recommended at dinner. Breakfast F$9–F$16; burgers and salads F$15–F$20; main courses F$15–F$25. AE, DC, MC, V. Mon–Wed 7am–10pm; Thurs–Sat 7am–11pm (bar later).

Tiko's Floating Restaurant BARBECUE/GRILL/SEAFOOD   Locals like to take out-of-town guests to this floating restaurant, which served years ago with Blue Lagoon Cruises. One hopes they don't lean to seasickness, for the old craft does tend to roll a bit when freighters kick up a wake going in and out of the harbor. Your best bets are the nightly seafood specials, such as *walu* (Spanish mackerel) and *pakapaka* (snapper). The fish is fresh, the service is attentive, and a terrific musician-singer, usually performs at dinner—all of which makes for a pleasant night out.

Stinson Parade at Sukuna Park. ℂ **331 3626.** Reservations recommended. Main courses F$18–F$60. AE, MC, V. Mon–Fri noon–2pm; Mon–Sat 6–10pm.

Inexpensive

Bad Dog Cafe ★ BARBECUE/GRILL/PIZZA/SEAFOOD   Expatriate residents and professional Suvans—from their mid-20s on up—congregate in this sophisticated pub for after-work drinks and then hang around for good food, including some of Fiji's best pizzas. One pie will feed two adults of moderate appetite. Served in a sandwich or as a main course, the sushi-grade yellowfin tuna is the best in town. An attractive, energetic, and good-natured waitstaff help make this Suva's top pub. The bar area in front can get thick with cigarette smoke, so head for the rear dining room.

Victoria Parade, at MacArthur St. ℂ **331 2884.** Burgers, sandwiches, and salads F$1–F$15; pizza F$12–F$18; main courses F$13–F$25. AE, MC, V. Mon–Wed 11am–11pm; Thurs–Sat 11am–1am; Sun 5–11pm.

Hare Krishna Restaurant ★ 🍴 VEGETARIAN INDIAN   This clean, casual restaurant specializes in a wide range of very good vegetarian curries—eggplant, cabbage, potatoes and peas, okra, and papaya to name a few—each seasoned delicately and differently from the others. Interesting pastries, breads, side dishes, and salads (such as cucumbers and carrots in yogurt) cool off the fire set by some of the curries. The items are displayed cafeteria-style near the entrance to the second-floor dining room, or get the all-you-can-eat *thali* sampler and try a little of everything. Downstairs has an excellent yogurt and ice-cream bar; climb the spiral stairs to reach the air-conditioned dining room. The Hare Krishna ownership allows no alcoholic beverages or smoking.

16 Pratt St., at Joske St. ℂ **331 4154.** Curries F$4–F$11. No credit cards. Dining room Mon–Sat 11am–2:30pm. Downstairs snack bar Mon–Fri 8am–6pm; Sat 8am–3pm.

Maya Dhaba ★★★ 🎁 INDIAN   This chic, sometimes noisy Victoria Parade bistro is Suva's most urbane restaurant and purveyor of its best Indian food. Regardless of ethnicity, local couples and families all flock here for authentic subcontinent fare at extraordinarily reasonable prices. The menu runs the gamut from Punjabi Tandoori chicken *tikka* to huge vegetarian *masala dosa* (rice-flour pancakes wrapped crepelike around potato curry). In fact, vegetarians will have many choices here. My old standby, butter chicken, has a wonderful smoked flavor here. Little guess work is required since the menu explains every dish. There's a take-away branch in the Morris Hedstrom City Centre food court (see below).

281 Victoria Parade, btw. MacArthur and Loftus sts. ℂ **331 0045.** Reservations recommended. Main courses F$10–F$20. MC, V. Daily 11am–3pm and 5:30–10pm.

10

Old Mill Cottage ★★★ 🍴 PACIFIC RIM/INDIAN/INTERNATIONAL   One of the few remaining late-19th-century houses left in Suva's diplomatic-government section, these adjoining two-room clapboard cottages offer some of the most extraordinary home cooking in the South Pacific. Order at the cafterialike counters—one for breakfast, one for lunch—from among a choice of daily specials such as Fijian *palusami* (taro leaves in coconut milk), mild Indian curries, or European-style mustard-baked chicken with real mashed potatoes and peas. The vegetable plate is a good value, as you can pick and choose from more than a dozen European, Fijian, and Indian selections. Diplomats (the U.S. Embassy is out the back door) and government executives pack the place at midday.

47–49 Carnavon St., near corner of Loftus St. ℂ **331 2134.** Breakfasts F$5–F$8; meals F$7–F$10. No credit cards. Mon–Fri 7am–6pm; Sat 7am–5pm.

Palm Court Bistro LIGHT FARE   When I'm not having breakfast at the Old Mill Cottage you will find me at this walk-up carryout in the open-air center of the Palm Court Arcade. Continental breakfasts are served all day, as are a variety of other snacks and light meals. Order at the counter and then eat at plastic tables under cover, or go sit in the shade of the namesake palm in the middle of the arcade.

Victoria Parade, in the Palm Court Arcade, Queensland Insurance Centre. ℂ **304 4662.** Reservations not accepted. Most items F$3.50–F$10. No credit cards. Mon–Fri 7am–6pm; Sat 7am–3pm.

Food Courts & Coffee Shops

I could eat for a week at the excellent **MHCC Food Court,** on the top level of the modern Morris Hedstrom City Centre shopping mall, on Thomson Street at Nubukalou Creek. The wonderful **Maya Dhaba** (see above) has an outlet here, and a branch of Nadi's excellent **Restaurant 88** (see p. 114) has both a lunch area and a more refined dining room. There are several other Indian counters, and others offer Fijian, Filipino, and other Asian cuisines. The court is open daily from 9am to 10pm.

If you're hankering for a Big Mac, head for the **McDonald's** on Victoria Parade at the northern edge of Sukuna Park. A **Kentucky Fried Chicken** is on Victoria Parade next to the General Post Office.

Esquires Coffee Shop COFFEEHOUSE   This branch of the nationwide coffee shops occupies the triangular corner of FNPF Place, on the Victoria Parade side of Dolphins Food Court. You can listen to recorded jazz while drinking your latte or cappuccino and eating your brownie, cake, or quiche at the tall tables by the big storefront windows. Both this and a second Suva location, on Renwick Road at Pratt Street (© **330 0082**), have Wi-Fi for your laptop, and it's free if you make a purchase.

Victoria Parade at Loftus St., in FNPF Place Building. (© **330 0333.** Pastries and sandwiches F$3.50–F$7. No credit cards. Mon–Fri 7am–9pm; Sat 7am–9pm; Sun 7am–6:30pm.

NIGHTLIFE IN SUVA

Nocturnal activities in Suva revolve around going to the movies and then hitting the bars—until the wee hours on Friday, the biggest night out.

Movies are a big deal, especially the first-run Hollywood and Indian "Bollywood" flicks at **Village 6 Cinemas** (© **330 6006**), on Thomson Street at Nubukalou Creek, a modern, American-style emporium with six screens and a games arcade upstairs. Check the newspapers for what's playing and show times. Locals flock here on Sunday afternoon, when these plush, air-conditioned theaters offer a comfortable escape from Suva's sunshine and humidity.

Most bars worth frequenting are on Victoria Parade, opposite the Suva City Carnegie Library, between MacArthur and Loftus streets.

Trap's Bar, 305 Victoria Parade (© **331 2922**), is a popular watering hole where you're not likely to witness a fight. A band usually plays in the back room on weekends. **O'Reilly's,** on MacArthur Street off Victoria Parade (© **331 2968**), is an Irish-style pub that serves Guinness stout and sports on TVs (and it can get a bit rough, depending on who's winning the rugby matches).

Also on this block are loud **discotheques** frequented by a young, noisy crowd.

Remember: Suva has a crime problem, so be careful when bar hopping. Guard your valuables, and always take a taxi to and from your hotel after dark, particularly if you've had a few drinks.

RAKIRAKI & NORTHERN VITI LEVU

ew travelers are disappointed by the scenic wonders on the northern side of Viti Levu. Cane fields climb valleys to green mountain ridges. Dramatic cliffs and spires bound a stunning bay. A narrow mountain road winds along the Wainibuka River, once called the "Banana Highway" because, in preroad days, Fijians used it to float their crops down to Suva on disposable *bilibilis* (rafts made of bamboo).

A relatively dry climate beckons anyone who wants to catch a few rays—so many rays that modern real estate developers call this the "Sun Coast." Local English-Fijian families appreciated the dryness—and the cooling breezes which seem to constantly blow up here—long before the developers arrived, and some bought land and built vacation homes, especially on hilly **Nananu-I-Ra Island,** off the big island's northernmost point. They chose not to build along the main coast, which, with a few exceptions, is skirted by mangrove forests.

One family created the 6,800-hectare (17,000-acre) **Yaqara Estate,** Fiji's largest cattle ranch. Cowpokes still tend the steers, but the area is best known now for Fiji Water, which comes from artesian wells up in the hills above the ranch. A constant parade of trucks rumbles along the King's Road, either hauling bottles of Fiji Water to the port at Lautoka, and from there primarily to the United States, or bringing back empty containers for more.

During World War II, American soldiers built an airstrip near the Fijian village of **Rakiraki,** the chiefly headquarters from which Viti Levu's northern tip gets its name. The air base is long gone, but the charming hotel they frequented is still in business. Now the Tanoa Rakiraki Hotel, it's the last accommodations left from Fiji's colonial era.

Like the English-Fijians before them, today's sun-seeking visitors are attracted to a small peninsula near Rakiraki, to Nananu-I-Ra Island, and to great diving on the reefs offshore. Thanks to prevailing trade winds funneling between Viti Levu and Vanua Levu, this also is the windsurfing capital of Fiji—or surf kiting, the latest version of this arm-building sport. Despite the mangroves elsewhere, **Volivoli Point,** the island's northernmost extremity, has one of Fiji's best beaches.

There is only one drawback: It's a long way from Rakiraki to anywhere else in Fiji, and because there is no longer an airport up here, you must go to and fro by car or bus via the King's Road. Consequently, most visitors are serious divers, windsurfers, and Australians and New Zealanders enjoying taking a break in the sun during the austral winter from June through August.

GETTING TO & AROUND RAKIRAKI

Some local hotels and backpackers' resorts either provide or arrange for their guests' transportation from Nadi, and it's always best to ask when you make your reservations. All transfers are by rental car, taxi, or bus. Rakiraki is about a 2½-hour drive from Nadi International Airport.

The **King's Road** runs for 290km (180 miles) from Nadi Airport around the island's northern side to Suva—93km (58 miles) longer than the Queen's Road to the south. A 30km (18 miles) unsealed portion through the central mountains between Rakiraki and Nausori can be treacherous, so I am extremely cautious when driving this way, especially during the rainy season from November through April, when bridges can wash out. I never drive this road at night.

Taxi fares from Nadi to Rakiraki are about F$100 each way.

Ellington Wharf, Volivoli Beach Resort, and the Tanoa Rakiraki Hotel are regular stops for **Feejee Experience** (© 672 5959; www.feejeeexperience.com), the backpacker bus that circles Viti Levu counterclockwise (p. 49).

Sunbeam Transport Ltd. (© 666 2822), **Reliance Transport Bus Service** (© 666 3059), and **Akbar Buses Ltd.** (© 669 4760) have express and local service via the King's Road between the Lautoka market and **Vaileka,** a predominately Indian town 1km (½ mile) off the King's Road near Rakiraki village. The one-way fare from Lautoka to Vaileka is about F$20.

Local taxis are available in Vaileka. The one-way fare from there to Ellington Wharf or the northern tip of Viti Levu is about F$12.

See "Getting Around Fiji," in chapter 3, for more information.

EXPLORING RAKIRAKI

The King's Road officially begins at Lautoka. To reach it by car from Nadi, follow the Queen's Road north and take the second exits off of both traffic circles in Lautoka.

From Lautoka, the King's Road first crosses a flat, fertile plain and then ascends into hills dotted with cattle ranches before dropping to the coast and entering Fiji's "Sugar Belt," its most productive sugar-growing area.

Ba & Tavua

The gorgeous steep hills of the **Ba Valley,** populated mostly by Fiji Indians, are second only to Suva in economic importance. The town of **Ba,** a prosperous farming and manufacturing community on the banks of the muddy Ba River, has one of Fiji's five sugar mills, and many of the country's most successful businesses are headquartered here. While most Fijian towns have the Western air of the British Raj or Australia, the commercial center of Ba is a mirror image of India. **Note:** The King's Road bypasses Ba, so watch for the exit leading into town.

Gravel roads twisting off from Ba into the valley offer some spectacular vistas. One of these roads follows a tributary into the central highlands and then along the Sigatoka River down to the Coral Coast. You can explore the Ba Valley roads in a rental car, but take the cross-island route only if you have a four-wheel-drive vehicle and a very good map.

From Ba, the King's Road continues to **Tavua,** another predominately Indian sugar town backed by its own much smaller valley reaching up to the mountains and the **Vatukoula Gold Mine,** whose workers lend a certain Wild West flair to Tavua. Although the mine has been troubled in recent years, it has produced more than 7 million ounces of gold since 1935. It's not open for tours, so don't bother driving up here.

Personally I wouldn't attempt this route, but the main road to Vatukoula, 8km (5 miles) inland, continues from the mine and crosses the central mountains to Suva. Along the way it passes the **Monasavu Hydroelectric Project,** which supplies much of Viti Levu's electrical power. The Monasavu Dam creates a lake directly in the center of Viti Levu, but it's so remote it has no facilities for visitors and is not worth the difficult trip to see.

Back on the King's Road, the enchanting peaks of the **Nakauvadra Range** keep getting closer to the sea as you proceed eastward. Legend says the mountains are home to Degei, the prolific spiritual leader who arrived with the first Fijians and later populated the country (see "The Dreaded Degei" box, in chapter 5). Where the flat land is squeezed between foothills and sea, cane fields give way to the grasslands and mesas of the Yaqara Estate cattle ranch. Offshore, conelike islands begin to dot the aquamarine lagoon.

Rakiraki

Although everyone refers to northernmost Viti Levu as Rakiraki, the commercial and administrative center is actually **Vaileka,** a predominately Indian town about 1km (½ mile) off the King's Road. Vaileka is home to the **Penang Mill,** the only one of Fiji's five sugar mills that produces solely for domestic consumption (the others export all their sugar). The 9-hole **Penang Golf Course** is near the mill; visitors who want to play it can make arrangements at their hotel (see "Where to Stay & Dine in Rakiraki," below).

With its fair share of the car-destroying road humps that populate every Fijian village, **Rakiraki** is on the King's Road, about 1km (½ mile) past the Vaileka junction. It's home of the *Tui Ra,* the high Fijian chief of Ra district, which encompasses all of northern Viti Levu.

Beyond the village, an unsealed gravel road makes a loop around the peninsula at the top of Viti Levu. Kept in reasonably good condition for the Feejee Experience buses, this road is a marvelously scenic drive. At the northeastern corner, you'll come to **Vilivoli Beach ★★★**, now occupied by the inexpensive Volivoli Beach Resort.

Rakiraki & Nananu-I-Ra

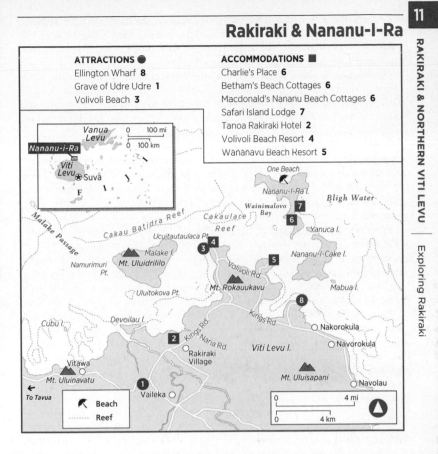

ATTRACTIONS ●
Ellington Wharf **8**
Grave of Udre Udre **1**
Volivoli Beach **3**

ACCOMMODATIONS ■
Charlie's Place **6**
Betham's Beach Cottages **6**
Macdonald's Nananu Beach Cottages **6**
Safari Island Lodge **7**
Tanoa Rakiraki Hotel **2**
Volivoli Beach Resort **4**
Wananavu Beach Resort **5**

From Volivoli, the gravel road runs along the shoreline to the peninsula's eastern side and Wananavu Beach Resort. Some of the freehold land up here has been sold as lots for vacation homes, which sit up on the hillsides.

East of the peninsula, a paved road leads off the King's Road to **Ellington Wharf,** the jumping-off point for **Nananu-I-Ra,** the semiarid island that has inexpensive retreats (see "Nananu-I-Ra Island," below).

Rakiraki to Suva

From Ellington Wharf, the King's Road rounds the island's north point into **Viti Levu Bay,** whose surrounding mountains topped with basaltic cliffs, thumblike formations, and spires give it a tropical splendor. In my opinion, the British should have put the capital here rather than in damp Suva. About 15km (9⅓ miles) from Rakiraki stands **St. Francis Xavier Church,** home of the unique *Naiserelagi,* or Black Christ mural painted by artist Jean Charlot in 1963.

From the head of the bay, the road begins to climb through rice paddies and more cattle country to the head of the winding **Wainibuka River.** This "Banana Highway" is a major tributary of the mighty Rewa River, which eventually flows into the sea through a broad, flat delta northeast of Suva. The cool, often cloudy highlands of the Wainibuka Valley are old Fiji, with traditional Fijian villages perched on the slopes along the river.

Be careful on the many switch-back curves above the river. An often-delayed project is slowly improving the King's Road through the mountains, but there are still no shoulders to pull off on, and you will encounter one-lane wooden bridges, which can be icy slick during the frequent rains. Also watch out for the huge buses that regularly ply this route, taking up the entire road as they rumble along at breakneck speeds. Plan on taking 1 hour to get through the 30km (18 miles) of unpaved road.

Beyond the Wainibuka lies the dairy farming region of eastern Fiji, source of the country's fresh milk and cheeses (be alert for cows on the road!). The small town of **Korovou,** 107km (66 miles) from Rakiraki, is the major junction in these parts. At the dead end, a left turn will take you to **Natovi Wharf,** an outpost in the middle of nowhere where ferries depart for Savusavu and Taveuni. Turn right at the juncture to continue on to Nausori and Suva. (If you are driving south to north, don't believe the road signs at the traffic circle on the northern end of the Korovou bridge; go halfway around the circle to resume on the King's Road.)

You will now go directly south for 25km (16 miles) until the King's Road meets the junction of the Wainibuka and Rewa rivers, now a meandering coastal stream. You soon come to bustling Nausori, the delta's main town. Bear right at the traffic circle to reach the four-lane bridge to Suva.

WATERSPORTS

Although not as dramatic or scenic as in the Somosomo Strait between Vanua Levu and Taveuni (see chapter 14), the reefs off northern Viti Levu have colorful soft corals. And this is the closest land to the sites out in Bligh Water, the passage between Viti Levu and Vanua Levu. The reefs up here are relatively undiscovered, and because the currents are not as strong as at other soft coral spots, there's a greater chance that you will see really good color at any time. Most require a boat ride, but the hulk of the cargo ship *Papuan Explorer* lies in 22m (72 ft.) of water only 150m (492 ft.) off Nananu-I-Ra Island. It was sunk in 1990 to create a reef, and experienced divers can swim inside the wreck. Also nearby is the upside-down carcass of the *Ovalau,* an inter-island ferry that went down in 2005.

The top dive operator in the area is **Ra Divers** (© **669 4622;** www.ra-divers. com), at Volivoli Beach Resort (see below).

The strong trade winds, especially from June to August, put this area on the world's windsurfing maps. **Safari Island Lodge** on Nananu-i-Ra Island (© **669 3333;** www.safarilodge.com.fj) rents Windsurfers, sea kayaks, sailboats, snorkeling gear, and other toys (see "Nananu-I-Ra Island," below). Owner Warren Francis conducts Fiji's only **kite-surfing school** here.

While the wind often whips from the southeast, Nananu-I-Ra and adjacent Nananu-I-Thake Island protect a usually quiet lagoon, creating a great spot for day sailing and kayaking. The islands are surrounded by fringing reefs, but the waters in between are deep enough to be dark blue.

WHERE TO STAY & DINE

Some of the new houses on the northern peninsula are available to rent as vacation homes, which appeal to Australians and New Zealanders on quick, get-away-from-it-all holidays. One is **Star Fish Blue** (© 828/277-7800 in the U.S.; www.star fishblue.com), a three-bedroom luxury villa adjacent to Wananavu Beach Resort, which manages a few others (see below). Star Fish Blue has its own swimming pool.

Tanoa Rakiraki Hotel ★ ✦ Frequented primarily by business travelers, this establishment is one of the few remaining colonial-era hotels in Fiji. The two clapboard roadside buildings were built as guesthouses when U.S. soldiers were stationed at an airstrip nearby during World War II. The original building houses a tongue-and-groove-paneled bar and dining room (with a very limited menu). Another is used as housing by Australian-Pacific Technological College, which trains hospitality students here. Out back, three modern two-story motel blocks have rooms outfitted to international standards, with air-conditioned units, phones, and tiled shower-only bathrooms. The staff will arrange excursions to Vaileka and to Fijian villages, horseback riding, golfing, scuba diving, and treks into the highlands. You will not be able to log on the 'net here unless you have your Blackberry or iPhone.

P.O. Box 31, Rakiraki (Rakiraki village, on King's Rd., 2.5km/1½ miles east of Vaileka, 132km/82 miles from Nadi Airport). © **800/448-8355** or 669 4101. Fax 669 4545. www.tanoahotels.com. 24 units. F$130 double. AE, DC, MC, V. **Amenities:** Restaurant; bar; babysitting; outdoor pool; tennis court. *In room:* A/C, TV, fridge, hair dryer.

Volivoli Beach Resort ✦ This is both Rakiraki's top choice among backpackers and a good option for anyone wishing to stay in a bungalow with a fine view out over Bligh Water. Opening to a large swimming pool (with swim-up bar), the sand-floor restaurant and bar are around a bend from Volivoli Beach. This strip of white sand leads directly into deep water (no tidal flat here) and has a great vista back across a bay to Viti Levu's mountains. Budget travelers can opt for four rooms (sharing two bathrooms) or one of 64 dorm beds, all in hillside buildings with sea views from their long front porches. The 11 bungalows (or "villas") are all modern and well equipped, including full kitchens.

P.O. Box 417, Rakiraki. © **669 4511.** Fax 669 4611. www.volivoli.com. 19 units, 64 dorm beds. F$105 double; F$220 bungalow; F$26 dorm bed. MC, V. **Amenities:** Restaurant; 2 bars; outdoor pool; watersports equipment/rentals; Wi-Fi (in main bldg.; free). *In room:* A/C (in bungalows), ceiling fan, kitchen (in bungalows), no phone.

Wananavu Beach Resort ★ The area's most luxurious accommodations are here near Viti Levu's northernmost point. "Beach Resort" is a bit of a misnomer, for the resort's beach as well as its marina were created by removing a chunk of mangrove forest, leaving gray sand and a mud flat behind. Accordingly, Wananavu has strong appeal to divers headed to the colorful reefs offshore, but it's not the best choice for beach-exclusive vacationers. Perched on a hillside, the dining room, bar, and most of the duplex bungalows have fine ocean views. A few *bures* are down by the beach, including a honeymoon unit whose private garden has a plunge pool and an outdoor shower. Three hillside honeymoon bures also have plunge pools and al fresco showers. With separate living and sleeping areas, they are much larger and more charming than the other units here, most of which are duplexes constructed of knotty pine. Wananavu is popular with American dive groups.

P.O. Box 305, Rakiraki. © **669 4433.** Fax 669 4499. www.wananavu.com. 34 units. F$325–F$760 double. Rates include breakfast. AE, MC, V. **Amenities:** Restaurant; bar; babysitting; Internet (dial-up; F$18/hour); Jacuzzi; outdoor pool; spa; tennis court; watersports equipment/rentals. *In room:* A/C, ceiling fan, hair dryer, minibar, no phone.

NANANU-I-RA ISLAND

Hilly, anvil-shaped Nananu-I-Ra island, a 15-minute boat ride from Ellington Wharf, has long been popular as a sunny retreat for local Europeans who own beach cottages there (the island is all freehold land), and three local families still operate low-key resorts beside a long beach in the center of the island's western side. This is the narrowest part of the island, and you can walk over a hill to **Mile Long Beach** (yes, it actually is 1.5km/1 mile long) on the exposed eastern shore, Fiji's windsurfing headquarters. Although the lagoon is shallow at low tide, snorkeling is very good off the south coast.

Nananu-I-Ra once was on the backpackers circuit around Fiji, but today the young folks are more likely to stop at Volivoli Beach on the mainland. In addition to windsurfing enthusiasts, most visitors are Australian and New Zealand couples, some of whom return year after year for inexpensive holidays in the sun. Indeed, this is one of the most cost-friendly places in Fiji to spend a quiet beachside vacation. Consequently, reserve well in advance from June through August.

Where to Stay & Dine on Nananu-I-Ra Island

The three properties listed below sit side-by-side on the island's western shore. Fronted by a long beach, the land was once one parcel but the former owner divided it in sections, one for each of three sisters of the Macdonald clan, one of Fiji's most prominent European families. Their children, and their spouses, operate them today.

Over on the eastern side, avid windsurfers stay at Warren Francis' **Safari Island Lodge** (© **669 3333;** www.safarilodge.com.fj) to take advantage of the usually strong prevailing trade winds, especially from June through August. The eclectic property sits beside appropriately named Mile Long Beach. Accommodations are more modern than at the others, and they have hot-water showers.

All send open boats to pick up their guests at Ellington Wharf, 15 minutes away. Only Macdonald's Nananu Beach Cottages has a pier, elsewhere you will wade ashore.

Betham's Beach Cottages On the beach next door to Charlie's Place, Rob and Katie Pitts have five cottages, two rooms, and a four-bed dormitory. Built of concrete block or timber, the one-bedroom cottages have kitchens and covered verandas, while the two rooms share a kitchen and a veranda. The dorm has its own bathroom and porch. A two-story house can be rented whole or as up- or downstairs. Every unit has an electric fan, but their showers are cold-water. A pleasant restaurant-bar by the beach has picnic tables and Adirondack chairs for lounging while taking in the view of Viti Levu. A small store sells groceries and gift items.

P.O. Box 5, Rakiraki. ©/fax **628 0400** or 992 7132. www.bethams.com.fj. 7 units, 4 dorm beds. F$65 double; F$110–F$150 cottage; F$28 dorm bed. MC, V. **Amenities:** Restaurant; bar; watersports equipment/rentals. *In room:* Kitchen, no phone.

Charlie's Place Louise Anthony has two cottages for rent on her end of the beach on Nananu-I-Ra's western side. Both are built of concrete blocks and stand up on a hill. They do not have fans, but from this perch they are more likely to catch the prevailing breezes than the units at Betham's Beach Cottages and Macdonald's Nananu Beach Cottages, which are down by the beach and thus shaded from the trade winds. Although simply furnished, the cottages are spacious. Each has a bedroom and a bathroom with a cold-water shower. The higher unit has a sun porch with a fine view of the lagoon and Viti Levu, but mango and plumeria trees partially block the vista from the other bungalow's veranda. Louise doesn't have a restaurant, but you can walk to Betham's and Macdonald's, which do (be sure to reserve for dinner by 3pm at either of them).

P.O. Box 407, Rakiraki. (C) **628 3268.** charlie's@connect.com fj 2 units. F$120 double. No credit cards. *In room:* Kitchen, no phone.

Macdonald's Nananu Beach Cottages   Maxine Macdonald's pleasant beachside property has a sand-floor restaurant serving very good burgers and pizzas. Accommodations consist of two-bedroom cottages, a larger A-frame bungalow dressed up Fijian style, two rooms (each with two single beds), and a four-bunk dorm. Most do not have covered verandas like those at Betham's, but they are a bit more spacious and airy. The cottages have kitchens, and a small, well-stocked shop sells groceries. All units have bathrooms with showers that dispense cold water. The lagoon here is shallow at low tide, but you can swim and snorkel off the end of the resort's long pier, which reaches deep water.

P.O. Box 140, Rakiraki. (C) **628 3118** or 993 5004. www.macsnananu.com. 7 units, 4 dorm beds. F$85 double; F$145 cottage; F$26 dorm bed. MC, V. **Amenities:** Restaurant; bar; babysitting; watersports equipment/rentals. *In room:* Ceiling fan, no phone.

LEVUKA & OVALAU ISLAND

You may think you've slipped into the "Twilight Zone" as you stroll through the streets of **Levuka,** Fiji's first European-style town. Everything in this historical jewel seems to be frozen at a moment just before the government moved to Suva in 1882: ramshackle dry-goods stores with false fronts, clapboard houses with tin roofs to keep them dry and shaded verandas to keep them cool, and the round clocks in the baroque tower of Sacred Heart Catholic Church, which seem to have stopped working more than a century ago. In contrast to bustling Suva, Levuka remains a charming example of what South Sea towns were like in the 19th century.

Part of the reason Levuka isn't still Fiji's capital is that it resides on ruggedly beautiful **Ovalau,** the largest of the Lomaiviti Group of islands, some 32km (20 miles) east of Viti Levu. Where its regular streets end, Levuka's "step streets" climb the base of the jagged cliffs which tower over the town. These 360m-tall (1,200-ft.) walls of basalt caused Levuka's ultimate demise by preventing its expansion, but they create a soaring backdrop that ranks Ovalau in the big leagues of dramatic tropical beauty.

Not that Levuka hasn't changed at all since its days as one of the South Pacific's most notorious seaports. All but one of the 50 or more hotels and saloons that dispensed rum and other pleasures disappeared long ago. The sole survivor—the Royal Hotel—is now a quiet, family-run establishment.

Despite its history, extraordinary scenery, and extremely hospitable residents, Levuka is relatively off the beaten tourist track. The volcano that created Ovalau has eroded into such rugged formations that it has left very little flat land and no decent beach; therefore, the island has not attracted resort or hotel development. But Levuka does have comfortable and charming accommodations in which to stay while meeting the friendly locals, learning about Fiji's history and culture, and diving over some of the country's best reefs.

Within sight of Levuka lies **Wakaya Island,** another historic outpost which now is home to the Wakaya Club, one of Fiji's finest little resorts.

GETTING TO & AROUND LEVUKA & OVALAU

Getting There

Pacific Sun (© **800/294-4864** in the U.S., or 672 0888; www.pacificsun.com.fj) has early-morning, midday, and late-afternoon flights from Nausori Airport at Suva to Bureta airstrip, on the Ovalau's west coast. The round-trip fare from Suva is about F$180.

Patterson Shipping Services (© **331 5644;** patterson@connect.com.fj) has bus-ferry connections from Suva to Buresala Landing, north of the airstrip.

The airstrip and ferry landing are at least 45-minute rides from Levuka via the very rough road that circles Ovalau; nevertheless, the ride to Levuka, on the other side of the island, is a sightseeing excursion in its own right. Bus fare from the airstrip or ferry landing into town is F$10; taxis cost about F$35.

For more information, see "Getting Around Fiji," in chapter 3.

Getting Around

Levuka is a small town, and you can get to most places in 25 minutes by foot. Numerous taxis congregate on Beach Street; be sure you and the driver agree on a fare before departing.

Given the poor condition of Ovalau's roads, four-wheel-drive trucks with seats in the back—called "carriers" here—serve as the local bus service. They don't run after dark, so find out from the driver when—and whether—he returns to Levuka at the end of the day.

EXPLORING LEVUKA & OVALAU

A Walking Tour of Town

A walking tour of Levuka (pop. 3,745) should take about 2 hours. Begin at **Ovalau Watersports,** on the south end of Beach Street (© **344 0166;** www.owlfiji.com), the only scuba diving operation here; it also rents bicycles, does laundry, provides Internet access, books tours, and generally is the focal point for all visitors. German owners Andrea and Noby Dehm and their staff are fonts of information.

LEVUKA COMMUNITY CENTER ★★

Next door is the **Levuka Community Centre** (© **344 0356**), where you can explore the town's small but interesting history museum. In addition to displaying real Fijian war clubs and an excellent collection of shells (including ancient mother-of-pearl buttons), the museum chronicles Levuka's earliest European settlers, such as American David Whippy and Englishman Henry Simpson, who arrived on ships in the 1820s and stayed to found two of the country's most prominent families.

The center occupies the quaint old **Morris Hedstrom** store built in 1878 by two other early arrivals, Percy Morris and Maynard Hedstrom. The trading company they founded is now Fiji's largest department store chain ("MH" stores are all over the country). The company donated this dilapidated structure to the National Trust of Fiji. The Levuka Historical and Cultural Society raised money throughout the country to restore it and install a small branch of the Fiji Museum, a public library, a meeting hall, and a crafts and recreational center. The furniture is made of timbers salvaged from the rotting floor. Admission is F$2. The center is open Monday through Thursday from 8am to 1pm and from 2 to 4:30pm, Friday from 8am to 1pm and from 2 to 4pm, and Saturday from 8am to 1pm.

NASOVA & THE DEED OF CESSION ★★

South of the museum, the post office stands at the entrance to the **Queens Wharf.** The drinking fountain in front marks the site of a carrier-pigeon service that linked Suva and Levuka in the late 1800s. The Queens Wharf is one of Fiji's four ports of entry (Suva, Lautoka, and Savusavu are the others), but along with domestic cargo, it now primarily handles exports from the **tuna cannery,** established by the Pacific Fishing Company (Pafco) in 1964. Follow your nose to the cannery in the industrial buildings south of the pier.

Keep going to **Nasova,** a village on the shore of the little bay about half a mile south of the cannery. The **Cession Monument ★★** now marks the site where Chief Cakobau signed the deed ceding Fiji to Great Britain. Three stones in the center of the grassy park at the water's edge commemorate the signing ceremony that took place on October 10, 1874, as well as Fiji's independence exactly 96 years later and the 1974 centennial celebration of the Deed of Cession. Two meeting-houses—one traditional Fijian-style, the other a modern building—stand across the road. The new one was built in anticipation of a meeting of the Great Council of Chiefs in early 2007, but the coup in December 2006 put an end to those plans.

South of Nasova, the **Old Levuka Cemetery** is tended to perfection by prison inmates. Tombstones bear the names of many Europeans who settled here in the 19th century—and some who met their demise instead.

BEACH STREET ★

Backtrack to the weathered storefronts of Levuka's 3-block-long business district along **Beach Street.** Saloons no longer line this avenue; instead, the Indian- and Chinese-owned stores now dispense a variety of dry goods and groceries. On the horizon, beyond the ficus trees and park benches, lie the smoky-blue outlines of Wakaya, Makogai, and other Lomaiviti islands. The green cliffs still reach skyward behind the stores, hemming in Levuka and its narrow valley. Walk along the waterfront, and don't hesitate to stick your head into the general stores for a look at their amazing variety of goods: You could see an old-fashion kerosene lantern displayed next to a modern DVD player.

You'll soon come to the **Church of the Sacred Heart,** a wooden building fronted by a baroque stone tower. It was built by the Marist Brothers who came to Levuka in 1858. The clock in the tower originally struck once on the hour, and again—in case residents missed the number of chimes marking the time—1 minute later. Across Beach Street stands a **World War I monument** to the Fijian members of the Fiji Labour Corps who were killed assisting the British in Europe.

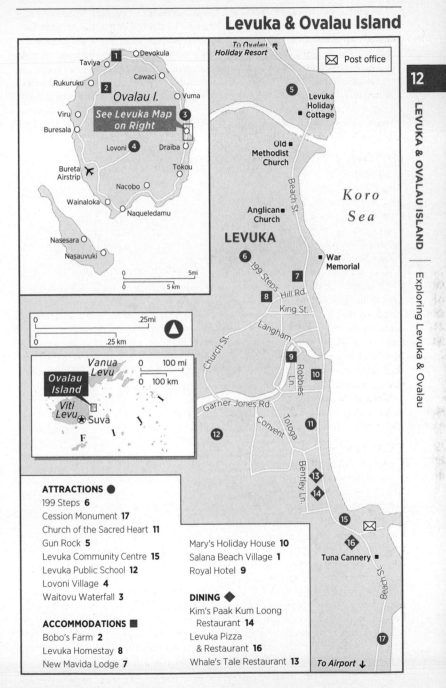

Levuka & Ovalau Island

⊠ Post office

To Ovalau Holiday Resort

Devokula
Taviya
Cawaci
Rukuruku
Ovalau I.
Vuma
See Levuka Map on Right
Viru
Buresala
Lovoni
Draiba
Bureta Airstrip
Tokou
Nacobo
Wainaloka
Naqueledamu
Nasesara
Nasauvuki

0   5mi
0   5 km

Levuka Holiday Cottage

Old Methodist Church

Koro Sea

Anglican Church

LEVUKA

199 Steps

War Memorial

Hill Rd.

King St.

Langham

Church St.

Robbies Ln.

Garner Jones Rd.

Totoga

Convent

Bentley Ln.

Beach St.

Tuna Cannery

To Airport ↓

0   .25mi
0   .25 km

Vanua Levu

0   100 mi
0   100 km

Ovalau Island

Viti Levu
★ Suva

F

ATTRACTIONS ●
199 Steps **6**
Cession Monument **17**
Church of the Sacred Heart **11**
Gun Rock **5**
Levuka Community Centre **15**
Levuka Public School **12**
Lovoni Village **4**
Waitovu Waterfall **3**

ACCOMMODATIONS ■
Bobo's Farm **2**
Levuka Homestay **8**
New Mavida Lodge **7**

Mary's Holiday House **10**
Salana Beach Village **1**
Royal Hotel **9**

DINING ◆
Kim's Paak Kum Loong Restaurant **14**
Levuka Pizza & Restaurant **16**
Whale's Tale Restaurant **13**

Walk on across **Totoga Creek,** from whose bridge local youth like to dive off for a swim, to low **Niukaubi Hill,** on top of which is another World War I monument, this one to Levukans of English ancestry who died fighting as British soldiers in that conflict. Parliament House and the Supreme Court building sat on this little knoll before the capital was moved to Suva. They had a nice view across the town, the waterfront, and the reef and islands offshore. At the bottom of the hill is the **Levuka Club,** a colonial-era social club established by Indians, who weren't allowed in the European-dominated Ovalau Club.

Keep going north on Beach Street, which soon passes the 1904-vintage **Anglican Church** before arriving in the original Fijian village known as **Levuka.** The Tui Levuka who lived here befriended the early European settlers. Later, Chief Cakobau worshiped in the Methodist church that was built on the south side of the creek in 1869. John Brown Williams, the American consul, is buried in the village's Old Cemetery near the church. (Remember, good manners dictate that you request permission before entering a Fijian village.)

To the north, **Gun Rock** towers over Levuka village. In order to show the chiefs just how much firepower it packed, a British warship in 1849 used this steep headland for target practice. Beach Street now runs under the overhang of Gun Rock, where the Marist Brothers said their first Mass. The road didn't exist then, only a shingled beach where the sea had worn away the base of the cliff.

INLAND

Beyond Gun Rock lies the village of **Vagadaci,** where the Duke of York—later King George V—and his brother, the Duke of Clarence, once played cricket (the field is now covered by a housing project), but I usually turn around at Gun Rock and return to Hill Road, the first street inland south of the hospital. It leads to the **199 steps** that climb Mission Hill from the Methodist church to the collection of buildings comprising **Delana Methodist School.** For the energetic, the view from the 199th step is worth the climb.

From the church, cut down Chapel and Langham streets and take a look in the historic **Royal Hotel,** a sightseeing attraction in its own right (see "Where to Stay in Levuka," below). Even if you don't stay at Fiji's oldest operating hotel, have a look at its public rooms, for this ancient establishment is as much attraction as accommodations. It dates to about 1860 but was rebuilt in 1917 after a fire destroyed the original building. Except for installing ceiling fans and bathrooms, little seems to have been done to it since then. Not much imagination is required to picture W. Somerset Maugham or Robert Louis Stevenson relaxing in the comfortable rattan chairs in the charming lounge, slowly sipping gin-and-tonics at the polished bar, or playing a game of snooker at the antique billiards table. Note the large piece of tapa cloth, which was part of the bridal train of the late Queen Salote of Tonga.

After visiting the hotel, keep going south along the banks of Togoga past the burned carcass of the **Masonic Temple,** which looks as if it could be a Grecian ruin, to the **Town Hall,** built in 1898 in honor of Queen Victoria's 50 years on the British throne; it still houses most of Levuka's city offices. Next door is the **Ovalau Club,** built in 1904 as a social club for British colonials. Behind the Town Hall, **Nasau Park** provides the town's rugby and cricket fields, bowling green, and tennis courts.

Cross the bridge and head uphill on Garner Jones Road along the creek until you get to the lovely white Victorian buildings with broad verandas of **Levuka Public School,** Fiji's first educational institution (opened in 1879) and still one of its best. A row of mango and sweet-smelling frangipani trees shade the sidewalk known as Bath Road between the school and the rushing creek. Walk up Bath Road, which soon turns into a "step street" as it climbs to a waterfall and concrete-lined swimming hole known as the **Bath.** Cool off at this refreshing spot before heading back down the steps to Beach Street.

Attractions Beyond Levuka

St. John's College, in the village of Cawaci north of Levuka, was founded by the Marist Brothers in 1884, primarily to educate the sons of ranking Fijian chiefs. The school sits on the grounds of **St. John's Church,** a Gothic Revival building typical of Catholic missions in the South Pacific. On a bluff overlooking the sea, the **Bishop's Tomb** holds the remains of Dr. Julian Vidal, the first Catholic bishop of Fiji.

Yavu, south of Levuka, is a hilltop overlooking the sea where, according to legend, a newly arrived chief lit a fire, which caught the attention of a chief who was already here. The two met at Yavu and agreed that one would be chief of the interior, while the other would rule the coastline. They placed two sacred stones at the spot to mark their agreement. The hilltop isn't marked, so go there with a guide (see "Organized Tours," below).

Waitovu, about a 50-minute walk north of town (look for its mosque), has the town's nearest waterfall. Ask permission, and the residents will show the way. You can dive into the top pool from the rocks above.

Rukuruku village on the northwest shore has a waterfall and Ovalau's sole swimming beach.

Lovoni Village ★

A picturesque Fijian village in the crater of Ovalau's extinct volcano, **Lovoni** was the home of ferocious warriors who stormed down to the coast and attacked Levuka on several occasions in pre-colonial times. Chief Cakobau settled that problem in the 1840s by luring them into town to talk peace; instead, he captured them all and deported them to other parts of Fiji. Lovonians still bear a grudge against their coastal brethren. Some of them came down to Levuka during the 2000 insurrection and torched the Ovalau Club and the Polynesia Masonic Lodge, until then two of the town's landmarks. My friend Christine Moore Green and I took a bus up to Lovoni in 1977; it has changed little since then. The houses still are built of wood with corrugated iron roofs. Today's Lovonians have seen so many travelers wandering around their village that most are adept at pleasantly smiling while ignoring you. It rains a lot up in the crater, whose walls are carpeted with tropical rainforests.

Organized Tours

The best way to see the town and environs on foot is in the company of a Levuka native. The **Levuka Community Centre** (✆ **344 0356**) has 1-hour guided walking tours of town Monday to Friday at 10am. They cost F$10 per person.

Noa "Nox" Vueti of **Nox Walking Tours** ★ leads a 2-hour historical walking tour of town well worth the F$10 per person. He also leads walks to Waitovu waterfall and climbs up to the top of the peak overlooking town; these trips cost F$15 per person. The climb to the peak takes 1½ hours each way and is not for anyone who is out of shape. Book either through **Ovalau Watersports** (© 344 0166).

Epi's Inland Tour ★ (© 362 4174) departs at 11am and goes by truck to Lovoni village, up in the central crater. The visit includes a *sevusevu* (kava) welcoming ceremony and lunch of traditional Fijian food in the village, then a walk into a nearby rainforest. The trips cost between F$60 and F$80 per person, depending on how many go. You'll get back to town about 6pm. Reservations are required, so call Epi or book at the Royal Hotel (see "Where to Stay in Levuka," below).

Ovalau Watersports (© 344 0166) organizes **Tea and *Talanoa*** visits with veteran Levuka resident "Bubu" Kara, who serves tea and tells tales about the island's old days and explains Fijian culture and customs. *Talanoa* is Fijian for sitting down and having a long talk, and it's well worth F$15 to do just that with these knowledgeable locals.

For a guided tour of the island, contact **Lloyd's Transport** (© 344 0331 or 925 2226), which is operated by a Levuka native whose real name is Subbayia but who was dubbed Lloyd by his school classmates. The English name stuck. Lloyd will take you around in his air-conditioned van on a 2-hour tour F$150, or for F$200 he will escort you all day.

DIVING, SNORKELING & HIKING

Ovalau's lack of beaches means that water sports are limited here. One exception is the ubiquitous **Ovalau Watersports** (© 440 611; www.owlfiji.com), which offers **scuba diving** and teaches PADI courses. Owner Noby Dehm pioneered diving in the Lomaiviti Islands and knows the area better than anyone. Nearby dive sites are in and near Levuka harbor, including Levuka Pass, with its multitude of fish and sharks. Weather permitting, Noby also takes divers to Wakaya Passage, where manta rays and hammerhead sharks congregate. This area is not crowded with other divers, so you will be with small groups. Noby charges F$170 for a two-tank dive, and he teaches PADI open-water courses. Snorkelers can go along on the nearby dive trips for F$40 each.

Ovalau is a fine place to go **hiking,** whether it's a long walk along the shoreline on either side of Levuka, or climbing into the mountains above the town. However, I don't advise wandering into the mountains by yourself; instead, go with **Nox Walking Tours.** You'll be rewarded with some terrific views on his hike to the peak overlooking Levuka and the Lomaiviti Islands. **Epi's Inland Tour** to Lovoni village includes rainforest hikes followed by a dip in the cool stream flowing through the village. See "Organized Tours," above.

WHERE TO STAY IN LEVUKA

Two local families welcome visitors on Ovalau's northern coast. **Silana Beach Village** is a seaside homestay with four *bures* (bungalows) and 10 dorm beds near Arovundi village, while **Bobo's Farm** has one Western-style cottage on a riverbank in the Rukuruku Valley. Both charge about F$70 per double, including meals.

Contact **Ovalau Watersports** (© **344 0166;** www.owlfiji.com) for more information and reservations.

Andrea and Noby Dehm of Ovalau Watersports also rent their **Gun Rock Cottage,** a two-bedroom house at the base of Gun Rock and across the main road from
the lagoon. It has a full kitchen and a bathroom with hot-water shower. They charge
F$85 a night.

Levuka Homestay ★★★ After vacationing in Fiji several times, John and
Marilyn Milesi gave up on the fast lane and relocated here from Perth, Australia.
One of the top bed-and-breakfasts in Fiji, John and Marilyn's home overlooking
Levuka is far and away the best place to stay here. You climb up stairs bordered by
tropical foliage past three of their hotel-style rooms to the main house, where Marilyn serves breakfast on the veranda, whose view almost matches the quality of her
cooking. The three units below the house are staggered down the hill and each has
a porch, so they seem almost like small bungalows. They have old Levuka touches,
such as tongue-and-groove plank walls, and windows that push out in the colonial
style (they are not screened, but these units are air-conditioned). A fourth room is
on the first floor of the Molesi's upstairs quarters. Although it is less private and not
air-conditioned, it's carved out of the hill, which moderates the temperature. It also
has twin beds, while the others have one queen-size bed each. Every unit has a ceiling fan and a small desk.

P.O. Box 50, Levuka, Ovalau. © **344 0777.** www.levukahomestay.com. 4 units. F$160 double. Rates
include full breakfast. MC, V. **Amenities:** Free Wi-Fi. *In room:* A/C (3 units), ceiling fan, fridge, no phone.

Mary's Lodge This house on Beach Street has been attracting backpackers for 3
decades. A central hallway passes basic but clean rooms, most of which have double
beds. Others with cots serve as dormitories. The breezy living room fronts Beach
Street. Guests share toilets, showers, and a primordial communal kitchen in the rear
of the house.

P.O. Box 90, Levuka, Ovalau. © **344 0013.** 13 units (none with bathroom), 20 dorm beds. F$50 double;
F$20 dorm bed. Rates include continental breakfast. No credit cards. *In room:* No phone.

New Mavida Lodge Levuka's only modern motel opened in 2006 on the site of
the original Mavida Lodge, a terrific Fijian guesthouse where I spent Christmas of
1977, and which, unfortunately, burned down a few years ago. On Beach Street, this
incarnation is entered via a two-story lobby with gleaming white-tile floors. Hallways
lead off to the rooms, each with a TV, telephone, and modern bathroom. The most
expensive rooms have balconies, but I prefer to opt for one on the second floor with
a lagoon and sea view. A large, fan-cooled room serves as a privacy-deprived dormitory with 10 cots; it has both male and female bathrooms en suite and two more
across the backyard. Guests are served complimentary breakfast in the meeting
room, but there is no restaurant on-site.

P.O. Box 4, Levuka, Ovalau. © **344 0477.** Fax 334 0533. newmavidalodge@connect.com.fj. 11 units, 10
dorm beds. F$80–F$120 double; F$25 dorm bed. Rates include continental breakfast. No credit cards.
Amenities: Internet (F$1/minute). *In room:* A/C, TV.

Royal Hotel ★ One of Levuka's fine old families, the Ashleys, has owned and
operated this historic attraction for more than half a century with such attentive care
that it seems more like a pension full of antiques than a hotel. Creaking stairs lead

to the 15 rooms in the original building. Basic by today's standards, they are charming and all have ceiling fans, shower stalls, and toilets. Their unscreened windows push out, and some rooms have small sun porches with white wicker furniture (you can watch the local rugby matches from those on the backside of the building). A mosquito net hangs romantically over the queen-size bed in the honeymoon room, which has a fridge and sun porch. The largest room is the family unit on the north end of the building; it has a queen-size bed in a large room, two single beds in its sunroom, a sink, and a fridge. Much more modern and spacious, six clapboard cottages between the old structure and Beach Street were built in 1998. Five of these are air-conditioned, although their louvered windows usually let in the sea breeze, and five have kitchens. Each has a front porch. Preferable to me are the Winifred, Ed, and Dot cottages, which face Beach Street and have kitchens. Next would be Kie and Kiku, beside the hotel's outdoor pool. The dining room here serves breakfast all day but no other meals.

P.O. Box 47, Levuka, Ovalau. © **344 0024.** Fax 344 0174. www.royallevuka.com. 15 units, 6 cottages. F$42–F$65 double; F$85–F$123 cottage. MC, V. **Amenities:** Restaurant (breakfast only); bar; bikes; exercise room; outdoor pool; Wi-Fi (F$5/hour). *In room:* A/C (in 5 cottages); ceiling fan, fridge (in 2 rooms and all cottages); kitchen (3 cottages); no phone.

WHERE TO DINE IN LEVUKA

None of Levuka's hotels serve lunch or dinner, so you will have to head to one of the following on Beach Street.

Kim's Paak Kum Loong Restaurant CHINESE/INDIAN   The best tables in this upstairs restaurant are out on the front porch overlooking Beach Street. The menu offers something for everyone in town: Fried fish and chips for Europeans, spicy curries for Indians, and *ika vakalolo* (fish steamed with coconut milk) for Fijians, plus several Chinese dishes including good won ton soup. Pan-fried fish in herbs and garlic and spicy Thai curries also are served.

Beach St., middle of town. © **344 0059.** Reservations not accepted. Main courses F$6.50–F$14. No credit cards. Mon–Sat 7am–2pm and 6–9pm; Sun 6–9pm.

Levuka Pizza & Restaurant PACIFIC RIM/PIZZA   Crews from the tuna boats docking at the nearby cannery frequent this establishment for pizza, served in small and medium sizes with familiar toppings. They're not the best pies in the world, but they beat the basic local dishes such as fish, chicken, or beef stir-fries served with rice.

Beach St. (opposite main wharf). © **344 0429.** Reservations not accepted. Pizza F$8.50–F$19; sandwiches F$3.50–F$7.50; main courses F$7–F$15. No credit cards. Mon–Sat 7am–2pm and 6–9pm; Sun 6–9pm.

Whale's Tale Restaurant PACIFIC RIM   This cramped but pleasant restaurant in one of Beach Street's old storefronts is the best place to dine in Levuka. Australian Liza Ditrich and Fijian partner Sai Tuibua serve continental breakfasts as well as sandwiches, burgers, and pastas at lunch. At night they put cloths on the tables and offer omelets, burgers, pastas, stir-fries, and three-course dinners from a chalkboard menu, which usually includes a vegetarian selection.

Beach St., middle of town. © **344 0235.** Reservations not accepted. Most items F$7.50–F$13. No credit cards. Mon–Sat 11am–8pm.

WAKAYA ISLAND'S SUPER-LUXURY RESORT

Within sight of Levuka, **Wakaya Island** is an uplifted, tilted coral atoll in the Koro Sea. Beaches fringe Wakaya's north and east coasts, and cliffs fall into the sea on its western side. Relics of a Fijian fort still stand on the cliffs. Legend says a chief and all his men leapt off the cliff to their deaths from there rather than be roasted by a rival tribe; the spot is now known as Chieftain's Leap. The only way to visit Wakaya, however, is to stay at:

The Wakaya Club ★★★ A 20-minute flight by private plane from Nausori Airport, 50 minutes from Nadi, this super-deluxe beachside facility is the brainchild of Canadian entrepreneur David Gilmour, who also introduced us to "Fiji" bottled water. Gilmour has sold off pieces of Wakaya for deluxe getaway homes. For a small fortune, you can rent one of these villas, including *Vale O,* Gilmore's own Japanese-influenced mansion high on a ridge overlooking the resort. Nicole Kidman (a regular guest) and other Hollywood types who don't own a private villa—or can't borrow a friend's—feel right at home in the club's large, super-luxurious bungalows. The gourmet food here is outstandingly presented. Guests dine in a huge thatched-roof beachside building or outside, either on a patio or under two gazebolike shelters on a deck surrounding a pool with its own waterfall. The Fijian staff delivers excellent, unobtrusive service. Only the humongous Governor's and Ambassador's bures have TVs for DVD viewing. The latter, a 418-sq.-m (4,500-sq.-ft.) retreat, is the largest bure here.

P.O. Box 15424, Suva (Wakaya Island, Lomaiviti Group). ℭ **344 0128.** Fax 970/920-1225 or 344 0406. www.wakaya.com. 9 units. US$1,900–US$7,600 bungalow. Rates include meals, drinks, and all activities except deep-sea fishing, scuba diving courses, and massages. AE, DC, MC, V. **Amenities:** Restaurant; bar; babysitting; bikes; 9-hole golf course; health club; Internet; Jacuzzi; outdoor pool; room service; spa; tennis court; watersports equipment/rentals; free Wi-Fi. *In room:* A/C, ceiling fan, TV/DVD (some units), minibar, MP3 docking station.

SAVUSAVU

To me, the pristine islands of northern Fiji are what the old South Seas are all about. Compared to busy Viti Levu, "The North" takes us back to the old days of *copra* (dried coconut meat) planters, of Fijians living in small villages in the hills or beside crystal-clear lagoons. You will get a taste of the slow, peaceful pace of life up here as soon as you get off the plane.

The rolling hills of northern **Vanua Levu,** the country's second-largest island, are devoted to sugar-cane farming and are of little interest to anyone who has visited Nadi. **Labasa,** a predominately Indo-Fijian town and Vanua Levu's commercial center, reminds me of Dorothy Parker's famous quip, "There is no there there."

But Vanua Levu's southern side is quite another story. From Labasa, the paved Cross-Island Road traverses the rugged central mountains, where cheerful villagers go about life at the ageless pace of tropical islands everywhere. The Cross-Island then drops down to an old trading town with the singsong name **Savusavu.**

GETTING TO & AROUND SAVUSAVU

Getting There

Pacific Sun serves Savusavu from both Nadi and Suva. It does not fly directly between Savusavu and Taveuni, however, so you will have to go back to Nadi in order to get between the two. The tiny Savusavu airstrip is on Vanua Levu's south coast. Hotel representatives meet guests who have reservations. A few taxi drivers usually meet the flights.

Bligh Water Shipping Ltd. and **Venu Shipping Ltd.** operate ferries between Savusavu and Suva. **Patterson Shipping Services** has bus-ferry connections from Natovi Wharf (north of Suva on eastern Viti Levu) to Nabouwalu on Vanua Levu. You connect by bus from Suva to Natovi and from Nabouwalu to Labasa. Local buses connect Labasa to Savusavu.

The small ferry *Amazing Grace* (© **927 1372** in Savusavu, 888 0320 on Taveuni) crosses the Somosomo Strait between Buca Bay and Taveuni 4 days a week. The one-way fare is F$25, including the 2½-hour bus ride between Savusavu and Buca Bay and the 1½-hour ferry trip across the strait. Call for schedules and reservations.

See "Getting Around Fiji," in chapter 3, for more information.

Getting Around Savusavu

Rock 'n Downunder Divers, on the main street (℗ **885 3447;** www.dive-savusavu.com), rents bicycles and is the local agent for **Budget Rent A Car** (℗ **800/527-0700** in the U.S., or 672 2735 in Nadi; www.budget.com). **Trip n Tour,** a travel agency in the Copra Shed (℗ **885 3154;** tripntours@connect.com. fj), rents bikes (F$25 a day), scooters (F$50 a day), and cars ($F132).

An incredible number of **taxis** gather by the market in Savusavu. The cars of **Paradise Cab** (℗ **885 0018** or 956026), **Michael's Taxi** (℗ **995 5727**), and **Blue Lagoon Cab** (℗ **997 1525**) are air-conditioned. Fares from Savusavu are about F$5 to the airstrip, F$7 to Namale Resort, F$12 to Koro Sun Resort, and F$6 to the Jean-Michel Cousteau Fiji Islands Resort on Lesiaceva Point.

Local buses fan out from the Savusavu market to various points on the island. Most of them make three or four runs a day to outlying destinations, but ask the drivers when they will return to town. The longest runs should cost about F$6, with local routes in the F55¢ to F$1 range.

[FastFACTS] SAVUSAVU

The following facts apply to Savusavu. If you don't see an item here, check "Fast Facts: Fiji" in chapter 15.

Currency Exchange ANZ Bank, Westpac Bank, and **Colonial National Bank** have offices with ATMs on the main street.

Emergencies In case of an emergency, phone ℗ **917** for the police, and ℗ **911** for **fire** or **ambulance.** The **police station** (℗ **885 0222**) is east of town.

Healthcare If he hasn't retired by the time you arrive, **Dr. Joeli Taoi** (℗ **885 0721**) has an office and pharmacy in the Palm Court shops, on the main street. The **government**

hospital (℗ **885 0800**) is east of town, in the government compound.

Internet Access Xerographic Solutions, in the Copra Shed (℗ **885 3253**), has a Wi-Fi hotspot and broadband access in air-conditioned comfort for F$4 an hour.

Mail The post office is on the main street east of the downtown commercial district. It's open Monday to Friday 8am to 5pm, Saturday 8am to noon.

Safety Savusavu generally is a safe place to visit,

but you should always keep an eye on your personal property.

Visitor Information Your best bet for local information are **Trip n Tour,** in the Copra Shed (℗ **885 3154**), and **Rock 'n Downunder Divers,** on the eastern end of main street (℗ **885 3447**). You can find information on the Web at the Savusavu Tourism Association's site (**www.fiji-savusavu.com**).

Water The tap water in town and at the resorts is safe to drink.

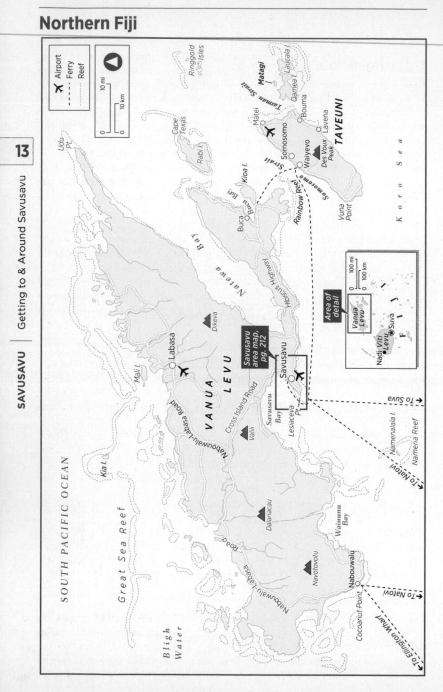

EXPLORING SAVUSAVU

For practical purposes, Savusavu has only one street, and that runs along the shore for about 1.5km (1 mile). It has no official name, but everyone calls it Main Street. About midway along the shore stands the **Copra Shed,** an old warehouse that has been turned into modern shops, offices, two restaurants, and the Savusavu Yacht Club. A bit farther along is **Waitui Marina,** where cruising yachties come ashore.

Highlights of a stroll along the bay-hugging street are the gorgeous scenery and the volcanic **hot springs.** Steam from underground rises from the beach on the west end of town, and you can see more white clouds floating up from the ground between the sports field and the school, both behind the BP service station. A concrete pot has been built to make a natural stove in which local residents place meals to cook slowly all day. Overlooking the springs and bay, the **Savusavu Hot Springs Hotel** has great views (see "Where to Stay in Savusavu," later in the chapter).

Organized Tours

More than likely your hotel will have a choice of guided excursions in and around Savusavu. If not, **Trip n Tour,** in the Copra Shed (✆ **885 3154;** tripntours@connect.com.fj), has a series of tours and excursions. One spends half a day in a Fijian village and costs F$5 per person. Another goes in search of the red prawns that grow in lakes on southeastern Vanua Levu (F$55 per person). A third takes you to a copra and beef plantation, where you can see the modern-day version of the old South Seas coconut plantation. It costs F$50 per person.

Best of all is a full-day trip to **Waisali Rainforest Reserve** ★★ (✆ **330 1807;** www.nationaltrust.org.fj), a 116-hectare (290-acre) national forest up in the central mountains; the outing, which includes a hike to a waterfall, costs F$125. The park has well-maintained gravel pathways. Reservations for the tour are essential. You can also take a taxi to the reserve and do it yourself. If so, admission is F$8 for adults, F$4 for children, or F$20 for a family. The reserve is open Monday to Saturday from 9am to 3pm.

Rock 'n Downunder Divers, on the eastern end of main street (✆ **885 3447;** www.dive-savusavu.com), has half-day Fijian village visits for F$60. It also offers half- and full-day boat tours around Savusavu Bay for F$70 and F$120, respectively, and full-day cruises up a river on the bay's north shore for F$100 per person.

OUTDOOR ACTIVITIES

The gray-sand beaches around Savusavu aren't the main reason to come here. The nearest beach to town is a shady stretch on Lesiaceva Point just outside the Jean-Michel Cousteau Fiji Islands Resort, about 5km (3 miles) west of town, which is the end of the line for westbound buses leaving Savusavu market.

Adventure Cruises ★★★

Ecotourism takes to sea with **Tui Tai Expeditions** (✆ **253/617-1035** in the U.S., or 885 3032; www.tuitai.com), which uses the luxurious, 42m (140-ft.) sailing schooner *Tui Tai* to make 7- and 10-day voyages from Savusavu. The boat goes to Taveuni, where you visit Bouma Falls; Kioa, where you spend time in that island's one village; and Rabi Island, which is inhabited by Micronesians who were relocated

Savusavu

here after World War II when their home island of *Banaba* (Ocean Island) was made uninhabitable by phosphate mining. Some cruises go into the Lau Islands in eastern Fiji. The *Tui Tai* carries mountain bikes for land excursions as well as kayaks and diving and snorkeling gear for exploring the shoreline and reefs. The *Tui Tai* can accommodate 24 guests in air-conditioned cabins. Rates range from US$3,900 to US$11,400 per cabin double occupancy, depending on the length of voyage and type of stateroom, and including all meals and activities.

Fishing

Ika Levu Fishing Charters (© **944 8506;** www.fishinginfiji.com) uses 7.2 and 12m (24- and 41-ft.) boats for sportfishing excursions in the bays and offshore. Rates start at F$1,500 for half a day. Each boat can take up to four fishers.

Hiking & Mountain Biking

The best way to explore Vanua Levu's mountains is on foot or by bike, especially on a tour offered by Sharon Wild and Scott Smith of **Naveria Heights Lodge** (© **885**

0348; www.naveriaheightsfiji.com). They will tailor hiking and biking excursions to your schedule and include accommodation at the lodge (see "Where to Stay in Savusavu," below).

Scuba Diving & Snorkeling ★★★

A very long boat ride is required to dive on the Rainbow Reef and Great White Wall, which are more easily reached from Taveuni than from Savusavu. But that's not to say that there aren't plenty of colorful reefs near here, especially outside the bay along the island's southern coast. The beautifully preserved Namena Barrier Reef, a wonderful formation nearly encircling Moody's Namena, is a 2½-hour ride away (see "A Resort on Namenalala Island," later in the chapter). Namena trips are not always possible, as it can be too rough to cross if the trade winds are blowing strongly out of the southeast. Most of the resorts have complete diving facilities (see "Where to Stay in Savusavu," below).

The best dive operators here are **L'Aventure Dive Shop** at Jean-Michel Cousteau Fiji Islands Resort (© **885 0188;** www.fijiresort.com) and **Koro Sun Dive** (© **885 2452;** www.korosundive.com) at Koro Sun Resort. The latter is on the south coast, thus has shorter boat rides to the colorful reefs in the Somosomo Strait. See "Where to Stay in Savusavu," later in this chapter.

The best spot for snorkeling is over **Split Rock,** off the Jean-Michel Cousteau Fiji Islands Resort, but to access it you will have to stay at the resort or go on a snorkeling expedition with Savusavu town–based **Rock 'n Downunder Divers** (© **885 3447;** www.dive-savusavu.com), which also has scuba diving, teaches PADI diving courses, and rents snorkeling gear, kayaks, and bicycles.

SHOPPING IN SAVUSAVU

Marine biologist Justin Hunter spent more than 10 years working in the U.S. before coming home to Savusavu and founding Fiji's first black-pearl farm out in the bay. You can shop for the results—including golden pearls unique to Savusavu—at **J. Hunter Pearls** ★★, on the western end of town (© **885 0821;** www.pearlsfiji. com; Mon–Fri 8am–5pm, Sat 8am–1pm). Prices range from F$20 up to F$2,000 for loose pearls. Justin has them set in jewelry, too, as well as selling some interesting items made from the mother-of-pearl shells (I prize my salad forks made from gleaming shells with tree-branch handles). For F$25, you can take a 30-minute boat tour of the farm at 9:30am and 1:30pm weekdays.

The mother-son team of Karen and Shane Bower display their paintings and sculpture, respectively, at the **Art Gallery,** in the Copra Shed (© **885 3054**). They also carry J. Hunter black pearls and shell jewelry. Gallery hours are Monday Friday from 9:30am to 1pm and 2 to 4:30pm. Karen and husband Edward Boy also operate Trip n Tour in the Copra Shed.

Next door, **Taki Handicrafts** (© **885 3956**) sells quality woodcarvings, cloth, shell jewelry, and other Fiji-made items (Mon–Fri 8am–1pm and 2–4:3(Sat 9:30am–noon).

Also look in **Waterfront Home & Garden** (© **885 3220**), upstairs in th commercial building at the eastern end of the main street. Owned by Am expatriate Denise Melinski, it carries unique Savusavu-made home furnishin some handicrafts you may not see elsewhere, such as baskets from Kioa Island. Open Monday to Friday 9am to 4pm, Saturday 10am to 1pm.

When you tour the **Savusavu Municipal Market,** on Main Street, go into the **Savusavu Town Council Handicraft Center** (no phone) on the eastern side of the building. It's open Monday to Friday 7am to 5pm, and Saturday from 6:30am to 3pm.

WHERE TO STAY IN SAVUSAVU

Expensive

Jean-Michel Cousteau Fiji Islands Resort ★★★ ☺   The finest family resort I have ever seen bears the name of Jean-Michel Cousteau (son of the late Jacques Cousteau), who convinced the owners that a tropical resort could be both environmentally friendly and profitable. It is indeed environmentally friendly, from wastewater-treatment ponds inhabited by frogs (nature's own mosquito control) to the lack of energy-guzzling air-conditioners (except in the plush honeymoon villa). With its own swimming pools, the outstanding Bula Camp is like a little resort within the resort. Exiled here, children under 13 years old learn about the tropical environment and are taken on their own snorkeling and other adventures.

With the kids thoroughly occupied and mostly out of sight from 8:30am until 9pm, depending on their parents' wishes, this also is an excellent couples resort. Guests of any age can take part in environmentally oriented activities such as visits to rain- and mangrove forests. An on-site marine biologist gives lectures and leads bird-watching expeditions and visits to Fijian villages. And divers are accompanied by guides skilled in marine biology.

The property looks like an old-time Fijian village set in a flat palm grove beside the bay near Lesiaceva Point. Reception and the resort's bar and dining areas (one for families, another for couples) are under large thatched roofs built like Fijian chiefs' and priests' houses. These impressive buildings sit next to an infinity pool just steps from one of the better beaches in the area.

The thatched-roof guest *bures* (bungalows) have ceiling fans to augment the natural breezes flowing through the floor-to-ceiling wooden jalousie windows comprising the front and rear walls. Most bures have porches strung with hammocks, and some of the smaller units have been enlarged to include a separate bedroom, a plus for families. It's worth paying extra for more space and privacy in the split-level "villas" isolated at the end of the property. The award-winning honeymoon villa has its own swimming pool and a spa tub in its large bathroom. It's the only unit here with a phone.

You can get massages and treatments in beachside bures, which become private dining venues after dark. Even the kids' cuisine is outstanding here.

Post Office, Savusavu (Lesiaceva Point). ☎ **800/246-3454** or 885 0188. Fax 885 0430. www.fijiresort. com. 25 units. US$690–US$2,470 double. Rates include meals, soft drinks, Bula Club for kids, and all activities except scuba diving, fishing, massage. AE, MC, V. **Amenities:** Restaurant; bar; babysitting; children's center; 3 outdoor pools; tennis court; free airport transfers; watersports equipment/rentals; free Wi-Fi. *In room:* A/C (in honeymoon villa), ceiling fan, hair dryer, minibar, no phone.

Koro Sun Resort   This sprawling property on Vanua Levu's southern coast has been considerably upgraded in recent years by its owner, American architect Jack

Savusavu Town

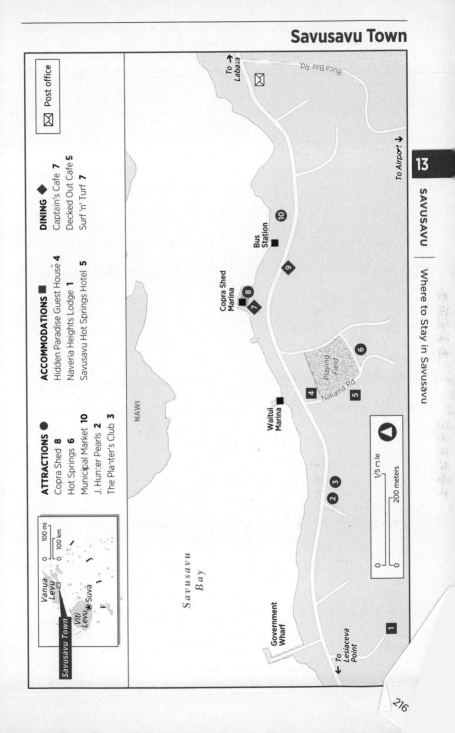

⊠ Post office

ATTRACTIONS ●
Copra Shed **8**
Hot Springs **6**
Municipal Market **10**
J. Hunter Pearls **2**
The Planter's Club **3**

ACCOMMODATIONS ■
Hidden Paradise Guest House **4**
Naveria Heights Lodge **1**
Savusavu Hot Springs Hotel **5**

DINING ◆
Captain's Cafe **7**
Decked Out Cafe **9**
Surf 'n' Turf **7**

Vanua
Levu
Savusavu Town
Viti
Levu ⊛ Suva

0   100 mi
0   100 km

Savusavu
Bay

NAWI

Copra Shed
Marina

Bus
Station

Waitui
Marina

Playing
Field

Nakama Rd.

Buca Bay Rd.

To →
Labasa

To Airport →

Government
Wharf

To
Lesiaceva
Point

0   1/5 mile
0   200 meters

Young, who will gladly sell you a piece of paradise and build a custom-designed home on it (the resort rents luxury villas already built by its landowners). Jack's trademark is the round window, and you will see many of them here, including in the floors of the two-bedroom Edgewater Villas extending over the lagoon. Similar villas stand over a stream dammed to form a large lily pond. Along with those at **Likuliku Lagoon Resort** (p. 127), these are the only overwater units in Fiji. The Hibiscus Highway runs through the property along the shoreline, which turns quickly from flat coastal shelf to hills, where most of the smaller guest bungalows are perched, thus commanding views through the palms to the sea. All the hillside units have screened porches. One has a separate bedroom, another has two bedrooms. The octagonal honeymoon bure is the most deluxe and private. Down at sea level, the "garden" units lack views but have small front yards behind picket fences, plus four-poster beds with mosquito nets. All units have outdoor showers behind high rock walls. The resort offers a bit of beach, and a swimming hole has been dredged into the shallow reef. A weekend-only restaurant and bar sit on a landfill by a marina, also blasted into the reef. Koro Sun sports two outdoor pools (the more attractive reserved for adults only), and a 9-hole, par-3 golf course. A dirt track leads around the course and through a rainforest to the resort's own refreshing cascades, where you can take a cold dip or be pampered in the spa's two screened bungalows.

Private Mail Bag, Savusavu (Hibiscus Hwy.). © **877/567-6786** or 885 0262. Fax 885 0355. www.koro sunresort.com. 24 units. US$400–US$550 bungalow; US$650–US$1,200 villa. Bure rates include meals and nonmotorized water sports. AE, MC, V. **Amenities:** 2 restaurants; 2 bars; babysitting; bikes; children's programs; 9-hole golf course; health club; Jacuzzi; 2 outdoor pools; spa; 2 tennis courts; free airport transfers; watersports equipment/rentals; Wi-Fi (F$20/hour). *In room:* A/C, ceiling fan, TV, TV/DVD (in villas), fridge, hair dryer, kitchen (in villas), no phone.

Namale – The Fiji Islands Resort & Spa ★★★

Both luxurious and eclectic, this resort is owned by toothy American motivational author and speaker Anthony Robbins, who visits several times a year and operates his get-a-grip Oneness University–Fiji across the road (most participants sleep up there, but those willing to pay a lot extra stay in the resort). Robbins obviously finds any dull moment distasteful, for he has built an air-conditioned gym with a wall-size TV for watching sports via satellite, an indoor basketball court, an electronic golf simulator, and a full-size bowling alley. As my travel-writing colleague "Johnny Jet" DiScala once wisecracked, this is "the kind of place Americans come when they really don't want to leave home."

This area has been geologically uplifted, so all buildings are on a shelf 3 to 6m (10–20 ft.) above sea level. The guest quarters are widely scattered in the blooming tropical gardens, thus affording honeymoonlike privacy, if not a setting directly beside the lagoon. The crown jewel is the "Dream House," a two-bedroom, two-bathroom minimansion with a kitchen, its own small pool, a whirlpool bathtub, and indoor and outdoor showers. Similarly equipped, the "Bula House" has only one bedroom, but its rental includes the two guest bungalows outside, and it has a Jacuzzi on its deck. Now listen up, you Hollywood types: Both the Dream and Bula houses have drop-down movie screens with wraparound sound systems. Two more "Grand Villas" have their own pools, separate buildings for sleeping and living, and a treehouselike platform for lounging with sea views. Among the bungalows, the deluxe honeymoon bure also has its own swimming pool. Four more honeymoon units have bathrooms with Jacuzzi tubs, separate showers with indoor and outdoor entrances, and their own ceiling fans. Six older bures are much less spectacular, but they are attractively appointed nonetheless. You'll have a walkie-talkie instead of a phone.

P.O. Box 244, Savusavu (Hibiscus Hwy.). © **800/727-3454** or 885 0435. Fax 885 0400, or 619/535-6385 in the U.S. www.namalefiji.com. 15 bungalows, 3 houses. US$900–US$1,250 double in bungalow; US$2,000–US$2,500 house. Rates include meals, drinks, and all activities except spa services, scuba diving, and fishing. AE, MC, V. No children 11 and under accepted. **Amenities:** Restaurant; 2 bars; bikes; health club; Jacuzzi; 2 outdoor pools; spa; tennis courts; free airport transfers; watersports equipment/ rentals; free Wi-Fi. *In room:* A/C (in houses and deluxe bungalows), ceiling fan, TV/DVD (some units), hair dryer, minibar, no phone.

Inexpensive

The least expensive place to stay in town is the **Hidden Paradise Guest House** (© **885 0106;** hp@connect.com.fj), on the main street in front of the hot springs. It is plain, simple, and a bit dark, but owners Graham and Elenoa Weatherall keep it very clean. Their six small rooms all have air-conditioners. Not so in the dormitory, but it usually gets a good breeze. Everyone shares toilets, showers, and a kitchen. Rates are F$40 per person in rooms, F$25 in dorms, including full breakfast. No credit cards.

Daku Resort ♦ This former church camp is now owned by Britons John ("J.J.") and Delia Rothnie-Jones, who renovated it and now use it as a base for their Paradise Courses offering a variety of educational classes such as creative writing, quilting, bird-watching, sketching, and gospel singing (see www.paradisecourses.com for more activities). There is no beach here, but the tin-roof accommodations, main building with restaurant and bar, and outdoor pool sit in a lawn across Lesiaceva Point Road from the lagoon. Ranging from hotel rooms to three-bedroom houses, the units are simple but clean and comfortable. Some units have outdoor showers. Savusavu town is a 25-minute walk from here.

P.O. Box 18, Savusavu (Lesiaceva Point Rd.). © **885 0046.** Fax 885 0334. www.dakuresort.com. 19 units. F$180–F$350 double. AE, MC, V. **Amenities:** Restaurant; bar; babysitting; Internet (F$10/hour); outdoor pool; free airport transfers; watersports equipment/rentals. *In room:* A/C (3 units), ceiling fan, fridge, kitchen (2 villas), no phone.

Naveria Heights Lodge ★ You will need a stout heart or four-wheel-drive vehicle to climb the steep hill up to this charming little bed-and-breakfast, but you will be rewarded with spectacular views of Savusavu Bay. It's the creation of partners Sharon Wild and Scott Smith, who settled here from Canada and Scotland, respectively. The central building, with a kitchen and TV lounge, opens to a view-filled veranda, which holds a small plunge pool and wraps around in front of the three bedrooms. One unit has a queen-size bed, while the others have kings. The unit next to the pool also has a jetted tub in its bathroom. Sharon and Scott organize hiking, mountain biking, and other excursions, and they will let you ride into town with them and—more importantly—back up the hill. If you do climb it yourself, relieving massages are available.

P.O. Box 437, Savusavu (in town). © **885 0348** or 936 4808. www.naveriaheightsfiji.com. 3 units. F$160–F$200 double. Rates include breakfast. MC, V. Biking, hiking, other packages available. **Amenities:** Bikes; outdoor pool; free airport transfers; free Wi-Fi. *In room:* Ceiling fan, no phone.

Savusavu Hot Springs Hotel 🔔　Once a Travelodge motel, this three-story structure sits on a hill in town, and its motel-style rooms afford the view through sliding glass doors opening to balconies. Units on the third and fourth floors have the best vantage. The less-expensive rooms on the lower levels are equipped with ceiling fans but lack air-conditioners. Some ground-floor rooms are devoted to dormitory-style accommodations, which makes this the most comfortable backpacker's choice in the area. Most of the dorms have double beds, while two are equipped with four bunk beds each. The pool is surrounded by a wooden deck and overlooks the bay. This establishment needs some maintenance, but it's clean, comfortable, friendly, and a very good value.

P.O. Box 208, Savusavu (in town). ©️ **885 0195.** Fax 885 0430. www.hotspringsfiji.com. 48 units. F$115–F$175 double; F$37 dorm bed. AE, MC, V. **Amenities:** Restaurant, bar; babysitting; outdoor pool. *In room:* A/C (most units), fridge.

Cottage Rentals

As on Taveuni (see "Where to Stay on Taveuni," in chapter 14), a number of expatriates who have purchased land here have constructed rental cottages on their properties. Others rent out their homes when they're not here, either through rental programs such as at Koro Sun Resort (see above) or on the Internet.

Deserting the deserts of New Mexico, owners Susan Stone and Jeffery Mather relocated to this lush setting in 2001 and built **Tropic Splendor** (©️ **851 0152** or 991 7931; www.tropic-splendor-fiji.com), on the north shore of Savusavu Bay, a 20-minute drive from town. Their guest bungalow sits beside a beach of powdery, cocoa-colored sand. It has ceiling fans, a TV with DVD player, wireless Internet access, a king-size bed, a big wraparound porch with hammock, outdoor shower, and other amenities. They charge F$360 per day, with discounts for longer stays. MasterCard and Visa credit cards are accepted.

Another option is **Fiji Beach Shacks** (©️ **885 1002;** www.fijibeachshacks.com), whose "House of Bamboo" between town and Lesiaceva Point is anything but a shack. This two-level, two-bedroom, two-bathroom luxury home with outdoor pool is perched high on a hill overlooking Savusavu Bay. Rates are F$275 for a double per night, with a 3-night minimum stay required.

Karen and Edward Bower, who own **Trip n Tour,** in the Copra Shed (©️ **885 3154;** tripntours@connect.com.fj), rent their Bayside Bure next to Jean-Michel Cousteau Fiji Islands Resort for F$30 per person per night.

WHERE TO DINE IN SAVUSAVU

Captain's Cafe INTERNATIONAL　With seating inside the Copra Shed or outside on a deck over the bay, this cafe is a pleasant place for a morning coffee, an outdoor lunch, and good steaks at dinner. Fresh fish is surprisingly tasty, too, especially the mahimahi in lemon butter. Other offerings are sandwiches, burgers, side salads, garlic bread, and reasonably good pastas and pizzas.

Main Street, in the Copra Shed. ©️ **885 0511.** Breakfast F$5–F$10; burgers and sandwiches F$8–F$12; pizza F$10–F$34; main courses F$9–F$20. MC, V. Daily 7:30am–10:30pm.

Decked Out Cafe ★ PACIFIC RIM　A tin roof covers the patio of this open-air restaurant nearly hidden behind a stone wall. The menu is all over the place, with a wide selection of burgers, sandwiches, chili hot dogs, Tandoori chicken wraps, and main courses such as sesame-breaded fried fish served with a papaya salsa. I was thoroughly satisfied with the chef's salad, a refreshing mix of avocado, orange pieces, apple slices, tomatoes, and lettuce tossed with a light vinaigrette. You can slake a thirst in the bar with a big TV for watching rugby games.

Main street, opposite Copra Shed. © **882 2033.** Sandwiches and salads F$6–F$13; pizza F$15–F$20; main courses F$15–F$25. No credit cards. Mon–Sat 8am–11pm; Sun 6–11pm.

Surf 'n' Turf ★★ BARBECUE/GRILL/INDIAN/SEAFOOD   Formerly a chef at Jean-Michel Cousteau Fiji Islands Resort, Vijendra Kumar now puts his skills to good use at this waterfront restaurant in the Copra Shed. As the name implies, a combination of steak and tropical lobster tail leads the list here. This is one of my favorite places to eat *ota,* the young shoots of the wood fern. It's often offered here in a lobster salad appetizer, of which I order two to make a main course. Vijendra also cooks very good Indian curries. His specialty is a six-course dinner cooked at your bayside table.

Main street, in Copra Shed. © **881 0966.** Reservations required for fixed-priced dinner. Main courses F$10–F$40; fixed-course dinner F$50. MC, V. Mon and Thurs–Sat 10am–2pm and 5:30–9:30pm; Tues 6–10pm; Sun 5:30–9:30pm.

NIGHTLIFE IN SAVUSAVU

The resorts provide weekly Fijian *meke* nights and other entertainment for their guests. Otherwise, not much goes on in Savusavu after dark except at one local **nightclub,** which I have not had the courage to sample, and at three local **bars,** which I have.

For a step back in time, visit the **Planter's Club** ★ (© **885 0233**), an ancient clapboard building near the western end of town. It's a friendly holdover from the colonial era, with a snooker table and a pleasant bar, where you can order a cold young coconut—add gin or rum, and you've got a genuine island cocktail. It's open Monday to Thursday from 11am to 9pm, Friday and Saturday 11am to 10pm, Sunday 10am to 8pm. You'll be asked to sign the club's register.

Yachties and the numerous expatriates who live here congregate at the wharfside bars of the **Savusavu Yacht Club,** in the Copra Shed (© **885 3057**), which is open Monday to Saturday 10am to 10pm and Sunday 11am to 9pm.

TAVEUNI

One of my favorite places to hang out in Fiji is cigar-shaped Taveuni, just 6.5km (4 miles) from Vanua Levu's eastern peninsula across the Somosomo Strait. The country's third-largest island is one of the world's most famous scuba-diving spots. Although it is only 9.5km (6 miles) wide, a volcanic ridge down Taveuni's 40km (25-mile) length soars to more than 1,200m (4,000 ft.), blocking the southeast trade winds and pouring as much as 9m (30 ft.) of rain a year on the mountaintops and the island's rugged eastern side. Consequently, Taveuni's 9,000 or so residents (three-fourths of them Fijians) live in villages along the gently sloping, lush western side. They occupy some of the country's most fertile and well-watered soil—hence Taveuni's nickname: the Garden Isle.

Thanks to limited land clearance and the absence of the mongoose, Taveuni is the best place in Fiji to explore the interior on foot in **Bouma National Heritage Park** and the gorgeous **Lavena Coastal Walk.** It still has all the plants and animals indigenous to Fiji, including the unique Fiji fruit bat, the Taveuni silktail bird, land crabs, and some species of palm that have only recently been identified. The **Ravilevu Nature Preserve** on the east coast and the **Taveuni Forest Preserve** in the middle of the island help protect these rare creatures. Even part of the offshore reef is protected by the **Waitabu Marine Park & Campground.**

In a volcanic crater atop the mountains at an altitude of more than 810m (2,700 ft.) is **Lake Tagimaucia,** home of the rare *tagimaucia* flower that bears red blooms with white centers.

The surrounding waters are equally fascinating. With dozens of fabulous dive sites nearby, including the Rainbow Reef and its Great White Wall, Taveuni is the best place to explore Fiji's underwater paradise.

The little airstrip and most of Taveuni's accommodations are at **Matei,** on the northeastern corner of the island facing the small, rugged islands of **Qamea** and **Matagi,** homes of two of my favorite little offshore resorts (see "Resorts on Matagi & Qamea Islands," later in this chapter).

GETTING TO & AROUND TAVEUNI

Pacific Sun flies to Taveuni from Nadi and Suva. There is no direct service between here and Savusavu. The hotels send buses or hire taxis to pick up their guests.

The large ferries from Suva stop at Savusavu before arriving at Waiyevo, and the small *Amazing Grace* crosses the Somosomo Strait between Waiyevo and Buca Bay daily.

See "Getting to & Getting Around Savusavu," in chapter 13, and "Getting Around Fiji," in chapter 3, for details.

Taxis don't patrol the roads here, but your hotel staff can summon one. I have been satisfied with **Taveuni Island Tours** (℅ **888 0221**), **Nan's Taxi** (℅ **888 0705**), and **Ishwar's Taxi** (℅ **888 0464**). None of the taxis have meters, so negotiate for a round-trip price if you're going out into the villages and having the driver wait for you. The fare from the airstrip is about F$2 to Maravu Plantation and Taveuni Island resorts, F$17 to Bouma Falls, and F$20 to Navakoca (Qamea) Landing, or Waiyevo. A taxi and driver cost about F$150 for a full day.

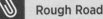

Rough Road

Taveuni's main road, which runs along the west and north coasts, is paved between Waiyevo and Matei, but elsewhere it's rough gravel, winding, often narrow, and at places carved into sheer cliffs above the sea. Even if there were car rental firms here, I would take taxis everywhere I cannot walk.

Local **buses** fan out from Naqara to the outlying villages about three times a day from Monday to Saturday. For example, a bus leaves Naqara for Bouma at 8:30am, 12:15pm, and 4:30pm. The one-way fare to Bouma is no more than F$5. Contact **Pacific Transport** (℅ **888 0278**) opposite Kaba's Supermarket in Naqara.

Coconut Grove Beachfront Cottages in Matei (℅/fax **888 0328**) rents bicycles for F$25 a day. See "Where to Stay on Taveuni," later in the chapter.

[FastFACTS] TAVEUNI

The following facts apply to Taveuni. If you don't see an item here, see "Fast Facts: Fiji" in chapter 15.

Currency Exchange Colonial National Bank (℅ **888 0433**) has an office and an ATM at Nagara. It's open Monday to Friday from 9:30am to 4pm.

Electricity The resorts and hotels have their own generators because only Taveuni's villages have public electricity. Most generators are 220 volts but a few are 110 volts, so ask before plugging in your electric shaver.

Emergencies In an emergency, phone ℅ **917**

for the **police,** ℅ **911** for **fire** or **ambulance.** The **police station** (℅ **888 0222**) is in the government compound. Taveuni is relatively safe, but exercise caution if you're out late at night.

Healthcare The **government hospital** (© **888 0222**) is in the government compound in the hills above Waiyevo. To get there, go uphill on the road opposite the Garden Island Resort, and then take the right fork.

Mail The **post office** is in Waiyevo (Mon–Fri 8am–4pm, Sat 8am–noon).

Visitor Information There is no visitor information office on the island, but the **Taveuni Tourism**

Association has a website at **www.puretaveuni.com**.

Water The tap water is safe to drink at the hotels on Taveuni but not elsewhere.

EXPLORING TAVEUNI

Taveuni is famous for shallow **Lake Tagimaucia** (*Tangi*-maw-thia), home of the rare *tagimaucia* flower bearing red blooms with white centers. Its sides ringed with mud flats and thick vegetation, the lake sits in the volcanic crater of **Des Voeux Peak** at more than 800m (2,700 ft.) altitude. It's a rare day when clouds don't shroud the peak.

The three-level **Bouma Falls** are among Fiji's finest and most accessible waterfalls, and the area around them is included in the **Bouma National Heritage Park** (see below). Beyond Bouma at the end of the road, a sensational coastal hiking track begins at **Lavena** village and runs through the Ravilevu Nature Reserve.

Yesterday & Today

The 180th meridian would have been the international date line were it not for its dividing the Aleutians and Fiji into 2 days, and for Tonga's wish to be on the same day as Australia. Even so, I love to stand here on Taveuni with one of my feet in today, the other in yesterday.

By tradition, Taveuni's **Somosomo** village is one of Fiji's most "chiefly" villages; that is, its chief is one of the highest ranking in all of Fiji, and the big meetinghouse here is a prime gathering place of Fiji's Great Council of Chiefs. Although Somosomo has a modern Morris Hedstrom supermarket, the predominately Indo-Fijian **Nagara** village next door is the island's only commercial center.

The administrative village of **Waiyevo** sits halfway down the west coast. A kilometer (½ mile) south, a brass plaque marks the **180th meridian** of longitude, exactly halfway around the world from the zero meridian in Greenwich, England. In addition to the aptly named Meridian Cinema, the village of **Wairiki** sports the lovely **Wairiki Catholic Mission,** built in the 19th century to reward a French missionary for helping the locals defeat a band of invading Tongans. A painting of the battle hangs in the presbytery.

The main road is rough, slow-going gravel from Wairiki to **Vuna Point** on Taveuni's southeastern extremity. On the way, it passes **Taveuni Estates,** a real-estate development with a 9-hole golf course (you, too, can own a piece of paradise).

Bouma National Heritage Park ★★★

One attraction on everyone's list is **Bouma National Heritage Park** (© **888 0390;** www.bnhp.org) on Taveuni's northeastern end, 18km (11 miles) from the airstrip, 37km (23 miles) from Waiyevo. The government of New Zealand provided funds for the village of Bouma to build trails following the Tavoro River to the three

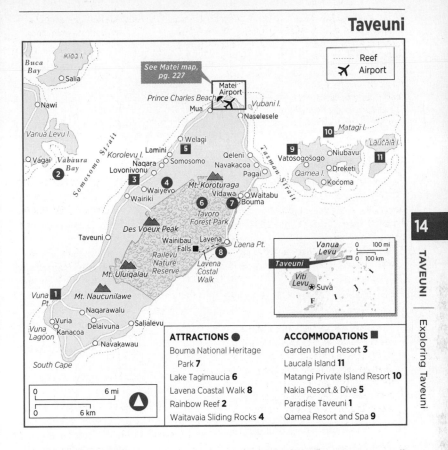

Taveuni

Reef
Airport

Buca Bay
KIOA I.
Salia
See Matei map, pg. 227
Matei Airport
Prince Charles Beach
Mua
Vubani I.
Naselesele
Nawi
Vanua Levu I.
Welagi
Matagi I.
Laucala I.
Vagai
Vabaura Bay
Korolevu I.
Lamini
Somosomo
Qeleni
Navakacoa
Pagai
Vatosogosogo
Niubavu
Dreketi
Qamea I.
Kocoma
Naqara
Lovonivonu
Waiyevo
Wairiki
Mt. Korotaraga
Vidawa
Waitabu
Bouma
Tavoro Forest Park
Des Voeux Peak
Taveuni
Wainibau Falls
Lavena
Laena Pt.
Railevu Nature Reserve
Lavena Costal Walk
Mt. Uluiqalau
Vanua Levu
Taveuni
Viti Levu
Suva
Vuna Pt.
Mt. Naucunilawe
Naqarawalu
Vuria
Kanacoa
Delaivuna
Salialevu
Vuna Lagoon
Navakawau
South Cape

0   6 mi
0   6 km

Somosomo Strait
Tasman Strait
0   100 mi
0   100 km

ATTRACTIONS ●

Bouma National Heritage Park **7**
Lake Tagimaucia **6**
Lavena Coastal Walk **8**
Rainbow Reef **2**
Waitavaia Sliding Rocks **4**

ACCOMMODATIONS ■

Garden Island Resort **3**
Laucala Island **11**
Matangi Private Island Resort **10**
Nakia Resort & Dive **5**
Paradise Taveuni **1**
Qamea Resort and Spa **9**

levels of **Bouma Falls,** also known as Tavoro Waterfalls. It's a flat, 15-minute walk along an old road from the visitor center to the lower falls, which plunge some 180m (600 ft.) into a broad pool. From there, a trail climbs sharply to a lookout with a fine view of Qamea and as far offshore as the Kaibu and Naitoba islands east of Taveuni. The trail then enters a rainforest to a second set of falls, which are not as impressive as the lower cascade. Hikers ford slippery rocks across a swift-flowing creek while holding onto a rope. This 30-minute muddy climb can be made in shower sandals, but be careful of your footing. A more difficult track ascends to yet a third falls, but I've never followed it, and people who did have told me it isn't worth the effort.

Another park trail, the **Vidawa Rainforest Walk,** leads to historic hill fortifications and more great views. Guides lead half-day treks through the rainforest, but you'll need to book at your hotel activities desk or call the park's **visitor center** (© **888 0390** or 822 0361) at least a day in advance. The trek ends at Bouma Falls. The hikes cost F$40 per person.

The park is open daily from 8am to 5pm. Admission is F$8 per person without a guide, F$15 with a guide. See "Getting to & Getting Around Taveuni," above, for information about how to get here.

Hiking ★★★

In addition to the short walks in the Bouma National Heritage Park (see above), three other treks are worth making, depending on the weather. The relatively dry (and cooler) season from May to September is the best time to explore Taveuni on foot.

Best of all is the **Lavena Coastal Walk ★★★**. It follows a well-worn, easy-to-follow trail from the end of the road past the park for 5km (3 miles), and then climbs to **Wainibau Falls.** The last 20 minutes or so of this track are spent walking up a creek bed, and you'll have to swim through a rock-lined canyon to reach the falls (stay to the left, out of the current). The creek water is safe to drink, but bring your own bottled water if you want to be on the safe side. You can do it on your own, but it's much more rewarding to go with a Lavena village guide for F$15 plus the F$12 per person trail fee.

Positioned on a peninsula, Lavena village has one of Taveuni's best beaches and a lodge where hikers can overnight for F$30 per person, including the trail fee (© **820 3639** for reservations). On the beach side of the trail, the lodge has simple rooms with their own hand basins. Everyone shares communal toilets and cold-water showers.

> ### Actors in Paradise
>
> On a clear day you can see **Naitaba Island**—once owned by the late Raymond Burr—from up the hills of Bouma National Heritage Park. Another actor, Mel Gibson, owns **Mago Island,** which lies beyond Naitaba.

High in the center of the island, a rough road leads to the top of **Des Voeux Peak** and **Lake Tagimaucia,** home of the famous flower that blooms from the end of September to the end of December. This crater lake is surrounded by mud flats and filled with floating vegetation. Beginning at Somosomo village, the hike to the lake takes about 8 hours round-trip. The trail is often muddy and slippery, and—given the usual cloud cover hanging over the mountains by midmorning—you're not likely to see much when you reach the top. Only hikers who are in shape should make this full-day trek. You must pay a F$25-per-person "custom fee" to visit the lake, which includes a guide—an absolute necessity. Your hotel will make the arrangements. An alternative is to take a four-wheel-drive vehicle up Des Voeux Peak for a look down at the lake. The drive is best done early in the morning, when the mountain is least likely to be shrouded in clouds.

OUTDOOR ACTIVITIES

The hotels and resorts will arrange all of Taveuni's outdoor activities, although you should book at least a day in advance.

Game Fishing

Two charter boats will take you in search of big game fish offshore: New Zealander Geoffrey Amos's **Matei Game Fishing** (© **888 0371**) and American John Llanes's **Makaira Charters** (© **888 0686;** makaira@connect.com.fj). They charge about US$400 for half a day for up to four fishers. Call for reservations, which are required.

Golf

The real-estate development known as **Taveuni Estates,** about 7km (4⅓ miles) southeast of the 180th meridian, has a scenic 9-hole golf course skirting the island's eastern shore. Reserve at the clubhouse (© **850 3437**), which serves lunch and has a bar. The greens fee is F$40, including clubs and a pizza.

Horseback Riding

Maravu Plantation Beach Resort & Spa (© **888 0555**) has horseback riding along a trail leading to the resort's wedding chapel on a ridge with views of both sides of Taveuni. See "Where to Stay on Taveuni," later in the chapter.

Jet-Skiing

Paradise Taveuni (© **888 0125;** www.paradiseinfiji.com) has jet-skiing expeditions across the Somosomo Strait to Vanua Levu, a 45-minute ride each way. These cost F$400 per person, including lunch. Reserve at least 2 days in advance. See "Where to Stay on Taveuni," later in the chapter.

Kayaking

It's great fun to kayak to the three little rocky islets off the north shore, near the airstrip. You can land on the islands for a bring-your-own picnic. **Coconut Grove Beachfront Cottages & Restaurant** (© **888 0328;** see "Where to Stay on Taveuni," later in the chapter), rents two-person ocean kayaks for F$35 per half day, F$55 per full day. Owner Ronna Goldstein will prepare a picnic lunch with advance notice.

Scuba Diving ★★★

The swift currents of the Somosomo Strait feed the soft corals on the Rainbow Reef and its White Wall between Taveuni and Vanua Levu, making this one of the world's most colorful and famous scuba-diving locales. As a diver I met said, "It's like when you buy a pack of coloring pencils, except there aren't enough colors."

The Rainbow Reef and its Great White Wall are only 6.4km (4 miles) off Waiyevo, so the **Garden Island Resort** (see "Where to Stay on Taveuni," below) is the closest dive base, a 20-minute boat ride across the Somosomo Strait. You need not stay here to go with the resort's own dive operation.

Almost as close is **Taveuni Ocean Sports** (© **867 7513;** www.taveunioceansports.com), operated by Julie Kelly, daughter of Jim and Robin Kelly at Nakia Resort & Dive (see "Where to Stay on Taveuni," below). She has the newest boats and equipment here, and she takes only small parties diving.

>
> ### It All Depends on the Tides
>
> Because of the strong currents in the Somosomo Strait, dives on Taveuni's most famous sites must be timed according to the tides. You can't count on making the dives you would like if the tides are wrong when you're here. A very good friend of mine spent 10 days on Matangi and Qamea islands and never did get out to the Rainbow Reef.

The other close operator is Carl Fox's **Taveuni Dive** (© 828 1063; www.
taveunidive.com), which has a base at Wairiki and also serves Taveuni Paradise (see
"Where to Stay on Taveuni," below), where it operates as **Pro Dive Taveuni.**

All operators charge about F$120 for a one-tank dive.

Snorkeling & Swimming

If they aren't too busy with serious divers, most of the scuba operators will take
snorkelers along. It's worth asking at your hotel or calling them.

The best snorkeling is around **Korolevu Island,** off Waiyevo. Most resorts will
arrange trips to this rocky outcrop surrounded by a colorful reef.

You can also snorkel from a Fijian *bilibili* (bamboo raft) over the **Waitabu
Marine Park & Campground** ★★ (© 8208 1999; www.bnhp.org), a part of
Bouma National Heritage Park (see above). The marine park was founded in 1998
to protect the reefs off northern
Taveuni. The hard corals here attract
some of the largest fish in Fiji. These
half-day bilibili ventures cost F$40
per snorkeler. For F$50 per person
you get refreshments and music by
Fijian villagers. The trips only go at
high tide, so call for reservations. Also
call in advance if you want to camp by
the beach (villagers will cook your
meals). The campground has tents,
showers, and toilets.

> **Beware of "Jaws"**
>
> Ancient legend says that Taveuni's par-
> amount chief is Fiji's highest ranking
> because sharks protect the island from
> enemies. True or not, shark attacks
> have occurred here. So be careful when
> you're swimming and snorkeling in the
> Somosomo Strait, and don't, under any
> circumstances, swim out to the edge of
> the reef. Swim and snorkel between
> 9am and 3pm to minimize the risk of a
> dangerous encounter.

Some of the best do-it-yourself
snorkeling is at the foot of the cliff off
Tramontu Bar & Grill (see "Where
to Dine on Taveuni," later in the chap-
ter), and in the three little rocky islets off the north shore, near the airstrip (provided
kelp from the nearby seaweed farms isn't drifting by). Also good for both snorkeling
and swimming are **Prince Charles Beach, Valaca Beach,** and the lovely, tree-
draped **Beverly Beach,** all south of the airstrip.

A fun outing is to **Waitavaia Sliding Rocks,** near Waiyevo (no phone), where
you can literally slide over the rocks down a freshwater cascade. Be prepared to get
a few bruises! The rocks are off the side road leading to Waitavala Estates, and
admission is free.

WHERE TO STAY ON TAVEUNI

The majority of Taveuni's accommodations are near the airstrip at Matei, on the
island's northeastern corner. A few small planes arrive and depart about 9:30am and
again about 2:30pm, so it's not as if you're sleeping under the flight path of an international airport. I like to stay at Matei because I can walk to the airstrip-area hotels
and restaurants in no more than 20 minutes. The stroll along the lagoon from the
airstrip east toward Naselesele village is one of my favorites in Fiji.

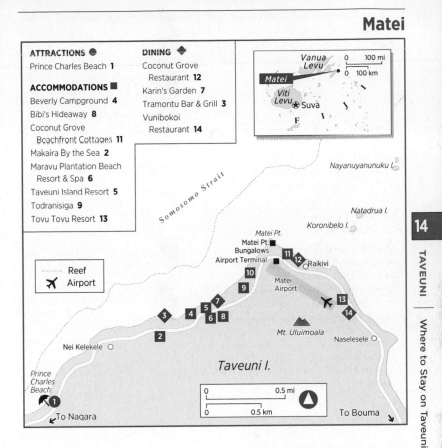

ATTRACTIONS ●
Prince Charles Beach **1**

ACCOMMODATIONS ■
Beverly Campground **4**
Bibi's Hideaway **8**
Coconut Grove
 Beachfront Cottages **11**
Makaira By the Sea **2**
Maravu Plantation Beach
 Resort & Spa **6**
Taveuni Island Resort **5**
Todranisiga **9**
Tovu Tovu Resort **13**

DINING ◆
Coconut Grove
 Restaurant **12**
Karin's Garden **7**
Tramontu Bar & Grill **3**
Vunibokoi
 Restaurant **14**

Reef
✈ Airport

Somosomo Strait

Vanua Levu
0   100 mi
0   100 km
Matei
Viti Levu ★ Suva
F

Nayanuyanunuku I.
Natadrua I.
Koronibelo I.
Matei Pt.
Matei Pt. ■
Bungalows
Airport Terminal ■ **11** **12** ○Raikivi
10
9 *Matei Airport*
7
3 **4** **5** **13**
 6 **8** ▲ **14**
Mt. Uluimoala
2 *Naselesele* ○
Nei Kelekele ○

Taveuni I.

0   0.5 mi
0   0.5 km ▲

Prince Charles Beach
1
↙To Naqara
To Bouma ↘

14

TAVEUNI | Where to Stay on Taveuni

Other accommodations are in Waiyevo village, about halfway along Taveuni's northern coast, and near Vuda Point, on the southeastern end. Vuda Point is at least an hour's drive from the airstrip.

At Matei

Bibi's Hideaway   Jim Bibi (prounced *Bim*-bee), who describes himself as "100% Fijian," retired as a lecturer at the Marist Training Center on Taveuni and bought this 32-hectare (20-acre) coconut plantation. He cleared away the brush by hand with a machete, and built five plywood-and-tin cottages, one for each of his children (they later added a sixth). They are simple but clean and fairly spacious structures. Not all of their windows are screened, but mosquito nets hang over the beds, which range from two singles to a queen-size. One bungalow dedicated to backpackers has a kitchen and an outdoor shower. All showers here dispense cold water. This is a good place to get to know local residents.

P.O. Box 80, Waiyevo, Taveuni. ☎ **888 2014** or 888 0443. 6 units. F$50–F$110 double. No credit cards. *In room:* Fans, fridge (some units), no phone.

Coconut Grove Beachfront Cottages ★★★ 🏝

Ronna Goldstein, who named this little gem not for the palm trees growing all around it but for her home-town in Florida, has three *bures* (bungalows) set beside a fine little beach next to her restaurant (see "Where to Dine on Taveuni," below). Although this is the only hotel on Taveuni sitting directly beside a beach, the ambience here is more like a country inn than a resort, for Ronna lives here, and the restaurant is on her big, breezy front porch with a terrific view of the sea and offshore islets. Next door, the Mango cottage has a great sea view from its large front porch. My favorite is the Banana bure; it's right by the beach. The Papaya bure is the smallest, but it's also the most private. All three have CD players, a collection of books, and outdoor showers. Veteran staffers Bimla, Sera, Vina, Kata, Rosie, and Longi also will make you feel at home. Her friendly, shoe-munching pooch, Millie, is in charge of guest relations. You will get complimentary kayaks, snorkeling fins (bring your own mask), a 30-minute massage on arrival, and village visits. This is one of Fiji's great values. *Note:* Children 6 and under are not accepted here.

Postal Agency, Matei, Taveuni. ☎/fax **888 0328**. www.coconutgrovefiji.com. 3 units. US$175–US$225 double. Rates include full breakfast, afternoon tea, and 30-min. massage. MC, V. No children 6 and under accepted. **Amenities:** Restaurant; bar; bikes; free airport transfers; watersports equipment/rentals; Wi-Fi (in main house; free). *In room:* Ceiling fan, fridge, no phone.

Maravu Plantation Beach Resort & Spa ★ 🏝

Although it has its own lovely beach across the road (a 5-min. downhill walk), this unusual retreat is set among 36 hectares (90 acres) of palms on a former *copra* (dried coconut meat) plantation. Most of the bures are laid out among grounds carefully planted with bananas, papayas, and a plethora of ginger plants and wild orchids. This plantation setting blocks the prevailing breezes, which means the property can get warm and humid during the day. Built in the style of South Seas planters' cottages, the guest bungalows have thatch-covered tin roofs and reed or mat accents that lend a tropical ambience. Situated about a 5-minute walk from the main complex via wooden pathways spanning a small ravine, six honeymoon units have sea views and are my favorites. These all have outdoor showers, Jacuzzis, and sun decks. Only a few older "planters bures" close to the main building don't have outdoor showers. The largest unit here is the "Treehouse" bungalow; it stands on pilings and has a tree growing through its sun-deck. With an emphasis on very good "nouvelle Fijian" cuisine, the dining room under the high thatched roof looks out to the lawns and a pool surrounded by an expansive deck. Wine lovers are in for a treat here, for owner Jochen Kiess, a German lawyer, has accumulated a fine list. Because most of Maravu isn't directly on the beach, Jochen doesn't charge an arm and a leg, which makes it a good value. Horseback riding is included in the rates here, too.

Postal Agency, Matei, Taveuni. ☎ **866/528-3864** or 888 0555. Fax 888 0600. www.maravu.net. 21 units. US$130–US$325 per person double occupancy. Rates include full breakfast. AE, DC, MC, V. **Amenities:** Restaurant; bar; babysitting; bikes; health club; Internet (in main bldg.; free); Jacuzzi; outdoor pool; spa; free airport transfers; watersports equipment/rentals. *In room:* A/C, ceiling fan, hair dryer, minibar, no phone.

Nakia Resort & Dive ★

Jim and Robin Kelly were stuck in a traffic jam in Hawaii one morning when they decided to relocate to Taveuni and build this little resort, up in a coconut grove with a view of Somosomo Strait. Their central restaurant, with excellent home cooking utilizing produce from an organic garden, overlooks a swimming pool and is flanked by the plantation-style guest bungalows. Three of them have queen-size beds and are suited to couples, while their larger family unit has both king-size and double beds. All have porches with hammocks. A steep stairway leads down to a small beach (at low tide, at least), but like Taveuni Island Resort (see below), the hillside location means this is not the place for a typical beachside vacation. It is an excellent choice for divers, however, as daughter Julie Kelly operates her excellent Taveuni Ocean Sports here (see "Scuba Diving," earlier in this chapter).

P.O. Box 204, Waiyevo, Taveuni. 🄒 **888 1111.** Fax 888 1333. www.nakiafiji.com. 4 units. US$200–US$300. AE, MC, V. **Amenities:** Restaurant; bar; babysitting; Internet (computer in main house; free); outdoor pool; free airport transfers; watersports equipment/rentals. *In room:* Ceiling fan, fridge, no phone.

Taveuni Island Resort ★★
Ric and Do Cammick's resort offers honeymooners and other romantic couples (no kids 14 and under are allowed) a very private, pampered stay with a fabulous view. You will be sorely disappointed if you expect to step out of your bungalow onto the beach, however, for this property sits high on a bluff overlooking Somosomo Strait, and you will have to climb down it to reach the sand. To compensate, a hilltop pool commands a stunning view over the strait, as do the central building and the guest bungalows. Six of the units are hexagonal models built of pine with side wall windows that let in the view and the breeze. The most stunning view of all is from the spacious deck of the Veidomoni bure—or you can take in the vista from its open-to-the-sea outdoor shower. All other units also have outdoor showers as well as separate sleeping and living areas. One deluxe unit has a separate bedroom, and the luxurious Matalau villa has two master bedrooms and its own private pool.

Postal Agency, Matei, Taveuni. 🄒 **877/828-3864** or 888 0441. Fax 888 0466. www.taveuniislandresort. com. 12 units. US$830–US$1,495 double. Rates include all meals. AE, MC, V. Children 14 and under not accepted. **Amenities:** Restaurant; bar; bikes; free Internet; Jacuzzi; outdoor pool; room service; spa; free airport transfers; watersports equipment/rentals. *In room:* A/C, ceiling fan, hair dryer, minibar.

Taveuni Palms ★★
This private little retreat in a coconut grove specializes in pampering guests in its two private villas, each with its own expansive deck, swimming pool, and small beach among the rocks and cliffs lining the coastline. Owners Tony and Kelly Acland have no need for a restaurant or bar. Instead, their staff prepares and serves your meals in your own dining room, on your deck, down by the beach, or just about any place you choose. The bungalows have sea views from their perches above the shoreline. Each also has two air-conditioned bedrooms with king-size beds, a big-screen TV to play DVDs, an outdoor shower, an intercom for ordering your meals, and its own kayaks and snorkeling gear. Taveuni Palms has its own dive master, and you can have your massage or spa treatment down by the beach. Other than your having to pay for it, staying here is like residing in your very rich uncle's seaside guest house.

P.O. Box 51, Matei, Taveuni. 🄒 **888 0032.** Fax 888 2445. www.taveunipalmsfiji.com. 2 units. US$1,195 double. Minimum 5-night stay required. Rates include meals, nonalcoholic beverages, and most activities. AE, MC, V. **Amenities:** Babysitting; Internet; Jacuzzi; outdoor pool; room service; free airport transfers; watersports equipment/rentals. *In room:* A/C, ceiling fan, TV/DVD, movie library, hair dryer, kitchen, minibar, MP3 docking station, free Wi-Fi.

Tovu Tovu Resort   Spread out over a lawn across the road from the lagoon, the Peterson family's simple but attractive bungalows have front porches, reed exterior walls, tile floors, ceiling fans, and bathrooms with hot-water showers. Three of them also have their own private cooking facilities. The Vunibokoi Restaurant is here, and it's a scenic walk to Coconut Grove Restaurant and others near the airport (see "Where to Dine on Taveuni," below).

Postal Agency, Matei, Taveuni. **℃ 888 0560.** Fax 888 0722. www.tovutovu.com. 5 bungalows. F$95–F$130 bungalow. AE, MC, V. **Amenities:** Restaurant; bar; free airport transfers; Wi-Fi (F10¢/minute). *In room:* Ceiling fan, kitchen (in 3 units), no phone.

At Waiyevo

Garden Island Resort ★   Built as a Travelodge in the 1960s, this waterside motel received a serious makeover in 2008 and is now flashy and modern throughout. There is no beach here, but all rooms face a fine view of the Somosomo Strait to Vanua Levu. Each medium-size unit has a queen-size bed and a sofa, and ground-floor units add spa tubs on their patios. Most of the clientele are divers, as this is the closest accommodations to the White Wall and its Rainbow Reef (a 20-min. boat ride away in normal conditions), but the friendly staff welcomes everyone. Guests and nonguests can rent kayaks and go on snorkeling trips to Korolevu islet offshore and even to the Rainbow Reef with the hotel's own dive operator. The staff also arranges hiking trips and other excursions.

P.O. Box 1, Waiyevo, Taveuni. **℃ 888 0286.** Fax 888 0288. www.gardenislandresort.com. 28 units. US$200 double room. Rates include continental breakfast. AE, MC, V. **Amenities:** Restaurant; bar; babysitting; outdoor pool; room service; free airport transfers; watersports equipment/rentals; Wi-Fi (in lobby; F$15/day). *In room:* A/C, ceiling fan, TV/DVD, fridge, hair dryer.

In Southeastern Taveuni

Paradise Taveuni ★★ 🐟   An hour's drive south of the airport (or by jet ski or speed boat, if you prefer), this pleasant lagoonside property is remote but enjoys a fine view of the Somosomo Strait. It was a backpacker resort until present Australian owners Allan and Terri Gorten took over and seriously upgraded it. This paradise doesn't have its own beach, but you can climb down a ladder from the rocky shoreline and go swimming and snorkeling in the crystal clear lagoon. It's like having the world's largest swimming pool at your door steps. Or you can swim in the real pool or walk 5 minutes to a black-sand beach. The thatched-roof guest bures are reasonably spacious, with king-size beds and outdoor showers. The oceanfront models add Jacuzzis. Allan is a chef, so the Pacific Rim cuisine served in the central building is very good. Masquerading as Pro Dive Taveuni, Carl Fox's Taveuni Dive (p. 226) has a base here. It's a long way to the Great White Wall from here, but the Vuna Lagoon reefs are close at hand.

P.O. Box 69, Waiyevo, Taveuni. **℃/fax 888 0125.** Fax 888 0456. www.paradiseinfiji.com. 10 units. F$300 per person. Rates include meals. AE, MC, V. **Amenities:** Restaurant; bar; babysitting; outdoor pool; spa; free airport transfers (by road); watersports equipment/rentals; Wi-Fi (in main bldg.; F50¢/minute). *In room:* Ceiling fan, fridge, hair dryer, no phone.

Cottage Rentals

Several expatriate landowners on Taveuni rent out their own homes when they're away, or they have cottages on their properties to let. None of them accepts credit cards.

One owner who did not move here from someplace else is Fiji-born May Goulding, who has two cottages at **Todranisiga** (© **888 0680** or 941 3985; todrafj@ yahoo.com), her property south of the airstrip. The land slopes through coconut palms from the road down to the top of a seaside cliff, from where her planter-style bungalows look out over the Somosomo Strait. One of them has an alfresco shower—and I do mean alfresco, as nothing blocks you from the view, or the view from you. You'll spend most of your time out on the porches enjoying the breeze, taking in the view, and perhaps cooking a light meal on the gas camp stove. May charges F$155 for a double.

Two other cottages with views are at American Roberta Davis's **Makaira By the Sea** (© **888 0686;** www.fijibeachfrontatmakaira.com), sitting above a cliff with a 180-degree view down over Prince Charles Beach and the sea (notwithstanding the website address, this is not a beachfront property). Built of pine, the cottages have both indoor and outdoor showers. Tramontu Bar & Grill is across the road (see "Where to Dine on Taveuni," below). Roberta charges US$135 to US$210 per double, with discounts for longer stays.

Also with Somosomo Strait view is the one cottage at **Karin's Garden** (© **888 0511;** www.karinsgardenfiji.com), which Peter and Karin Uwe rent for US$185 per night. Peter gave up the high-tech fast lane in 1994, when he and Karin relocated from Germany to Taveuni and bought this lovely property. Given Peter's computer background, it's not surprising you'll have Wi-Fi here. They also serve meals at night (see "Where to Dine on Taveuni," below).

Camping

Campers who like to sleep by the sea and be near resorts and restaurants can find a beautiful (if not insect-free) site at Bill Madden's **Beverly Campground** (© **888 0684**), on Beverly Beach about 1.5km (1 mile) south of the airstrip. Maravu Resort's beach is next door. Monstrous trees completely shade the sites and hang over portions of the lagoon-lapped shore. The campground is very basic, but it has flushing toilets, cold-water showers, and a rudimentary beachside kitchen. Rates are F$15 per person if you bring your own tent, or F$17 if you sleep in one of Bill's. A bed in the rustic dorm costs F$20.

More remote is **Waitabu Marine Park & Campground** (© **8208 1999;** www. bnhp.org), a part of Bouma National Heritage Park (see "Snorkeling," under "Scuba Diving, Snorkeling & Other Outdoor Activities," above). The park has a campground with tents, showers, and toilets, and the villagers provide meals.

WHERE TO DINE ON TAVEUNI

Don't be surprised if you are asked at breakfast what you would like to have at dinner. That's a fact of life on islands like this, where logistics can be problematic. Most of the restaurants require reservations for this same reason.

Coconut Grove Restaurant ★★ INTERNATIONAL   American Ronna Goldstein consistently serves Taveuni's best fare at her little enclave, where she also rents cottages (see "Where to Stay on Taveuni," above). She offers breakfasts (her banana, coconut, and papaya breads are fabulous) and salads, soups, burgers, and sandwiches for lunch. Dinner offerings include a variety of local seafood dishes, spicy and mild Fijian curries (I love the fish curry), and homemade pastas. Saturday night features a buffet and Fijian musicians. Dining tables are on Ronna's veranda, which has a great view of the little islands off Taveuni, making it a fine place not just for lunch or dinner but to sip a great fruit shake or juice while waiting for your flight. She can also set you up for a romantic dinner under a cabana by the beach.

Matei. ℂ **888 0328.** Reservations required by noon for dinner. Breakfast F$7–F$21; lunch F$12–F$26; main courses F$23–F$37. MC, V. Daily 7:30am–4pm and 6:30–9pm.

Karin's Garden INTERNATIONAL   Karin and Peter Uwe prepare meals from their native Europe in the dining room of their home overlooking the beach and Somosomo Strait (see "Cottage Rentals," under "Where to Stay in Taveuni," above). Dining here is much like attending a dinner party with these longtime residents. Reservations are required by noon.

Matei, south of airstrip. ℂ **888 0511.** Reservations required by noon. Full meals F$40–F$45. No credit cards. Seatings daily 7pm.

Tramontu Bar & Grill PACIFIC RIM   Having a sunset drink at this open-air, Fijian-owned cafe perch atop a cliff with a spectacular view overlooking the Somosomo Strait is always part of my Taveuni ritual. The local fare consists of the usual curries, grilled steaks, and chicken stir-fries, but I prefer the wood-fired pizzas.

Matei, south of airstrip. ℂ **888 2224.** Pizza F$25–F$30; main courses F$10–F$30. No credit cards. Tues–Thurs 11am–2pm and 6–9:30pm; Fri–Sun 10am–10pm.

> ### Audrey's Sweet Somethings
>
> **East of the airstrip, Audrey's Island Coffee and Pastries** (ℂ **888 0039**) really isn't a restaurant; it's the home of American Audrey Brown, Taveuni's top baker. She charges F$10 per serving for cakes with coffee, but doesn't accept credit cards. Audrey's is open daily from 10am to 6pm.

Vunibokoi Restaurant PACIFIC RIM   On the front porch of the main house at Tovu Tovu Resort (see above), this plain but pleasant restaurant serves breakfast, lunch, and dinner, with a blackboard menu featuring home-cooked Fijian, Indian, and Western fare. I always make sure my trip coincides with the Vunibokoi's Friday night Fijian *lovo* food buffet, one of the most authentic such traditional feasts in the islands.

Matei, in Tovu Tovu Resort, 1km (½ mile) east of airstrip. ℂ **888 0560.** Reservations required. Main courses F$20–F$25. AE, MC, V. Daily 8am–2pm and 6–9pm.

MATAGI & QAMEA ISLAND ★★★ RESORTS

The northern end of Taveuni gives way to a chain of small, rugged islands that are as beautiful as any in Fiji; especially gorgeous are Matagi and Qamea. Their steep, jungle-clad hills drop to rocky shorelines in most places, but here and there little shelves of land and narrow valleys are bordered by beautiful beaches. The sheltered waters between the islands cover colorful reefs, making the area a hotbed for scuba diving and snorkeling. It's unfortunate that geography places them at the end of my coverage of Fiji, for they are home to two of my favorite resorts, both of which are beside two of Fiji's best beaches.

OVER THE TOP ON "red bull's island"

Out past Qamea and Matagi islands sits **Laucala Island** (℃ **888 0007;** www.laucala.com), Fiji's most expensive resort. I haven't been to it, but several people I know on Taveuni have, and they all report that it has taken luxury over the top in Fiji. They also call it "Red Bull's Island" because it's owned by Deitrich Mateschitz, the Austrian founder of the Red Bull energy drink. (He bought it from the heirs of another famous owner, the late American publisher Malcolm Forbes, whose ashes are buried atop Laucala's highest hill.) Mateschitz took several years to construct his almost self-sufficient resort, which grows its own fruits and vegetables and raises its own cattle and chickens. The human equation works out to 25 superluxe villas ranging from one room to monstrous residences with their own swimming pools. One even has its own guest houses. The well-heeled guests can dine at four restaurants, with meal service available around the clock. There's an 18-hole golf course, a spa, a yoga pavilion, an equestrian center, a huge swimming pool, and a children's center. Those of you with a whole lot of dough—such as Mateschitz's Austrian buddy, California Gov. Arnold Schwarzenegger—can land your private jets on the island's strip. To use the old saw, if you have to ask how much Laucala costs, you can't afford it.

On Matagi Island

Matangi Private Island Resort ★★★ 🐦 Matangi ranks high in my book because of proprietors Noel and Flo Douglas and their daughter, Christine. Of English-Fijian descent, they own all of hilly, 104-hectare (260-acre) Matagi Island, a horseshoe-shape remnant of a volcanic cone, where, in 1987, they built their resort in a beachside coconut grove on the western shore. This luxury retreat is very much a family operation, with a resident collection of pet dogs, cats, and Flo's pet fruit bat. A lounge building with a deck hanging out over the lagoon takes full advantage of gorgeous sunset views of Qamea and Taveuni. The tin-roofed central restaurant and bar building lacks the charm of Qamea's, but it overlooks a beachside swimming pool. You can be taken to the spectacular half-moon-shape beach in aptly named Horseshoe Bay and be left alone for a secluded picnic on two of Fiji's outstanding beaches. Honeymooners also can escape to three romantic bures 6m (20 ft.) up in the air, one of them actually in a shady Pacific almond tree. These units all have outdoor showers, as do some of the deluxe units down in the coconut grove beside the beach. They also have the "Matangi Air-Conditioned Bed"—Noel's latest invention in which curtains resembling mosquito nets keep in cool air from a small air-conditioning unit over the head of the bed. The central building and many of the bungalows are round, in the Polynesian-influenced style of eastern Fiji. Umbrellalike spokes radiating from hand-hewn central poles support their conical roofs. One bure is equipped for guests with disabilities. Children 11 and under are not accepted here.

P.O. Box 83, Waiyevo, Taveuni (Matagi Island, 20 min. by boat from Taveuni). ⓒ **888/628-2644** or 888 0260. Fax 888 0274. www.matangiisland.com. 13 units. US$610–US$1,050 double. Rates include meals and all excursions and activities except scuba diving, water-skiing, sportfishing, and island trips. AE, DC, MC, V. Children 11 and under not accepted. **Amenities:** Restaurant; bar; outdoor pool; spa; watersports equipment/rentals; Wi-Fi (in main bldgs.; free). *In room:* A/C, ceiling fan, hair dryer, kitchen (1 unit), minibar, no phone.

On Qamea Island

Qamea Resort and Spa ★★★ ✦

This luxury property has the most stunning main building and some of the most charming bures of any resort in Fiji. In the proverbial lagoonside coconut grove beside a lovely beach, this entire property shows remarkable attention to Western comfort and Fijian detail. If I were to build a set for a South Seas movie, it would feature the original bungalows, all covered by 31-cm-thick (12-in.) Fijian thatch. Spacious and rectangular, each has an old-fashioned porch with a hammock strung between two posts. Each unit is large enough to swallow the king-size bed, two oversize sitting chairs, a coffee table, and several other pieces of island-style furniture, and their bathrooms include outdoor showers. If you need more space, you can rent a luxuriously appointed "premium villa," which has a large plunge pool sunken into its front porch. These are on the other side of a swamp on the far end of the property and are the most private here. Two honeymoon villas at the other end are split-level models with day beds out front and small plunge pools in their large outdoor bathrooms. Qamea's centerpiece is the dining room and lounge under a soaring, 16m-high (52-ft.) priest's bure supported by two huge tree trunks. Orange light from kerosene lanterns hung high under the roof lends romantic charm for feasting on gourmet quality meals. You won't find a children's menu on hand because kids 15 and under are not accepted at the resort.

P.O. Matei, Taveuni (Qamea Island, 15 min. by boat from Taveuni). ⓒ **866/867-2632** or 888 0220. Fax 888 0092. www.qamea.com. 16 units. US$650–US$950 double. Rates include meals and all activities except diving, sportfishing, and island tours. AE, MC, V. Children 15 and under not accepted. **Amenities:** Restaurant; bar; health club; Internet (in office; F25¢/minute); Jacuzzi; outdoor pool; spa; free airport transfers; watersports equipment/rentals. *In room:* A/C, ceiling fan, TV/DVD (in premium villas), hair dryer, minibar, MP3 docking station (in premium villas), no phone.

FAST FACTS: FIJI

The following facts apply to Fiji in general. For more destination-specific information, see the "Fast Facts" sections in individual chapters.

Area Codes Fiji does not have domestic area codes. The country code for calling into Fiji is **679**.

Business Hours Stores are generally open Monday to Saturday from 8am to 5pm, but many suburban stores stay open until 6pm and even 8pm. Sunday hours are from 8:30am to noon, although some tourist-oriented stores are open later. Shops in most hotels stay open until 9pm every day. Government office hours are Monday to Thursday from 8am to 4:30pm. Banking hours are Monday to Thursday 9:30am to 3pm, Friday 9:30am to 4pm.

Drinking Laws The legal age for the purchase and consumption of alcohol is 18. Bars are supposed to close no later than 2am; most do, some don't. Most grocery stores sell beer, spirits, and wines from Australia and New Zealand. Both beer and spirits are produced locally and are considerably less expensive than imported brands, which are taxed heavily.

Drug Laws Marijuana is grown illegally up in the hills, but one drive past the Suva Gaol will convince you not to get caught buying it—or smuggling narcotics or dangerous drugs into Fiji.

Electricity Electric current in Fiji is 240 volts, 50 cycles. Many hotels have converters for 110-volt shavers, but these are not suitable for hair dryers. The plugs are the angled two-prong types used in Australia and New Zealand. Outlets have on/off switches mounted next to them.

Embassies & Consulates The **U.S. Embassy** is at 31 Loftus St., Suva (© **331 4466;** www.amembassy-fiji.gov). Other major diplomatic missions in Suva are **Australia,** 37 Princes Rd., Tamavua (© **338 2211**); **New Zealand,** Reserve Bank of Fiji Building, 10th Floor, Pratt Street (© **331 1422**); **United Kingdom,** Victoria House, 47 Gladstone Rd. (© **331 1033**); **Japan,** Dominion House, Second Floor, Thomson Street (© **330 2122**); **France,** Dominion House, Seventh Floor, Thomson Street (© **331 2233**); **People's Republic of China,** 147 Queen Elizabeth Dr. (© **330 0215**); and **South Korea,** Vanua House, Eighth Floor, Victoria Parade (© **330 0977**).

Emergencies The **police** emergency number is **917** throughout Fiji. The emergency telephone number for **fire** and **ambulance** is © **911.**

Holidays Banks, government offices, and most private businesses are closed for New Year's Day, Good Friday, Easter Saturday, Easter Monday, Ratu Sukuna Day (May 30 or the Mon closest thereto), the Prophet Mohammed's Birthday (a Mon in mid-July), Fiji Day (the Mon closest to Oct 10), Deepawali (the Indian festival of lights in late Oct or early Nov), Christmas Day, and December 26 (Boxing Day).

Banks take an additional holiday on the first Monday in August, and some businesses also close for various Hindu and Muslim holy days.

And if Fiji wins a seven-man rugby tournament, don't expect anyone to be at work the next day!

Insurance   Given the relatively poor standard of medical care in Fiji, and the fact that my health insurance policy does not cover me outside the United States, I always buy a travel insurance policy that provides evacuation if necessary.

For information on traveler's insurance, trip cancellation insurance, and medical insurance while traveling, please visit **www.frommers.com/tips**.

Language   English is an official language of Fiji and most residents can speak it to some degree.

Mail   All the main towns have post offices operated by **Post Fiji** (www.postfiji.com.fj), and there is a branch at Nadi International Airport, across the entry road from the terminal. Post offices usually are open Monday to Friday from 8am to 4pm.

At press time, international postage rates were F$1.50 for a letter to the U.S. and Europe; F$1.25 to Australia and New Zealand. It cost F$1 to mail a postcard anywhere.

FedEx, UPS, and **DHL Express** all have express service into and out of Fiji.

Measurements   Fiji is on the metric system. See the chart on the inside front cover of this book for details on converting metric measurements to nonmetric equivalents.

Passports   See "Embassies & Consulates," above, for whom to contact if you lose your passport while traveling in Fiji. For other information, contact the following agencies:

For Residents of Australia   Contact the **Australian Passport Information Service** at ✆ **131-232,** or visit www.passports.gov.au.

For Residents of Canada   Contact the central **Passport Office,** Department of Foreign Affairs and International Trade, Ottawa, ON K1A 0G3 (✆ **800/567-6868;** www.ppt.gc.ca).

For Residents of Ireland   Contact the **Passport Office,** Setanta Centre, Molesworth Street, Dublin 2 (✆ **01/671-1633;** www.foreignaffairs.gov.ie).

For Residents of New Zealand   Contact the **Passports Office,** Department of Internal Affairs, 47 Boulcott Street, Wellington, 6011 (✆ **0800/225-050** in New Zealand, or 04/474-8100; www.passports.govt.nz).

For Residents of the United Kingdom   Visit your nearest passport office, major post office, or travel agency, or contact the **Identity and Passport Service (IPS),** 89 Eccleston Square, London, SW1V 1PN (✆ **0300/222-0000;** www.ips.gov.uk).

For Residents of the United States   To find your regional passport office, check the U.S. Department of State website (travel.state.gov/passport), or call the **National Passport Information Center** (✆ **877/487-2778**) for automated information.

Police   The nationwide emergency police number is ✆ **917** throughout Fiji. The non-emergency numbers are ✆ **670 0222** in Nadi, 334 3777 in Suva.

Smoking   Smoking is legally prohibited in government buildings in Fiji and in most indoor public spaces in hotels, businesses, and restaurants. Many hotels are now smoke-free, and those which are not have nonsmoking rooms.

Taxes   Fiji imposes a 12.5% value added tax (VAT) on most goods and services. These "VAT-inclusive prices," or VIP, are included in most prices. In addition, you will pay a 5% hotel tax. Hotels are not required to include the VAT and hotel tax in the rates they quote outside Fiji, so be sure to ask whether a quoted room rate includes all taxes and fees.

You can claim a **VAT refund** of 10%—not the full 12.5%—when you leave the country on up to F$500 spent per day. You must have (1) VAT forms filled out by the merchants at the time of purchase, and (2) your original receipts. The refund desks are to the right of the airline check-in desks at Nadi International Airport and immediately after you clear Immigration.

Time Normal local time in all of Fiji is 12 hours ahead of Greenwich Mean Time. Although the 180° meridian passes through Taveuni, all of Fiji is west of the international date line, so it's 1 day ahead of the United States and shares the same day with Australia and New Zealand. Fiji observed daylight saving time from the last Sunday in November 2009 until the last Sunday in March 2010. Whether it will do so again had not been decided when we went to press.

Tipping Tipping is discouraged throughout Fiji unless truly exceptional service has been rendered. That's not to say that the porter won't give you that where's-my-money look. Many resorts have staff Christmas funds in lieu of tipping.

Visitor Information Known prior to 2009 as the Fiji Visitors Bureau, **Tourism Fiji,** P.O. Box 9121, Nadi Airport, Fiji Islands (© **672 2433;** fax 672 0141; www.bulafiji.com), sends out maps, brochures, and other materials from its head office in the Colonial Plaza shopping center, on the Queen's Road in Namaka, about halfway between Nadi Airport and Nadi Town.

Tourism Fiji's award-winning website is a trove of up-to-date information and is linked to the home pages of the country's airlines, tour operators, attractions, and hotels. It also has a directory of e-mail addresses.

Other office locations are:

- **United States and Canada:** 5777 West Century Blvd., Ste. 220, Los Angeles, CA 90045 (© **800/932-3454** or 310/568-1616; fax 310/670-2318; www.bulafijinow.com)
- **Australia:** Level 12, St. Martins Tower, 31 Market St., Sydney, NSW 2000 (© **02/9264-3399;** fax 02/9264-3060; www.bulafiji-au.com)
- **New Zealand:** 33 Scanlon St., Grey Lynn (P.O. Box 1179), Auckland (© **09/373-2533;** fax 09/376-4720; info@bulafiji.co.nz)
- **Germany:** Petersburger Strasse 94, 10247 Berlin (© **30/4225-6026;** fax 30/4225-6287; www.bulafiji.de)
- **Japan:** Noa Building, 14th Floor, 3–5, 2 Chome, Azabuudai, Minato-Ku, Tokyo 106 (© **03/3587-2038;** fax 03/3587-2563; www.bulafiji-jp.com)
- **United Kingdom:** Lion House, 111 Hare Lane, Claygate, Surrey KI 0QF (© **0800 652 2158** or 1372 469818; fax 1372 470057; fiji@ihml.com)

The Fiji government's information website is at **www.fiji.gov.fj**.

Many bookstores and hotel gift shops in Fiji sell maps, and the Fiji telephone directory has colorful city and town maps in the front.

The best place to order quality maps of the region is from **Maptown Ltd.** (www.maptown.com). The **Perry-Castañeda Library** at the University of Texas at Austin posts free maps of the region on its website at www.lib.utexas.edu/maps/australia.html. Other free sources are **www.mapsouthpacific.com**, **www.maps-pacific.com**, and **www.worldatlas.com**.

Water Except during periods of continuous heavy rain, the tap water in the main towns and at the major resorts is safe to drink. Nevertheless, I drink the famous "Fiji" or other bottled water, widely available at shops and hotels.

Index

See also Accommodations and Restaurant indexes, below.

General Index

Accommodations

Restaurants